STUDIES IN IMPERIALISM

General editor: Andrew S. Thompson

Founding editor: John M. MacKenzie

When the 'Studies in Imperialism' series was founded
by Professor John M. MacKenzie more than thirty
years ago, emphasis was laid upon the conviction that
'imperialism as a cultural phenomenon had as significant
an effect on the dominant as on the subordinate societies'.
With well over 100 titles now published, this remains
the prime concern of the series. Cross-disciplinary work
has indeed appeared covering the full spectrum of cultural
phenomena, as well as examining aspects of gender and sex,
frontiers and law, science and the environment, language
and literature, migration and patriotic societies, and much
else. Moreover, the series has always wished to present
comparative work on European and American imperialism,
and particularly welcomes the submission of books in these
areas. The fascination with imperialism, in all its aspects,
shows no sign of abating, and this series will continue to
lead the way in encouraging the widest possible range of
studies in the field. 'Studies in Imperialism' is fully organic
in its development, always seeking to be at the cutting edge,
responding to the latest interests of scholars and the needs
of this ever-expanding area of scholarship.

Hong Kong and British culture, 1945–97

MANCHESTER
1824

Manchester University Press

SELECTED TITLES AVAILABLE IN THE SERIES

WRITING IMPERIAL HISTORIES
ed. Andrew S. Thompson

MUSEUMS AND EMPIRE
Natural history, human cultures and colonial identities
John M. MacKenzie

MISSIONARY FAMILIES
Race, gender and generation on the spiritual frontier
Emily J. Manktelow

THE COLONISATION OF TIME
Ritual, routine and resistance in the British Empire
Giordano Nanni

BRITISH CULTURE AND THE END OF EMPIRE
ed. Stuart Ward

SCIENCE, RACE RELATIONS AND RESISTANCE
Britain, 1870–1914
Douglas A. Lorimer

GENTEEL WOMEN
Empire and domestic material culture, 1840–1910
Dianne Lawrence

EUROPEAN EMPIRES AND THE PEOPLE
Popular responses to imperialism in France, Britain, the Netherlands,
Belgium, Germany and Italy
ed. John M. MacKenzie

SCIENCE AND SOCIETY IN SOUTHERN AFRICA
ed. Saul Dubow

Hong Kong and British culture, 1945–97

Mark Hampton

MANCHESTER UNIVERSITY PRESS

The right of Mark Hampton to be identified as the author of this work has been asserted by him in accordance with the Copyright, Designs, and Patents Act 1988.

Published by Manchester University Press
Altrincham Street, Manchester M1 7JA
www.manchesteruniversitypress.co.uk

British Library Cataloguing-in-Publication Data
A catalogue record for this book is available from the British Library

ISBN 978 1 5261 1672 7 paperback

First published by Manchester University Press in hardback 2016

This edition first published 2017

The publisher has no responsibility for the persistence or accuracy of URLs for any external or third-party internet websites referred to in this book, and does not guarantee that any content on such websites is, or will remain, accurate or appropriate.

Typeset by Out of House Publishing

永遠懷念我的岳丈 – 羅勝先生 (1932–2015)

In loving memory of my father-in-law, Low Shing
(1932–2015)

CONTENTS

List of illustrations – viii
Preface and acknowledgements – ix
Abbreviations – xi

	Introduction: Britishness, empire, and Hong Kong	1
1	Hong Kong and British culture: postwar contexts	15
2	The discourse of unbridled capitalism in postwar Hong Kong	42
3	A man's playground	72
4	The discourses of order and modernisation	100
5	Good governance	131
6	Chinese Britishness	160
7	Narratives of 1997	186
	Epilogue: postcolonial hangovers	211

Select bibliography – 219
Index – 230

ILLUSTRATIONS

1 Crowds at South Wigston Station to see the 1st Battalion depart for Hong Kong, 11 May 1949. (Leicestershire, Leicester and Rutland Record Office, reproduced with permission of TopFoto) *page 8*

2 Illegal Immigrants, Hong Kong, 1962. (Hong Kong Museum of History) 24

3 Street Trading, Hong Kong, c. 1950s. (Hong Kong Museum of History) 55

4 Cartoon by Mac [Stan McMurtry]: 'Well done Geoffrey – now I want you to hammer out a similar agreement with Arthur Scargill.' (*Daily Mail*, 28 September 1984.) (British Cartoon Archive, reproduced with permission of Solo Syndication, the *Daily Mail*, and Stan McMurtry) 63

5 UNDATED BLACK AND WHITE PHOTO. Night shot of one of the Wan Chai bars where Suzie Wong and her mates used to enjoy clients, Oct. 64. (*South China Morning Post*) 83

6 Squatters, Tiu Keng Leng, Kowloon, c. 1952. (Hong Kong Museum of History) 108

7 Resettlement Estate, Wang Tau Hom, Kowloon, 1960s. (Hong Kong Museum of History) 110

8 Riots in Hong Kong, 1967. (Hong Kong Museum of History) 139

9 Demonstrations in Kowloon, 1968. (Hong Kong Museum of History) 140

10 Beatles in Hong Kong, July 1965. (Hong Kong Museum of History) 179

11 Visit of Mrs Margaret Thatcher to Hong Kong, September 1982. (Hong Kong Museum of History) 189

PREFACE AND ACKNOWLEDGEMENTS

This book originates in personal motivations as well as scholarly ones; as it happens, it also originates about a mile away from the Manchester University Press editorial office. As an American post-graduate student in 1996, researching what became an article about the *Manchester Guardian*'s coverage of the South African War of 1899–1902, I met a young woman from Hong Kong who was pursuing a master's degree at the University of Manchester. My knowledge of Hong Kong was strikingly limited; it is embarrassing to recall that I was surprised to discover that she considered herself Chinese rather than British. It was, of course, a lively period in Sino-British relations, less than a year before the change of sovereignty. My new-found awareness of Hong Kong fortuitously coincided with the colony's growing prominence in the news. I became increasingly interested in the history of Hong Kong, and my interest was only piqued as my new friend followed me to the United States and, eventually, agreed to marry me.

Still, I put this interest on hold. The pressures of teaching, and publishing material relating to my Ph.D. thesis, occupied my time, and beyond that, the idea of writing a book on Hong Kong seemed daunting, not least because I had never been to Asia, nor did I have a clear idea how, from my position at a small teaching-oriented college in Georgia, I would fund the necessary research trips.

Through a stroke of fortune (and David Pomfret's grantsmanship), during a 2005–06 sabbatical I had the opportunity to spend a term as a visiting faculty member at the University of Hong Kong. My first introduction to Hong Kong only reinforced my interest in studying its history. I immediately fell in love with the city, and within five days of arriving as a visitor had applied for the position I have now held for eight years, at Lingnan University. And in 2007 I began researching this book.

In writing this book, I have benefited greatly from the generous research support provided by Lingnan University's Research Committee, which made it possible for me to visit archives in the United States, Britain, and Australia. The logistics of managing research funding were entirely straightforward thanks to the efficient professionalism of Connie Lam in Lingnan's Office of Research Support. The book has benefited as well from research assistance by Timothy Wales in London, and Penelope Ching-yee Pang, Zou Yizheng, Ceci Tam, Peter Law, and James Fellows in Hong Kong. Simon Case helped with formatting and with preparing the index.

I am very fortunate to have been helped enormously by knowledgeable and generous colleagues at Lingnan University. Mette Hjort and Paisley Livingston have been invaluable mentors. Grace Ai-Ling Chou and Poon Shuk-wah have shared their knowledge of Hong Kong and Chinese history. Richard Davis, Niccolò Pianciola, and James Fichter provided crucial non-specialist perspectives on my interpretations. Law Wing Sang and Hui Po-keung shared their theoretical expertise and deep knowledge of Hong Kong culture. Vincy Au and Ann Wong run the Lingnan History Department office with a tremendous efficiency that makes it possible for me to find time to write, and with a cheerfulness that makes it a pleasure for me to come to work each day.

In moving into a new research field, I have benefited from a multi-continental network of colleagues both old and new. Simon Potter and Adrian Bingham, both of whom I met through my earlier interest in journalism history, gave me valuable advice, respectively, on the histories of empire and sexuality. Chi-kwan Mark and Ray Yep answered my naive queries. David Clayton shared his encyclopedic knowledge of Hong Kong-related archives and challenged me to keep my ideas of 'culture' firmly grounded (I doubt I succeeded); he also generously shared his unpublished research and helpfully critiqued my earliest writings on Hong Kong history. Barry Crosbie and Stuart Ward helped me place Hong Kong within a wider imperial context, both through conversations and through comments on specific chapters. Patrick Hase lent his expertise both as an historian and as a former colonial official. Christine Loh, during an interview at her office, very kindly answered my questions about her political activities and motivations in the late colonial period. John Carroll read the entire manuscript, answered dozens of my very specific queries, and more than anyone else convinced me that I could write this book.

I am very grateful to the archivists and librarians at some three dozen institutions whose holdings are cited in this book, and to the editorial and production team at Manchester University Press. I am also grateful to audiences at conferences and seminars at the University of Hong Kong, the University of Copenhagen, Hong Kong Baptist University, the University of York, the International Convention of Asian Scholars, the Crossroads Cultural Studies conference, the Empire State of Mind conference, the International Association for Media and History, and my post-graduate reading group in the spring 2014 term. A shorter version of Chapter 2 appears in Barry Crosbie and Mark Hampton (eds), *The Cultural Construction of the British World* (Manchester: Manchester University Press, 2016); I am grateful to the publisher for permission to reprint it.

Researching a book requires not only the cooperation of specialist scholars in sharing their knowledge, but also supportive friends and colleagues to help with various logistical matters and moral support during overseas research trips. Rohan McWilliam and Kelly Boyd have, since 1995, made me feel at home in London, and seeing them is always the high point of my trip. Peter Mandler introduced me to High Table at Cambridge, and also kindly shared research material. Tom O'Malley hosted me in Aberystwyth. Simon Potter hosted me in both Oxford and Bristol.

I dedicated my first book to Ring Mei-Han Low. Although she inspired me to write this one, I am sure she will forgive me for dedicating it instead to her father, Low Shing. As a child in Guangdong at the end of the Second World War, he escaped particularly fraught circumstances to make his way quasi-legally into Hong Kong. Despite limited education, and often having to work in the colony's shadow economy, he managed to support his daughter's earning three degrees on three continents, in Hong Kong, Manchester, and Buffalo. When colonial officials said that, in addition to the British genius of administration, it was the tremendous energies of their Chinese subjects that transformed Hong Kong from a barren rock into one of the world's great cities, they were talking about him.

ABBREVIATIONS

ANA	Australian National Archives
BBC WAC	British Broadcasting Corporation Written Archives Centre
BDTC	British Dependent Territories Citizen
BG	Bernie Grant papers, Bishopsgate Institute
BNO	British National Overseas
BUTT	Herbert Butterfield Papers, Cambridge University Library
CCP	Chinese Communist Party
CDO	City District Officers
CHAS	China Association collection, School of Oriental and African Studies, University of London
CO	Colonial Office
CUHK	Chinese University of Hong Kong
EEC	European Economic Community
FAULDS	Andrew Faulds papers, LSE
FCO	Foreign and Commonwealth Office
FEER	*Far Eastern Economic Review*
FO	Foreign Office, TNA
FS	Fabian Society papers, LSE
GIS	Government Information Services
HKBU	Hong Kong Baptist University
HKPRO	Hong Kong Public Records Office (Hong Kong Government Records Office)
HKTA	Hong Kong Tourist Authority
HKU	University of Hong Kong
HS	Han Suyin Collection, Howard Gotlieb Archival Research Center, Boston University
ICAC	Independent Commission against Corruption
JC	James Clavell collection, Howard Gotlieb Archival Research Center, Boston University
JCWI	Joint Council for the Welfare of Immigrants
KNKK	Neil Kinnock papers, Churchill College, Cambridge
KW	Kaye Webb collection, Seven Stories Archive, Newcastle
LMA	London Metropolitan Archives
LSE	London School of Economics
NLW	National Library of Wales
OMELCO	Office of the Members of the Executive and Legislative Councils
PLA	People's Liberation Army
POLL	Enoch Powell Papers, Churchill College, Cambridge
PRC	People's Republic of China
RTHK	Radio Television Hong Kong
SAR	Special Administrative Region

ABBREVIATIONS

SCMP	*South China Morning Post*
SHORE	Peter Shore papers, LSE
SIU	Special Investigation Unit
TNA	The National Archives, Kew, London
UMELCO	Unofficial Members of the Hong Kong Executive and Legislative Council
WYAS	West Yorkshire Archive Service

Introduction: Britishness, empire, and Hong Kong

Every Guy Fawkes Day, five bonfire societies in Lewes, Sussex, lead processions of men dressed in Cavalier costumes, accompanied by bands and bonfires, to celebrate the discovery of the 1605 Gunpowder Plot. During the Grand United Procession, four of the five societies join together, along with visiting societies from other nearby towns, marching from one end of the town to the other. According to Jim Etherington, writing in 1993, with 'over two thousand society members, accompanied by fifteen to twenty bands and being a mile or more in length, the procession can take over thirty minutes to pass one point'. Afterwards, the various societies split into their own Grand Processions, marching, followed by crowds, to separate venues at the edge of town, where members dressed in clerical garb rail against unpopular politicians and enemies of Britain, as well as opponents of the bonfire itself.[1] Following the denunciations, effigies of these enemies, along with effigies of Guy Fawkes, are ignited.

In November 1997, a little more than four months after Britain's exit from Hong Kong and the latter's establishment as a Special Administrative Region (SAR) of the People's Republic of China (PRC), as well as just over two months after Princess Diana's death, Hong Kong featured in the Lewes Bonfire celebrations. While one of the Bonfire Societies played 'Candle in the Wind' in memory of Princess Diana, two of them commemorated Hong Kong's Handover, with one of these, that of Commercial Square, depicting Governor Christopher Patten's crushing by a Chinese tank.[2] According to the local *Sussex Express*, the Patten 'tableau had forcefully delivered the society's message: anger that the last major colony was no more'.[3]

The *Express* did not explain the precise reason for the Commercial Square Bonfire Society's anger. Was it in recognition that Britain's imperial retreat was finally complete and its 'decline' fully accomplished, a quarter of a century after what John Darwin terms the end of

[1]

the 'British World-System'?[4] Was it dismay at the handing-over of six million imperial subjects to a Communist regime, barely eight years after the Tiananmen Square massacre? Was it a protest against what many regarded as a humiliating retreat following Margaret Thatcher's failed negotiations in the early 1980s, symbolised by the public spill the Prime Minister took at one of the meetings?[5] Certainly these themes had featured in the coverage in the national press a few months earlier, at the time of the Handover itself. To *Daily Mail* journalist Ann Leslie, 30 June was the date when 'at the stroke of midnight this wild, hot, steamy and neurotically glittering enclave of 6.3 million free, feisty and precarious people is thrust, willy-nilly, into the hands of the murderous and corrupt regime of communist China'.[6] Fellow *Daily Mail* writer Paul Eastman focused less on the Communist Party itself than on the People's Liberation Army (PLA), which 'owns nightclubs, pig farms, ice cream parlours and brothels. They are the most corrupt force on earth ... and tonight they get their hands on Hong Kong.'[7] Reporting on the Handover ceremony, Leslie expressed hurt feelings on Britain's behalf, criticising Chinese Communist Party (CCP) Secretary Jiang Zemin's speech for omitting any mention of Britain's role in 'helping to make this once "barren rock" in the South China Sea one of the most vibrant and free-living, free thinking economies in the world'.[8] To Alan Massie, Prince Charles's 'glum' look at the ceremonies reflected the 'diminished state of the monarchy itself'.[9]

While the *Daily Mail* nursed a hurt pride, the *Sun* and the *Mirror* both emphasised British accomplishments. To the *Sun*, what stood out among Britain's achievements were a 'fair and respected legal system', the conquest of corruption, the establishment of a true free market, and the sheer scale of development.[10] Far from expressing sorrow, the paper combined its characteristic flippancy (including numerous headline puns) with goodwill, concluding 'the people of Hong Kong mostly welcome new management ... So long, Hong Kong. It's been good to know you.' It even devoted its trademark topless 'page 3 girl' to the occasion, featuring a British-born Chinese whose parents had come from Hong Kong. Under the picture, the caption read: 'Here's a little Hong Kong phewy to mark today's transfer of the colony to Beijing rule – 23-year-old Ivy Yeung, whose parents are Chinese. Of course, our new Page 3 girl, who lives in the Lake District, would be worth Peking at ANY day. Just look what she has her handover [i.e., her breasts].'[11] The *Mirror*, while noting the sadness of the occasion, emphasised the success of British imperialism and its ending: 'none of us who watched that final ceremony could fail to be proud to be British ... Hong Kong symbolised how this nation was able to help other countries achieve so much for themselves'.[12]

[2]

A person judging only from the popular press coverage surrounding the Handover could be excused for thinking that the small Chinese colony was central to Britain's national identity. Conversely, a regular newspaper reader who happened to miss those few days of coverage in late June and early July 1997 would be forgiven for assuming that Hong Kong was almost entirely absent from the British consciousness. As Roger Buckley pointed out that year, Hong Kong often lacked salience within British society. He noted, for example, that an April 1963 Commons debate concerning Hong Kong began with only a dozen MPs in attendance, a figure that rose only to twenty-three by the debate's end. More broadly,

> Rarely was interest much above the level of interest that led the Hong Kong government to report that 'less dog was eaten nowadays' or junior minister John Profumo's reply in March 1957 that 'modern ideas are gradually doing away with concubinage and I think that may prove the best way to deal with it'.[13]

Former Governor Alexander Grantham, similarly, told an interviewer in 1968 that one of the reasons the Colonial Office (CO) was willing (on Grantham's advice) to retreat from plans to introduce democratising constitutional reform was that the British electorate 'didn't care a brass fa[r]thing about Hong Kong'.[14]

If Hong Kong often eluded public interest, it also has been largely absent in historical studies of British culture; still less has it featured in the scholarship on Britishness. This is not surprising. During the late Victorian zenith of imperial consciousness, when empire arguably had its most pronounced effect on British national identity, Hong Kong was a quite minor colony. During the interwar period, when Britain's Empire reached its greatest geographical extent, Hong Kong became, as Robert Bickers argues, a 'backwater'. Hong Kong's importance was rarely as a thing-in-itself; it was as an access point to China, and in this regard it was, by the interwar years, a poor second to Shanghai.[15] After the Communist victory in 1949, as David Clayton points out, Hong Kong became 'the most attractive base for economic contact with China', and the retention of the colony was regarded in the early 1950s as a vital economic interest, one that shaped British policy toward China.[16] Yet Hong Kong's postwar importance ran counter to more prevailing narratives, especially after 1956, of decolonisation, affluence, and the welfare state consensus. Indeed, Hong Kong's relative unimportance within the 'imperial mind' has been echoed in the relative neglect of Hong Kong within the historiography of the British Empire, in which India, Africa, the West Indies, and the Dominions have predominated.[17]

If Hong Kong plays a negligible part in the scholarship on British culture and Britishness in the late nineteenth and early twentieth centuries because of its relative neglect even within imperial scholarship, its absence from studies of the late twentieth century stems from a different cause: decolonisation. Richard Weight argues that even as early as 1940, empire lost whatever significance it had previously held within British national identity; he cites, for example, the declining use of empire in advertisements after 1930, as well as the demise of Empire Day.[18] Catherine Hall, in a different context, notes that 'in white England, amnesia about empire' was widespread during the era of decolonisation.[19]

The ways in which metropole and empire were 'mutually constitutive' has become something of a truism in studies of the nineteenth century; indeed, the point has been sufficiently well established to have prompted its own revisionism.[20] By contrast, historiography of the era of decolonisation has been slower in coming to terms with the interactions between domestic and imperial cultures. Certainly the gap has narrowed since Stuart Ward wrote in 2002 that, in contrast to the Victorian and interwar periods,

> As far as the post-1945 era is concerned, the rigid conceptual barriers between metropole and periphery are still very much intact. There remains a firmly entrenched assumption that the broad cultural impact of decolonisation was confined to the colonial periphery, with little relevance to post-war British culture and society. No attempt has been made to examine the cultural manifestations of the demise of imperialism as a social and political ideology in post-war Britain. Indeed, as far as empire and metropolitan culture are concerned, it is as though the end of empire has signalled the end of the subject.[21]

Indeed, recent books by Bill Schwarz, Wendy Webster, and James Chapman and Nicholas Cull have illuminated the cultural impact of empire in the post-1945 period, with particular attention to the question of national identity.[22] Yet Hong Kong – the most obvious counter-trend to the story of decolonisation for several decades after the war – has not factored into British cultural historiography in any significant way. This point is amply illustrated by Jordanna Bailkin's important book, *The Afterlife of Empire*. Bailkin offers an innovative and broadly convincing argument that the Welfare State and decolonisation were intertwined in the 1950s and 1960s, so that the postcolonial was an important component of the postwar. Her argument steers clear of Hong Kong, which throughout the 1970s remained both a solidly British colony (if only by Chinese acquiescence) and a self-conscious exemplar of pre-Welfare State Britishness.[23]

[4]

One possibility, of course, is that Hong Kong has been largely absent from postwar British cultural *historiography* for good reason: its relative insignificance in British cultural *history*. There is a prima facie case for this view. Aside from the famous inability of large numbers of Britons to name a single colony in a survey taken in 1947, Hong Kong itself arguably lacked resonance to the British public.[24] Harold Ingrams, writing in 1952, told the story of a postal worker who challenged a customer's claim that Hong Kong was part of the British Empire; upon verifying that the customer was correct, the worker insisted that it must have been a recent development.[25] The Hong Kong Association, a London-based organisation created in 1961 to promote Hong Kong industry and trade, was deemed necessary because of 'widespread ignorance about the Colony and much hostility towards it. It was largely considered to be a place of sweated labour, dope and vice, and complaints of unfair competition were rife.'[26] A 1969 memo by the Association noted that little about Hong Kong was reported in the British press 'save complaints about toys or accusations from Lancashire of the dumping of textiles'.[27] Nigel Cameron justified his 1978 history of Hong Kong by citing a widespread ignorance of the colony that co-existed with a collage of fleeting images, such as the drug trade, corrupt policemen, 'super-luxury', and Suzie Wongs.[28] A 1981 *Far Eastern Economic Review* (*FEER*) correspondent noted that stories about Hong Kong rarely appeared in the British press, but those that did appear portrayed it 'as a sweatshop colony in the grip of corrupt policemen and a prime breeding ground for triads operating in London's Chinatown'.[29]

The potential loss of such a colony could not be expected to trouble Britons unduly, particularly in the context of a general indifference toward empire. Not only, in the words of Wm. Roger Louis, did the 1960s' 'dismantling of the Empire' in Aden, Sarawak, and North Borneo occur 'with hardly a flicker of attention from the British public'.[30] A July 1967 assessment by the American Central Intelligence Agency, made during the height of the riots, or 'disturbances', concluded as well that the loss of Hong Kong to mainland China would not constitute a 'serious psychological blow to Britain or to the Labor government', but would be accepted 'philosophically as an inevitable part of the winding up of Empire to which all political parties have been at least resigned'.[31] The perception of British indifference to Hong Kong was so strong that, in advocating in the late 1960s that the adjective 'Royal' be added to the Hong Kong Police Force's title, one of the arguments put forward was that such a move would 'remind the people of Hong Kong, in their remote and isolated position, that Her Majesty and Her Majesty's Government continue to take a deep interest in the well-being of the Colony and its inhabitants'.[32] A person seeking to argue how little Hong Kong mattered to British culture would, then, have little difficulty finding supporting quotations.

Yet such assessments considerably understate Hong Kong's place within postwar British culture and national identity. Indeed, Hong Kong, as a colony whose spectacular development under British auspices contrasted sharply with the contemporary retreat elsewhere, offered just as pointed an opportunity for reflecting on Britishness as did the 'betrayal' of the 'white man's world' so richly detailed by Bill Schwarz. But whereas the British surrender of Kenya and Rhodesia chiefly afforded an occasion for contrasting the 'real' whiteness of settlers abroad (and ordinary Britons confronting immigrants at home) with feckless politicians and bureaucrats, Britain's continuing management of Hong Kong, decisively challenged only in the early 1980s, offered a site in which supposed British virtues could be more positively showcased. Preparation for the 1997 Handover lacked the same acrimony as the retreat from Kenya or Rhodesia, at least among white Britons. Virtually no commentators entertained the fantasy of resisting the Chinese takeover, and the signing of the Joint Declaration in December 1984 gave Britons more than a dozen years to resign themselves to reality; the ongoing 'localisation' of the civil service from the early 1970s meant that, unlike in 1930s Shanghai, few Britons stood to face real loss from the end of British Hong Kong.[33] The Handover, rather, provided an occasion to reflect upon British accomplishment in establishing markets; rule of law; and effective, corruption-free government: properties that could be extended rhetorically to the entire British Empire.

Hong Kong was, of course, most important among the British who lived and worked there, and their voice will be the most prominent in this story. The number of British expatriates and settlers varied over time, and in some years official statistics lumped Britons and Commonwealth citizens together. In 1969, more than 5,000 Britons served in the Hong Kong Police Force alone, representing some 5 per cent of the force.[34] In 1975, the number of British in Hong Kong, excluding the Armed Forces, stood at 18,994; by 1982 it had risen to an estimated 21,900, but by the end of 1985, following the Sino-British Joint Declaration, that number was down to 14,900 (by which point the number of British civilians had been surpassed by Americans, up from only about 1,800 in 1975).[35] At its peak, therefore, Hong Kong's British civilian population was equal to that of a modest provincial town – Tyldesley, for example. Moreover, because Hong Kong's British population was often transient, the number of Britons who spent significant time in Hong Kong vastly exceeded the number who lived there at any given moment.

[6]

Although Hong Kong figured most prominently in the experience of settlers and expatriates, it was far from absent from the metropolitan consciousness. In national contexts, Hong Kong became discursively prominent at certain atypical moments: when a visiting MP railed against its working conditions; when a crisis of rule confronted the Colonial Government, as in the 'Disturbances' of 1967; during negotiations in the early 1980s concerning the end of British rule; and above all during the Handover itself. The BBC, for example, featured a dozen news stories on Hong Kong on one day in May 1967 – having featured only a couple of dozen in all of 1959.[36]

These exceptional events were not, of course, the only time that Hong Kong appeared in Metropolitan discourse. In local contexts, Hong Kong became relevant when a regional military regiment began its two-year assignment in Hong Kong and local crowds saw them off at the train station from which they would travel to the docks of Liverpool; or when (for example) a 1960 London church's Missionary Pageant, entitled 'Hong Kong Epiphany', comprised an 'Exhibition of pictures and articles of interest on life in Hong Kong'; or when a 1965 Surrey tea event featured a 'Talk by Miss Kiddle on Her Holiday to Hong Kong' (accompanied by a cancer fundraiser and a 'Competition – My Prettiest Cup and Saucer').[37] In addition, periodically, Hong Kong was the setting of popular novels, such police-themed television series as the BBC's *Hong Kong Beat* and ITV's *Yellowthread Street*, or the topic of a BBC programme such as *Woman's Hour*. During the 1980s and 1990s, the University of Wales awarded a significant number of postgraduate degrees for theses comparing Wales and Hong Kong. Nor did students have to wait for university to be introduced to the colony. One forty-two-page 'Upper Intermediate' children's storybook from 1991, *Adventure in Hong Kong*, featured young Jack and Anna, in a stopover with their parents during their return from Australia, helping the police to thwart a terrorist group's attempt to blow up their plane. Despite its brevity, the book managed to feature a Lion Dance and a pick-pocket, visits to the Night Market and the Peak, and to convey that Hong Kong was an electronics emporium and that it was crowded with Chinese people.[38] Postwar children were often acquainted with Hong Kong through the labels on their toys, even if not always directly; David Cannadine has written of his childhood toys identified as ' "Empire Made" – an explicit acknowledgement that the empire still existed, but a euphemism for the fact that such goods invariably originated in Hong Kong'.[39] Yet if the labels were sometimes euphemistic, readers of William Marsden's *Living in Hong Kong*, a short 1991 children's picture-book, were confronted with pictures of Batman toys accompanied by the caption: 'These toys were made in Kowloon.

Figure 1 The departure of a local regiment could remind a town of Hong Kong's existence. Crowds at South Wigston Station to see the 1st Battalion depart for Hong Kong, 11 May 1949.

People in Britain buy many goods which are made in Hong Kong.'[40] According to Nigel Whitely, writing in 1989 in the *New Statesman & Society*, plastic's public-relations problem following the Second World War stemmed from the 'rash of cheap-and-nasty plastic toys and trinkets' from Hong Kong, so that 'in the post-war age, "plastic", "Hong Kong", and "inferiority" congealed in the public's collective unconscious'.[41] Not that plasticity was the worst feature attributed to Hong Kong toys; the BBC in 1965 and 1966 reported on their toxicity, including rumours that children 'all over the world [were] suffering poisoning by sucking some of the Hong-Kong-made toys'.[42]

This book examines depictions of Hong Kong within domestic British discourse, and a range of commentary by British people in Hong Kong, moving fluidly between the two sites as convenience requires. Covering the period between the fall of two imperial regimes, Japanese and British, this book is not intended as a comprehensive history of British Hong Kong even during this short half-century. Rather, it

[8]

examines the place of Hong Kong within the British imagination from the time the British reclaimed Hong Kong from the Japanese to the time they relinquished it to the PRC. Although the book considers culture in the broadest sense, it focuses above all on the relationship between Hong Kong and Britishness, drawing on a catholic range of primary sources, including British and Colonial Government documents, private correspondence, novels, memoirs, news media, and contemporary journalistic and academic accounts, just to name the most important types. Some of the stories have not been previously told, while others, such as the war on corruption, are familiar to Hong Kong specialists but are considered here within a new context. It is worth emphasising, moreover, that my focus is on the stories that the British told about themselves and what they were trying to accomplish.

Two other points about the sources deserve emphasis. First, although most of their authors can fairly unproblematically be called 'British', I also draw on relevant sources whose authors belonged to the broader 'British world', including Australia, Canada, and Rhodesia, as well as Americans.[43] Of these, Australia is, not surprisingly, the most important. Stuart Ward has shown that until the early 1960s, Australian national identity was largely constructed through an engagement with Britishness, shifting to a more exclusivist Australian nationalism in response to Britain's closer ties to Europe. Similarly, John Darwin has underscored that the Dominion ideal was central to postwar attempts to fashion a 'fourth British empire'.[44] In the discourse that explained Hong Kong to British readers, not only did such Australian writers as James Clavell and Richard Hughes feature prominently, but Clavell – before eventually becoming a naturalised US citizen – provided some of the most pronounced iterations of overt Britishness. Other, much less famous, examples surface in archives, whether the 1950s Australian tourist who visited Hong Kong en route to London, and whose complaints of loneliness prompted earnest correspondence between the Australian Government Trade Commissioner and Assistant Secretary, Department of Commerce and Agriculture, or the Australian expatriate whose very politicised (and pro-Patten) 1995 Christmas circular found its way into Martin Booth's archive.[45] Yet if Australians are the most frequent 'British world' figures to intrude into this book, others feature as well, including the Rhodesia-born novelist John Gordon Davis, and the Canadian-born self-proclaimed sex guru Roger Boschman.

The United States is a different case. My occasional quotations from American interlocutors do not reflect a Churchillian fantasy of their belonging to an Anglo-Saxon imagined community, but rather the fact that they shared a discursive (and physical) space with the Britons who are my main subjects. For the postwar United States, Hong Kong was a key cold war location: the site of the largest US Consulate, where 'China-watchers' could be based, and a notorious leave destination for American soldiers during the Vietnam War. It was also a place in which the American missionary engagement with China, more than a century old, could concentrate now that the mainland had been closed, as well as a crucial location for Sinophiles. Yet although the American engagement with Hong Kong had a very different provenance than the British one did, it necessarily informed the British understanding of Hong Kong. In part this reflected the strong American presence in Hong Kong, and the prominent American role in creating discourse about Hong Kong; even the British Council's Representatives felt constrained to see their mission in Hong Kong through comparison to the United States Information Services.[46] More broadly, of course, it stemmed from the increasing American cultural presence in Britain itself, as in so many other countries. Yet while American sources (like Australian ones) come into this story from time to time, the focus remains on the British cultural engagement with Hong Kong.

A second point bears emphasising: this book is based entirely on English-language sources. In large part this is the simple result of my own linguistic deficiencies, but in turn it follows naturally from this study's focus on British culture (and my own primary interest in modern British history). I have no doubt that there are extant Chinese sources that would enrich this story, particularly with respect to Chapter 6, but, *faute de mieux*, I will leave it to other scholars to decide whether they are worth pursuing.

At the heart of this book is the interplay among three somewhat contradictory themes: Hong Kong as the site of an unbridled capitalism, in happy contrast to the increasingly 'managed' post-1945 metropole; as the recipient of modernisation projects, often initiated by the Government; and as the focus of good governance, in which legitimacy was made compatible with non-democratic rule. Although in practice these three motifs often overlapped, they will for analytical purposes be discussed in separate chapters (2, 4, and 5). All three themes featured in the recurring trope, common in the postwar era, of Hong Kong as a 'barren island' upon which Britons had imposed order and modernity. Trea Wiltshire's 1971 coffee-table book, for example, subtitled 'An Impossible Journey through History,' begins with a section entitled 'Barren Island,' and proceeds to chronicle all of the factors, including recurring bad luck and a lack of natural resources, that conspired against Hong Kong's triumph. Noting Lord Palmerston's displeasure at Captain Elliot's taking Hong Kong, 'a barren island with hardly a house upon it', as a poor spoil of the Opium War, she avers simply,

'He was wrong.' Her point is not to criticise Palmerston's lack of fore-
sight, but to highlight it as a reasonable assessment of Hong Kong's
prospects: 'one can almost sympathize with Palmerston's pessimism,
for failure would have been easier to explain than success'.[47] Wiltshire
is not alone. Palmerston's quotation – often with 'barren rock' substi-
tuted for 'barren island' – repeatedly features as the foil against which
those celebrating British rule in Hong Kong rate its impressiveness.[48]

Hong Kong was not, of course, only a site for serious British accomplishments; it was also a place of masculine leisure, including sport,
clubs, and sexuality – the subject of Chapter 3. After Hong Kong's place
within the British imagination has been established, Chapter 6 considers the phenomenon – limited though it was – of Chinese Britishness,
focusing both on the extent to which British commentators envisioned
its possibility and on the extent to which Chinese subjects embraced it.
Finally, Chapter 7 examines the discourse surrounding the Handover in
1997, a discourse that wavered between celebration of Britain's achievement and remorse or even bitterness over its potential destruction.
First, however, Chapter 1 considers Hong Kong and Britishness within
the contexts of postwar decolonisation, the cold war, demographic
explosion, and economic miracle – a period in which Hong Kong went
from being a quite minor colony to being far and away Britain's most
important remaining colony, in fact its last major colony.

Notes

1 Jim Etherington, *Lewes Bonfire Night* (Seaford: S. B. Publications, 1993), p. 9.
2 'Wet, Wet, Wet, but It Was Still Superb', *Sussex Express* (7 November 1997), p. 23.
3 'Tableau Marks Retreat from Hong Kong', *Sussex Express* (7 November 1997), p. 25.
4 John Darwin, *The Empire Project: The Rise and Fall of the British World-System, 1830–1970* (Cambridge: Cambridge University Press, 2009).
5 See Mark Roberti, *The Fall of Hong Kong: Britain's Betrayal and China's Triumph* (New York: John Wiley and Sons, 1996), Chapter 4; John Flowerdew, *The Final Years of British Hong Kong: The Discourse of Colonial Withdrawal* (New York: St Martin's Press, 1997), Chapter 3; David Bonavia, *Hong Kong 1997: The Final Settlement* (Hong Kong: FEER, 1985), p. 99.
6 Special Report from Ann Leslie in Hong Kong, *Daily Mail* (28 June 1997), p. 10.
7 Paul Eastman, 'Howe Breaks Ranks over Colony Party', *Daily Mail* (30 June 1997), p. 21.
8 Ann Leslie, 'A Tearful Salute to the Last Jewel in the Crown', *Daily Mail* (1 July 1997), p. 1.
9 Allan Massie, 'The Flag Comes Down but We Can Hold Our Heads High', *Daily Mail* (1 July 1997), p. 8.
10 Robin Bowman, 'Why I'm Staying on in Hong Kong', *Sun* (30 June 1997), p. 6.
11 'The Tasty Chinese Takeaway/So Long, Hong Kong', *Sun* (30 June 1997), pp. 7–8. Oddly, the page 3 girl appeared on page 7, displaced by news that Mike Tyson had bitten off a piece of Evander Holyfield's ear.
12 'Look Back with Pride', *Mirror* (1 July 1997), p. 6. See also Mark Dowdney's pictorial, 'How We Turned Hong Kong ... from This to This', *Mirror* (28 June 1997), pp. 22–3.

13 Roger Buckley, *Hong Kong: The Road to 1997* (Cambridge: Cambridge University Press, 1997), pp. 76, 79. David Bonavia notes that in the House of Commons December 1984 debate on the Sino-British Joint Declaration, only 8 per cent of MPs bothered to attend. Bonavia, *Hong Kong 1997*, p. 144. According to Bernard Porter, Hong Kong was not unique in this regard; in the 1930s, imperial debates in general failed to attract the presence of very many MPs. Bernard Porter, *The Absent-Minded Imperialists: Empire, Society and Culture in Britain* (Oxford: Oxford University Press, 2004), pp. 269–72.

14 Rhodes College, Oxford, MS Brit. Emp. Si 288, Alexander Grantham, interview by D. J. Crozier, 21 August 1968, p. 12.

15 Robert Bickers, 'The Colony's Shifting Position in the British Informal Empire in China', in Judith M. Brown and Rosemary Foot (eds), *Hong Kong's Transitions, 1842–1997* (Basingstoke: Macmillan, 1997), pp. 33–61 (pp. 39–40). See also Jan Morris, *Hong Kong: Epilogue to an Empire* (New York: Random House, 1997), p. 182 (future references are to the 1997 edition unless stated otherwise); Bonavia, *Hong Kong 1997*, p. 69. Lawrence Kadoorie said of interwar Hong Kong, 'If Shanghai was London then Hong Kong was Hastings.' Quoted in Kevin Rafferty, *City on the Rocks: Hong Kong's Uncertain Future* (New York: Viking, 1989), p. 136.

16 David Clayton, *Imperialism Revisited: Political and Economic Relations between Britain and China, 1950–54* (Basingstoke: Macmillan, 1997), p. 99.

17 There are, of course, distinguished exceptions, including work by Philippa Levine, Susan Pedersen, Wm. Roger Louis, John Carroll, David Clayton, and Chi-kwan Mark. In a collection of essays published in 1997, the year of the Handover, John Darwin argued that Hong Kong does not fit into the conventional decolonisation narrative, not least because Hong Kong did not achieve independence; John Darwin, 'Hong Kong in British Decolonisation', in Brown and Foot, *Hong Kong's Transitions*, pp. 16–32. Hong Kong is, of course, the subject of an increasingly sophisticated scholarship focusing on the development of its political and civic institutions, its relationship with mainland China, or its emergence as a global city; this scholarship, which has been highly formative in my own understanding of Hong Kong history, is scarcely noticed by historians of Britain and the British Empire.

18 Richard Weight, *Patriots: National Identity in Britain, 1940–2000* (Basingstoke: Macmillan, 2002), pp. 286–7.

19 Catherine Hall, *Civilising Subjects: Metropole and Colony in the English Imagination, 1830–1867* (Chicago: The University of Chicago Press, 2002), p. 5.

20 On the interplay between imperial and domestic cultures, see especially John M. MacKenzie, *Propaganda and Empire* (Manchester: Manchester University Press, 1990); John MacKenzie (ed.), *Imperialism and Popular Culture*; Andrew Thompson, *The Empire Strikes Back? The Impact of Imperialism on Britain from the Mid-Nineteenth Century* (Harlow: Longman, 2005); Hall, *Civilising Subjects*; Antoinette Burton (ed.), *After the Imperial Turn: Thinking with and through the Nation* (Durham, NC: Duke University Press, 2003); Catherine Hall and Sonya M. Rose (eds), *At Home with the Empire: Metropolitan Culture and the Imperial World* (Cambridge: Cambridge University Press, 2006). For an argument that the influence of empire on metropolitan life has been significantly overstated, see Porter, *The Absent-Minded Imperialists*. See also Richard Price, 'One Big Thing: Britain, Its Empire, and Their Imperial Culture', *Journal of British Studies* 45 (2006): 602–27.

21 Stuart Ward, 'Introduction', in Stuart Ward (ed.), *British Culture and the End of Empire* (Manchester and New York: Manchester University Press, 2001), pp. 1–2.

22 Bill Schwarz, *The White Man's World* (Oxford: Oxford University Press, 2011); Wendy Webster, *Englishness and Empire, 1939–1965* (Oxford: Oxford University Press, 2005); James Chapman and Nicholas J. Cull, *Projecting Empire: Imperialism and Popular Cinema* (London: I. B. Tauris, 2009).

23 Jordanna Bailkin, *The Afterlife of Empire* (Berkeley: University of California Press, 2012).

24 Weight, *Patriots*, p. 286.

25 Harold Ingrams, *Hong Kong* (London: HMSO, 1952), p. 43.

[12]

26 CHAS, SI 17, 'Draft Letter to Mrs S. Yuen, Hong Kong', n.d. (1968?). According to the Colonial Secretary, C. B. Burgess, speaking in August 1962, this hostility to Hong Kong was a new development in the late 1950s, after a sympathetic world opinion at the time of the Shek Kip Mei fire in 1953. C. B. Burgess, *Hong Kong's Image: An Address Given to the Rotary Club of Hong Kong by the Colonial Secretary the Honourable C. B. Burgess, C.M.G., O.B.E. on Tuesday, 28th August, 1962* (Hong Kong: Government Printer, 1962), pp. 7–8.

27 CHAS, SI 17, 'Hong Kong's Public Relations in the UK', 18 February 1969.

28 Nigel Cameron, *Hong Kong: The Cultured Pearl* (Hong Kong: Oxford University Press, 1978), pp. ix, xiv.

29 Dinah Lee, 'The London View: What Does Talk of Greater Democracy Mean Here?', *FEER* (13 March 1981): 64–6.

30 Wm. Roger Louis, 'The Dissolution of the British Empire in the Era of Vietnam', in Wm. Roger Louis, *The Ends of British Imperialism: The Scramble for Empire, Suez and Decolonization* (London and New York: I. B. Tauris, 2006), pp. 557–86 (pp. 585–6). He cites Rhodesia as a counterexample to this general picture. See also Ritchie Ovendale, 'The End of Empire', in Richard English and Michael Kenny (eds), *Rethinking British Decline* (Basingstoke: Macmillan, 2000), pp. 257–78.

31 Quoted in Catherine R. Schenk, 'The Banking and Financial Impact of the 1967 Riots in Hong Kong', in Robert Bickers and Ray Yep, *May Days in Hong Kong: Emergency and Riot in 1967* (Hong Kong: Hong Kong University Press, 2009), pp. 105–26 (p. 107).

32 TNA, FCO 40/ 226, A. L. Mayall to Michael Adeane, 6 February 1969.

33 See Robert Bickers, *Britain in China: Community, Culture and Colonialism, 1900–1949* (Manchester and New York: Manchester University Press, 1999), pp. 170–218. Chi-kwan Mark has argued that Hong Kong was effectively 'decolonised' in the decade after 1957, despite continued British administration; see Chi-kwan Mark, 'Lack of Means or Loss of Will? The United Kingdom and the Decolonization of Hong Kong, 1957–1967', *The International History Review* 31 (March 2009): 45–71.

34 Draft notes for supplementaries, n.d. (1969). TNA, FCO 40/ 226.

35 *Report for the Year 1975* (Hong Kong: Government Printer, 1976), p. 181; *Hong Kong 1983: A Review of 1982* (Hong Kong: Government Printer, 1983), p. 238; *Hong Kong 1986: A Review of 1985* (Hong Kong: Government Printer, 1986), p. 269.

36 See the BBC radio schedule, available at the British Broadcasting Corporation Written Archives Centre (BBC WAC).

37 LMA, N/C/63/095, leaflet for a missionary pageant; Surrey History Centre, 1587/1/347, talk on holiday in Hong Kong.

38 Stella Martin, *Adventure in Hong Kong* (London and Basingstoke: Macmillan, 1991).

39 David Cannadine, *Ornamentalism: How the British Saw Their Empire* (Oxford: Oxford University Press, 2001), p. 186.

40 William Marsden, *Living in Hong Kong* (Edinburgh: Oliver and Boyd, 1991), p. 13.

41 Nigel Whitely, 'The Plastic Years', *New Statesman & Society* 2 (17 November 1989), p. 40.

42 BBC WAC, N1094, Hong Kong Government Office, Part I, [??] May 1965–21 December 1989, 'Story as attached to the script for 19th May 1965'. See also BBC WAC, N1094, Hong Kong Government Office, Part I [??] May 1965–21 December 1989, B. I. Barlow to O. J. Whitley, 24 June 1965; B. I. Barlow to O. J. Whitley, 24 June and 13 August 1965; and Ronald Boxall (Principal Information Officer) to O. J. Whitley (Chief Assistant to the Director-General, BBC) 12 January 1967.

43 On the British world, see, for example, Kate Darian-Smith, Patricia Grimshaw, and Stuart Macintyre (eds), *Britishness Abroad: Transnational Movements and Imperial Cultures* (Melbourne: Melbourne University Press, 2007); Phillip Buckner and R. Douglas Francis (eds), *Rediscovering the British World* (Calgary: University of Calgary Press, 2005); Kent Fedorowich and Andrew S. Thompson (eds), *Empire, Migration and Identity in the British World* (Manchester: Manchester University Press, 2013); Barry Crosbie and Mark Hampton (eds), *The Cultural Construction of the British World* (Manchester: Manchester University Press, 2016).

44 Stuart Ward, *Australia and the British Embrace: The Demise of the Imperial Ideal* (Melbourne: Melbourne University Press, 2001); Darwin, *The Empire Project*. See also A. James Hammerton and Alistair Thompson, *Ten Pound Poms: A Life History of British Postwar Immigration to Australia* (Manchester: Manchester University Press, 2005); Simon J. Potter, *Broadcasting Empire: The BBC and the British World, 1922–1970* (Oxford: Oxford University Press, 2012); A. G. Hopkins, 'Rethinking Decolonization', *Past & Present* 200 (2008): 211–47.

45 ANA, A609 552/108/1, H. Sullivan to Assistant Secretary, Department of Commerce and Agriculture, 12 February 1953; Martin Booth collection, 1998/67 Box 6, Penny Forster, 'Christmas, Hong Kong, 1995'.

46 See Mark Hampton, 'Projecting Britishness to Hong Kong: The British Council and Hong Kong House, 1950s–1970s', *Historical Research* 85 (2012): 691–709.

47 Trea Wiltshire, *Hong Kong: An Impossible Journey through History. Hong Kong: 1841–1971* (Hong Kong: Serasia, 1971), pp. 15–17. The phrase 'A barren island' also appears at the beginning of the book's inside jacket flap.

48 For example, it appears in the British Central Office of Information's 1976 twelve-page 'Fact Sheet' on Hong Kong. See Central Office of Information, *Hong Kong* (London: HMSO, 1976), p. 4. Other examples include Nora Clarke, *Living in Hong Kong* (Hove: Wayland, 1980), p. 6; James Kirkup, *Cities of the World: Hong Kong and Macao* (London: J. M. Dent and Sons, 1970), p. 14; Morris, *Hong Kong*, p. 18; 'Outguessing the Cassandras', in 'Hong Kong: A Survey by the *Economist*', *The Economist* (19 October 1968), p. iii. For a discussion of the trope of Hong Kong as a formerly 'barren rock', see C. K. Lau, *Hong Kong's Colonial Legacy: A Hong Kong Chinese's View of the British Heritage* (Hong Kong: Chinese University Press, 1997), pp. 187–90.

CHAPTER ONE

Hong Kong and British culture: postwar contexts

International and local contexts

In the summer of 1945, neither Hong Kong's prospects, nor its continued status as a British colony, were assured. At the end of the Second World War, Hong Kong's population stood at barely 600,000 (down from a prewar high of perhaps 1.8 million). British expatriates who might contemplate resuming life there faced the daunting challenge of rebuilding. The BBC war correspondent Edward Ward, perhaps best known for his March 1940 scoop that Finland and the Soviet Union had reached a peace agreement, arrived in Hong Kong in early September 1945, shortly before the Japanese surrender ceremony. Ward, who had spent three-and-a-half years in Italian and German prison camps following his capture by Italian troops at Tobruk, described the 'beautiful houses' in Victoria as being 'in ruins' – not because of bombs, but because of wartime 'Chinese looting, unchecked by the Japanese', a practice that continued at least a month after British reoccupation of Hong Kong. At the same time, 'one-time gardens' had become 'jungly wildernesses', and 'Rank vegetation had grown almost completely across the roads.'[1] Not even Hong Kong's premier gentlemen's club was immune to wartime destruction, albeit of a distinctive nature: an entry in *Time* magazine's 1945 'Time Capsule' reported that 'When the conquerors took over the swank Hong Kong Club in 1941, they sawed six inches off the legs of the Club's billiard tables, so that stubby Jap officers could play. Last week, long-legged Britons were back at their billiards, kneeling and stooping to cue.'[2] Although most obviously noticeable to Britons on the scene, news of such deterioration made it to at least one metropolitan household, by way of Sydney. Soldier Billy Moore, anticipating a short assignment in Hong Kong while awaiting demobilisation from the Pacific theatre, wrote to his wife Vera of rumours that the homes previously inhabited by Europeans had mostly been looted and turned into firewood.[3]

Such images would be recalled decades later. In his 1962 account of three years spent in late-1950s Hong Kong directing a fisheries research team, F. D. Ommaney recalled his first arrival in August 1945 as part of the liberation force: 'The population was starving and people were dying in the gutters. In order to provide firewood during four winters, the great deserted mansions of the rich on the Peak had been stripped of doors, doorposts, flooring, stairways and all woodwork. Most of them stood in ruins.'[4] According to Alexander Grantham, reflecting in 1968 upon his return to Hong Kong as governor in 1947, as a result of the war, three-quarters of the 'tenement type of buildings were not fit for human habitation'.[5] This was, moreover, before the tremendous influx of refugees beginning after 1949.[6] Writing in the early 1980s, the missionary-turned-political-activist Elsie Elliott remembered passing through Hong Kong in 1947: 'Hong Kong in those days was just a sleepy replica of present-day Macao on a larger scale, with four-storey buildings of colonial style. People scurried everywhere carrying goods in baskets on the ends of bamboo poles.'[7] A late 1947 memo outlining the Commonwealth Bank of Australia's prospects for trade in Hong Kong called the colony 'fortunate in that it suffered comparatively little war damage', but most observers seem to have been less impressed by its comparison to other East Asian cities than with the absolute level of destruction.[8]

Not only did Hong Kong face physical ruin, but Britain's continued possession of Hong Kong was not assured, even after the Allied victory over Japan. In 1943, Chiang Kai-shek's Nationalist Government had pressed Britain for a return of Hong Kong, linking the question to the ending of extraterritoriality, but the British successfully deferred the Hong Kong issue until victory. Although, with American acquiescence, the British arranged that they, rather than Chiang, would receive the Japanese surrender, the British Government understood that the matter was not resolved, and that the Chinese could raise the issue at any moment.[9] In 1946, a secret memorandum issued jointly by the Foreign Office and the CO weighed the merits of raising the question, as uncertainty was undermining investors' confidence, and thus Hong Kong's postwar recovery. British policymakers viewed administration and material interests, not sovereignty, as the crucial point, and believed there was some ground for thinking that the Chinese would accept a compromise along those lines. At the same time, the wider imperial context had to be considered, as it was feared that a change of Hong Kong's sovereignty would open the questions of Gibraltar, the Falklands, Cyprus, and other colonies; in addition, the Americans might disapprove of a British concession. Against these complications, ultimately, the joint memorandum counseled against

[16]

raising the issue with Chiang, while at the same time recommending that the Government clearly state British intention to remain in Hong Kong.[10] Over the next several years, the British Government established its commitment to the defence of Hong Kong, a process that Chi-kwan Mark has situated within the context of Anglo-American relations in the early years of the cold war.[11] The Australian and New Zealand Governments, moreover, reflecting their continuing support for what John Darwin has called 'the fourth British Empire', asserted their commitment to the defence of Hong Kong, even if, in practical terms, there were limitations to that commitment.[12]

Despite the demonstrated intention to retain Hong Kong, and temporary Chinese acquiescence in the status quo, Hong Kong's long-term future remained uncertain. Japanese initial success in the war had undermined European empire in Asia, and both the Nationalists and Communists indicated a commitment to Hong Kong's eventual return to China, no doubt to the chagrin of Shanghai capitalists who, the Australian journalist Peter Russo noted in September 1946, were steadily moving capital to Hong Kong and lamenting the loss of foreign management of Chinese affairs.[13] Chinese immigrants may have been seeking British management, but they brought Chinese cultural practices with them. An August 1946 article in Australia's *Sunday Mail*, for example, noted that Hong Kong's Chinese Maritime Customs Office had since the war increasingly been subjected to 'the gentle intrusion of Chinese ways into the office's normal routine' with the 'tacit suggestion that the foreigner is on his way out'. According to the article, the establishment of a Monday 'staff joss meeting', the presence of Chinese flags and Sun Yat-sen's picture, and the regular singing of the Chinese national anthem had alienated foreign staff, so that the typical foreign official would 'be ready to go, were it not for the loss of his pension.'[14] As Jan Morris wrote – perhaps with some overstatement – although after the war the 'pageantry of Government was soon restored … this was never again to feel quite like a British colony'.[15]

After the emergence of the PRC in 1949 most observers realised that British rule was in perpetual jeopardy, though it was often suggested that economics could trump nationalism or ideology for Mao's regime. As Australian Prime Minister Ben Chifley suggested to Clement Attlee in 1949, the 'accumulated experience and unrivalled facilities of Hong Kong as a trade entrepot' offered the 'best hope' that the Chinese Communists would leave it alone.[16] Still, many took for granted that the Chinese would resume control in 1997, with the expiration of the New Territories lease, if not before.[17] Malcolm Muggeridge, describing Hong Kong in 1958 as a 'curious little capitalist enclave [that] has managed to survive – like those tenacious maiden ladies who continue to make their afternoon tea and exercise their dogs despite wars, revolutions and other cataclysms', nonetheless thought that the colony's days were numbered. Speaking less than a year after his sacking by the BBC for criticising the Royal family in an American periodical, he said of Hong Kong that '[e]veryone knows that the place has no permanence. It may end next week or in thirty years' time, but it is doomed.'[18] According to Cecil King, Chairman of the Mirror Newspaper Group, during his visit to Hong Kong in March 1967, Governor Sir David Trench told him that he thought the British would continue to govern Hong Kong for 'about 30 years' so long as the British did not 'provoke a situation'.[19] Two months later, in the context of the 1967 riots, *New Statesman* editor Paul Johnson suggested that Mao was unlikely to 'push us out just yet', because of the 'gold' Hong Kong brought in vast quantities, necessary for grain and capital goods purchases; Johnson presciently believed the 'real difficulties' would begin to arise around fifteen years before 1997 as investment would fall sharply in the face of a shrinking window of opportunity.[20] The Australian journalist Richard Hughes captured this impermanent status in the evocative title of his 1968 book, *Borrowed Place, Borrowed Time*. As Hughes wrote, Hong Kong

> is the only human habitation in the world that knows when it will die – 1997, when the lease on the ceded New Territories expires and nine-tenths of the colony must be handed back to China. But no one broods over this deadline – which can be advanced whenever Peking has a change of policy and a change of mind.[21]

This idea of a sudden PRC attack on this most visible legacy of the nineteenth century's unequal treaties is a recurring theme in the 1950s and 1960s. Richard Mason's 1957 novel, *The World of Suzie Wong*, features this exchange between an American visitor and the British protagonist, Robert Lomax:

> Rodney sat down again, puckered his brow, and leaned across the table towards me. 'Look, Bob, there's something I want to ask you', he said, with the earnest humility of a student addressing a learned professor. 'Now, don't get angry with me – remember I'm just a stupid hysterical American. But I confess it's got me beat. All right, now to start – how far would you say it is from here to the China border?'
> 'I suppose about thirty miles', I said.
> 'About thirty miles. O.K. Right. And what's the population of Red China?'
> 'Say four hundred million.'
> 'Say four hundred million. O.K. Right. So that makes four hundred million Reds thirty miles away across the border – as against a few thousand

of you British sitting here in Hong Kong. And yet to judge by that race-track this afternoon, there's not a goddam [sic] one of you turning a hair. Well now, Bob, what I want to know is this. Just how the hell is it done? Are you crazy – or am I?'[22]

The idea of a sudden takeover by China features, two decades later, in John le Carré's 1977 cold war spy novel, *The Honourable Schoolboy*. When central character Jerry Westerby perceives, on a night in which his own plans appear to have gone sour, that the streets are uncharacteristically empty, he naturally infers that

> it's the Colony's last day ... Peking has made its proverbial telephone call. 'Get out, party over'. The last hotel was closing; he saw the empty Rolls-Royces lying like scrap around the harbour, and the last blue-rinse round-eye matron, laden with her tax-free furs and jewellery, tottering up the gang-way of the last cruise ship; the last China-watcher frantically feeding his last miscalculations into the shredder; the looted shops, the empty city waiting like a carcass for the hordes.[23]

Westerby self-consciously places this assumption in the context of the apparent eviction of the Anglo-American partnership from all of Southeast Asia, including Vietnam. He is, needless to say, mistaken; by the end of the novel, Westerby has been killed by his confederates, but British Hong Kong survives. The point that is relevant in the present context, though, is that Hong Kong's precarious status in the face of the Chinese threat remained an easily referenced meme for British novelists.

Of course, while to outward appearances Britain and China were cold war enemies, Britain the hated imperialist power, and Hong Kong a perpetual affront to China's dignity and sovereignty, the reality was that the colony was well integrated into China's economy, with clear benefits to both sides; beyond that, Hong Kong was dependent upon mainland China then, as it is now, for food and water. British Hong Kong's continued viability depended on PRC forbearance; far from requiring a military action to overthrow British rule (which was as militarily indefensible in the postwar era as it had been in 1941), it would be a simple matter of closing the water spigots or, conversely, opening the refugee floodgates.[24] Yet according to F. D. Ommaney, writing in 1962, the prospect of 1997 seemed, if anything, to bother people in England more than people in Hong Kong; at least for the Chinese in Hong Kong, most of whom were sojourners who had 'never really regarded the place as their home anyhow and have not quite begun to do so even now, though they will', the possibility of Hong Kong's return to China was not particularly arresting. The only visible effect, he wrote, was that rents were very high as landlords determined to squeeze as much profit as soon as possible.[25] As Richard Hughes said even in 1976, '1997 is still two enigmatic decades away. Borrowed time is as good as any.'[26] Just two years earlier, a confidential British Council report had expressed doubt that China would seek to absorb Hong Kong any time soon, not only because of the benefits it gained from the colony's existence but also because it seemed 'unlikely that [Communist China would] have an appetite for such an indigestible slice of mammon' in the near future.[27]

As we will see in Chapter 7, the early postwar argument that, although China could reclaim Hong Kong any time it wanted, it was unlikely actually to do so in the near future, was echoed by assertions in the 1980s and 1990s that, although China was, after all, going to reclaim the colony, self-interest would ensure that the Communists did not impose radical change on it. In both cases, the assertion was often disputed, and in both cases one gets the impression of wilful optimism. Yet the optimism died hard. As late as 1980, shortly before the negotiations between Margaret Thatcher and Deng Xiaoping over Hong Kong's post-1997 status had begun, but after Governor MacLehose had raised the issue with Beijing, Nora Clarke's picture book for children complacently assured her intended British audience that 'The lease of this land [New Territories] runs out in June 1997. The "New Territories" as they are called, must then be returned to China if demanded. But Hong Kong Island and the town of Kowloon will continue to be British.' To be sure, few commentators shared Clarke's view that Hong Kong and Kowloon could be feasibly separated from the New Territories; as Clarke herself noted a few pages later, the separation of the leased part from the ceded part would separate the territory's financial and industrial centres.[28] But Clarke was hardly alone in believing, even at this late date, that the British presence in Hong Kong could be extended; it was only after 1982 that the change of sovereignty became a certainty.

As Ommanney implied, the prospect that 'borrowed time' would have to be returned may well have shaped the attitude of many Britons (and Chinese) that Hong Kong was a location for making quick profits rather than a long-term future, one of the topics of Chapter 2.[29] As *The Economist* put it in 1957, 'Not all of Hongkong's feverish activity is hay-making while the sunshine lasts, but much of it is'; the article cited building developers who aimed 'to recoup their capital outlay in not more than seven years, and often in two or three years'.[30] At the same time, this prospect formed the backdrop to all plans for development on the part of Government officials as well. Reflecting in 1999 on his arrival in Hong Kong in the early 1960s, the retired colonial official Ian MacPherson contrasted Hong Kong with Tanganyika, the former colony of his previous assignment. It was clear that the object in Hong Kong was not to prepare the colony for independence; as a result, he wrote, 'in my early days here we didn't really discuss 1997'.[31] The diplomat Percy Cradock, in his 1994 memoir, noted that in the late 1960s the topic of the lease 'would crop up briefly at dinner parties and then be pushed out of sight'.[32] Similarly, James Pope-Hennessy, grandson of the nineteenth-century Governor, wrote in 1969 of his expectation of a future of 'many more' British Governors of Hong Kong.[33] On the other hand, for the celebrated missionary to prewar China, Gladys Aylward, the prospect of Communist takeover gave an added urgency to Hong Kong's evangelisation. Writing in 1960, just a few years after her portrayal by Ingrid Bergman in the film *The Inn of the Sixth Happiness*, Aylward noted that the colony could be closed to missionaries at any time.[34] Likewise, the historian and former civil servant Dan Waters noted that his decision to accept a CO post in 1950s Hong Kong met with 'adverse comments' from acquaintances who assumed that Hong Kong, like the rest of the Far East, was destined for Communist takeover.[35]

Britain's position in Hong Kong not only depended on Chinese acquiescence, but was crucially shaped by domestic events within China. The political violence, famine, and general instability of the Chinese Civil War and the first decade of Communist rule undergirded the mass immigration. The Great Proletarian Cultural Revolution directly inspired the 1967 riots (even though Mao himself did not back the rioters); these riots, in turn, exposed a crisis of legitimacy for British rule in Hong Kong. Deng's establishment of political stability and gradual opening of China's economy to private enterprise and global trade ultimately led to the deindustrialisation of the territory and required Hong Kong once again to reinvent itself, while also raising the long-term prospect that the colony's economic niche could be made redundant. Following the 1984 Joint Declaration, which established the framework for the resumption of Chinese sovereignty in 1997, the 1989 killing of hundreds of unarmed protesters in Beijing's Tiananmen Square (and injury to thousands) shaped the relations between the Colonial Government and its people during the final decade of British Hong Kong. At the same time, the events of Tiananmen Square reinforced the growing sense that Hong Kong people were culturally distinct from their mainland counterparts, in ways that had doubtless been shaped by the experience of British rule. These themes will be further developed in subsequent chapters in the context of analysing the British cultural engagement with Hong Kong.

At the same time, Britain's position in Hong Kong was influenced by its own domestic politics, albeit to a much lesser extent. As noted

[21]

in the introduction, during the first three postwar decades, Hong Kong remained, like the rest of the Empire even during its late Victorian heyday, of only intermittent interest to the British public 'at home'. As with other colonies, the cultural engagement with Hong Kong was of greatest importance to those who, for one reason or another, were *in* the colony. Still, Hong Kong occasionally became the subject of parliamentary inquiry and interest-group politics as Labour activists worried about sweatshop working conditions and, not incidentally, their effect on British wages, while manufacturers worried about being undercut in their own domestic market. Conversely, the low taxes and light regulations of Hong Kong exerted an obvious appeal to the minority that did not support the Labour Government's revolution of 1945–51, in which large sections of the economy were nationalised and confiscatory taxes supported a 'cradle-to-grave' Welfare State and a sharp reduction in income inequality. The prospect of imperial retreat from Hong Kong may not have bothered most Britons, but the prospect of handing over several million British subjects to a tyrannical Communist regime (particularly after the Tiananmen Square massacre) disturbed many, obviously conflicting as it did with the prevailing narratives of 'honourable' decolonisation and nation-building. At the same time, Britain's apparent obligations to its Hong Kong subjects raised the prospect of mass Chinese immigration to Britain, a prospect that was interpreted within Britain's exclusionary racial politics. As with the mainland Chinese developments highlighted in the previous paragraph, these themes will be examined further in subsequent chapters.

In addition to pressures specific to Hong Kong, the wider global context became increasingly inhospitable to colonialism, and Hong Kong gradually transformed over a quarter-century from one of Britain's lesser colonies to its most important remaining colony. Notwithstanding Winston Churchill's famously proclaiming in 1942 that he had not become Prime Minister to preside over the liquidation of Empire, the first two postwar decades were characterised by retreat on the part of European imperial powers, with Britain itself surrendering independence to India, withdrawing from the Suez Canal Zone, pulling out of Africa, and abandoning its 'East of Suez' military commitments in fairly rapid succession. In this context, Hong Kong was not merely an anomaly, but a downright counter-point, emerging from obscurity to claim its place as an exemplar of British colonial achievement.

The cold war formed another key context. Much of the impetus to decolonisation arose from cost–benefit analysis driven by events outside British control. In the same way that no great master plan had existed for empire-building, none drove the decolonisation process; the late-nineteenth-century 'scramble for empire' was followed by a similar scramble to decolonise.[36] Decolonisation reflected the attempt by British strategists to manage emergent colonial nationalisms, Britain's loss of economic means, and the expectations of the United States, upon which Britain's global power increasingly depended.[37] While Britain gave up most of its imperial possessions readily, the cold war contributed to a context in which the PRC did not push to regain Hong Kong immediately, instead treating it as the site for an updated Canton System in which China could maintain trade with the outside world and earn vital foreign currency, particularly when the United States embargoed China during the Korean War.[38] It contributed as well to a context in which the United States supported Britain's imperial claim, with Hong Kong as a base for China-watching – the Consulate in Hong Kong was the United States' largest one for this very reason – and as a Vietnam War-era destination for US soldiers on leave.[39]

In addition to these global influences, the British cultural engage-ment with Hong Kong has to be situated within the colony's demo-graphic change, economic development, and political structure, even as these contexts themselves were constructed within the cultural frameworks described in the remainder of this book.[40] Hong Kong dur-ing this period was ruled by a London-appointed governor who enjoyed virtually absolute powers. Although responsible to London, in prac-tice the Colonial Government enjoyed increasing autonomy and often pursued local interests even to the detriment of metropolitan British interests.[41] The Colonial Government ruled through an appointed Legislative Council and Executive Council representing primarily the financial and merchant elites, both of which were disproportionately (but not exclusively) British, in a type of co-opting that Ambrose King has called the 'administrative absorption of politics'.[42] Industrial inter-ests, disproportionately Chinese, were decidedly subordinated, and (Chinese) labour interests were almost entirely unrepresented. The only elected body was the Urban Council, which was created in 1936 as a replacement for the Sanitary Board and continued to reflect its ori-gins as a body narrowly concerned with providing municipal services.[43] Unusually for the early postwar era, Hong Kong officially identified with laissez-faire, standing in sharp contrast with the developmental-ist model adopted in the Third World and the Keynesian mixed econo-mies of Western Europe. In reality, Hong Kong was less of a free market economy than one designed to 'promote trade and economic growth at the lowest possible costs', and the Government did not hesitate to intervene in the economy when the interests of colonial and Chinese elites required it.[44]

In the years immediately following the Second World War, Hong Kong's population grew from around 600,000 to over 2 million by 1950;

Figure 2 As Colonial Secretary Claude Burgess said, it was 'a problem of people'. Illegal immigrants, Hong Kong, 1962.

by 1960 it had reached 3 million and approached 4 million by 1966.[45] Much of the initial increase consisted of refugees from mainland China, particularly following the famines of the late 1950s. Many of the refugees lived at the barest subsistence level and did not necessarily intend to remain permanently in Hong Kong; they demanded little in the way of Government services. Thanks to a postwar baby boom, however, by the mid-1960s a sizeable population had grown up for whom Hong Kong was the only home they had ever known.[46] Among Hong Kong's Chinese inhabitants, then, the 1960s were the decade in which a society of transients gave way to one dominated demographically by native Hong Kong people. This transformation would have political consequences, as we will see in Chapter 5. It would also see the emergence of a distinct and widely shared Hong Kong identity.[47]

This change in popular subjectivity was reflected in, and facilitated by, the tightening of the border with mainland China. Until the early 1950s, Hong Kong had maintained an open border with China; as Frank Leeming put it in 1977, '[i]solation from Kwangtung [Guangdong] and China is a feature of the system which is new since 1949'.[48] In light of the influx of refugees (or, in official language, immigrants) following 1949, the border was restricted on both sides, though not fully closed; indeed, as Steve Tsang notes, the Hong Kong Government generally interpreted the immigration laws liberally.[49] Faced with the continuing influx of immigrants – especially in the wake of the Cultural Revolution – in 1974 the Colonial Government enacted the popularly named 'Touch Base' policy, whereby illegal immigrants discovered in the territory would be deported back to China unless they reached Kowloon and presented themselves to immigration officials. Following a spike in illegal immigration in 1978, and a backlash by the Hong

Kong Chinese, in 1980 the 'Touch Base' policy was discarded, Hong Kong residents were required to carry identification cards, and the border was more vigorously policed.[50] In the space of a generation, Hong Kong transformed from a city thoroughly integrated within southern Chinese society, to a city of Chinese immigrants, to a prosperous and exclusive community effectively set apart from its nation of origin.

Not only did the population grow dramatically during the first two postwar decades, but the economic growth was even more rapid. Following the American-inspired blockade of China during the Korean War, Hong Kong's position as an entrepot chiefly for the China trade was destroyed almost overnight, and thanks to the influx of Shanghai capital and a vast supply of cheap labour, Hong Kong was able to expand its industrial base dramatically in a few short years. Following impressive economic growth in the 1950s, Hong Kong's GDP tripled between 1961 and 1970, far outpacing the rate of population growth.[51] This already impressive economic growth continued into the 1970s, making possible a significant expansion of the Government's housing and education programmes as it sought to rebuild legitimacy following the 1967–68 riots.

Personal contexts: Britons in Hong Kong

The British cultural engagement with Hong Kong was shaped not only by local and international contexts; it was mediated, above all, by British people who spent time in Hong Kong – people who, as a result, are the dominant voices in this book. In *Britain in China*, Robert Bickers distinguishes between settlers and expatriates, arguing that the 'nationalisation' of Britain's informal empire in China after the late 1920s threatened the former's way of life even as it promoted the interests of the latter who, working for multi-national companies saw their positions in China as transitory.[52] A similar distinction makes sense in postwar Hong Kong, though in practice, of course, the distinction is not always clear, as those intending only a brief stay ended up remaining for many years, and vice versa. Yet there were British settlers who developed a complex expatriate society centred around racial distinction, clubs, the civil service, sport, and other cultural practices and institutions. According to Dan Waters, some of the British in the early 1950s distinguished between those like himself who had arrived since the war, and those who had spent time in the Japanese prison camp at Stanley, the latter constituting a sort of old boys' network.[53] Nor was this the only source of tension among British in Hong Kong. To the soldier Billy Moore, only briefly stationed in Hong Kong, the British living in Hong Kong were a spoiled lot, their character having been harmed by the abundance of 'cheap native labour' to do all the housework. The result was a social snobbery even on the part of children.[54] Eurasian doctor and novelist Han Suyin, writing in 1951, noted that 'Old China hands' continued anachronistically to assert their pre-war racial privileges.[55]

Yet the British in Hong Kong, even more than their Chinese counterparts, were generally sojourners. Many were soldiers. During the postwar period, the number of military personnel in Hong Kong ranged from around 30,000 in the late 1940s to as low as 4,000 Britons complemented by '5,000 Gurkhas and 1,300 locally recruited soldiers as well as a small naval and RAF contingent' at the time of the 1967 riots; the numbers dropped precipitously in the early 1990s as Britain prepared for withdrawal, so that only 1,920 troops remained by 1996.[56] They were, of course, rotated, generally holding two-year assignments during the early postwar years; as a result, the number of British soldiers who spent some time in Hong Kong would have been considerable.

How did British soldiers see their role in Hong Kong? Although direct evidence is difficult to locate, we can see how governmental and military spokespeople described their function. Despite the official commitment to Hong Kong's defence, as we have seen, Hong Kong was not realistically defendable, and in any invasion by the PRC, Hong Kong would be quickly overrun.[57] As early as 1955, when the British reduced the size of the Hong Kong garrison from twelve army units, a Royal Air Force Squadron, and an Auxiliary Squadron, to four army units and an Auxiliary Air Force Squadron, a Commonwealth Relations Office memorandum noted that this represented a 'calculated risk of reducing the Garrison to the force required for internal security'. It justified the British decision by pointing out that even before the reduction the Garrison would be insufficient to repel a direct attack; its real value followed from what its presence represented, as it conveyed to the Chinese that 'such an attack would precipitate a full-scale war'.[58] A leftist pamphlet published in the early 1970s described the military's role in less flattering terms:

> What is involved is simply a brief delaying operation while the Europeans and a few wealthy right-wing Chinese make their escape. But even this scenario is considered highly unlikely by most observers. The main role of the military is to appear 'credible' – for a basically incredible purpose; while in fact hovering menacingly over the Colony's population.[59]

Leaving aside the pamphlet's inflammatory language, it is true that the military's purpose was not genuinely defensive, but a combination of display and to support the police in the case of civil disturbance. According to the *New Statesman* in 1978, the purpose of the British military force was 'so that the Governor will sleep easier at nights knowing that he has a force at his disposal more reliable than the Hong Kong police'.[60] Similarly, Mary Lee reported in the *FEER* in 1980 that 'leftwing MPs' in Britain argued that Britain's contribution to Hong Kong defence was 'being spent "to protect the merchant bankers of Hong Kong"'.[61] According to a staff officer quoted in a 1979 *Spectator* article, the reason for the military presence was to 'reassure the local Chinese businessmen. That's the be-all and end-all of our military presence in Hong Kong. That's why the locals here pay three-quarters of our costs.'[62]

Indeed, the Commander British Forces confirmed both of these purposes – credible display and support for the police – in a speech to the Hong Kong Rotary Club in 1975. Not only did he underscore the support the military could give to the police, but he also argued that the military, by its 'very presence', provided 'the outward and visible manifestation that the British Government intends to live up to its responsibilities towards Hong Kong', a role that he believed was 'useful for business confidence'.[63] A classified 1962 military publication, *Keeping the Peace in Hong Kong (Duties in Support of the Civil Power)*, explained clearly the military's role in supporting the police: 'The sole aim of this Military support is the restoration of law and order and the return to normal conditions in which the Police can re-assume control in the shortest possible time.' The short book emphasised the need to understand police methods, and how to cooperate with the police so that 'initiative should be swiftly seized and held by the Police and Military'. Some police methods would not be used by the military: rather than coming into physical contact with a crowd, or employing 'Police methods of shield and baton', 'the aim of the Commander must be to dominate the crowd from a distance'. Yet the Military Commander was called upon to remember that in subduing a riot, he was 'NOT dealing with the Queen's enemies, but with citizens of the British Commonwealth who are behaving unlawfully. **Only the minimum amount of force necessary to restore law and order will be used.**' The book explained such tasks as 'dispersing a crowd', 'sealing off an area', and 'enforcing a curfew'.[64]

Whatever their views on Hong Kong, soldiers constituted an obvious category of sojourners, unlikely to develop long-term attachments to the colony. Indeed, their frequent relocation prompted comparisons to other assignments. In 1956, the younger soldiers in the Staffordshire Regiment's 1st Battalion reportedly 'preferred the more objective life in Korea [their previous post] to their present one in Hong Kong'. The 'C' Company noted that 'Despite the fact that we have barrack rooms instead of tents, live in a warmer climate and have good shower baths, etc., many men keep saying "We prefer Korea."' This may have been a result of the camp's remote location in the New Territories, still primarily a mixture of wilderness and agrarian villages: 'The big city is some twenty-five miles away and we seldom have the chance of seeing it.'[65] The Royal Warwickshire Regiment's 1st Battalion found Hong Kong a bit disappointing following 'a great build up when the Battalion was in Aden and a number of people expected a demi-Eden set in the China seas'; still, after 'initial disillusionment ... it is fair to say that the pendulum has swung the other way and that everyone is now enjoying the many attractions which the station offers'.[66]

Civilians were more likely to remain for several years, yet both in government and in the private sector, Hong Kong was often a short-term appointment, lasting from a few years until, at the latest, eligibility for retirement. That this was a well-known trope can be seen in a 1954 report in London's *Daily Mirror* that the publicity director for Worthing, a seaside town in Sussex, planned to contact 'each English-named Hong Kong telephone subscriber' to try to convince at least some of them to move to 'Sunny Worthing' upon retiring. This campaign was part of a broader effort to increase Worthing's population from 70,000 to 100,000.[67] Felix Patrikeeff, a long-time Hong Kong resident of Russian descent whose parents came to Hong Kong as refugees from Communist China, commented that expatriates working in the Hong Kong Government viewed Hong Kong as a 'glorified transit camp: a place to earn and save and perhaps even to enjoy life, but never to regard as home'.[68] Jan Morris, also writing in the 1980s, claimed that most British bourgeoisie in Hong Kong felt 'no profound loyalty' to the place, while some even 'detest[ed]' it: 'They are essentially transients anyway, and long ago many of them prepared for the future by buying one of those nice small properties in the vicinity of Grasse, where the food will still be good, the sun will shine a little like the eastern sun, and they can keep a boat in a marina somewhere.'[69] Jane Gardam's 2004 novel, *Old Filth*, depicts such a character, a retired judge named Sir Edward Feathers, returning to a comfortable retirement in Dorset.[70]

The title of Gardam's novel refers to the acronym for 'Failed In London, Try Hongkong', which, as historian May Holdsworth notes, 'cropped up in the local parlance in the 1980s'.[71] It would certainly be an overstatement to suggest that the primary reason that a British person would move to Hong Kong was to escape failure at home. Still, a big part of Hong Kong's attraction was the expatriate's ability to elevate his or her status considerably. This type of elevation was not unique to Hong Kong historically; for example, Elizabeth Buettner describes Britons in India in similar terms.[72] In the postwar period, though, Hong Kong gradually became a chief arena for such colonial status-climbing.

Contemporary accounts accordingly noted the social opportunities afforded by Hong Kong. A late 1960s book recruiting police officers from Britain noted that most Europeans in 'the Colony' enjoyed a higher standard of living than that in Britain: 'Most run a car, employ a servant and entertain more than they normally do at home.' Government employees paid 'nominal' rents, and income taxes were low.[73] Not only did expatriates often earn much greater salaries than they would have at home, but the accoutrements of expatriate life were, to use Felix Patrikeeff's word, 'intoxicating'. He described one man from a working-class part of Lancashire: 'There he had, in his own words, been climbing telephone poles for the Post Office. In Hong Kong he was in charge of hundreds of workmen, enjoyed seductive evenings and weekends at a club, on the tennis courts and beside the swimming pool. Such a transformation, he said, was unthinkable in Britain.' This elevation constituted a type of colonial privilege. According to the *Times* correspondent David Bonavia, writing in 1985, the 'big banks and trading firms continue to hire young Britons – not necessarily graduates – with qualifications patently lower than those of many experienced local employees'; Bonavia regarded this as a racial 'caste system'. Walter Easey, a police inspector in Hong Kong between 1962 and 1968 who in the 1970s formed the radical Hong Kong Research Project as his 'chosen form of therapy' in his quest to 'reform [him]self away from [his] previous criminal ways' – a task he supported by working as a barman at the School of Oriental and African Studies – presented a similar picture of the attractions of Hong Kong life for the British expatriate. Writing in 1980, in the context of speculating over the end of British rule (a prospect he welcomed enthusiastically), he warned that not only would opportunities decline for Britain's 'upper-middle class remittance-men', but so would the job's attractions: 'white priviledge [sic], servants, exclusive clubs, cheap prostitutes, gambling and liquor'. With British expatriates attaining a much higher status than they could in the UK, there was, according to Holdsworth, 'no escaping the suspicion that British mediocrity may have thrived in Hong Kong because citizens of the United Kingdom did not require permits to live and work in the colony before 1997, which gave them an unfair advantage over the nationals of other countries when it came to competing for jobs'. According to Stephen Vines, a former *Independent* correspondent and an editor for the short-lived *Eastern Express*, the lavish living standards of expatriates who would have been 'little more than clerks' at home contributed to arrogant behaviour on the part of many of them.[74]

Among its other characteristics, an elevated status depends upon one's ability to command the labour of others. Descriptions of expatriate life in Hong Kong – at the higher end, at least – regularly note the ubiquitousness of servants. A 1954 Post Report on Hong Kong provided by the Australian Trade Commissioner Service opined that there was 'no shortage of servants in Hong Kong' and that 'Chinese servants are amongst the best in the world.' The Report did, however, advise that servants would inevitably help themselves to 'small quantities of sugar, soap, etc., from their employer's pantry', and that strenuous efforts to prevent this would usually result in a servant's resigning; it also suggested having the servants examined for tuberculosis.[75] Servants were frequently remarked, too, in more casual observations. For example, Dorothy Needham, former Associate Director of the Sino-British Cooperation Office and wife of Joseph Needham, in her diary of her 1971 visit described her evening at the home of the bursar of the Chinese University and, three days later, another expatriate's home; both entries noted a 'charming' or 'eager' Chinese amah.[76]

For those on lucrative expatriate salary packages, servants and clubs were standard. Yet the low prices meant that even less well appointed Britons, including tourists, could enjoy a greater degree of consumption in Hong Kong than at home. The colony was regularly evoked as a shopper's paradise, in which everything was for sale and often at a bargain. As early as September 1947, while Britain languished in postwar rationing, the *Daily Mirror*'s Cassandra (Bill Connor) noted the prevalence of nylons, shoes, wool and cloth, and a diverse range of groceries in a Hong Kong only two years removed from occupation and torture by 'Johnny Japs'.[77] By the early 1960s, the colony's reputation for cheap electronics could make it seem worthwhile to take complex measures in order to take advantage. For example, in 1961 a Farley Motors employee wrote from Brisbane asking Stan Bullen of the Hong Kong branch office of Standard-Triumph Sales if he would purchase a Canon camera on behalf of a friend, to be collected by the latter's other friend who would be passing through Hong Kong shortly. Bullen apparently knew neither the ultimate recipient of the camera nor the person who would be collecting it on his behalf.[78]

Three decades later, following Hong Kong's economic miracle, such evocations of abundance remained common. Gunvor Edwards, in a 1995 letter to Puffin Books editor Kaye Webb, noted the Mong Kok Night Market's energy and wide variety of cheap products. Edwards recounted her son's experience arriving in Hong Kong for an interview for a BBC World Service position, and having his luggage go missing, leaving him with only £10 and nothing to wear to the interview. Luckily, at the Night Market, he sorted himself out, with enough change left over for a modest dinner.[79] Similarly, a 1985 children's book entitled *A Family in Hong Kong* aimed, perhaps, at advanced primary school children in the UK, described the view in Aberdeen Harbour:

> In the main streets, thousands upon thousands of neon advertising signs, in huge Chinese characters, dominate the scene. Small shops, crammed up together, jostle for space. Their windows are packed with cameras, lighters, radios, watches, jade and other duty-free luxury goods at the world's lowest prices. On every corner there are street restaurants, where the food is cooked and eaten in the open air. Other restaurants are the size of a small dining-room, but serve a huge number of dishes, from frog's legs to Peking duck, and all incredibly cheaply.[80]

Another children's book quoted a recent illegal immigrant from rural China, Suen Hung Wing, who in 1985 described being helped by another recent immigrant upon his arrival in 1978. 'He took us to his home and fed us. We hadn't eaten so well for years, but he said it was nothing special. We had duck, rice and vegetables; he said his family ate a meal like that about three times a week. We were in a different world.'[81]

Yet although bargains were to be had, Hong Kong was also known for lavish and ostentatious display. Like the Chinese immigrant quoted above, British visitors to the territory often noted the food. Dorothy Needham's description of an early-1970s dinner party at the home of the bursar of the Chinese University, already mentioned above, noted the elaborate Chinese banquet including Peking duck.[82] Other observers described the luxury cars, available to the wealthiest Chinese and expatriates alike.[83] Financial means had another benefit; notwithstanding the colony's high population density, the well appointed could enjoy retreat from the crowds. For example, Joseph Needham, describing his 1981 visit to Hong Kong in a letter to his wife, Dorothy, observed of an evening spent at the Kowloon home of a friend in finance and chemicals that the latter lived behind a remote-controlled gate with his Chinese-Indonesian wife, two cars, and extensive library.[84]

If we can distinguish between expatriates and settlers, an equally important distinction can be made between those willing to embrace Chinese culture and those who tried at all costs to recreate British ways of life overseas. In this respect, Britons in Hong Kong were not entirely typical. As John Darwin has noted, the British in much of the Empire were characterised by a 'growing tendency in the later nineteenth century to define Britishness more restrictively in racial and ethnic terms'. Robert Bickers has argued that among Britons throughout the Empire in the twentieth century, 'Nothing perhaps better prompts the articulation of identity, or the mobilisation of organised discontent, than the threat – or perceived threat – of dissolution.'[85] As already seen, the British in post-1945 Hong Kong were regularly confronted with the dissolution of *their* Hong Kong, but unlike Britons in the settler colonies of Kenya and Rhodesia during the same years, the British in Hong Kong did not particularly articulate their Britishness primarily in racial and ethnic terms.[86] Not that these factors were absent – far from it. Rather, what surfaces in much of the postwar commentary is the idea that racial exclusiveness is old-fashioned, and those who held to it were relics and objects of scorn. British administrators borrowed from Chinese traditions of governance, laws reserving residence on Victoria Peak to Europeans (and their domestic servants) were repealed after the war, and even interracial marriage became increasingly accepted.[87] As the *FEER* argued in its inaugural editorial in 1945, Hong Kong's importance lay in its status as a ' "civilisation exchange" between West and East'.[88]

A progressive attitude toward borrowing from Chinese culture and interracial sexuality, including marriage, can be seen in several of the period's novels; in many cases, a novel's protagonist appears as the champion of intercultural relationships against the bigotry of his fellow Britons who, it is implied, should be safely relegated to the dustbin of history. James Clavell's *Tai-Pan* will be discussed more thoroughly in Chapter 2, but in the present context we may note that the novel's hero, instrumental in the (fictionalised) creation of Hong Kong, possesses an open-mindedness toward interracial love more characteristic of the year in which the novel was published (1966) than the 1840s, in which it is set. Dirk Struan would like to marry his Chinese concubine, May-may, whom he had purchased as a fifteen-year old; he is hindered only by his recognition that an intolerant society would scorn this marriage, thereby endangering his larger goals for Anglo-Chinese partnership.[89] In *The World of Suzie Wong*, Richard Mason's minor character O'Neill, an 'old China hand', scandalises the company at a dinner party by pretending to have a grandmother who had been a Chinese mistress. Admitting afterward to Mason's narrator/protagonist, Robert Lomax, that he was just 'having a lark', he elaborates on the backwardness of the party's other attendees:

> Of course you don't want to take those people too seriously. They don't mean so much nowadays. That mentality's as doomed as the Empire which bred it – and which they have somehow got the impression bred the Empire, though of course it did nothing of the kind. In fact it has done a great deal, with its inflexibility, to hasten the losing of it. With due apologies to our hosts, I am afraid that most of our fellow-guests to-night were second-raters. And the real Empire-builders, in their own way, were first-raters.[90]

These examples should not be equated with another theme, to be explored in Chapter 3, of the easy availability of Asian female sexuality.

Rather, they refer to a more thorough racial and cultural integration. Alexander Grantham, who spent time in the Hong Kong Government in the 1920s and returned as Governor in 1947 after service in Bermuda, Jamaica, Nigeria, and Fiji, claimed in his autobiography to have observed 'a greater mixing of the races' than previously, 'but then Hong Kong has never had a colour problem like the African colonies, and the Chinese have as much racial pride as the Europeans'. He did allow, though, that European racial arrogance persisted in some quarters, 'taking such forms as the exclusion of Asians from clubs, downright rudeness or a patronizing manner'. Still, he argued (writing in 1957), 'the age of the "blimps" is over, though a few of them still remain, even in Hong Kong'.[91]

Yet if old-fashioned racialism was increasingly rejected, and a measure of social interaction between Britons and Chinese became more normal than previously, that is not to deny that the British tended to socialise mainly among themselves. Writing in 1970, James Kirkup, a prolific poet and travel writer who would later attain notoriety as the author of the 1976 poem 'The Love that Dares to Speak Its Name', whose publication in *Gay News* led to the editor's prosecution under British blasphemy law, noted Britons' continued segregation from Chinese society:

> They belong to a privileged class, with their own residential regions, golf and swimming clubs, beaches, shops and other areas of influence. One hardly ever sees a Chinese with a 'Whitey'. Europeans and Americans make little attempt to live a 'Chinese' existence: the British in particular conserve their class distinctions and insularity.[92]

The segregation of Europeans and Chinese was particularly true of marriage, a point rendered memorably in Han Suyin's 1952 autobiographical novel, *A Many-Splendored Thing*.[93] Suyin (the name of the first-person narrator as well as the author) portrays interracial sexual relationships as something that can be done discreetly, but would have significant consequences if discovered.[94] Suyin, herself Eurasian, agrees to marry British journalist Mark after his divorce; moreover, her uncle in Szechuan, days before the Communist takeover of his city, gives his blessing, reasoning that society itself is in upheaval and the old rules no longer apply. Their discovery by the Hong Kong rumour mill, though, threatens Mark's career, forcing him to leave Hong Kong. Upon his return, Suyin cautions him against acting too hastily:

> We must not be madly romantic. You may be losing your head over some cheap woman. I am Eurasian, and the word itself evokes in some minds a

sensation of moral laxity. People never think about words, they only feel them. I am Chinese, and at a certain moderate middling level, people do not marry Chinese girls. Neither, in China, do girls marry foreigners. It's only big enough people who can afford, occasionally, to be untrammeled by ordinary prejudice.[95]

The prejudice against interracial romantic relationships is confirmed by memoirs and contemporary accounts. The politician, activist, and historian Christine Loh, who spent part of her own childhood in a multiracial home and neighborhood, has written that 'In the mid-1960s, for an expatriate working for one of the hongs to marry an Asian was still considered "inappropriate" and mixed marriages were "discouraged".'[96] Dan Waters has said the same about the Colonial Service, noting that upon his 1960 marriage, his supervisor told him he was 'letting the side down'.[97] As late as 1972, radical writer John Walker claimed that 'European executive employees, on arrival in Hong Kong, are "warned of" Chinese girls by being told that their promotions will be slowed up if they have a Chinese wife or fiancee [sic].'[98]

Racial segregation was not one-sided; according to a 1951 article in the FEER, several local hotels, restaurants and tea rooms refused to serve Europeans, advertising the ban either by a posted sign or simply by turning them away at the door. The journal considered this an anachronistic practice that conflicted with Hong Kong's general reputation for tolerance, as well as the progressive reforms that had taken place since the war.[99] James Kirkup's 1970 travel book claimed that since the 1967 riots, which could always recur, 'fewer and fewer Chinese want to be seen associating with foreigners', excepting foreign missionaries, especially the Jesuits. Still, Kirkup noted, there were 'some Chinese, however, who do not mind being seen associating with foreigners, especially foreigners with lots of money, and they are the good-time girls, bar ladies and hostesses'.[100]

As early as 1962, by contrast, a history of Hong Kong designed for Form IV students (aged between ten and twelve), contrasting the 'present friendliness' of Chinese–European relations with nineteenth-century 'mutual contempt', noted didactically that the two races 'not only work together in business, in hospitals, in schools, in offices, but they often mix together outside their work, they play together, they visit each other, and more and more frequently they marry each other'.[101] The Hong Kong-based sociologist Henry Lethbridge noted in 1968 that interracial marriage had become more widely accepted in recent years, a development that he attributed largely to the changes in the way the two races now perceived each other.[102] Holdsworth confirms that by the 1970s, 'Gone were the days when juniors [working for the British hongs] were told to give a wide berth to local girls.'[103] Her assessment is supported by the pictures of numerous high-end balls and cocktail parties that filled the pages of *Hong Kong Tatler* after it began publication in 1977: most of the faces were European, but images of European men with Asian wives or dates were hardly rare.[104] In a very different setting, Lan Kwai Fong, which had emerged in the late 1970s as a leisure site associated in the Chinese mind mostly with such 'others' as homosexuals and drunken westerners, during the 1980s transitioned into a neighbourhood of relatively expensive restaurants, bars, and clubs in which Chinese and westerners intermingled, albeit within the framework of various hierarchies.[105]

If interracial romantic relationships, even marriage, became increasingly acceptable by the 1970s, this fact could put expatriate single women at a perceived disadvantage, particularly in those cases in which a western male attraction to Chinese women combined with a preference for women who were not seen as professional rivals, as well as a tendency to avoid long-term commitments. May Holdsworth's chapter on 'Trailing Spouses and Single Women' describes an Australian lawyer, Deborah Glass, who arrived at age twenty-nine in 1989. In Glass's words, her 'new male friends seemed much more taken with the many charming Cathay air hostesses in our midst' than with highly educated professionals such as herself. Holdsworth argues that Glass was 'not the first foreigner to find herself competing with the Hong Kong version of the "dumb blonde" – a compliant "China doll"'.[106] Expatriate British novelist John Burdett put similar words in the mouth of one of his female characters, a drunken and eager white police officer named Angie: 'Ain't that easy, mate. The white men chase Asian women like there's no tomorrow, and the best Chinese stick to their own.'[107]

Conclusion

Britain's cultural engagement with Hong Kong was shaped by several contexts and factors: the demographic explosion caused by crisis in mainland China; the economic miracle that accompanied the population growth; cold war influences that made Hong Kong useful to China even as China remained essential to Hong Kong's existence; Britain's decolonisation and general retreat from global power; China's resumption of political stability and its re-engagement with the international economy from the late 1970s; the Tiananmen Square massacre in 1989 and the politics of the Handover. This cultural engagement took place both in the metropole and within Hong Kong, though it was driven by commentators based in the colony.

We have seen that one of Hong Kong's attractions for expatriate Britons was the possibility of elevating one's economic position and social status, even while the prospect of an early end-date argued for aiming at quick profits rather than building a long-term business model. Both of these themes were consonant with the idea of Hong Kong as a site for unbridled capitalism, one of the chief tropes in the postwar British conceptualisation of Hong Kong, and the subject of Chapter 2.

Notes

1 Edward Ward, *Chinese Crackers* (London: John Lane and Bodley Head, 1947), pp. 14–15; Leonard Miall, 'Obituary: Edward Ward', *Independent* (10 May 1993). For the story of the Japanese occupation, see Philip Snow, *The Fall of Hong Kong: Britain, China and the Japanese Occupation* (New Haven and London: Yale University Press, 2003).

2 Quoted in *The Club: Special Commemorative Issue, 1879–1981* (Hong Kong: Club Publications, 1982), p. 9.

3 WYAS, William Moore Collection, 108D77/ 354, Billy Moore to Vera Moore, 17 September 1945, from British Fleet Mail Office, Sydney.

4 F. D. Ommanney, *Fragrant Harbour: A Private View of Hong Kong* (London: Hutchinson, 1962), p. 13.

5 Alexander Grantham, interview by D. J. Crozier, 21 August 1968, Rhodes College, Oxford, MS Brit. Emp. Si 288, p. 9.

6 Chi-kwan Mark, '"The Problem of People": British Colonials, Cold War Powers, and the Chinese Refugees in Hong Kong, 1949–62', *Modern Asian Studies* 41.6 (2007): 1145–81; Glen Peterson, 'To Be or Not to Be a Refugee: The International Politics of the Hong Kong Refugee Crisis, 1949–55', *The Journal of Imperial and Commonwealth History* 36 (June 2008): 171–95.

7 Elsie Elliott, *Crusade for Justice: An Autobiography* (Hong Kong: Heinemann Asia, 1981), p. 85.

8 ANA, A609 552/108/1, F. R. Wood and R. H. Star, 'Hong Kong', 21 November 1947, p. 1.

9 For the wartime diplomacy concerning the future of Hong Kong, see Andrew Whitfield, *Hong Kong, Empire and the Anglo-American Alliance at War, 1941–1945* (Basingstoke: Palgrave Macmillan, 2001); Kent Fedorowich, 'Decolonization Deferred? The Re-Establishment of Colonial Rule in Hong Kong, 1942–45', in Kent Fedorowich and Martin Thomas (eds), *International Diplomacy and Colonial Retreat* (London: Frank Cass, 2001).

10 The joint memorandum, as well as background material, and the response of the Cabinet's Far Eastern (Official) Committee to the memorandum, are included in British Library, IOR/L/PS/12/2298, 'The Future of Hong Kong', 9 December 1946–21 December 1947.

11 Chi-kwan Mark, *Hong Kong and the Cold War: Anglo-American Relations, 1949–1957* (Oxford: Clarendon Press, 2004); Wm. Roger Louis, 'Hong Kong: The Critical Phase, 1945–49', in Wm. Roger Louis, *Ends of British Imperialism: The Scramble for Empire, Suez and Decolonization* (London and New York: I. B. Tauris, 2006), pp. 339–78.

12 John Darwin, 'Was There a Fourth British Empire?', in Martin Lynn (ed.), *The British Empire in the 1950s: Retreat or Revival?* (Basingstoke: Palgrave Macmillan,

2006); Stuart Ward, *Australia and the British Embrace: The Demise of the Imperial Ideal* (Melbourne: Melbourne University Press, 2001). On the Australian and New Zealander support for Hong Kong in the late 1940s, see the newspaper clippings collected in ANA, A5954/2110/1. See also confidential Australian Cabinet memorandum, ANA, A2700/1512B, 'Cabinet – 19th August, 1949', for a demonstration of the limitations of Australia's commitment.

13 Peter V. Russo, 'Transition Period in China: No Real Evidence of Any Disillusionment', *Argus* (14 September 1946) (ANA, A373/11705).

14 R. J. C., 'Will Britain Give Back Hong Kong to the Chinese?' *Sunday Mail* (11 August 1946) (ANA, A373/11705).

15 Jan Morris, *Hong Kong: Epilogue to an Empire* (New York: Random House, 1997), p. 261.

16 ANA, A5954/1932/2, Ben Chifley to Clement Attlee, n.d. (*c.* June 1949).

17 The Crown Colony comprised Hong Kong Island and Kowloon, ceded in separate treaties in 1842 and 1860, respectively, and the much greater land mass of the New Territories, leased to Britain in 1898 for ninety-nine years. It was the approaching expiration of the New Territories lease, and the practical impossibility of detaching the ceded territories from the leased territories, that made 1997 appear a likely terminal year for the colony as a whole.

18 'Muggeridge Says H. K. Is Doomed', *SCMP* (9 June 1958) (ANA, 528/1/5). On Muggeridge's sacking by the BBC, see Richard Ingrams, *Muggeridge: The Biography* (San Francisco: HarperSanFrancisco, 1995), pp. 181–4.

19 Cudlipp Archive, Cardiff University, HC 2/2, Cecil King to Hugh Cudlipp, 10 March 1967.

20 Paul Johnson, 'London Diary', *New Statesman* (19 May 1967), p. 680.

21 Richard Hughes, *Borrowed Place, Borrowed Time: Hong Kong and Its Many Faces*, 2nd edn (London: André Deutsch, 1976), pp. 13–14.

22 Richard Mason, *The World of Suzie Wong* (London: Fontana, 1959 [1957]), p. 176.

23 John le Carré, *The Honourable Schoolboy* (New York: Pocket Books, 2002 [1977]), p. 539.

24 For early postwar musings on the possibility of a sudden takeover of Hong Kong, see ANA, A461/P350/1/9, Office of the High Commissioner for the United Kingdom, Canberra, 'Appreciation of the Situation in Hong Kong', 9 September 1949.

25 Ommanney, *Fragrant Harbour*, pp. 134–5. In 1961, half of Hong Kong's residents were emigrants from mainland China. Stephen Constantine, 'Migrants and Settlers', in Judith M. Brown and Wm. Roger Louis (eds), *The Oxford History of the British Empire: The Twentieth Century* (Oxford: Oxford University Press, 2001), p. 182.

26 Hughes, *Borrowed Place, Borrowed Time*, pp. 13–14.

27 TNA, BW 94/9, 'General Policy Inspection of Hong Kong, 27–31 October 1973: Report by Assistant Director-Regional (Regional)' February 1974, p. 1.

28 Nora Clarke, *Living in Hong Kong* (Hove: Wayland, 1980), pp. 4, 48–9.

29 See also Harold Ingrams, *Hong Kong* (London: HMSO, 1952), p. 66; Trea Wiltshire, *Hong Kong: An Impossible Journey through History. Hong Kong: 1841–1971* (Hong Kong: Serasia, 1971), p. 21.

30 'Hongkong: The Persistent Colony', *The Economist* (19 January 1957), p. 209.

31 Ian F. C. MacPherson, 'Aspects of Crown Service', in Elizabeth Sinn (ed.), *Hong Kong, British Crown Colony, Revisited* (Hong Kong: Centre of Asian Studies, University of Hong Kong, 2001), p. 119.

32 Percy Cradock, *Experiences of China*. new edn (London: John Murray, 1999), p. 163.

33 James Pope-Hennessy, *Half-Crown Colony: A Hong Kong Notebook* (London: Cape, 1969), p. 44.

34 Oldham Local Studies, AAL 11/5/1, Michael John Chen and Gladys Aylward, *Good Hope: The Hope Mission's Work in Hong Kong*, no. 1, August 1960.

35 Dan Waters, 'Hong Kong in the 1950s and '60s: Reminiscences', *Journal of the Hong Kong Branch of the Royal Asiatic Society* 42 (2002): 323–43 (324).

36 Ronald Hyam, *Britain's Declining Empire: The Road to Decolonisation, 1918–1968* (Cambridge: Cambridge University Press, 2006), pp. 398–410.

[37]

37 John Darwin, *The Empire Project: The Rise and Fall of the British World-System, 1830–1970* (Cambridge: Cambridge University Press, 2009); John Darwin, *Britain and Decolonisation: The Retreat from Empire in the Post-War World* (Basingstoke: Macmillan, 1988); P. J. Cain and A. G. Hopkins, *British Imperialism, 1688–2000* (New York: Longman, 2002).

38 David Clayton, *Imperialism Revisited: Political and Economic Relations between Britain and China, 1950–54* (Basingstoke: Macmillan, 1997).

39 Mark, *Hong Kong and the Cold War*; Chi-kwan Mark, 'Vietnam War Tourists: US Naval Visits to Hong Kong and British–American–Chinese Relations, 1965–1968', *Cold War History* 10 (February 2010): 1–28; Grace Ai-Ling Chou, *Confucianism, Colonialism, and the Cold War: Chinese Cultural Education at Hong Kong's New Asia College, 1949–1963* (Leiden: Brill, 2011).

40 This paragraph and the subsequent one are taken from Mark Hampton, 'Early Hong Kong Television, 1950s–1970s: Commercialization, Public Service, and Britishness', *Media History* 17 (August 2011), 305–22 (307).

41 Leo Goodstadt, 'Fiscal Freedom and the Making of Hong Kong's Capitalist Society', in Ray Yep (ed.), *Negotiating Autonomy in Greater China: Hong Kong and Its Sovereign before and after 1997* (Copenhagen: NIAS Press, 2013).

42 Ambrose King, 'Administrative Absorption of Politics in Hong Kong: Emphasis on the Grass Roots Level', *Asian Survey* 15 (1975), 422–39; Ma Ngok, *Political Development in Hong Kong: State, Political Society, and Civil Society* (Hong Kong: Hong Kong Univeristy Press, 2007), pp. 17–31.

43 John M. Carroll, *A Concise History of Hong Kong* (Lanham, MD: Rowman and Littlefield, 2007), pp. 117, 163.

44 Steve Tsang, *A Modern History of Hong Kong* (London and New York: I. B. Tauris, 2004), p. 197.

45 *Hong Kong Statistics, 1947–1967* (Hong Kong: Census and Statistics Department, 1969), p. 13.

46 Suzanne Pepper, *Keeping Democracy at Bay: Hong Kong and the Challenge of Chinese Political Reform* (Lanham, MD: Rowman and Littlefield, 2008), p. 171.

47 See Judith Agassi, 'Social Structure and Social Stratification in Hong Kong', in Ian C. Jarvie and Joseph Agassi (eds), *Hong Kong: A Society in Transition* (New York: Frederick A. Praeger, 1968); Tsang, *A Modern History of Hong Kong*, pp. 181–96; Carroll, *A Concise History of Hong Kong*, pp. 167–89; Li Pang-kwong, *Hong Kong from Britain to China: Political Cleavages, Electoral Dynamics and Institutional Changes* (Aldershot: Ashgate, 2000), pp. 28–30. John Carroll has shown, however, that the roots of a distinct Hong Kong bourgeois civic identity date to the late nineteenth century, even if it did not become a mass phenomenon until the mid-1960s. See John M. Carroll, *Edge of Empires: Chinese Elites and British Colonials in Hong Kong* (Cambridge, MA: Harvard University Press, 2005).

48 Frank Leeming, *Street Studies in Hong Kong: Localities in a Chinese City* (Oxford: Oxford University Press, 1977), p. 176.

49 Tsang, *A Modern History of Hong Kong*, p. 193; see also 'The Exodus to Hongkong', *The Economist* (19 May 1962), p. 677.

50 Helen F. Siu, 'Positioning "Hong Kongers" and "New Immigrants"', in Helen F. Siu and Agnes S. Ku (eds), *Hong Kong Mobile: Making a Global Population* (Hong Kong: Hong Kong University Press, 2008); Tsang, *A Modern History of Hong Kong*, pp. 193–4; Athena Chiu, 'A History of Refugees in Hong Kong', *Time Out Hong Kong* website (18 June 2013), www.timeout.com.hk/feature-stories/features/59040/a-history-of-refugees-in-hong-kong.html (accessed 14 January 2014); 'Swimming Season', *The Economist* (15 May 1971), pp. 40, 48; Mary Lee, 'Fed up with Poor Relations', *FEER* (21 March 1980), p. 22; Mary Lee, 'Don't Leave Home without It', *FEER* (2 November 1981), p. 34.

51 Gary McDonogh and Cindy Hing-Yuk Wong, *Global Hong Kong* (London: Routledge, 2005), pp. 67–84, 92.

52 Robert Bickers, *Britain in China: Community, Culture and Colonialism, 1900–1949* (Manchester and New York: Manchester University Press, 1999). See also Robert

Bickers, 'Shanghailanders and Others, 1843–1957', in Robert Bickers (ed.), *Settlers and Expatriates: Britons over the Seas* (Oxford: Oxford University Press, 2010), p. 297.
53 Waters, 'Hong Kong in the 1950s and '60s', p. 326.
54 WYAS, William Moore Collection, 108D77/379, Billy Moore to Vera Moore, 10 November 1945.
55 HS, Box 73, Han Suyin to Jonathan Cape, n.d. (mid-1951).
56 Louis, 'Hong Kong: The Critical Phase'; Georgina Sinclair, '"Hong Kong Headaches": Policing the 1967 Disturbances', in Ray Yep and Robert Bickers (eds), *May Days in Hong Kong: Emergency and Riot in 1967* (Hong Kong: Hong Kong University Press, 2009), p. 98 (quotation from Sinclair); *Parliamentary Debates*, Commons, 5th series (1909–80), Vol. CCLXXVIII, col. 337W.
57 A March 1946 Defence Office memorandum to the Australia and New Zealand Governments contemplated an external attack by a 'major power' in the context of a foreign invasion of the Chinese mainland, and concluded that Hong Kong could not be defended against such an attack. ANA, A3317 337/1946, Defence Office to Australia and New Zealand, 15 March 1946.
58 ANA, A1209 1957/4556, Commonwealth Relations Office, 'Reduction of the Hong Kong Garrison', 7 December 1955, p. 1.
59 *Hong Kong: A Case to Answer* (Hong Kong: Hong Kong Research Project, 1974), p. 19.
60 'Red Flags, Running Dogs and Air Conditioned Horses', *New Statesman* (26 May 1978), p. 703. The article mentioned the recent police mutiny described in Chapter 5.
61 Lee, 'Fed up with Poor Relations', p. 22.
62 Anthony Mockler, 'The Gurkhas' Front Line', *Spectator* (17 February 1979), p. 13.
63 HKU Special Collections, Sir Edwin Noel Westby Bramall, *Address to the Rotary Club of Hong Kong by Commander British Forces, Tuesday 27 May 1975*, pp. 5–6. The Commander agreed that the military's primary role was not defensive, but attributed this not to the colony's indefensibility but to 'excellent' tripartite relations among the UK, the PRC, and the colony.
64 Surrey History Centre, ESR/25/BOTT/3, British Forces Hong Kong, *Keeping the Peace in Hong Kong (Duties in Support of the Civil Power)*, 1962, pp. 3–4, 29. Bold in original.
65 'Battalion Notes', *The China Dragon* 27 (May 1955), p. 46; '"C" Company', *The China Dragon*, 27 (May 1955), p. 48 (Staffordshire Regiment Museum).
66 *The Antelope* 31 (May 1961), p. 3 (Royal Regiment of Fusiliers Museum [Royal Warwickshire]).
67 'Seaside Town Sends "Ads" to Hong Kong', *Daily Mirror* (1 March 1954), p. 5.
68 Felix Patrikeeff, *Mouldering Pearl: Hong Kong at the Crossroads* (London: George Philip, 1989), p. 89.
69 Jan Morris, *Hong Kong* (New York: Viking, 1988), p. 100.
70 Jane Gardam, *Old Filth* (London: Chatto and Windus, 2004).
71 May Holdsworth, *Foreign Devils: Expatriates in Hong Kong* (Oxford: Oxford University Press, 2002), p. xii.
72 Elizabeth Buettner, *Empire Families: Britons and Late Imperial India* (Oxford: Oxford University Press, 2004), p. 200.
73 TNA, FCO 40/226, policing Hong Kong, n.d. (1968/69), p. 8.
74 Patrikeeff, *Mouldering Pearl*, p. 25; David Bonavia, *Hong Kong 1997: The Final Settlement* (Hong Kong: FEER, 1985), pp. 12–13; Walter Easey, *Ducking Responsibility: Britain and Hong Kong in the '80s* (Manchester: *Christian Statesman*, 1980), pp. 26, 46; Peter Victor, 'Obituary: Walter Easey', *Independent* (2 April 1998), www.independent.co.uk/news/obituaries/obituary-walter-easey-1153959.html (accessed 5 October 2012); Holdsworth, *Foreign Devils*, p. xii; Stephen Vines, *Hong Kong: China's New Colony* (London: Orion Business), p. 71.
75 ANA, A1838/530/4, Commonwealth of Australia, Trade Commissioner Service, 'Post Report on Hong Kong – January, 1954', p. 6.
76 Girton College, Cambridge, Dorothy Needham Papers, GCPP Needham 5/1/12, Dorothy Needham diary, 8 and 11 September 1971.

77 'John Bull's Other Island', *Daily Mirror* (30 September 1947), p. 2.
78 Modern Records Office, University of Warwick, Standard-Triumph (Far East) Ltd., MS 226/ST/3/0/FE/1, Jack Carter to S. N. Bullen, 9 January 1961.
79 Seven Stories Archive, Newcastle, KW/01/02/25/07, Peter and Gunvor Edwards to Kaye Webb, 17 January 1995.
80 Peter Otto Jacobsen and Preben Sejer Kristensen, *A Family in Hong Kong* (Hove: Wayland, 1985), p. 11.
81 Suen Hung Wing, in Chris Fairclough, *We Live in Hong Kong* (Hove: Wayland, 1985), p. 6.
82 Girton College, Cambridge, Dorothy Needham Papers, GCPP Needham 5/1/12, Dorothy Needham diary, 10 September 1971.
83 Morris, *Hong Kong*, pp. 46, 63, 164; Anthony Shang, *Living in Hong Kong* (London and Sydney: Macdonald, 1985), p. 27. Shang went on to claim that 'the "rags to riches" dream of a poor refugee becoming a millionaire is less likely to come true today [1985]'.
84 Girton College, Cambridge, Dorothy Needham Papers, GCPP Needham 1/4/1/19/7, Joseph Needham to Dorothy Needham, 21 October 1981.
85 John Darwin, 'Orphans of Empire', in Bickers, *Settlers and Expatriates*, pp. 239–45 (p. 338); Robert Bickers, 'Introduction: Britain and Britons over the Seas', in Bickers, *Settlers and Expatriates*, pp. 1–17 (p. 16).
86 Dane Kennedy, *Islands of White: Settler Society and Culture in Kenya and Southern Rhodesia, 1890–1939* (Durham, NC: Duke University Press, 1987); Bill Schwarz, *The White Man's World* (Oxford: Oxford University Press, 2011).
87 On prewar segregation, see John M. Carroll, 'The Peak: Residential Segregation in Colonial Hong Kong', in David S. G. Goodman and Bryna Goodman (eds), *Twentieth-Century Colonialism and China: Localities, the Everyday, and the World* (Oxford: Routledge, 2012), pp. 81–91.
88 Quoted in '*Far Eastern Economic Review* – Into the Seventh Year', *FEER* (16 October 1952), p. 488.
89 James Clavell, *Tai-Pan: A Novel of Hong Kong* (London: Michael Joseph, 1966), pp. 341, 676.
90 Mason, *The World of Suzie Wong*, pp. 188–9.
91 Alexander Grantham, *Via Ports: From Hong Kong to Hong Kong* (Hong Kong: Hong Kong University Press, 1965), p. 104. See also Alexander Grantham, interview by D. J. Crozier, 21 August 1968, Rhodes College, Oxford, MS Brit. Emp. Si 288, p. 9. Henry Lethbridge in 1968 referred to the remaining 'minority of racialists' who, 'like museum pieces, are permanently on exhibition'. H. J. Lethbridge, 'The Best of Both Worlds?', *FEER* (10 October 1968), p. 130.
92 He went on to say 'Most of them look with dismay upon the recent invasions of American tourists, big business, and troops on leave.' James Kirkup, *Cities of the World: Hong Kong and Macao* (London: J. M. Dent and Sons, 1970), pp. 43–4.
93 When she pitched the novel to publisher Jonathan Cape, she openly described it as autobiographical. HS, Box 73, Han Suyin to Jonathan Cape, 8 January 1951.
94 Han also feared the consequences of her book's publication, insisting that there be no editing, cutting, or the like without her express approval, and was cautious about serial or cinema rights. She worried that the book might be transformed into pro-American propaganda, and told Jonathan Cape that she worried that her family in China might be killed in retaliation. HS, Box 73, Han Suyin to Jonathan Cape, 25 April 1951.
95 Han Suyin, *A Many-Splendored Thing* (Boston: Little, Brown, 1952), p. 167.
96 Christine Loh, *Being Here: Shaping a Preferred Future* (Hong Kong: SCMP Books, 2006), p. 126.
97 Dan Waters, *One Couple, Two Cultures: 81 Western–Chinese Couples Talk about Love and Marriage* (Hong Kong: MCCM Creations, 2005), p. 11.
98 J. Walker, *Under the Whitewash*, rev. and enlarged edn (Hong Kong: *70s Biweekly*, 1972), p. 89.
99 'Anachronistic Racial Discrimination in Hongkong', *FEER* (16 August 1951), p. 196.

100 Kirkup, *Cities of the World*, p. 44.
101 G. B. Endacott and A. Hinton, *Fragrant Harbour: A Short History of Hong Kong* (Hong Kong: Hong Kong University Press, 1962), p. 183.
102 Lethbridge, 'The Best of Both Worlds?', p. 129.
103 Holdsworth, *Foreign Devils*, p. 17.
104 Just to take one example, see the pictures of the 'Post Macau GP Party', which was held at the Hong Kong Club, in *Hong Kong Tatler* 1 (January 1978), pp. 40–1.
105 Sea-ling Cheng, 'Consuming Places in Hong Kong: Experiencing Lan Kwai Fong', in Gordon Mathews and Tai-Lok Lui (eds), *Consuming Hong Kong* (Hong Kong: Hong Kong University Press, 2003), pp. 237–62.
106 Holdsworth, *Foreign Devils*, pp. 216–17.
107 John Burdett, *The Last Six Million Seconds: A Thriller* (New York: William Morrow, 1997), p. 71.

CHAPTER TWO

The discourse of unbridled capitalism in postwar Hong Kong

Writing in 1983, against the backdrop of the negotiations that would result in the 1984 Sino-British Joint Declaration and the 1997 Handover, the historian Gregor Benton argued that Hong Kong's postwar economic miracle should not be attributed to British rule in Hong Kong, 'which at best provided the arena' within which fairly unusual contingent factors could operate. These factors included a regional instability that prompted capital inflows into a relatively stable Hong Kong, as well as China's supply of cheap raw materials and immigrant labour, and they would not necessarily continue into the future.[1] Within this atypical context, Hong Kong's economic triumph was, above all, a Chinese accomplishment. Benton's explanation echoed a characteristic 1974 memorandum from a British Council Regional Assistant Director General, J. D. B. Fowells, not intended for public consumption, which explained Hong Kong's achievement simply, as the result of 'wits and hard work' – implicitly, the efforts of the young and rapidly growing immigrant population.[2] Similarly but more explicitly, the British Council's Hong Kong Representative, also in a confidential report in 1971, entirely credited the 'energy, skill, and hard work' of the Chinese population, many of whom were refugees from the PRC, with Hong Kong's economic miracle.[3] A decade earlier in 1961, Hong Kong's financial secretary, A. G. Clarke, in his final official speech, confessed his inability to comprehend how, in the hands of Hong Kong's people, 'new and successful industries can be created out of nothing, in face of every possible handicap', and predicted that his successor would be just as incapable of understanding the foundations of Hong Kong's economic success.[4]

Most British commentators, though, were much more willing to credit distinctly British virtues with the making of Hong Kong, that formerly 'barren rock'.[5] To be sure, they were often willing to admit the obvious fact that Hong Kong's success owed a great deal to Chinese

[42]

industriousness and Chinese capital; numerous writers took apparent pains to remind their readers that Hong Kong was a 'Chinese city', as if this point could easily be forgotten. Some writers, for example James Clavell, went so far as to imply that Hong Kong's success was the product of the best qualities of both the Chinese and the British: for him, an important characteristic of Britishness was its ability to assimilate the best of other cultures. Eurasian novelist Han Suyin, in an article written for *Life Magazine* in 1959, described an English friend who, while acknowledging the contribution of Hong Kong's Chinese inhabitants, 'smugly' attributed Hong Kong's success to British 'healthy neglect'.[6] The anthropologist Marjorie Topley (1963) credited the 'relatively greater public security and emphasis on economic development' with encouraging both capital and labour to settle in Hong Kong and Singapore; the good fortune had spread to Shanghai thanks to extra-territoriality.[7] A Hong Kong Government Information Services (GIS) booklet, *An Introduction to Hong Kong* (1983), attributed Chinese emigration to 'liberal British rule', which facilitated the 'blend of British administration and industrial expertise, and Chinese energy and enterprise, which explains the Hong Kong phenomenon'.[8] Similarly, as John Flowerdew notes, Christopher Patten, the final British Governor of Hong Kong, regularly attributed Hong Kong's spectacular achievement to the character of Hong Kong's people, acting within the political framework provided by the British.[9] Such quotations as these lend support to David Faure's characterisation of the thesis that 'British institutions and Chinese hard work created the very wealthy city which reverted to China in June 1997' as 'Hong Kong's colonial myth' – one that, as all myths do, 'twists partial reality to fit a political end'.[10]

But notwithstanding an admission of the Chinese role in the making of modern Hong Kong, what unites most British commentators during the postwar years is their insistence on ultimate British responsibility for Hong Kong's economic rise. Indeed, many would have taken issue with Benton's basic formulation: even leaving aside the role of British trading companies and merchants, what Benton termed 'at best provid[ing] the arena' was a decisive contribution. Vice-Admiral Harcourt, the Commander-in-Chief of Hong Kong's military Government immediately after the war, told New Zealand official James Bertram in 1946 that he expected China to continue acquiescing in British rule, in light of its demonstrable benefit to China. In making this case, he told Bertram ' "that all we got from China was a barren rock". From this start, a hundred years of British rule had built-up the most important entrepot port of the Far East.'[11] As the *Daily Mirror*'s 'Cassandra' (William Connor) put it in 1949, 'Down the great arc of the China Coast, with its piracy,

[43]

its corruption, its armed smuggling and its infamous reputation for lawlessness and disorder, Hong Kong is the one precious tiny site where trade and business can be done on honourable and dependable terms.' This being the case, the Chinese, 'with their sharp zest for a deal, have swarmed into it', producing a 'most comforting entry on the books of the British Empire'.[12] In the words of a 1949 article by Hong Kong's Public Relations Office, 'Almost a century of uninterrupted peaceful development' followed the British takeover of Hong Kong, and the British-enforced

> freedom of the port ensured the role of entrepot both for the trade and for the labour of China's southern provinces. Reclamations were carried out, roads built, and anti-malarial measures initiated; ship yards capable of constructing 10,000 ton ships, docks to accommodate the world's largest liners, and light industries all developed with the years.[13]

Similarly, W. Y. Willetts, reviewing S. G. Davis's *Hong Kong in Its Geographical Setting* in the *Spectator* in 1950, noted the 'forceful' proposition that 'Hong Kong is an original creation, out of next to nothing, of British mercantile genius.'[14] A review in the same magazine of Harold Ingram's CO-commissioned 1952 book on Hong Kong began with the question, 'How many people realise that only 110 years ago Hong Kong was nothing more than a home for fishermen and a refuge for pirates – a barren brown rock?'.[15] Subsequent chapters will address the theme of Hong Kong as a British creation, virtually *ex nihilo*, in the context of tropes of modernisation and good government. This chapter, by contrast, will emphasise the discourse of economic freedom. Hong Kong was imagined as a site characterised by 'unbridled capitalism', and an example of the economic dynamism – but also the extremes of wealth and poverty – that could also be unleashed in Britain by a return to pre-Keynesian economics.

During the period examined in this book, Hong Kong was often portrayed as a territory free of the rules that constrained economic choices elsewhere. Such portrayals were by no means the unique province of British commentators – they were a staple of American cold warriors and anti-Keynesians – but their articulation takes on a distinct resonance within the context of concerns about Britishness, the English national character, and the post-1945 Welfare State 'consensus'. Although this 'unbridled capitalism' motif contained its share of myth, it contributed to the idea of Hong Kong as a place in which British qualities and liberties that were stifled in the metropole could be given free rein. Moreover, in the context of the Thatcherite attack on the Welfare State from the mid-1970s onward, Hong Kong was frequently cited as a salutary model.

Recent scholarship has questioned the myth of Hong Kong as a laissez-faire colony, emphasising Government intervention in the housing market and the development of 'New Towns', for example.[16] This new scholarly emphasis has largely replaced an older view that not only accepted laissez-faire as an apt description of the Government's policies, but also saw it as a reflection of Hong Kong people's low expectations for Government intervention. Lau Siu-kai argued that Hong Kong Chinese political apathy derived from 'utilitarian familialism', in which they pursued material benefit while looking to family networks, rather than the State, for any necessary assistance. The Hong Kong-born and UK-based political historian Steve Tsang has situated British non-intervention within Confucian expectations of government, arguing that non-interference was one of the major attributes by which Chinese judged their rulers; he argues that, judged by these Confucian ideals, the Colonial Government was one of the most successful in China's history.[17]

Leo Goodstadt neatly reconciles these two conflicting assessments of Hong Kong's non-interventionist vision. While accepting the general idea that the Colonial Government pursued non-intervention, he underscores that its commitment to laissez-faire was 'not a matter of principle but motivated by political convenience and economic expediency'. Championing laissez-faire ideals served as a legitimising tactic, while pragmatism meant that the Government did not need to be bothered by theoretical inconsistencies. At the same time, a general lack of proactive Government support for business was offset by a lack of generous social welfare spending as a compromise that maintained Hong Kong's delicate political balance. Similarly, David Davies, Goodstadt's former colleague on the progressive/liberal *FEER*, noted in 1971, in the context of Murray MacLehose's replacement of David Trench as Governor, the disjunction between official commitment to laissez-faire and actual Government activism. In Davies's view, Trench's Financial Secretary, Sir John Cowperthwaite, had 'specialised in intellectualising with awesomely convoluted logic around the case for noninterference' even as the Government had intervened strategically in key economic sectors.[18] Goodstadt's and Davies's formulation goes a long way toward explaining the expansion of the State in the 1970s and 1980s, as well as the coexistence of a seemingly strident laissez-faire approach with fairly extensive housing and infrastructure projects beginning as early as the 1950s.[19]

My concern here is not to settle the question of the nature of the Colonial State. This chapter treats colonial non-interventionism neither as a quality to be measured nor, strictly speaking, as a political ideology, as, for example, in the assertion by Tak-Wing Ngo that laissez-faire was a legitimating tool for British rule.[20] Rather, it approaches laissez-faire as a particular way in which commentators on Hong Kong articulated a particular vision of Britishness that championed the individual against the State and the man of action against mass mediocrity.

More British than Britain: Hong Kong's Victorian economy

Most observers cited in this chapter celebrated Hong Kong's economic freedom. Following the creation of the post-1945 British Welfare State, embattled capitalists could look to Hong Kong as a sort of colonial 'world we have lost', in which taxes were low, profits were high, labour was quiescent, and the State's reach was limited.[21] As Harold Ingrams wrote in 1952, 'It is not only in the material things of life – the many surviving *large* rooms, the *fat* newspaper with porridge, *two* eggs and bacon and *very* fragrant coffee for breakfast – and all the rest – that Hong Kong offers to those who can afford it, an escape to the past, but in much of its atmosphere.'[22] The 'atmosphere' was one that encouraged, even demanded, true British virtues. While the climate in postwar Britain itself was, according to the economist Joseph Schumpeter, actively hostile to entrepreneurship or any sort of income-earning not directly tied to labour, Hong Kong remained a site in which the industrialists, merchants, and entrepreneurs could succeed – or fail.[23] Although the setting was very different, Hong Kong thus joined the settler colonies in postwar Africa as a place in which the 'best elements in "the British culture"' could continue to flourish, in contrast to idle and effeminate Britain, which was 'no longer fully British'.[24]

This paradoxical idea that Hong Kong was more British than Britain contributed to ambivalent feelings toward the metropole on the part of Britons in Hong Kong, often veering toward *Schadenfreude*. A member of Britain's Department of Health and Social Security, S. M. Davies, reporting on a 1970 trip to Hong Kong to promote Britain's lagging medical supplies industry, noted that 'Expatriate Britons are notorious for their masochistic delight in denigrating their home country.'[25] Similarly, John le Carré's fictional 1977 depiction of the Hong Kong Club portrayed *Telegraph* readers grousing about Britain's ubiquitous strikes and the decline of the pound.[26] More than a matter of declinism, it was frequently observed that Britons in Hong Kong were increasingly alienated from postwar British life. In 1970, for example, the British Council's Hong Kong Representative claimed that 'citizens of Great Britain living in Hong Kong tend to think, with a curious dichotomy of mind, of Britain as a foreign country (which, by comparison, it is)'.[27]

Yet paradoxically, it was Hong Kong that was the more classically British, while Britain itself had changed. In the title of one 1960s pamphlet published by a pro-free-market think-tank, the Institute of Economic Affairs, Hong Kong was 'John Stuart Mill's Other Island', and the only question was whether or not it was an appropriate model for other developing economies.[28] The peripatetic British political scientist Peter Harris, who founded the University of Hong Kong's (HKU) Political Science Department after stints in Rhodesia and London (and degrees from Wales, London, and Natal), described in 1978, in more dispassionate terms, the prevailing view of an administrative State in which the Financial Secretary could enforce a laissez-faire line by his ability to say 'no'; he quoted the American scholar Alvin Rabushka, shortly to be known for his championing of a 'flat tax' for the United States, as referring to Hong Kong's 'official line' as 'Gladstone reincarnated'. By the late 1970s, of course, Harris could note that this picture of Hong Kong's Government had grown somewhat outdated: the

> would-be authoritarian Financial Secretary ... is faced with a luxuriant proliferation of organizational growth. There are many more centres of power than there were, and London may even recall him by air to render an account of his stewardship ... The governorship, too, has changed its character and has assumed a more active role.[29]

Chapter 5 will describe some of these changes in the nature of Hong Kong's Government in the 1970s. Nonetheless, even with recent changes and assorted caveats, Financial Secretary C. P. Haddon-Cave could still credibly claim that the Government 'consciously refrain from substituting a bureaucratic decision-making process for the process of market determination'.[30]

Evocations of Hong Kong's continuing adherence to nineteenth-century economic values took their place within a wider range of claims concerning the superiority of Hong Kong's British credentials to those of a home country in which they had disappeared. This can be seen, for example, on the invitation to a 1977 Christmas party that, according to *Hong Kong Tatler*, attracted 500 guests. The invitation's first page included a quotation from Sir Winston Churchill, affirming the importance of a unified British Empire. The second page revealed the evening's programme, which included the 'Royal Fanfare' and the National Anthem, as well as separate toasts to the Queen and the Empire; it also announced a dress code of 'hunting or tweeds' for the gentlemen, and 'scarves, twin sets and pearls' for the ladies. Yet the hosts' self-conscious articulation of their superior Britishness came most clearly in a ten-line poem that contrasts Britain's diminishing power, the collapse of the pound sterling, and Urdu signs on British streets on the one hand, with, on the other hand, the remaining 'British Bulldogs' who, far from 'dead', live in Hong Kong, where they 'stand for what is British, what is noble, just and right'.[31] In the context of a caricaturistic display of Hong Kong Britishness, the dig at Britain's currency crisis reaffirmed the wisdom of Hong Kong's rejection of the Welfare State of Britain itself.

Yet even those who spoke about Hong Kong with a critical voice generally affirmed its identification with pre-Attlee economic and social policies, even if only in order to lambaste their retrograde character. This point is illustrated by a 1974 pamphlet, anonymously written by Jon Halliday and published by a radical London-based organization called the Hong Kong Research Project that was founded by former Hong Kong policeman Walter Easey. This pamphlet essentially saw Hong Kong as a repressive colonial police state whose chief function was to transform a thorough exploitation of Chinese workers into 'high levels of capital accumulation, and high profits'.[32] John Gordon Davis's 1979 novel *Typhoon* includes a scene in which senior police inspector Bernard Champion lectures an American journalist that Hong Kong 'exists for one reason only. Money!'. He elaborates, saying that corruption, triad criminality, and philanthropy were all intertwined and embodied in the same social elites, while British hypocrisy recognised such figures with knighthoods and honours – specifically in the case of the novel's villain, Sir Herman Choi. John le Carré's *The Honourable Schoolboy* includes a similar, though less cartoonish, character in Drake Ko, O.B.E., described by one character as 'to all outward purposes ... something of a Hong Kong prototype: Steward of the Jockey Club, supports the charities, pillar of the integrated society, successful, benevolent, has the wealth of Croesus and the commercial mentality of the whorehouse'.[33] Such stereotypes appear just as frequently in non-fiction. For example, according to Nigel Cameron, the long-time art critic of the *South China Morning Post* (*SCMP*), writing in 1978, Hong Kong's 'frenetic commerce' was 'carried on largely without British restrictions', because elites were able to operate without the constraints imposed by twentieth-century popular movements on their counterparts in Britain. As a result, in Hong Kong, 'just as in the heyday of Victorian capitalist expansion during that seemingly eternal and God-countersigned sunshine of the peak of empire, if you can do it and have enough money to do it, then you can probably get away with it'.[34]

Indeed, for Hong Kong's critics, the lack of (modern) British-style social welfare and more equitable distribution of income was directly related to its lack of popular representation. For example, in April

1969, during the House of Commons Oral Answers concerning the conferring of the title 'Royal' upon the Hong Kong Police, one Labour member, John Rankin, objected that Hong Kong 'as a State stands for everything that we in this country reject' and noted that this un-British system was 'loyally backed up by the Hong Kong Police Force'.[35] According to Duncan Campbell, writing in the *New Statesman* in 1980, this wealth-serving police state was further supported by a thorough surveillance network that, in the words of his article's title, contributed to a 'secret plan for dictatorship' in case the normal measures of repression failed.[36] Yet it was not only critics who linked a lack of democracy with Hong Kong's economic success. Peter Bauer, in an admiring review of the American political scientist Alvin Rabushka's *Hong Kong: A Study in Economic Freedom*, linked Hong Kong's success to its minimal government and low taxes, and cited the 'absence of election promises' as one of the key factors in discouraging political activism aimed at interventionist economics.[37]

The idea of Hong Kong as a site for unrestrained wealth-building was built into its founding mythologies. For example, in his 1985 book *Hard Graft in Hong Kong*, a sympathetic scholarly account of the creation of the Independent Commission against Corruption (ICAC), Henry Lethbridge described nineteenth-century Hong Kong's European society as a 'distorting mirror of mid-Victorian England – outwardly respectable, conservative, snobbish, and Sabbatarian'. Yet beneath this 'lacquer', he wrote, life entailed a 'frantic scramble for wealth, with the intruding reminder that life was short on the China coast'. According to Lethbridge, early Hong Kong was a virtually lawless society or, more precisely, one in which merchants were 'prepared to cut corners, to sail close to the law'.[38] Jan Morris's sensationalist mass-market history of Hong Kong, first published in 1988 and reprinted in 1997 a few months before the Handover, similarly portrays nineteenth-century Hong Kong as uniquely concerned with the pursuit of wealth, so that even when 'evangelical improvement was a powerful motive of imperialism, the merchants of Hong Kong abided by the principles of laissez-faire at their most conscienceless'. More broadly, she concluded that 'Like it or not, there was never anywhere quite like Hong Kong for instant opportunities ... It is like a mammoth game of Monopoly, tinged with enigma.'[39] Naturally, she attributed Hong Kong's economic success to its having been 'relatively free from government interference'.[40] Anthony Shang, in his 1985 children's book entitled *Living in Hong Kong*, in a section headed 'Get It while You Can', opined that 'Hong Kong society encourages many people to see making a lot of money as the most important thing in life. Younger Chinese people tend to be particularly influenced by this.'[41]

[49]

James Clavell's Hong Kong

Yet nowhere was the identification of Hong Kong with quick money, earned in a virtually lawless environment, more evocatively rendered than in two novels by Australian-born writer James Clavell. *Tai-Pan*, published in 1966, mythologises the nineteenth-century founding of British Hong Kong and its leading company engaged in the China trade, Jardine Matheson; while *Noble House*, published in 1981, provides a vivid portrayal of Hong Kong capitalism in 1963. Born in 1924 in Australia, Clavell served in the British military in the Asian theatre during the Second World War. Enlisting in the Royal Artillery at age sixteen, by the end of the war he had been wounded by gunfire and imprisoned in Japanese prisoner-of-war camps in Java and Singapore. According to literary critic Gina Macdonald, his experience in Singapore's Changi prison, in which 'unholy realities of a Japanese prison camp' tested the idealistic British military values he had been taught by his patriotic father, underlies his lifelong commitment to the value of individual freedom and private enterprise.[42] Clavell's championing of the heroic side of British imperial history may well have reflected an attempt to escape from what he considered Britain's loss of its way; as he told an interviewer in 1966, he felt that since the Second World War 'the country had lost its morality and sense of obligation'.[43]

Despite being an opium trader, the hero of *Tai-Pan*, Dirk Struan, embodies the best of Britishness: rule of law, the anti-slavery movement, fair play, and support for free trade and peace. At the same time, he willingly borrows from the best of Chinese civilisation – tea instead of water, hygienic practices, medicines such as quinine – and regards China and Britain as partners in advancing human civilisation. In Clavell's typically didactic manner, we learn Struan's thoughts:

> Stop it, he said to himself. You're acting like a madman. Aye, and they'd all think you mad if you told them that your secret purpose was not just to get rich on trade and to leave. But to use riches and power to open up China to the world and particularly to British culture and British law so that each could learn from the other and grow to the benefit of both. Aye. It's a dream of a madman.
>
>   But he was certain that China had something special to offer the world. What it was, he did not know. One day perhaps he would find out.[44]

Clavell's narrative does not shy away from the sordid aspects of British imperialism – the drug trade, the exploitative side of profit-seeking, the brutality. Clavell appears to endorse the school of imperial thought that making omelettes requires breaking a few eggs.[45] As one prepublication review noted, 'Some of the merchants' actions verge on piracy, some of their cargo is opium, but they are brave and resourceful in facing their trade risks, their precarious position on the verge of a vast empire which hates them, and the personal danger to themselves and their families.'[46] The end result is that Hong Kong – that barren rock – is established as a beneficent site of British and Chinese cooperation. Again, we see Struan's thoughts upon the founding of Hong Kong:

> The treaty would stand because it was fair. Then, over the years, the Chinese would gradually open their ports willingly – seeing that the British had much to offer: law, justice, the sanctity of property, freedom.
>
> For the ordinary Chinese want what we want, he thought, and there's nae difference between us. We can work together for the benefit of all. Perhaps we'll help the Chinese to throw out the barbaric Manchus. That's what will happen so long as there's a reasonable treaty now, and we're patient, and we play the Chinese game with Chinese rules, in Chinese time. Time measured not in a day or year, but in generations. And so long as we can trade while we're waiting. Without trade the world will become what it was once – a hell where only the strongest arm and the heaviest lash was law. The meek will never inherit the earth. Aye, but at least they can be protected by law to live out their lives as they wish.[47]

Where *Tai-Pan* argues the significance of Hong Kong's creation, *Noble House* shows the colony's flourishing just over a century later. It tells the story of an American businessman, Linc Bartlett, arriving in Hong Kong in 1963 (with his assistant Casey Tcholok) ostensibly to arrange a deal with Ian Dunross, a descendant of Dirk Struan and tai-pan of the firm Noble House. In fact, Bartlett schemes with Dunross's rival, Quillian Gornt, to take over Noble House – a plot that comes dangerously close to success before Dunross secures mainland Chinese backing. Dunross's Randian qualities are clear as he navigates Hong Kong's intricate cultural landscape and defeats his rivals, but in case any reader might miss the novel's patriotism toward British Hong Kong, Clavell offered as his dedication: 'I would like to offer this work as a tribute to Her Britannic Majesty, Elizabeth II, to the people of Her Crown Colony of Hong Kong – *and perdition to their enemies.*' Throughout the novel, the association of Hong Kong with money and, in particular, quick money, is clear, even heavy-handed. This association appears in the Americans' motivation for coming to Hong Kong: Casey is trying to score a quick US$2 million of 'drop dead' or 'screw you' money, and though she is unsure how to get it, she thinks 'somehow I know this is the place'.[48] Clavell assures us that she is right to think this way: upon the Americans' arrival by plane, Bartlett 'caught a strangeness on the wind, neither pleasant nor unpleasant, neither odor nor perfume – just strange and curiously exciting' – a smell noticed as well by Casey. Asking what the smell was, he was informed by the Superintendent, 'That's Hong Kong's very own, Mr. Bartlett. It's money.'[49] (Fragrant harbour, indeed!)

Nor is Casey wrong to hope for quick riches. As Dunross's sister, Kathren, explains to her, Hong Kong is a vengeful place, a 'piratical society with very few curbs'. It is a 'place of transit – no one ever comes here to stay, even Chinese, just to make money and leave'. Hong Kong's vengeful quality and air of quick money derive, in part, from foreboding: 'we live on the edge of catastrophe all the time: fire, flood, plague, landslide, riots'. In part they derive from Hong Kong's temporary status: 'China can swallow us any moment. So you live for today and to hell with everything, grab what you can because tomorrow, who knows?'[50]

Nor was Communist Chinese takeover the only threat to Hong Kong. Clavell contrasted his hero, Ian Dunross, with the periodic meddling of London politicians. In a characteristically didactic passage, Dunross, asked what his politics are, explains to Alan Grant that Hong Kong is apolitical, ruled on behalf of the Crown by a Governor whose despotism is not so much benevolent as benignly neglectful: 'Wisely he leaves things alone. He listens to the business community, makes social changes very cautiously and leaves everyone to make money or not make money, to build, expand, go broke, to go or to come, to dream or to stay awake, to live or die as best you can.' He goes on to boast of the low tax rate – applied only to money earned in Hong Kong – and asserts 'I'm royalist, I'm for freedom, for freebooting and free trade. I'm a Scotsman, I'm for Struan's, I'm for laissez-faire in Hong Kong and freedom throughout the world.'[51] This hectoring speech is reinforced several times throughout the novel, for example, in Dunross's views on Hong Kong: 'Here the strong survive and the weak perish but en route the government doesn't steal from you, or protect you. If you don't want to be free and don't like our rules, or lack of them, don't come.'[52] As Bartlett enthusiastically tells Casey, speaking of insider trading, 'Jesus, it's fantastic – wonderful – a great system! What they do here legally every day'd get you twenty years in the States.'[53]

Yet Hong Kong was not free from London's periodic intrusion, as seen in Clavell's explication of Dunross's thoughts as the latter talks with Robin Grey, a visiting Labour MP. Dunross chooses his words 'carefully', knowing that the 'anti-Hong Kong lobby in Parliament was strong'. Yet this latest threat to Hong Kong's status merely joined the list of surmountable obstacles Hong Kong had always faced: 'Never mind, he thought. Since 1841 we've survived hostile Parliaments, fire, typhoon, pestilence, plague, embargo, depression, occupation and the periodic convulsions that China goes through, and somehow we always will.'[54] During the course of the novel parliamentary interference

[52]

does not materialise and Clavell, writing much of this book against the backdrop of the 1979 election that brought Margaret Thatcher to power, clearly endorses this benign neglect.

Parliamentary interference did not, of course, exist only in Clavell's imagination. Although by the 1960s the Hong Kong Government was increasingly autonomous – and increasingly self-financing – questions of working conditions and corrupt oligopolistic dominance periodically attracted enquiry from London. In the 1970s, metropolitan pressure contributed to the social welfare reforms passed by Governor MacLehose, a 'reluctant reformer' in the words of Ray Yep and Tai-Lok Lui.[55] This could result from a Labour MP's ideological opposition to the very nature of Hong Kong's economy, or from pressure from British manufacturing interests concerned to protect their markets from 'dumping' of Hong Kong's wares, a topic to which we will return.[56]

No love of money

While Clavell's Ian Dunross sees parliamentary interference as a blow to freedom, he speaks from the position of the tai-pan of a long-enduring company. It is Casey's desire for the quick score – after which she could leave Hong Kong – that illustrates an oft-remarked quality of Hong Kong's economic life: the short-term focus. Marjorie Topley, writing in 1963, blamed Chinese investors' short-term focus for their general unwillingness to invest in industry, where 'profits may be slow in coming'. Even when investing in industry, investors tended to 'look for quick profits by whatever means present themselves as attractive in the short run rather than to look for opportunities for starting long-term investment'.[57] A 1967 Australian report on immigration reform argued that the impending 1997 expiration of the New Territories lease 'discourage[d] the kind of long-term projects' that normally employed science and engineering graduates in 'countries like Australia'.[58] Similarly, the British Council's Hong Kong Representative, in his 1971 Report, linked the Council's work to the gap that existed between 'commercial success' and 'social conditions' – a gap he attributed to the business community's 'excessive concentration' on short-term goals and unwillingness to plan for the longer term. Governor Trench disagreed with this characterisation, but the Representative was not the only one to note this tendency.[59] The *Times* correspondent David Bonavia, writing in the *FEER* in 1966, argued that Hong Kong's industries lacked 'long-term planning and long-term capital'; instead, they shifted from one product to another in a 'form of the bandwaggoning for which Hongkong is well known'.[60] Nor was short-term thinking attributed only to the private sector.

The pro-establishment *South China Sunday Post-Herald*, in a 1970 editorial, lamented the Government's apparent inability to consider long-term goals, tending instead to make plans on a 'piecemeal' or 'ad hoc' basis, and favouring initiatives that provided a 'speedy return that can readily be totted up on a balance sheet'.[61]

Where Clavell celebrated even the more sordid aspects of Hong Kong's commercial mentality, other writers were less enthusiastic about the colony's devotion to mammon. In 1975, during a series of high-profile police corruption trials, Robert Elegant noted in *The Australian* that the Royal Hong Kong Police Force was the 'best police force money can buy in Asia' – both because it was certainly one of Asia's top three police forces, and because 'many policemen, from constables to senior officers, are for sale to lawbreakers'. (He did argue, though, that Hong Kong was relatively less corrupt than most of Asia, but that a 'free press and a concerned government' talked about it more than their authoritarian and controlled counterparts elsewhere).[62] Political activist Elsie Elliott's anti-corruption rhetoric similarly often focused on the idea that legal justice and bureaucratic administration were, in effect, commercialised. More germane to the present discussion, she noted the extent to which even civil servants imbibed the commercial mentality. In her 1981 autobiography, she noted that on one occasion she applied to the Education Department for permission to erect some army huts, which she had acquired at a bargain price, to use as a new building for the charitable school she operated. The bureaucrat was less than sympathetic: 'The official who interviewed me (I remember his name but will not shame him by repeating it here) said, "Why don't you copy Mr So-and-so? He runs private schools, and now runs around in a big American car." He was not joking either.'[63]

No doubt such attitudes were particularly distasteful to someone like Elliott, who first arrived in Hong Kong in the early 1950s as a 'faith missionary' – i.e. one without a regular salary. Yet according to Marjorie Topley, writing in 1963, commercial considerations predominated. She quoted the prevalent Chinese observation that 'Most things are decided in Hong Kong on the basis of whether or not the abacus makes a satisfying click', and went so far as to claim that few religious goods existed 'that would not be sold if the price offered were sufficiently attractive'.[64] F. D. Ommanney, too, noted the predominance of commercial considerations in Hong Kong's public life. As he pointed out, the typical British tendency to plant trees wherever they went was defeated by Hong Kong's development: 'when the towns started to expand the speculative builder got to work and nobody worried about trees'. He lamented that most of Kowloon consisted of buildings with a 'quite unique soulless quality that depresses the spirit, towering

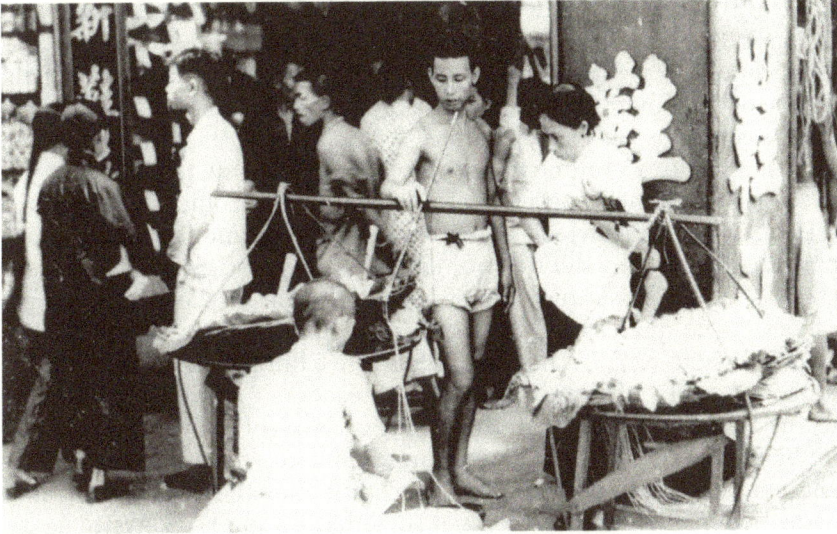

Figure 3 The source of Hong Kong's 'economic miracle': its people. Street trading, Hong Kong, *c.* 1950s.

flat surfaces pierced by hundreds of small windows soaring up giddily without regard to their neighbours'. Meanwhile, on the one stretch of Nathan Road that was, for a few hundred yards, a 'boulevard' contrasting with the city's general ugliness, a movement had recently arisen to cut down the banyan trees 'because it was said that they obscured the neon signs and were bad for business'; luckily, the Municipal Council retained a shred of feeling and the movement was defeated.[65] David Bonavia insisted that 'only the ignorant have written off Hong Kong as nothing but a money machine, a sweatshop or a sink of corruption and vice', but even he, noting (in 1985) the sad tendency of the 'most notable Victorian and Edwardian architectural monuments' to be torn down in service of commercial needs, concluded that 'Land is money, and money is Hong Kong's god.'[66] Piers Gray made a similar point in his review of the 1988 edition of Jan Morris's popular history: 'Buildings go up and buildings come down as, and how, the price suits the time', leaving Hong Kong 'utterly devoid of monuments'.[67] Similarly, the journalist Kevin Rafferty, writing in 1989, argued that even 'a cursory look around the territory' would reveal that Hong Kong's Chinese 'have virtually no hangups when it comes to making money'. He cited the entrepreneurial drive of illegal hawkers, many of whom 'stand warily behind unlicensed carts and quickly dart away whenever they spot a policeman coming their way'.[68]

[55]

Elsie Elliott's missionary career is a reminder that not all expatriates in Hong Kong were motivated primarily by money. Aside from soldiers, who were typically posted to Hong Kong for two years through no choice of their own, Hong Kong was home to missionaries and workers in non-governmental organisations. An example of the former is Jackie Pullinger, who, according to her autobiography, came to Hong Kong in 1966 with no official position or any source of income; she became a schoolteacher in Kowloon's lawless Walled City, and founded a youth organisation to minister to opium addicts and prostitutes.[69] Even more established organisations, though, depended on impecunious staffers as well as volunteers and charitable contributions, help that was not always easy to find. In the early 1950s, the Church Missionary Society noted difficulty in recruiting qualified teachers given the low salaries it was able to pay. In negotiating over the terms of the warden position for St Stephen's College, one leading candidate wrote that his acceptance of the position depended upon professional and financial concerns. After he ultimately refused the offer, Canon H. A. Wittenbach, the Society's East Asia Secretary, noted that this was probably for the best, since the candidate had been primarily concerned with 'his status and his allowances'.[70] Yet if Hong Kong's churches in the 1950s depended upon the missionary spirit of a certain type of British expatriate, by 1988, on the other side of Hong Kong's 'economic miracle', Hong Kong's advantage to British churches was that they were wealthy enough not to need metropolitan resources. For example, in proposing that its Diocese form links with the Diocese of Hong Kong and Macau, along with churches in Mozambique and Saxony, a Church of England Bishops' Council reasoned that 'neither Hong Kong nor Saxony needs money and Mozambique offers us more spiritually than we can ever give in cash'.[71] Yet such counterexamples for whom Hong Kong was an arena for Christian or philanthropic service not only went against the predominant character of the colony, but their presence was scarcely registered in the commentary about Hong Kong – and, when noted, normally appeared as a fly in the ointment rather than as something to be celebrated.

Laissez-faire and the Chinese character

Much more common, again, was the emphasis on Hong Kong as a site for financial gain. In part, this characteristic was attributable to the genius of British limited government, which not only stayed out of the way of economic incentives, but also was frequently linked to the character of either the Chinese or, more specifically, the Cantonese. For example, while F. D. Ommanney attributed Hong Kong's 'exaggeratedly commercial outlook' to sheer economic necessity for its population, at the same time he viewed the Cantonese work ethic as a 'natural' characteristic:

> Another characteristic of the Cantonese which strikes one on arrival in Hong Kong is their industry, which is astonishing. It is like that of the ant-heap, directed towards the same end: survival. Work is for them a natural bodily function, like breathing or the heart-beat. It is automatic and without it life stops.

For this reason, although he did not directly criticise western attempts to reduce Hong Kong people's working hours, he nonetheless concluded that 'If shorter hours are forced upon them by Welfare State legislation they fill the extra hours of enforced leisure with some other work.'[72] James Pope-Hennessy, writing in 1969, referred to such an attitude as one of the 'stock official answers' to any query he made 'about, say, restaurant working hours': not only did the Chinese 'like overworking', but even if legislation were passed that reduced working hours, it would be unenforceable since employers would have no difficulty finding workers who were willing to 'work the old excessive hours without lodging any complaints'. He concluded that, 'in fact, the tenets of the mill-owners of Victorian England still prevail'.[73] Jan Morris, in her popular history of Hong Kong, generalised that the Hong Kong Chinese 'are tireless workers'.[74] A Government-sponsored report on the 1967 riots, *Colony in Conflict*, claimed that 'To a race, which is so hard working by nature, long hours do not become a main source of discontent.'[75] Former Governor Alexander Grantham, in a 1968 interview, blamed the Chinese work ethic for the difficulty of finding a non-Hong Kong home for early 1950s refugees from the PRC: 'None of the countries in South-East Asia would have them because the Chinese are not popular there, they work too hard.'[76] A Cambodia-based journalist in John le Carré's *The Honourable Schoolboy* similarly evoked the Chinese work ethic, but put a more favourable spin on it, arguing that hard-working Chinese had 'fixed our [Cambodia's] money market, our transport monopoly, our rate of inflation, our siege economy'. As a result, Chinese controlled 80 per cent of Cambodian commerce, while 'lazy' Cambodians remained 'content to take [their] profit out of American aid'.[77] Such a British view of the Chinese labourer has a long history, of course, and one not limited to Hong Kong; early-nineteenth-century proposals to replace Trinidad's slave labour with Chinese workers on long-term contracts hinged on visions of Chinese natural industriousness, as did working-class resistance to importing Chinese labour to South Africa at the turn of the twentieth century.[78] It is striking, though, that these images continued late into the twentieth century to circulate in otherwise responsible accounts of Hong Kong.

Edward Szczepanik, a Polish-born economist who made an academic career in Britain and Hong Kong, in 1958 published what he called the first economic history of Hong Kong. For Szczepanik, the work ethic in Hong Kong went beyond any inherent Chinese qualities; these would not explain Hong Kong's recent economic growth and advantage over the rival ports Singapore and Macau. Rather, Hong Kong's Chinese population had a distinct 'historical structure'. Unlike Singapore and Macau, where the Chinese were 'descendants of settlers who gradually trickled away from their native villages as farmers, fishermen, craftsmen, or merchants', the Chinese in Hong Kong were, in the 1950s, disproportionately new arrivals fleeing Mao's China. Szczepanik, whose own country had only recently begun a tentative de-Stalinisation in the mid-1950s, said of these recent migrants: 'They came in bulk, frightened by Communism and prepared to work hard rather than live under terror again.'[79] Similarly, Marjorie Topley, writing in 1963, noted that observers often contrasted the materialism of Hong Kong Chinese with the character of more 'cultivated' northerners; she argued, however, that these observers unwittingly contrasted the northern upper classes with Hong Kong people of 'more humble origin'.[80] This type of specificity was, however, rare; most commentators, though they certainly would have understood that the Communist takeover in China was the reason for the flood of refugees, attributed their hard-work ethic to their Chineseness more generally, not to their social class or their fear of Communism.

Evocations of the Chinese work ethic co-existed nicely with the distinctive Hong Kong trope of civic familialism, noted above, as both justified inaction by the State in the face of widespread poverty. Hong Kong people, the thinking went, looked to their own efforts to pull themselves up by their bootstraps, and where they needed help, they looked to their extended families. British observers, particularly before the late 1960s, also emphasised the quiescent nature of Hong Kong's Chinese: however difficult their circumstances might appear to western sensibilities, the Chinese were content. For example, Kaye Webb, describing her visit in a BBC interview, noted that Hong Kong's surface prosperity belied scandalous conditions in which most people lived: entire families living in junks, or on the stairs of tenement buildings, in six square feet of living space per person. Nevertheless, she claimed, she saw no complaints, and only clean, quiet, and happy children.[81] This claim echoed that made by Zara Holt, wife of the future Australian Prime Minister, in her 1960 travel letter: although observing Hong Kong's living conditions bothered the Holts, she noted a low unemployment rate and a universal contentedness.[82] In his own 'travel diary', written in a tone that suggested it was designed for public consumption, Harold Holt similarly noted that the children, despite overcrowding, looked 'cheerful and amazingly healthy'.[83]

One can, to be sure, distinguish a refugee's incessant working born out of low wages and desperate poverty from a racial or cultural tendency to 'like overworking'. Urban Councillor Hilton Cheong-Leen noted in 1966 that many shop employees had complained to him about their long working hours, and called upon Britain, a signatory to the Universal Declaration of Human Rights, to uphold its position on reasonable working hours.[84] John Walker, writing in the early 1970s, argued that the long hours of the Chinese working classes came 'not out of some pernicious Chinese penchant for hard work, but for the more understandable human motive that they need the money ... people have to work very long hours merely to be able to continue to exist'.[85] As Robin Porter argued, in a 1975 pamphlet published by the Bertrand Russell Peace Foundation, 'low wages and inadequate social security', rather than Chinese culture, explained the tendency toward overworking, including child labour.[86] Anthony Shang, in a 1985 children's book, agreed: 'Hard work is a necessity. People need all they can earn to feed large families and save for the future; Hong Kong has no state pensions or unemployment benefits. People are expected to look after themselves in times of trouble and to provide for their elderly parents.'[87] Nigel Cameron similarly argued that the Hong Kong Chinese work ethic derived less from race or culture than from Hong Kong's structural arrangements, but emphasised the carrot as well as the stick:

> There is nothing like the prospect of making a lot of money, or of being destitute, for engendering hard work. And those prospects are both acutely present. So Hong Kong is on the whole one of the hardworking cities of the world. The contrast is sharply observable when you spend some time in the West, in London, for example, where it is impossible to starve, and rare to become as rich as that large segment of Hong Kong Chinese and Westerners who have bottomless bank balances.[88]

Yet pathologist-turned-crime-writer Feng Chi-shun, in his memoir of his youth in the squatter village of Diamond Hill in the 1950s, concurs with the idea that the Chinese of the era were motivated by opportunities to earn 'extra cash', even if getting rich did not appear to be on the cards. Describing his own teenage summer work as a domestic piece-worker in the plastic flower industry, he writes: 'We jumped at the opportunity to make the extra cash, even though we were not exactly starving. That was the mindset of the whole community at the time.'[89] In any case, it was not only the Chinese who grasped at every opportunity to earn money. The protagonist and first

[59]

person narrator of *The Great Hong Kong Sex Novel*, Nigel Trefford, describes his expatriate law firm's sending his secretary to visit him regularly in the hospital in which he is recovering from an emotional breakdown: 'Actually, I think it's to make sure I get some work done while I'm on the mend. The company's very happy I haven't lost my facility for totting up the bills.'[90]

The Government's declining to regulate working hours was not the only example of laissez-faire justified by the supposed Chinese character. In addition to their penchant for working, Hong Kong's Chinese loved gambling. This point is illustrated by Leo Goodstadt, who notes that in refusing to countenance Government insurance of bank deposits, officials not only made the familiar 'moral hazard' argument, but frequently argued that the Chinese had something of a gambler's mentality, and willingly entrusted their cash to the bank that would pay the highest interest rate, in full expectation of losing their entire capital from time to time.[91] This meme was conveyed at great length in John Gordon Davis's 1974 novel *The Years of the Hungry Tiger*, in protracted observations made by British banker Derek to Jake McAdam, fast-track police officer and first-person narrator. Derek's world-weary observations, set in the early 1960s, coherently tied together several themes: British Hong Kong's precarious existence, which Mao could end instantly 'with a telephone call'; Hong Kong's taste for luxury – in this case property; and the Chinese penchant for speculation and quick profits. In Derek's view, the luxury property market was in a decided bubble: properties flipped repeatedly at ever-higher prices, before they had even been conveyed. The problem was not only the speculative fever of the Chinese buyers, but that of the banks that lent, without adequate reserves, on the assumption the prices would keep rising, despite Hong Kong's precarious status; and also of depositors who sought out the banks with the highest interest rates without attention to the banks' soundness. Derek is quick to point out that his own bank, the Hong Kong Shanghai Bank, would not touch such loans, 'nor [would] any of the big established banks with economic know-how, we're not encouraging this madness: no, it's the goddam Chinese banks. The one-eyed pisspot family banks.'[92] McAdam's own musings, from his chair in the Hong Kong Club, highlight the downside of British non-intervention: prudent reserve requirements would prevent the bubble from developing, as would a willingness to prosecute the newspapers that, in pursuing circulation-grabbing headlines over responsible journalism, published unfounded rumours of bank insolvency and provoked ruinous bank runs. With its commitment to laissez-faire, of course, the Hong Kong Government chooses neglect over prudence.[93]

[60]

In *Typhoon*, published five years later, and set a decade later in Governor Murray MacLehose's reformist mid-1970s, Davis once again emphasises the speculative side of the Chinese pursuit of money, in this case through the stock market. As with housing and high-interest lending in the 1960s, the smart money either stays on the sidelines or gets out early, sometimes on the basis of insider information but often simply out of prudence, while the unconnected and impecunious working classes blindly chase unsustainable returns. For Jake McAdam – by now retired from the police force and living as an investor and philanthropic environmentalist – a quick 40 per cent based on an insider tip and a slight delay of releasing unfavourable news to the press were simply prudent (though hollow), but his moral code forces him to draw the line at issuing a public offering of his own business in order to cash in on the sort of unsophisticated Chinese investors who would lose everything when the stock market eventually crashed. In his thoughts, McAdam likened such investors to those who bet on horses: 'All he understood was that you buy, then sell at a profit; it was like betting on a winner at the races at Happy Valley except that at the stock exchanges all the shares were winners.'[94]

Horse racing was, of course, the perfect combination of ostentatious display and gambling fever. A common expression, cited by several writers of both fiction and non-fiction, was that Hong Kong was governed by the Hong Kong and Shanghai Bank, the Royal Jockey Club, and the Governor; the order varied but always with the Governor coming last. The Royal Jockey Club was an opportunity for social power, in which the wealthy and connected competed for positions as stewards, raced the horses they owned, and could be seen by the masses. It was a site of what Law Wing Sang calls 'collaborative colonial power' and John Carroll (speaking of an earlier period) refers to as 'patterns of collaboration and accommodation' between Chinese elites and British colonials.[95] It was also, though, for the masses, a regulated and legal form of gambling. John le Carré's *The Honourable Schoolboy* describes Happy Valley as offering the 'gambler's dream of instantaneous salvation' from 'grey skyscraper slums crammed so tight they seemed to lean on each other in the heat'.[96] The gambler's mentality was similarly noted in a 1978 *New Statesman* article that pointed out that nearby Macau attracted two million Hong Kong visitors per year to its casinos.[97]

Victorian values and their discontents

Hong Kong's labour conditions attracted the periodic attention of social reformers and manufacturing interests in Britain. In the mid-1960s, Elsie Elliott's campaigns included visits to London to encourage parliamentary intervention.[98] David Clayton has shown that British governmental pressure was crucial in pushing the adoption of the eight-hour day for female workers in the late 1960s, and London bureaucrats and social reformers took the Hong Kong Government's weakening of the new law as evidence of Hong Kong's retrograde (Victorian) social character.[99] Robin Porter, in a mid-1970s pamphlet already cited above, referred to Hong Kong as an exemplar of a modern industrial economy that had failed to shed its preindustrial acceptance of child labour. Instead, he wrote, 'traditional employment of children has been carried over into modern times with the excuse that it is the local cultural norm'. In Porter's view, Hong Kong was marked by a 'hybrid Nineteenth Century laissez-faire economy' in which desperate parents sent their children to work because they needed their wages in order to survive, and were able to do so because of inadequate workplace inspections that did not enforce even Hong Kong's minimal labour laws.[100] Yet for Keith Joseph, founder of the anti-Keynesian think-tank Centre for Policy Studies and a crucial champion of Margaret Thatcher's leadership campaign, Hong Kong offered a clear model for Britain itself, one in which Victorian economic arrangements facilitated dynamism and economic growth.[101] Hong Kong was one of three Asian territories (the others were South Korea and Singapore) that he cited in a January 1979 interview with *Forbes* magazine as favourable contrasts with the 'failure of the collectivist idea'; in Joseph's words, 'You'd think the contrast between what's happening there and elsewhere would have some effect.'[102] Speaking to the Hong Kong General Chamber of Commerce in 1981, Joseph congratulated Hong Kong on its achievements, which had, in certain key areas such as life expectancy and infant mortality, surpassed Britain's own, and which resulted from the operation of a 'market economy within the rule of law'. Reminding his audience that 'it was in the United Kingdom, in Scotland to be precise', that the benefits of these structures had first been articulated, he argued that 'we forgot the truths which we had been, through Adam Smith, the first to perceive'. Only with the coming of the Thatcher Government in 1979 had the British begun returning to their original wisdom, which, as he implied, the people of Hong Kong had never forgotten.[103]

Richard West made similar points in an article in the *Spectator* that same year. Responding to London politician Ken Livingstone's recent favourable contrast of Communist China with Hong Kong's 'rat race', West in turn contrasted Hong Kong's prosperity with British stagnation. Not only did the continuing importance of the extended family mean that Hong Kong did not have the same need for western-style,

'Well done Geoffrey—now I want you to hammer out a similar agreement with Arthur Scargill.'

Figure 4 The Thatcher Government ensured that Hong Kong would remain free of socialism; could it do the same for Britain?

State-provided social welfare, but Hong Kong's privatised transport was more efficient and its losses did not have to be covered by taxpayers. As a result,

> Low tax means that shops and businesses thrive, and provide employment even to most of the hundreds of thousands of refugees who have come to the colony in the last ten years. Because of the profitability of manufacture and retail business, these have attracted investment and capital which, in England, would go to property speculation.

Even the image of ' "sweated labor" – conjuring up a picture of stick-limbed, opium-crazed coolies, women and children at work in steamy rat-infested cellars beside the port', if it had ever been true, was now outdated. Instead, since 'British industry, backed by the British trade unions' had lost its ability to suppress competition, Hong Kong wages were 'high and increasing'. Accordingly, Ken Livingstone's referring to Hong Kong as a 'rat race' meant only that 'the Hong Kong Chinese work more than the English, and are getting paid for it'.[104]

Yet not all British commentary celebrated Hong Kong's 'Victorian values'. First, as already mentioned, as Hong Kong factories began competing for British textile markets in the 1950s, the Lancashire textile lobby became vocal critics.[105] Hong Kong's aggressive pursuit of the British market followed the US-imposed trade embargo during the Korean War, a move that severely curtailed the colony's position as an entrepot and prompted the expansion of its industrial economy. In this context, accusations of dumping put Hong Kong manufacturers on the defensive, leading them in the late 1950s voluntarily to 'temporarily restrict exports' to the UK as an act of goodwill, in order to mollify Lancashire complaints.[106] As late as 1983, a GIS booklet, *An Introduction to Hong Kong*, countered 'taunts and accusations' by western industrialists, 'who resented this new source of competition', that the cheapness of Hong Kong products derived from low wages produced by 'slave labour', noting that Hong Kong's manufacturing, like Japan's, became more sophisticated and attained higher levels of quality.[107]

Second, other commentators, often, but not uniformly, speaking from leftist perspectives, pointed to the precarious livelihoods and poor working conditions of the Hong Kong Chinese in this supposedly 'prosperous' colony. In 1957, George Edinger wrote in the *Spectator* that refugees in Hong Kong believed that it was 'amazing to feel free. And British justice too was admirable, if you could afford it. But you cannot eat freedom and, unhappily, a social conscience is one blessing you do not always find in Hong Kong.'[108] In a subsequent reply to readers' letters, Edinger elaborated on the causes of the 1956 Kowloon riot, citing the recently published Hong Kong *Annual Report*: 'Three hundred and fifty thousand homeless in warrens of shanty towns, some on the roofs of buildings! A quarter of a million more settled in slum conditions! And yet the luxury sky-scrapers go shooting up to wreck the beauty and open spaces on the Peak.'[109] More than two decades later, Walter Easey, shuddering at Keith Joseph's desire to introduce 'Hong Kong-style export zones' in British city centres, and Lord Trefarne's statement in the House of Lords that Hong Kong was a *'splendid example of the free enterprise system at its best'*, used colourful language in contrasting 'their Hong Kong' with the one he had observed:

> Their Hong Kong doesn't have tens of thousands of teenage prostitutes, no vast army of heroin addicts, no-one whose health has been broken in the dirty and dangerous factories owned by the legislators, no-one who has ever been insulted, squeezed or beaten-up in a police station, no-one commits suicide … and no-one complains save for a few idealists when an ugly old building is knocked down to make way for an

[64]

ugly new one, or the pollution around the beaches fouls the propel-
lors of their launches ... Their Hong Kong success story is the saga
of rags-to-riches and cites Sir Y. K. Pao rising from penniless refugee
to deputy-chairman of the Hong Kong and Shanghai Bank, shipowner
and multi-multi-millionaire. No-one features in their story who arrived
poor and homeless in 1949 and is still poor and homeless in 1980, whose
only change in life has been to see their daughter move from a factory
at age 11, to a massage parlour at age 13 and their son from school age
12 to heroin addicted triad-member by age 16.[110]

Similarly, John Walker, a writer for the short-lived Hong Kong-based
leftist magazine *70s Biweekly*, wrote in 1972 that the poor constituted
'the majority', and noted that the minimal provision for State-sponsored
social welfare left most of the social work in the hands of private agencies, 'often financed by money from overseas'. Unfortunately, by the
early 1970s it was becoming 'increasingly difficult for these agencies to
get funds from abroad, since the official line that Hong Kong is prosperous is gaining headway among the people who have never been here'.[111]
According to Walker, the poverty was exemplified by housing conditions, which included perhaps 500,000 squatters, compared to 300,000
in 1953 when resettlement began on a large scale, who lacked access
to running water and adequate provision for waste disposal. For those
who had been resettled in public housing, the standards for cleanliness were much improved, but the overwhelming impression was
overcrowding and noise, with communal lavatories and washrooms.[112]
More than a decade later, a picture book entitled *We Live in Hong
Kong*, aimed at British youth, quoted a young Australian missionary's
observation that 'Outsiders tend to view Hong Kong in terms of its
economic success, without seeing the human misery and suffering that
is also found here.'[113]

In the aftermath of the 1966–68 riots, critics became more vocal in not
only pointing out poverty, but demanding that the Government address
it. One member of the Urban Council, blaming the widening wealth
gap for the 1967–68 'disturbances', insisted that it was 'not enough' for
the Government to 'set up and maintain the framework to foster the
prosperity of Hong Kong'. Rather, ensuring that working people enjoyed
their 'rightful share of such prosperity' was the Government's 'fundamental obligation'.[114] As we will see in Chapter 5, faced with a perceived crisis of political legitimacy, and buttressed by torrid economic
growth, in the 1970s the Government became more willing to countenance a rudimentary safety net. Still, the identification of Hong Kong
with a more pristine, Victorian version of British capitalism endured
well beyond this era of reform. For its advocates, Hong Kong throughout
the postwar years was an arena in which British rule ensured economic

freedom so that entrepreneurs, both British and Chinese, could flourish in a way that they could not in post-1945 Britain, and in which workers were driven both by the hope of riches and the fear of penury. By the early 1970s, indeed, Hong Kong was increasingly a cudgel for those who wished to roll back the British Welfare State.

Notes

1 Gregor Benton, *The Hongkong Crisis* (London: Pluto Press, 1983), pp. 19–20.
2 TNA, BW 94/9, 'General Policy Inspection of Hong Kong, 27–31 October 1973: Report by Assistant Director-Regional (Regional)', February 1974, p. 1.
3 TNA, BW 94/11, British Council, Hong Kong Representative's Annual Report, 1970/71, p. 1. See also TNA, BW 94/9, [British Council], 'Brief for Policy Inspection of Hong Kong March 1980', p. 1; TNA, BW 94/12, [British Council], 'Country Brief for Hong Kong 1979/80', p. 5.
4 Roger Buckley, *Hong Kong: The Road to 1997* (Cambridge: Cambridge University Press, 1997), p. 54.
5 For discussions of the theme of Hong Kong as a formerly 'barren rock', see C. K. Lau, *Hong Kong's Colonial Legacy: A Hong Kong Chinese's View of the British Heritage* (Hong Kong: Chinese University Press, 1997), pp. 187–90; Tak-Wing Ngo, 'Industrial History and the Artifice of *Laissez-Faire* Colonialism', in David Faure (ed.), *Hong Kong: A Reader in Social History* (Hong Kong: Oxford University Press, 2003), pp. 543–71 (p. 544); Robert Bickers, 'Loose Ties that Bound: British Empire, Colonial Autonomy and Hong Kong', in Ray Yep (ed.), *Negotiating Autonomy in Greater China: Hong Kong and Its Sovereign before and after 1997* (Copenhagen: NIAS Press, 2013), pp. 29–54 (p. 43).
6 HS, Box 60, Han Suyin, 'Hong Kong, 1949–1959', unpublished MS.
7 Marjorie Topley, 'The Role of Savings and Wealth among Hong Kong Chinese', in Marjorie Topley, *Cantonese Society in Hong Kong and Singapore: Gender, Religion, Medicine and Money*, ed. and intro. Jean DeBernardi (Hong Kong: Hong Kong University Press, 2011), pp. 275–332 (p. 291).
8 *An Introduction to Hong Kong* (Hong Kong: Government Printer, 1983), p. 6.
9 John Flowerdew, *The Final Years of British Hong Kong: The Discourse of Colonial Withdrawal* (New York: St Martin's Press, 1997), pp. 91–2. According to Flowerdew, Patten's evocations of Hong Kong's political system often left its British provenance implicit.
10 David Faure, 'Rethinking Colonial Institutions, Standards, Life Styles and Experiences', in Helen F. Siu and Agnes S. Ku (eds), *Hong Kong Mobile: Making a Global Population* (Hong Kong: Hong Kong University Press, 2008), pp. 231–46 (p. 231). According to Faure, between 1870 and 1967, Hong Kong's hard-working Chinese for the most part worked hard 'within the framework of Chinese institutions' rather than British ones. Needless to say, Faure's argument further problematises the historical discourse of Hong Kong as a British achievement that I trace in this book. Cindy Yik-yi Chu has also noted that hard-working Chinese workers in the context of British administration constitute the 'most often cited' factors in Hong Kong's economic success; she argues, however, that such accounts have neglected the role of Chinese and CCP policy. See Cindy Yik-yi Chu, *Chinese Communists and Hong Kong Capitalists: 1937–1997* (Basingstoke: Palgrave Macmillan, 2010), p. 24.
11 ANA, A4534/44/11, James Bertram to Secretary, Department of External Affairs, 7 March 1946, 6. Bertram continued: 'This is the standard British argument, which is sometimes inclined to forget – or fail to emphasise – that the prosperity of Hong Kong has always been built on the wealth of China; and in particular, that the super-profits of the pre-war years were quite cynically gained from China's distress.'

12 Cassandra, 'The Ripe Plum', *Daily Mirror* (17 May 1949), p. 6.
13 ANA, A816/19/301/1093, 'Hong Kong', n.d. (1949).
14 W. Y. Willetts, 'The Future of Hong Kong', *Spectator* (29 December 1950), p. 767.
15 M. J. B., review of Harold Ingrams, *Hong Kong* (London: HMSO, 1952), *Spectator* (9 January 1953), p. 53.
16 John M. Carroll, *Edge of Empires: Chinese Elites and British Colonials in Hong Kong* (Cambridge, MA: Harvard University Press, 2005), pp. 7–8; Alan Smart, *The Shek Kip Mei Myth: Squatters, Fires and Colonial Rule in Hong Kong, 1950–1963* (Hong Kong: Hong Kong University Press, 2006).
17 Lau Siu-kai, *Society and Politics in Hong Kong* (Hong Kong: Chinese University Press, 1983); Steve Tsang, 'Government and Politics in Hong Kong: A Colonial Paradox', in Judith M. Brown and Rosemary Foot (eds), *Hong Kong's Transitions, 1842–1997* (Basingstoke: Macmillan, 1997), p. 62.
18 Leo Goodstadt, *Profits, Politics and Panics: Hong Kong's Banks and the Making of a Miracle Economy, 1935–1985* (Hong Kong: Hong Kong University Press, 2007), p. 16; Leo Goodstadt, 'Fiscal Freedom and the Making of Hong Kong's Capitalist Society', in Yep, *Negotiating Autonomy*, pp 81–109 (p. 83). David Davies, 'A Letter to the Governor', *FEER* (27 November 1971), p. 18.
19 Felix Patrikeeff put a slightly different spin on a similar point: by emphasising education and housing and de-emphasising spending that might constitute a 'safety net', the Government took a 'calculated gamble on the strong'. Felix Patrikeeff, *Mouldering Pearl: Hong Kong at the Crossroads* (London: George Philip, 1989), p. 71. And not surprisingly, a Hong Kong Research Project book, anonymously written by Jon Halliday, referred to public housing as the 'minimal dormitory accommodation for a super-exploited proletariat ... a rational capitalist calculation ... not a social service'. It also emphasised that public works projects constituted a way of transferring 'part of the Colony's huge budget surplus to favoured businesses'. [Jon Halliday], *Hong Kong: A Case to Answer* (Hong Kong: Hong Kong Research Project, 1974), pp. 23–4, 30.
20 Ngo, 'Industrial History', p. 566.
21 For conservatives of a more pastoral bent, Africa might be a more compelling model. 'Between 1945 and 1955, the white populations of Northern and Southern Rhodesia increased from 5,000 and 80,000 to over 60,000 and 200,000 respectively.' Dominic Sandbrook, *Never Had It So Good: A History of Britain from Suez to the Beatles* (London: Abacus, 2006), p. 309. As in Hong Kong, the European population were more prosperous than their counterparts 'back home'. Bill Schwarz notes that in postwar Salisbury, Rhodesia, 'Nearly every white family owned a car, long before car ownership in Britain was widespread. From the beginning of the 1960s swimming pools, particularly, became symbols of the new wealth, with a greater concentration of pools amongst white families in Salisbury than amongst the inhabitants of Beverly Hills.' Bill Schwarz, *The White Man's World* (Oxford: Oxford University Press, 2011), p. 408.
22 Ingrams, *Hong Kong*, p. 242. Italics in original. Among other things, Ingrams's idea of 'atmosphere' included antipathy to the Labour Government; see p. 241.
23 According to Schumpeter, writing in 1949, Britain's nationalisation policy was 'coupled with an attitude toward private enterprise in general that amounts to sabotage'. Joseph Schumpeter, 'English Economists and the State-Managed Economy', in Joseph Schumpeter, *Essays: On Entrepreneurs, Innovations, Business Cycles, and the Evolution of Capitalism* (Brunswick, NJ: Transaction Publishers, 1989), pp. 306–21 (p. 309).
24 Stephen Howe, 'When (if Ever) Did Empire End? "Internal Decolonisation" in British Culture since the 1950s', in Martin Lynn (ed.), *The British Empire since the 1950s: Retreat or Revival* (Basingstoke: Palgrave Macmillan, 2006), p. 219. See also Schwarz, *The White Man's World*, p. 212.
25 TNA, BN 76/29, 'Visit to Hong Kong, 11–18 September 1970', 2.
26 John le Carré, *The Honourable Schoolboy* (New York: Pocket Books, 2002 [1977]), p. 123.
27 TNA, BW 94/11, The British Council, Hong Kong Representative's Annual Report 1969/70, p. 3.

28 Henry Smith, *John Stuart Mill's Other Island: A Study of the Development of Hong Kong* (London: Institute of Economic Affairs, 1966). For a critical review, see L. F. Goodstadt, 'John Stuart Mill's Other Island', *FEER* (27 October 1966), pp. 237–8. According to Goodstadt, 'Mr Smith appears to have written in great haste and to have had problems in filling up his space ... Once again, we have been presented with an account of our economy written by someone who spent too little time here to acquire close familiarity with the local scene' (p. 238).

29 Peter Harris, *Hong Kong: A Study in Bureaucratic Politics* (Hong Kong: Heinemann Asia, 1978), pp. 130–1.

30 Quoted in Harris, *Hong Kong*, p. 131.

31 'A Perfectly British Party', *Hong Kong Tatler* 1 (February 1978), pp. 26–7.

32 [Halliday], *Hong Kong*, pp. 12–13, 16, 19 (quotation from p. 19). On Walter Easey, see Peter Victor, 'Obituary: Walter Easey', *Independent* (2 April 1998).

33 John Gordon Davis, *Typhoon* (New York: Dutton, 1979), pp. 11–13 (quotation on p. 12). Le Carré, *The Honourable Schoolboy*, p. 187.

34 Nigel Cameron, *Hong Kong: The Cultured Pearl* (Hong Kong: Oxford University Press, 1978), pp. 189–90.

35 TNA, FCO 40/226; *Parliamentary Debates*, Commons, 5th series (1909–80). Vol. DCCLXXXI (17 April 1969), col. 1333.

36 Duncan Campbell, 'A Secret Plan for Dictatorship', *New Statesman* 100 (12 December 1980), 8–9, 12.

37 Peter Bauer, 'The Lesson of Hong Kong', *Spectator* (19 April 1980), p. 10.

38 H. J. Lethbridge, *Hard Graft in Hong Kong: Scandal, Corruption, the ICAC* (Hong Kong: Oxford University Press, 1985), p. 25.

39 Jan Morris, *Hong Kong: Epilogue to an Empire* (New York: Random House, 1997), pp. 44, 158.

40 Morris, *Hong Kong*, p. 182. Morris was also fairly liberal in articulating the 'barren rock' theme; e.g. pp. 18, 293, 303.

41 Anthony Shang, *Living in Hong Kong* (London and Sydney: Macdonald, 1985), p. 13.

42 Gina Macdonald, *James Clavell: A Critical Companion* (Westport, CT: Greenwood Press, 1996), pp. 1–16 (quotation on p. 3). Macdonald describes Clavell as the type of Australian who was more British than the British. Not all Australians were of this type. Phillip Knightley, five years Clavell's junior, has written that Australians in the mid-1950s 'did not have a very high opinion of the British'; for Australians, 'the typical Englishman was short, cloth-capped, pasty-faced and whingeing'. Phillip Knightley, *A Hack's Progress* (London: Jonathan Cape, 1997), p. 61.

43 JC, 45, box 13, Ed Sheehan, 'Clavell: Each Moment Is Precious', *Honolulu Advertiser* (March 1966).

44 James Clavell, *Tai-Pan: A Novel of Hong Kong* (London: Michael Joseph, 1966), p. 75. Not everything about Chinese culture meets with Struan's approval. For example, he is disgusted by the chief mandarin of Macao, Wang Chu, who has four-inch fingernails; he pretends to beat his concubine so she can maintain face with the servants listening on the other side of a closed door, but he does not actually beat her as he believes it is barbaric. See *Tai-Pan*, pp. 53, 433–6.

45 Luckily, 'British justice, though quick and harsh, did not seem cruel to the Chinese ...'. Clavell, *Tai-Pan*, p. 440. Nor was Clavell alone in celebrating Hong Kong's origins in the drug trade; in the 1960s, Jardine Matheson ran a print advertisement with a full-page depiction of William Jardine, the notorious opium smuggler; it is reproduced in *'Far Eastern Economic Review': Telling Asia's Story for Fifty Years* (Hong Kong: Review Publishing Company, 1996). In the early 1980s, even as the future of Hong Kong was under negotiation, Margaret Thatcher rather tactlessly celebrated the nineteenth-century tai-pans at a banquet. Patrikeeff, *Mouldering Pearl*, p. 124.

46 JC, 45, box 13, Jessie Kitching, undated prepublication review circulated by Atheneum.

47 Clavell, *Tai-Pan*, p. 153. See also pp. 13–14 for the reflections of Struan's rival, Brock, on how poor a choice Hong Kong is for a colony. Writing in the 1960s, Clavell conveys that prosperous Hong Kong was created from virtual nothingness.

THE DISCOURSE OF UNBRIDLED CAPITALISM

48 James Clavell, *Noble House: A Novel of Contemporary Hong Kong* (New York: Delacorte Press, 1981), pp. 47–8.
49 Clavell, *Noble House*, p. 31.
50 Clavell, *Noble House*, pp. 226–7.
51 Clavell, *Noble House*, pp. 164–5.
52 Clavell, *Noble House*, p. 658.
53 Clavell, *Noble House*, pp. 656–7.
54 Clavell, *Noble House*, pp. 521–2.
55 Ray Yep and Tai-Lok Lui, 'Revisiting the Golden Era of MacLehose and the Dynamics of Social Reforms', in Yep, *Negotiating Autonomy*, pp. 110–41.
56 See, e.g., David Clayton, 'The Riots and Labour Laws: The Struggle for an Eight Hour Day for Women Factory Workers, 1962–71', in Robert Bickers and Ray Yep (eds), *May Days in Hong Kong: Emergency and Riot in 1967* (Hong Kong: Hong Kong University Press, 2009), pp. 127–44.
57 Topley, 'The Role of Savings and Wealth', p. 323. On the other hand, in her 1967 'Concluding Note' to the same essay, she blamed the 1965 bank crisis on the tendency of the affected banks to keep insufficient liquidity precisely by having too many long-term investments (p. 328).
58 ANA, A446 1970/95148, A. M. Harold and Kenneth Rivett, 'Immigration from Hong Kong', 3 October 1967.
59 TNA, BW 94/11, British Council, Hong Kong, Representative's Annual Report 1970/71, pp. 1–2. TNA, BW 94/11, Sir David Trench to G. A. Bridges, 1 May 1971.
60 David Bonavia, 'Enigmatic Exports', *FEER* (21 July 1966), pp. 125–7.
61 'Counting Costs', *SCMP* (6 September 1970) (TNA, BW 94/11). See also D. J. Dwyer, *People and Housing in Third World Cities: Perspectives on the Problem of Spontaneous Settlements* (London and New York: Longman, 1975), p. 179.
62 *The Australian* (30 January 1975) (ANA, A1533 1957/2133).
63 Elsie Elliott, *Crusade for Justice: An Autobiography* (Hong Kong: Heinemann Asia, 1981), p. 175.
64 Topley, 'The Role of Savings and Wealth', pp. 294, 305.
65 F. D. Ommanney, *Fragrant Harbour: A Private View of Hong Kong* (London: Hutchinson, 1962), pp. 21, 25.
66 David Bonavia, *Hong Kong 1997: The Final Settlement* (Hong Kong: FEER, 1985), p. 14.
67 Piers Gray, 'Wrong Mother?' *New Statesman & Society* 1 (30 September 1988), p. 45.
68 Kevin Rafferty, *City on the Rocks: Hong Kong's Uncertain Future* (New York: Viking, 1989), p. 18.
69 Jackie Pullinger, *Chasing the Dragon* (London: Hodder and Stoughton, 2010 [1980]).
70 Church Missionary Society Archives, University of Birmingham, AS 59 G1 CH1 e 6 1950–54, David S. Widdess to Canon Wittenbach, 22 April 1951; Canon Wittenbach to Bishop R. O. Hall, 21 June 1951.
71 LMA, DRO/101/267, 'Willesden and the World', n.d.
72 Ommanney, *Fragrant Harbour*, p. 44.
73 James Pope-Hennessy, *Half-Crown Colony: A Hong Kong Notebook* (London: Cape, 1969), p. 98. David Clayton's research supports this view; in the late 1960s, he argues, 'many female workers colluded with employers to undermine the spirit' of a newly passed eight-hour work day. Clayton, 'The Riots and Labour Laws', p. 127.
74 Morris, *Hong Kong*, p. 179.
75 John Cooper, *Colony in Conflict: The Hong Kong Disturbances, May 1967 – January 1968* (Hong Kong: Swindon, 1970), pp. 304–5. This passage is also quoted in J. Walker, *Under the Whitewash*, rev. and enlarged edn (Hong Kong: 70s Biweekly, 1972), p. 131.
76 Rhodes College, Oxford, Mss. Brit. Emp. Si 288, Alexander Grantham, interview by D. J. Crozier, 21 August 1968, p. 16. For attempts by the British Government in 1962 to find countries willing to accept Hong Kong's refugees, see the documents in ANA, A1209 1962/538, 'Assistance for Chinese Refugees in Hong Kong – Policy'.
77 Le Carré, *The Honourable Schoolboy*, p. 371.

78 James Epstein, *Scandal of Colonial Rule* (Cambridge: Cambridge University Press, 2012), pp. 211–12; Sascha Auerbach, *Race, Law, and 'The Chinese Puzzle' in Imperial Britain* (Basingstoke: Palgrave Macmillan, 2009), p. 30. For the wider context of Chinese labour within the Empire, see Rachel Bright, 'Asian Migration and the British World, c. 1850–c. 1914', in Kent Fedorowich and Andrew S. Thompson (eds), *Empire, Migration and Identity in the British World* (Manchester: Manchester University Press, 2013), pp. 128–49.

79 Edward F. Szczepanik, *The Economic Growth of Hong Kong* (Westport, CT: Greenwood Press, 1986), pp. 4–5.

80 Topley, 'The Role of Savings and Wealth', p. 280.

81 Seven Stories: National Centre for Children's Books, Newcastle, KW/14/01/119, 'Webb 1) Interviews 2) Firecrackers', n.d. (c.1964).

82 ANA, M2608/10, Zara Holt, Letter no. 1, September 1960.

83 ANA, M2608/9, 'Mr Harold Holt's Travel Diary', Instalment no. 1, p. 2, 2 September 1960.

84 FS J/74/1, 'Statement to the Press by Hilton Cheong-Leen, Elected Urban Councillor, Hongkong', 29 June 1966.

85 Walker, *Under the Whitewash*, p. 131.

86 Robin Porter, *Child Labour in Hong Kong* (Nottingham: Bertrand Russell Peace Foundation for the Hong Kong Research Project and *The Spokesman*, 1975), p. 10.

87 Shang, *Living in Hong Kong*, p. 26.

88 Cameron, *Hong Kong: The Cultured Pearl*, p. 194.

89 Feng Chi-shun, *Diamond Hill: Memories of Growing up in a Hong Kong Squatter Village* (Hong Kong: Blacksmith Books, 2009), p. 43. This observation has also been reflected in scholarly literature about Hong Kong people; see Benjamin K. P. Leung, *Perspectives on Hong Kong Society* (Hong Kong: Oxford University Press, 1996), pp. 57–8.

90 George Adams, *The Great Hong Kong Sex Novel: The Rise and Fall of a Hong Kong Chauvinist* (Hong Kong: AIP Publications, 1993), p. 228.

91 Goodstadt, *Profits, Politics and Panics*, p. 124.

92 John Gordon Davis, *The Years of the Hungry Tiger* (London: Michael Joseph, 1974), pp. 110–11.

93 Davis, *The Years of the Hungry Tiger*, pp. 198–9.

94 Davis, *Typhoon*, pp. 25–6, 134.

95 Law Wing Sang, *Collaborative Colonial Power: The Making of the Hong Kong Chinese* (Hong Kong: Hong Kong University Press, 2009); Carroll, *Edge of Empires*, pp. 12–13.

96 Le Carré, *The Honourable Schoolboy*, p. 168.

97 Murray Sayle, 'Red Flags, Running Dogs and Air Conditioned Horses', *New Statesman* (26 May 1978), p. 702.

98 See, e.g., Hong Kong Baptist University (HKBU), Elsie Tu collection, RG 13, Box 8, Folder 4, 'Visit to Britain', 26 January 1974.

99 Clayton, 'The Riots and Labour Laws', pp. 141–2.

100 Porter, *Child Labour in Hong Kong*, pp. 3, 4, 7, 20.

101 On the context of the emergence of anti-Keynesian think-tanks, see Richard Cockett, *Thinking the Unthinkable: Think-Tanks and the Economic Counter-Revolution, 1931–83* (London: Fontana Press, 1995).

102 Quoted in 'The Economics of Sir Fu Manchu', *New Statesman* (19 January 1979), p. 67.

103 Keith Joseph, 'Address by the Rt Hon. Sir Keith Joseph: To Members of the Hong Kong General Chamber of Commerce, 21st September, 1981', *The Bulletin* (November 1981): 31–3, available at http://sunzi1.lib.hku.hk/hkjo/view/17/1700951.pdf (accessed 23 April 2011).

104 Richard West, 'Livingstone's Hong Kong', *Spectator* (31 October 1981), p. 9.

105 See David Clayton, 'From "Free" to "Fair" Trade: The Evolution of Labour Laws in Colonial Hong Kong, 1958–62', *Journal of Imperial and Commonwealth History* 35 (2007): 263–82; David Clayton, 'Trade-Offs and Rip-Offs: Imitation-Led

Industrialisation and the Evolution of Trademark Law in Hong Kong', *Australian Economic History Review* 51 (2011): 178–98.

106 See, e.g., John Rylands Library, ACS/6/6/19, Cotton Board: Imports, 'Statement Issued by Mr T. Y. Wong, Chairman of the Hongkong Cotton Spinners Association, and Mr. N. C. Chang, Chairman of the Federation of Cotton Weavers', n.d. (late 1960).

107 *An Introduction to Hong Kong*, p. 16. *The Economist* made a similar point in 1971; see 'Just Another Typhoon', *The Economist* (11 September 1971): 83–4. See also 'That Hongkong Bull Will Be back', *The Economist* (31 March 1973): 60–1; 'Getting Heavier', *The Economist* (26 January 1974): 92.

108 George Edinger, 'Hong Kong, the Chance We Missed', *Spectator* (21 June 1957), p. 805.

109 George Edinger, letter, *Spectator* (9 August 1957), p. 190.

110 Walter Easey, *Ducking Responsibility: Britain and Hong Kong in the '80s* (Manchester: *Christian Statesman*, 1980), p. 48.

111 Walker, *Under the Whitewash*, pp. 106, 108.

112 Walker, *Under the Whitewash*, pp. 63–80.

113 Josephine Tanner, in Chris Fairclough, *We Live in Hong Kong* (Hove: Wayland, 1985), p. 30.

114 Quoted in Cooper, *Colony in Conflict*, p. 309.

CHAPTER THREE

A man's playground

If British commentators imagined Hong Kong as the site of an unbridled capitalism contrasting with the dreary Welfare State of post-1945 Britain, that did not mean that Hong Kong was purely a place of work. Alongside the glorification of the entrepreneurial hero went the British man at play. This meant reproducing British cultural practices such as club and sport, and it entailed the vision of Hong Kong as a sexual playground for the British man, one characterised by easy access to Asian women; the latter motif contrasted sharply with life in postwar Britain, where the emergence of a 'permissive society' was marked by at least as much challenge as opportunity for the British man.[1]

It is striking that the discourse on leisure was overwhelmingly masculinist. To say this is not to claim that portrayals of women at leisure were absent. We have already seen references, for example, to shopping and dinners, and the pages that follow include occasional glimpses of British women participating in club and sport. Certainly British women in Hong Kong *did* practise various forms of leisure, and some of them show up in the historical record. Yet what stand out in discourse surrounding British women in Hong Kong are the more serious pursuits: Jackie Pullinger trying to save souls and Elsie Elliott pushing political reform, for example. Similarly, Susanna Hoe's pioneering history of women in pre-1941 Hong Kong, despite its titular reference to 'private life', mostly describes political and social activism: campaigns against opium, foot-binding, 'little girl slavery' (the *mui tsai* system), and prostitution; or the founding of schools.[2] Nor should the heavily masculinist character of leisure discourse surprise us. As John Tosh has argued, 'more than most areas of national life, empire was seen as a projection of masculinity'; he quotes Clare Midgley's noting that British imperialism was 'an essentially masculine project'.[3] Writing of the late nineteenth century, Tosh argues that the nature of British masculinity was shaped by the perceived needs of empire, through encounters (depending on social class) with public schools, boys' story papers, and emigration. Empire, then, shaped a masculinity associated, among other qualities, with 'personal wealth, unchecked indulgence of the appetites, personal authority and boisterous homosociality'.[4] Postwar Hong Kong was regularly portrayed in similar terms. At the same time that Hong Kong preserved a Victorian model of capitalism, rendering it in some respects more truly British than Britain itself, Hong Kong in the era of decolonisation afforded the masculine leisure perquisites often elusive in the metropole.

Before turning to sport, clubs, and sexual bounty, it may be worth-while to highlight what the theme of British leisure did not entail: either high culture or British popular culture. As May Holdsworth notes, most western expatriates, at least until the 1980s, 'thought Hong Kong merely provincial and its denizens philistine. The place had no culture.' As an illustration, she tells the story of a Jardines executive giving a forty-eight-page booklet entitled *The Artistic and Cultural Life of Hong Kong* as a Christmas gift to office staff: all the pages were blank.[5] The town planner Sir Patrick Abercrombie, in his 1948 preliminary report on how to deal with the difficulties caused by Hong Kong's population density, observed that Hong Kong was 'perhaps more deficient in public buildings than any other town of comparable size in the world: there is no Town Hall, Civic Hall, Art Gallery, Museum, Public Library, Theatre or Opera House'.[6] A 1954 report, issued by the Australian Trade Commissioner Service, claimed that there were 'few cultural activities in Hong Kong. The Colony is really a trading centre, and, as might be expected, the main preoccupation is making money.'[7] According to the English journalist and historian Susanna Hoe, writing in January 1993, 'Until 15 years ago Hong Kong and Macau, a ferry ride apart, were noto-rious as a cultural desert. Now, we have so much choice from the inter-national music scene (as well as good local musicians) that people can afford to be blasé.'[8] Jonathan Dimbleby, in his 1997 account of Chris Patten's Governorship, echoed many of the observers cited in Chapter 2 in opining that if Hong Kong 'has any culture, it is that of the market-place – a free-for-all world where the pursuit of profit is unashamed and the possession of wealth is admired, not envied'.[9] John Burdett's Eurasian protagonist Jonathan Wong, in the 1997 novel *The Last Six Million Seconds*, ruminates while eating lunch in a high-end club:

> In total the men and women gathered at the club represented a wealth equal to the gross national products of some European countries. Together they could have bought Manhattan, if they had not done so already. But with all the frantic energy that Hong Kong created it had never made a single significant contribution to any form of science, art or literature, with the doubtful exception of Bruce Lee movies.[10]

[73]

To be sure, this theme of Hong Kong as a cultural wasteland can be exaggerated: until the early 1970s, when it shifted its focus more decisively toward commercial provision of English language teaching, the British Council regularly sponsored lectures, films, exhibitions, and concerts.[11] Still, Hong Kong prior to the 1980s did not strike British and other western commentators as a thriving scene of international culture.[12]

Leisure similarly did not involve easy access to the familiar comforts of British media culture. For example, during the early years of Hong Kong television, when Rediffusion held a monopoly, and access was disproportionately limited to elites and to Kowloon and Victoria, British viewers regularly complained that the English-language programming was dominated by American fare. The predominance of American programming is perhaps not surprising, given that television was organised on a commercial basis and American content was widely seen as less parochial than British; American content was, moreover, making significant inroads into Britain itself.[13]

Clubs and sport

In September 1945, shortly before being moved from Sydney to Hong Kong, en route to his demobilisation and return to England, soldier Billy Moore wrote to his wife that he was sorry to be leaving Australia just when cricket season was about to begin: 'May be we shall have some in Hong Kong! Chinese cricket where you use the wrong end of the bat or run backwards way [sic] or something.' He need not have worried; indeed, less than two months later he wrote to his wife from Hong Kong, describing a cricket match and reporting to his wife that he had been chosen captain of the Observatory cricket team; shortly afterward, he announced that he was among the leaders in the batting statistics, and reported that he was also playing football.[14]

Patrick McDevitt has argued of the period 1880–1935 that imperial sport was

> an expression of a worldview which held that participation in and success at athletic endeavors were primary measures of the worth of a man *as a man*. Games playing as defined by English rules and standards set the British and their subjects apart from effeminate continental Europeans, subjugated Africans, and effete Asians, and provided a forum for intra-imperial communication between the metropolitan center in England and the colonial periphery, as well as between peripheral nations themselves.

Further, they functioned as a 'tool of legitimation' for colonial elites, one in which indigenous populations' 'accommodation and half-conscious

[74]

complicity' featured.[15] These arguments are equally applicable to post-war Hong Kong.

British sport was ubiquitous in Hong Kong, kept up both by long-term civilian residents and by short-term military regiments.[16] The April 1956 issue of *The China Dragon*, a newsletter produced by the Staffordshire Regiment during its time in Hong Kong, devoted much of its battalion news section to sporting prowess. As the 1st Battalion reported, 'In the field of sport we have had an outstanding year, and we publish for information details of the Bn's performances and achievements of which we are justly proud of the record.' This was followed by several pages reporting the battalion's achievements in such sports as hockey, football, boxing, tennis, cross-country, cricket, and motor-cycling. Even defeat could spark a lengthy description. A full column was devoted to a single cricket match, in which the reader learned: 'The Sappers [i.e., the other side] are a good, strong, all-round team and we never thought of victory coming our way. We were, however, determined to fight in the true dogged Staffordshire fashion, and succeed in giving them quite a fright, as later statistics will show.'[17]

Similarly, the October 1961 issue of the *Queenshill Courier*, a mimeographed newsletter of about thirty pages reporting on the activities of the Royal Warwickshire Fusiliers, was overwhelmingly devoted to sport, including competitions among various battalions as well as against the police and even friendlies against Chinese sides. Different sports included rugby, cricket, football, bicycling, and even mountain climbing, which was depicted on the issue's cover. The regiment planned a Himalayan Expedition, 'the first of its kind sponsored by a British Regiment', but a training event on Tai Mo Shan, Hong Kong's highest peak, in which climbing leader Major Barrett fell more than 100 feet, 'endangered the future' of the expedition just one week before it was scheduled. 'It is to be hoped that the tragically unfortunate accident', explained an editorial entitled 'Expedition Crisis', 'will not prove to be an unsurmountable obstacle'.[18] Reports on battalion and platoon news were equally devoted to sport, including swimming, water polo, and of course, football and cricket.[19]

Sport's importance extended to civilian life as well as military. Former Attorney General and Chief Secretary Denys Roberts, perhaps a bit tongue-in-cheek, recalls working hard to impress the Establishment Officer with his cricket prowess, in order to ensure his promotion to Attorney General: 'I kept wicket with great enthusiasm. It would do no harm for the Establishment Officer to see that I was keen, active and fit.' His efforts paid off, as shortly afterward he received a telephone call learning that he would receive the

appointment: 'Hong Kong will support you. We badly need you as opening bat for the Wanderers. If we don't watch them, the CO might bring
in an A. G. who only played tennis. We can't have that.'[20] Similarly,
in January 1966 when the Hong Kong General Chamber of Commerce
announced its new appointment of a Resident Representative in
Europe, it thought it worth mentioning that he 'is keenly interested
in sport, particularly golf and cricket, and takes a very great interest
in social problems in Hong Kong'.[21] As in other colonies, and as it had
before the war, in Hong Kong sport afforded a means of maintaining
British culture abroad.

Like sport, clubs offered a venue for transplanting British culture to
Hong Kong; arguably, they were more distinctively a Hong Kong phenomenon. Neville Chesney, editor of the *Hong Kong Tatler*, claimed
in 1981 that clubs 'probably form a more important part of the social
life of Hong Kong than they do in any other major city'.[22] The magazine's June 1997 issue, published on the eve of the Handover, included
a twenty-two-page history of Victorian Hong Kong, taking stock of the
half-century in which the British began transforming the barren rock
into the 'strong, vibrant territory' that they were about to return to
Chinese sovereignty; four pages focused on the origins of club life in
Hong Kong, beginning with the aphorism that wherever Englishmen
gathered together, they were sure to form a club.[23] Amy Milne-Smith
has noted that in late Victorian London, clubs constituted a male space
joined both for convenience and affirmation of status. Only after the
Second World War did London's clubs begin admitting women as full
members, even as men increasingly withdrew from clubs in favour
of other sites of pleasure.[24] In postwar Hong Kong, gentlemen's clubs
retained much of their late Victorian character, despite the intrusion of
women in limited contexts.

Certainly clubs have a long history in Hong Kong, with the Hong
Kong Club founded in 1844, just three years after the colony's establishment. According to John Carroll, wealthy Britons in the late nineteenth and early twentieth centuries 'generally tried to live the life
they had enjoyed, or aspired to enjoy, in Britain'. This included 'large
English-style houses and villas, surrounded by well-manicured gardens, tennis greens, and croquet lawns'. It also included parties, formal
dinners, sport, and clubs, many of which centred on sport. Hong Kong,
Carroll writes,

> Had a club for every sport and a sport for every club: cricket at the
> Cricket Club, conveniently located among the office buildings of Central
> District; tennis at the Ladies Recreation Club, rowing at the Victoria
> Sailing Club and sailing at the Yacht Club on Kellett Island; polo in
> Causeway Bay, golf in Deep Water Bay; and hunting in Fanling.

Even more than the sporting clubs, the 'gentleman's club' was the 'most important mechanism for affirming status and prestige', and the Hong Kong Club was the oldest and most important of these; the Ladies' Recreation Club opened in 1884 as its counterpart for women. These clubs were, as late as the interwar period, closed to non-Europeans, but as Carroll notes, the response of Hong Kong's Chinese elites was not to try to end their exclusiveness, but to create an 'equally exclusive social world of their own', including their own restrictive social clubs, such as the Chinese Club and the Chinese Recreation Club.[25]

In the postwar era, clubs gradually became less exclusive, with women being accepted into men's clubs, and vice versa, at least on an 'associate member' basis, and with Chinese members being accepted into the most prestigious clubs. Yet several of the clubs retained their 'British' character until very late in the century. Susanna Hoe wrote in 1991 that dining at the Hong Kong Club 'if you are sensitive to issues of colonialism, race and gender is still to experience a slight shiver, though the external atmosphere is pleasant and the food superb'.[26]

The Hong Kong Club was, as indicated above, the most important of the gentlemen's clubs. Its premises included bowling alleys, a card room, a library, and a billiard room, and the Club operated its own pony race: in 1970, for example, Macau casino kingpin Stanley Ho's pony won the Hong Kong Club Cup. By 1970, the Club's active membership approached 1,000, prompting the administrative committee to introduce a waiting list and recommend closing membership. That same year's financial report presents a well-endowed institution: a budget surplus made possible not only by increases in the profit on bar sales and meal sales, but also by a substantial investment income.[27] A nostalgia-laden special issue of the Club's magazine, published in 1982 on the occasion of a relocation to a new building, evoked convivial drinking in the Main Bar or the Bowling Alley Bar, billiards, and darts. The Main Bar offered breakfast and a 'limited menu' for lunch, and served as a 'comfortable after business stop in the early evenings'. Indeed, the Bar 'provided a much appreciated venue to relax the tensions before facing the traffic that jams central from five to seven in the evenings'.[28] Not only the club's exclusivity, but even the building's physical structure contributed to the sense of retreat. Of the building's 'Main Entrance', the magazine noted, 'As we passed between them, the pillars seemed to close ranks behind us, their pitted faces giving an impression of strength and reliability and seeming to invite those who belonged to enter in the knowledge that the door was well guarded.' The reception lobby performed a similar function: 'As the front door swung shut behind us, we were immediately conscious of a dramatic change in environment. There was no more need to hurry, no urgency, we could take time to enjoy the privacy and tranquility which was the unique quality of the Club.'[29] Although women were admitted to the Club in 1997, some of its facilities remained off limits to them.[30]

Even the sporting clubs, despite their nominal purposes, often bore the character of the 'gentlemen's club'. Indeed, Denys Roberts quipped that his ability to play cricket was something of a disadvantage when he applied to the Cricket Club in the early 1960s, even though at the time the Club was struggling to attract new members. More broadly, Roberts claimed that at that time any new prospective member who did not play 'was admitted with enthusiasm, especially if he was a heavy drinker, since it would not be necessary to find a team for him'.[31] According to Roberts, who eventually became the Club's president, its popularity among younger members in the 1960s stemmed from its central location and low price for set lunches; it was convenient to lunch there during the working day. These advantages came at a price, though: in contrast to Hoe's description of the Hong Kong Club, at the Cricket Club the food was 'inedible, save for the toast which was excellent', while the meat pie caused 'severe flatulence of a particularly unpleasant kind'. Happily, the portions were generous.[32]

The increasing assertiveness of a Chinese Hong Kong civic identity took its toll on the Cricket Club, as the occupation of a sizeable piece of prime territory in the Central District by a club primarily serving privileged expatriates became a sore point for many Chinese; Legislative Councillor Ellen Li Shu-pui called the Club a symbol of 'racial discrimination' in the heart of the colony. Given this opposition, it is perhaps unsurprising that the Government decided in 1969 – in the aftermath of the 1966–68 riots – not to renew the lease when it expired.[33] The Club's 1975 move to a more remote location in Wong Nei Chong – in the middle of the island, and not convenient to the business district – coincided, according to Roberts, with its reinvention as 'more of a family club and less of a young man's sporting club'.[34]

Not all club life was purely recreational, nor were all clubs exclusively male. The Reform Club was founded in 1949 to promote social reform while increasing popular interest in public affairs.[35] Spearheaded by British lawyer Brook Bernacchi largely in order to promote the rehousing of squatters, by the 1960s it was advocating reforms in such areas as the tax code, policy toward hawkers, traffic safety, food safety, education, and criminal law, as well as introducing direct elections for some of the Legislative Council seats and bilingualism in Urban Council proceedings. In the 1960s it published a report on organised crime, and a free pamphlet called *When You Are Arrested*, offering 'practical suggestions on what immediate steps to take when confronted with the strong arm of the law. There was an exhortation not to panic, not to volunteer what was not necessary, to keep in mind certain inalienable civil rights of citizenship in a Britain [sic] political society, and to seek immediate professional legal help.' Given its purpose, it was not exclusive as other clubs discussed here were. By 1969 it claimed an impressive 35,000 members, and regular attendance of 1,000 at its meetings.[36]

In purpose, the Reform Club belongs more to Chapters 4 and 5 than to the present chapter, as it was less concerned with 'play' than with modernisation and good governance. Nevertheless, despite its serious purpose, the Reform Club was also part of the associational and leisure life of the Hong Kong middle classes – what the Victorian British would have called 'rational recreation'. Indeed, aside from its promotion of political reform, the Club held regular social meetings, dinners, and the like, and in 1964 even introduced a 'distinctive Club tie' whose 'sartorial elegance evoked much appreciation'. It also is a good example of the British club culture being spread to Hong Kong's Chinese. Its book commemorating its 'second ten years anniversary' in 1969 shows a mostly Chinese executive – only the Chairman (Bernacchi), one of three Vice-Chairmen (a woman, Alison Bell), and one other member were western.[37]

Clubs could also centre specifically round national identity. Scottishness was celebrated through both the Hong Kong St Andrew's Society, founded in 1881, and the Hong Kong Highlanders, founded in 1988. Hong Kong's St David's Society was established in 1911, among other reasons to 'provide a focus for the association for national and mutual purposes of men and women who are resident in or may sojourn in the Colony who are Welsh by origin, language or by association with Wales and the Welsh people' and 'to uphold and maintain and to promote the traditions, culture and spirit of the Welsh people in the Orient'. It included a provident fund for Welsh residents in Hong Kong who had fallen upon hard times.[38] The 1961 St David's Society Ball, attended by Governor Black, included a President's speech full of paeans to Welshness: for example, evocations of the brave warriors of Wales's past, including the ones who 'helped to put a Tudor king on the throne of England'. The address began by pointing out that all of the British countries except Wales had borrowed their patron saints from another, and noting that even Ireland's St Patrick came from Wales, before making a segue to celebrating the British nations' mutual borrowings; the Welsh had even made the sacrifice of embracing English gin, Scottish whisky, and Irish potatoes.[39] Yet however spirited the Society's Welshness, interest was, apparently, lacking. As the date of the ball approached, the number of registrants was unimpressive, prompting the Society's treasurer to speculate that paying for a ticket shortly after the Chinese New Year might be prohibitive for Society members, and to offer to let attendees pay for their tickets in the month following the ball.[40]

If clubs, like sport, afforded opportunities in Hong Kong to participate in a British masculine or (more rarely) mixed-company associational life, men's sexual opportunity paradoxically required the most discretion even as it attracted the most commentary.

Discourses of sexual opportunity

According to Ronald Hyam, 'sexual dynamics crucially underpinned the whole operation of British Empire and Victorian expansion', such that 'without the easy range of sexual opportunities which imperial systems provided, the long-term administration of tropical territories, in nineteenth-century conditions, might well have been impossible'. He argues further that an initial openness to cross-cultural sexual relations (though not marriage), including bisexual ones, began to close down in the wake of the late-nineteenth-century metropolitan 'purity' movement, so that by the 1920s 'the red-light districts of Bombay, Singapore and Hong Kong were all under moralistic scrutiny'.[41] Yet if British colonial sexuality had to become more discreet in its expression, the experience of Hong Kong suggests that the relationship between Empire and sexuality remained prominent. It is not too much to argue that, as in the nineteenth century Empire, in late twentieth-century Hong Kong sexual opportunities beckoned that would not have been as readily available in Britain, at least for men.

The idea of Hong Kong as a man's sexual playground, specifically as a site for the British man's conquest of Asian women, rested on a measure of knowingness and secrecy. On the one hand, it was commented on far too often for anyone to have illusions about its prevalence, and in many of the period's texts it was presented virtually as one of the perks of (male) Britishness. On the other hand, at least in many elevated circles, it was regarded as seedy, an affront to respectability and an obstacle to career success, so that enjoying sexual access to Asian women required discretion. F. D. Ommanney's observation, although not limited to British men, is relevant here. Noting that Victoria and Kowloon were, for all practical purposes, 'foreign soil' to each other, he allowed that there were two reasons for taking the ferry: 'for strictly business purposes or to sample entertainments at which they would prefer not to be recognised by acquaintances'.[42] This discretion can be seen as well in Ommanney's own text. His rich descriptions of bar girls are carefully coupled with assurances that he merely observed; he imagines that he could have become a 'dissipated old roué' under different circumstances, but that is as far as it goes. Rather, his engagement with the bar scene consisted of 'watching the game but not playing it'. At the same time, he developed a friendship with a bar girl, Linda, who regularly spent time at his apartment; his depictions are entirely chaste, leading the reader to believe that their friendship was platonic. Sexual dalliances with bar girls, he assures us, were the province of sailors, not the respectable westerner – even one who knew the scene intimately.[43] The Irish journalist Sean O'Callaghan, in his sensationalist 1968 exposé of trafficking and prostitution in several Asian cities, is similarly coy. O'Callaghan bases his revelations on sordid encounters that always seem to happen to his friends rather than himself; his own potentially compromising encounters arise only in the context of his attempts to obtain an innocent massage, and he rebuffs them either angrily or jadedly.[44] Breaking the code of discretion could lead to awkwardness; a small number of the HKU British staff in the 1970s shocked their Chinese colleagues when openly boasting of their Wanchai conquests.[45]

The trope of Hong Kong's sexual decadence was not only familiar to those who spent time in Hong Kong; it also emerged as a stock theme in depictions aimed at a British readership. Moreover, the discourse is overwhelmingly masculinist and uncritical. European female sexuality hardly surfaces in depictions of Hong Kong, while overt criticism of men who discreetly enjoyed Asian mistresses and prostitutes is equally rare. For example, popular historian Jan Morris, in referring to Hong Kong as a 'louche and lascivious city', singles out the male experience:

> From the beginning Hong Kong seems to have been more prurient even than most such colonial settlements, partly because of the climate perhaps, partly because European males have always been attracted by nubile Chinese females, partly because the early settlers were often men of vigorous appetite and flexible morals, and partly because the air of Hong Kong somehow seems to suggest that in sex, as in most other things, anything goes.[46]

According to O'Callaghan, by contrast, Hong Kong had only recently stolen the title 'the Cesspool of the Far East' from neighboring Macau, 'which, like a middle-aged courtesan who has entertained royalty, sits back, a trifle bewildered by it all, and watches her younger sister flounce jauntily past'.[47]

The easy availability of Asian women was a recurring theme in novels, journalistic accounts, memoirs, and letters in the postwar era. Not surprisingly, this theme intersected with the motif of commercialism that we explored in Chapter 2; sexual delights, like everything else, were for sale, whether directly through prostitution or less explicitly through keeping a mistress. In part this was a natural result of the juxtaposition of the relative wealth of colonial expatriate or visitor with the poverty of Hong Kong women, many of whom were refugees from postwar or Communist China. Billy Moore, upon arriving in Hong Kong en route to England after the war, described to his wife his initial sight: 'Immediately the ship had tied up in the harbour we were surrounded by small Chinese boats, trying to sell us things – including the good-looking daughters!!' Continuing the theme of Hong Kong as a shopper's paradise, he noted that cigarettes were in demand: 'I believe it is possible to get a watch (probably Japanese) for a few packets of cigarettes. No doubt you could get a young lady for even fewer packets.'[48] Poverty was also, famously, a motive behind the (fictitious) archetypal prostitute Suzie Wong's availability; she had a daughter to feed. Similarly, Anna, the seductress in Donald Moore's *The Striking Wind* (1959), turned to prostitution both to provide medicine for her parents and to trade desperate poverty for a comfortable flat, maid service, and elegant cheongsams. Missionary Jackie Pullinger's observations of the Kowloon Walled City in the 1960s confirm the link between poverty and prostitution, though the prostitutes she describes would have catered to less affluent Chinese men rather than to Europeans. James Bond creator Ian Fleming, visiting Hong Kong in 1959 for a travel article for *The Sunday Times,* learned from the Australian journalist Richard Hughes that the proliferation of massage parlours resulted from the 'traditional desire of Oriental womanhood to please, combined with unemployment and the rising cost of living'.[49] Nor was the choice always made by the woman herself. Pullinger described a mother who sold her daughter to a *mama-san* for 'lucky money': 'My husband left me, and as there were no social security payments in Hong Kong I had nothing to live on.'[50]

But the commercial availability of Asian women was not related only to their desire to escape a desperate poverty; in some cases it was the attraction of finer things rather than the wolf at the door that turned Asian women into commodities – sold, in most cases, of course, to Chinese rather than western men.[51] Harold Ingrams, in his comprehensive survey of Hong Kong in 1950, written for the CO, suggested that the two main reasons for prostitution were 'economic and personal': 'In the first case a woman or a girl is either sold or sells herself because of poverty ... In the second case a woman or girl is attracted by a life of prostitution or is mentally deficient.'[52] As George Adams's protagonist and first-person narrator in *The Great Hong Kong Sex Novel* (1993) put it, 'with some of the local girls, [the] moral imperative was "get something out of all this" '.[53] As he describes it

Figure 5 Night shot of one of the Wan Chai bars where Suzie Wong and her mates used to enjoy clients, October 1964.

elsewhere in the novel, it was 'very hard for a good girl with a bad job to dress reasonably in Hong Kong'; this was, he reasoned, a primary motivation to 'latch on to a sugar daddy type boyfriend or go one worse and take up part-time prostitution'.[54] Similarly, Suzie Wong was able, when engaging in sex with a man she did not love, to dissociate herself from her body: as she tells her sister, 'I'll just close my eyes and think, "What a nice easy way to get a new dress."'[55] The meme that prostitution was the best way to gain material comforts was widespread. For example, young girls working at a wig factory in Kwuntong, contesting their low pay during an industrial dispute in June 1970, were reportedly taunted with the question, 'If you're all so money-conscious, why don't you become bar girls?'.[56]

British representations of Hong Kong repeatedly portrayed the colony as a masculine space in which Asian women's bodies could be easily, if discreetly, enjoyed. Yet their commercial availability presented challenges as well as opportunity. Above all, it was crucial to weigh the advantages and disadvantages of various markets. John Gordon Davis's 1974 novel, written from the perspective of a first-person narrator describing his career as a member of the police force in the 1950s, casually noted that 'You can get almost anything in the Chungking Arcade. Upstairs in the many, many apartment houses you can get women, almost any kind you like. They are usually clean.'[57] For the well-heeled, a discreet mistress of relatively high status might be the best approach. Denys Roberts notes, for example, a judicial colleague in the 1960s who kept a Chinese mistress, and numerous examples appear in the fiction of the 1980s and 1990s.[58] On the other hand, more casual relationships, whether involving prostitution or not, could be more affordable. Yet in sex as in shopping more generally, one had to be careful not to overpay in establishments targeting tourists. Roberts described trying to track down a drunken prosecutor, one of the few who went to the bars for drink only. One of the bars – 'Ocean Bar. Topless Girls Inside' – Roberts described as a place in which 'the lights were dim, the drinks watered and the girls expensive'. Of the next bar, the Happy Bar, he observed, 'I could see that some of the girls were past their prime, if they ever had one. The girls at my table were young and eager for custom.'[59] James Kirkup's 1970 travel book warned of possible rip-offs, advising that 'In bars, it is best to pay for each drink as it comes, and if you don't like your bar girl, leave after buying her only one drink. It doesn't matter if you don't know where to go, or if she clings pleadingly to various parts of your anatomy; gently dissociate yourself and go out – in Wanchai, there's always another bar next door.'[60] In fact, if the girl was suspiciously inexpensive, young, and beautiful, warned Irish journalist Sean O'Callaghan in 1968, this could be an even bigger problem: she might well be a Communist agent attempting to pry military secrets from unsuspecting servicemen, not least Americans. He relayed the story of one of his American friends entertaining himself by combining a night of passion with the 'cheapest and best whore [he] ever had', one with a 'figure that many film stars would envy', with feeding her deliberate misinformation about the movements of his ship. Happily, O'Callaghan noted, the average tourist did not have to worry about these women, because they tended to give a wide berth to civilians. For civilians, the bigger worry was the use of violence on the part of waiters in order to enforce high payments for a hostess's time.[61]

Judy Bonavia's 1990 Automobile Association travel guide noted similarly that 'Wanchai is famous for its girlie bars – but be warned, this form of companionship is often very expensive.'[62] The journalist Kevin Rafferty developed this theme in his 1989 general account of Hong Kong, warning that 'Sitting close to a hostess in a darkened bar doesn't always come cheap. Letters frequently appear in the Hong Kong press filled with the moanings of visiting tourists who have paid US$100 for a single tepid drink of beer and not got more than a few words of broken English from their "middle-aged" painted companions in return.'[63] No doubt a local aficionado would not make this mistake, but not every tourist was fortunate enough, as Ian Fleming had been, to have an experienced guide. When Richard Hughes accompanied Fleming to the brothel/hotel that inspired Richard Mason's fictitious Nam Kok Hotel (in *The World of Suzie Wong*), Hughes assured Fleming that there were much better ones. Fleming insisted, though, that his interest was not prurient, but that Hughes had merely 'misunderstood one author's delighted interest in the brilliance of another author's myth'.[64]

For those tourists unaccompanied by a Richard Hughes, the 1981 publication of Roger Boschman's short book *Hong Kong By Night* might have proven helpful. Following chapters on 'The Chinese at Night' and 'The Tourist by Night', Boschman concluded with a chapter entitled 'The Fleeting World of Suzie Wong'. 'Whether it's your first time in Hong Kong or your fourth', Boschman wrote, 'if you're young and single, there's little doubt as to what you'll be wanting to do at night'.[65] Boschman, a Canadian by birth who, after teenage and young adult years spent in New Zealand and Australia among other places, wrote this book at the same time that, according to his 2014 recollections, he was 'master[ing] the art of the technique he would later call The Perfect Method™'.[66] In the concluding chapter, he listed several 'girlie bars' in both Wanchai and Tsim Sha Tsui, advised on the relative merits of paid sex versus trying one's luck in a disco, explained short-time hotels, and gave explicit information on prices of various bars and clubs. Perhaps most importantly, he warned, the hostess clubs, many of which had 'Japanese-sounding names, and that's because they cater to wealthy Japanese businessmen who seem to have unlimited expense accounts', were places to avoid, unless, of course, 'you want to blow a load of cash in a hurry without blowing anything else'.[67]

Joe Matyeh's *Bachelor's Guide to Hong Kong*, published the following year, was even more detailed. This obscure, locally published booklet offered itself as a handbook for successful pick-ups – a 'digest' of Matyeh's 'many years of experience and painstaking research'.[68] With chapters offering advice for different locations and different budgets, Matyeh promised the fruits of his hard-won knowledge, including his mistakes:

> To give you every possible detail (and to detail every possibility!) I have spent hundreds of hours cruising in and out of girlie bars, topless bars, saunas and massage parlours. I have drawn maps, made lists, dialled thousands of phone numbers, and engaged in hundreds of conversations. For your benefit I have walked mile upon mile in the city streets of Wanchai and Kowloon, have travelled internationally to report on the possibilities in Macau, and driven lonely miles in the dark of night through the jungles, forests and swamps of the New Territories to find you ladies in the countryside. And I have found them! They are there, and they are lovely, they are willing, and they are ready for anything.

But unfortunately, many women were also 'ready to take your money and give little in return'. Matyeh's book, therefore, showed the reader

> how to get value for your money, how to avoid being ripped off, and how to play the game. You see, you can learn by *my* mistakes! You don't have to go to ten bars in an evening as I did before finding the good ones. You can go directly to the right bar and act quickly, saving time and money.[69]

Among the other lessons taught in his book the reader learned that bar girls in the New Territories behaved more subtly than those in Kowloon, so that you might miss the opportunity for a pick-up if you were not alert; a short trip to Macau would bring you to Thai girls 'better endowed' than their Chinese counterparts; you should pay for your drinks as they arrive in order to avoid 'errors' in the bill; and 'non-professional companionship' could actually be 'a damn sight more expensive than the professionals', once expensive drinks and restaurants were tallied.[70] Perhaps such images of Macau were in Liberal MP Russell Johnston's mind when he playfully wrote to Labour MP Andrew Faulds, during their joint visit to Hong Kong in 1984, to suggest that Faulds had no doubt been engaging in 'various unmentionable activities in Macau' while Johnston had been 'calvinistically admiring [Hong Kong's] tramway system'.[71]

Nor was the Hong Kong Government oblivious to prostitution's role in promoting tourism revenue. The historian Chi-kwan Mark, in his study of American Vietnam War naval 'R and R' visits, notes that alongside the cold-war issues brought to the fore by these visits stood the Hong Kong Government's concern to protect the tourism revenue they generated. Although Hong Kong's attractiveness depended in large part on its additional amenities, such as shopping, tourist sites, and lack of overt anti-Americanism, brothels and bars were clearly at the centre of the attraction.[72] As we will see in Chapter 4, the presentation of Hong Kong as a British (or western) man's sexual playground, in which compliant Chinese and Asian women were readily available, was even tacitly endorsed by the Hong Kong Tourism Authority. The influx of American soldiers and sailors, along with the Tourism Authority's eye to the main chance, remind us that even while male sexual opportunity remained a key theme within British representations of Hong Kong, neither the discourse nor the opportunity belonged to Britons alone.

American intrusion into Wanchai exploded with the escalation of the Vietnam War. Yet it can be seen nearly a decade earlier in the most famous fictional portrayal of Hong Kong Chinese female sexuality, as well as prostitution, Richard Mason's *The World of Suzie Wong* (1957), and the sanitised 1960 Paramount film by the same name, starring William Holden and Nancy Kwan. The film itself can be seen as an American coopting of British discourse concerning Asian female sexuality. Whereas the novel humanises Suzie Wong, the film glamorises her; where the novel depicts deep social problems in British Hong Kong, the film concerns an individual damsel in distress. Above all, the film replaces the somewhat seedy British protagonist with a chivalrous American character played by one of Hollywood's most bankable stars.

The novel centres on the affair between a restless English novelist, Robert Lomax, and a desperately poor squatter and refugee who works as a prostitute at a thinly disguised brothel, largely catering to American and British sailors, operating out of the Nam Kok, the cheap hotel in which Lomax is staying. The hotel-brothel's very existence is a testament to what Lomax regards as British 'hypocrisy': a formerly well-regulated brothel system had been outlawed by meddling London politicians (goaded by 'a certain lady politician at home'), giving way to uncontrolled street-walking and disease. 'But now the licenses were no longer formally issued we could pretend it did not happen, wash our hands of it. Morality had been saved.' This, in turn, had led to the emergence of

> places like the Nam Kok, satisfying the letter of the law if not its spirit; and the police, one supposed, turned a blind eye, for the sailors would

find the girls somehow, and the girls the sailors, and here at least there could be control of a sort. This, of course, had to remain invisible, since there could be no conditions officially laid down for an activity that was not supposed to occur at all; there could be no ordinance about it, no direct communication between police and hotel.[73]

Mason vividly paints the hierarchy of Wanchai prostitution: dance-hall girls look down on the hotel girls who work 'short-times'; the bar-girls look down on the street girls. Indeed, 'a bar-girl considered herself as superior, socially, to a street-girl, as a respectable woman would consider herself superior to a whore'. The young women in the Nam Kok 'originated in about equal numbers from Canton and Shanghai, and most of the quarrels or jealousies arising in the bar were between girls of these two factions'. Yet despite their quarrels, the women 'were mostly generous, loyal to one another, and easily amused'. They also maintained a 'code of honour',

> according to which, once a sailor had committed himself by taking a girl upstairs, he thereafter became her property, to be reclaimed by her on his subsequent visits to the bar, and eschewed by the rest. They despised the 'butterfly' who liked a change of girl at each visit, and only the less scrupulous girls would contravene the code to oblige him.

These women, then, see themselves as better than mere prostitutes. Moreover, they often attempt to blend genuine romance with their commercial motivations:

> And their greatest pride and delight was to have a 'regular' boy-friend, which meant the same boy-friend for three or four days, or for whatever period his ship was in port; and a girl thus engaged would usually go far beyond her commercial obligations, providing not only sex but something like affection, besides all those little feminine attentions which were the lonely sailors' need. And she would boast of him to her girl-friends, become jealous of rivals, and bestow presents on him – if not actually shed tears – when he left.[74]

Of course, not all such 'boy-friends' are quite so transient. One of Suzie's regulars, an English businessman named Ben, engages in sailing as a weekend hobby and sublimation of sex; being with Suzie liberates him and restores his marital sex life. His experience with Suzie leads him to an epiphany that he shares with Lomax: Chinese society is on to something in openly accepting the keeping of mistresses. Man, he says, is a 'polygamous animal'. He continues:

> Of course in Europe we try and blind ourselves to the fact. Bloody stupid – why don't we accept it as a basic truth, like these Orientals? Their attitude is much more sensible. All the rich Chinese chaps keep

mistresses, and it's considered perfectly respectable. They do exactly as I'm doing. All right, so look at it statistically. On the one hand there are a few thousand Europeans in Hong Kong whom my behaviour would scandalise – and on the other hand several million Chinese who would accept it as perfectly natural.

Lomax does not appear convinced by Ben's reasoning.[75] His own desire for Suzie, eventually realised, is as a monogamous lover, one he is willing to take back to England despite social prejudice. Yet whatever its 'thesis' may be, the novel clearly portrays a field of great sexual opportunity for the unscrupulous European male. According to Sean O'Callaghan, moreover, this sexual opportunity came at a great cost to the real Suzie Wong, i.e., the character's real-life inspiration, whom a friend of his had located:

She was a fat, dirty, disease-ridden whore of about thirty-five, living in abject poverty in one of the back alleys of Wanchai. Once she may have looked like Nancy Kwan, who played the title role, but drink and disease had so transformed her that she looked like any of the other thousand or so prostitutes who beg or search the garbage tins for a living when their good looks are gone and they are no longer of any value to their masters, the traffickers.[76]

Historian May Holdsworth's take on Suzie Wong (offered in reference to the film), is that she represents a 'tenacious' stereotype of 'the Wan Chai bar girl on the lookout for a good catch and snaring some stupid besotted rich foreigner'.[77] George Adams's far less famous novel, *The Great Hong Kong Sex Novel*, illustrates this stereotype, but applied to Chinese women more broadly. It is a tongue-in-cheek morality tale about the hazards of playing the field, particularly where local women are concerned. Written in the form of a psychiatric patient's personal narrative, it tells the story of a prosperous and distinguished barrister, Nigel Trelford, who, despite having a beautiful live-in British girlfriend, naturally cannot resist the temptation of Asian women. The novel recounts Trelford's sordid and emotionally unsatisfying escapades – assuring us that the experiences he reveals are merely the tip of the iceberg, chosen for their representative nature – and ends with Trelford running from triad hitmen hired by a former conquest, a Hakka woman offended that he did not intend to marry her. This final act of attempted revenge follows an escalating series of harassments: vandalising his love nest in Tsim Sha Tsui, abusive telephone calls, and 'mysterious packets in the post: photomontages of myself in various postures of torture or obscene abandon; defamations in Chinese and English scrawled large with lurid inks; articles of underwear, soiled and torn; contraceptives used and knotted or blown into misshapen

comic balloons'.[78] Although Trelford ultimately gives up his enjoyment of the ever-available Asian women, and even conveys feelings of
'hideous forces of guilt' at having 'shamelessly exploited the precarious
economic and sociological situation of so many women' and having
'played on their naivety and abused their trust', his therapist finds the
repentance unconvincing.[79] Perhaps he is put off by Trelford's initial
self-justifying comparison of his situation to that of 'a man alone in
a girls' school for one night, many nights and the ugly prefects are
all sound asleep'.[80] In any case, for present purposes, the legitimacy
of Trelford's repentance is less important than the litany of clichés he
reveals. Moreover, if Trelford takes advantage of Chinese women for
whom sexuality and commerce are indistinguishable, his friend Larry
Snowdon, a policeman, typifies the middle-aged Englishman who has
let himself go after discovering Filipinas or, as he calls them, 'little
brown Eskimos'. Not only are they far less expensive than the local
women, but, as Snowdon notes, they 'love you fat and wrinkly. I can't
quite work out whether I remind them of their fathers or whether it's
that I'm just kind of safe-looking.'[81]

Indeed, particularly after the 1970s, non-Chinese Asian women,
especially domestic helpers on contingent visas, became a favourite
of many European men, as well as a recurring motif in fiction. They
show up in John Gordon Davis's 1974 novel, in which the first-person
narrator, describing his visit to a brothel staffed by Filipinas, notes that

> Most of them came from middle-class Manila families and they were just
> taking their two-weeks' vacation and paying their way. They did well in
> Hong Kong with the Europeans, because they were so happy about it,
> but probably not as well as the American and British girls who were par-
> ticularly popular with the Chinese, who will pay big money for a white
> woman, even if only out of curiousity.[82]

A generation later, John Burdett's apocalyptic Handover novel, *The
Last Six Million Seconds*, similarly describes the New Makati, not a
girlie bar but a 'genuine pickup joint' in Wanchai:

> Filipina maids with one night a week to spend finding a second financial
> source, maybe even a husband, crowded near the bandstand in groups of
> tens, chattering and laughing, their black eyes flickering over everyone
> who entered. Young Western men stood at the bar, grinning like sailors
> who have come across shoals of fish.[83]

The same year, American writer Paul Theroux's distasteful protagonist in the similarly apocalyptic *Kowloon Tong*, an Englishman living
with his mother and operating a crowded factory, not only loses his
virginity in a Mong Kok brothel and, later, makes one of his Chinese

employees his mistress, but in addition has regular dalliances with Filipina women. One of them occupies his mind during the funeral of his late business partner:

> All this while, in the church, surrounded by the Chinese mourners, Bunt was imagining the Filipino girl from last night, who called herself Baby, getting down on all fours, naked, presenting her bottom and looking back at him and saying, "Let we make puppies!"
> And he laughed, remembering that she had pronounced it *fuppies*.[84]

Leaving aside Theroux's unconvincing dialogue, this scene would not have surprised any male expatriate in 1997 who happened to read the novel. In their study of British expatriates in post-Handover Hong Kong, sociologists Caroline Knowles and Douglas Harper describe the continuing resonance of such scenes, particularly with domestic helpers who frequent the clubs in Wanchai. Although emphasising that most domestic helpers steer clear of these clubs and the men who frequent them, they note the symbiotic relationship between older and wealthier men and younger, attractive women: '[b]eautiful women with slender bodies and circumstances but with imagination and ingenuity, [who] detach themselves from Southeast Asian villages and set off abroad to make ends meet for those who stay behind.'[85]

If Hong Kong was presented as a place of sexual bounty for the western man, numerous commentators (including fictitious characters) were quick to warn against marrying Chinese women. To be sure, in the early postwar period, British (as well as Chinese) social custom strongly militated against intermarriage, a theme we saw in Chapter 1. But the warnings were not merely a reification of convention; they also followed from the belief that Chinese women were controlling and manipulative. In that sense, Nigel Trelford's fate is all the more unexpected: he has played by the rules of Hong Kong British male society, keeping his long-term relationship with a British woman separate from his mere dalliances with Asian (mostly Chinese) women, and has avoided any commitments to the latter, yet still is ensnared by a Chinese woman who refuses to play by the (tacit) rules.

At the same time they conveyed Hong Kong as a European man's sexual playground, writers routinely eroticised Asian women's appearance. Numerous writers noted the cheongsam. According to Ian Fleming, for example, it was the cheongsam that gave young Chinese women 'a deft and coltish prettiness which sends Western women into paroxysms of envy'. He contrasted the 'high, rather stiff collar' that gave 'authority and poise to the head and shoulders' with the 'flirtatious slits' of the garment's lower half.[86] Ommanney explained that 'It is distinctly bad style to have the skirt slit very high and is calculated to drive men mad. Naughty girls, however, do carry the slit very high indeed and men fall down in the street foaming at the mouth.'[87] Richard Mason's narrator-protagonist, Robert Lomax, noted of the prostitute Typhoo: 'She was as ugly as a little monkey, but had a beautiful figure and legs. The split in her skirt rose to immodest heights and showed a long white sliver of thigh.'[88] Denys Roberts, in his 2006 memoir, recalled his secretary from the 1960s, Margaret, a 'dark, handsome Eurasian girl. She wore glasses with black rims which made her look studious and a tight fitting cheongsam which did not.'[89] The cheongsam also figures prominently in Donald Moore's *The Striking Wind*: in describing hapless schoolteacher Hubert Phipps's succumbing at first sight to the charms of the Eurasian temptress Anna, the author lovingly details her cheongsams and her body: the slits in Anna's cheongsams

> were of intermediate length, sufficiently extended to be provocative, sufficiently restrained to be enticing. From his point of vantage Hubert could see the exposed part of her thigh, running in a narrowing V-shape from above her knee ... She was possessed of that rarity among Chinese women: a figure that was truly voluptuous ... He watched her furiously, his gaze moving from the shrouded nape of her neck between the high stiff collar and the softly billowing hair to the tips of her flimsy high-heeled shoes. The tightly stretched dress accentuated every part of her body and Hubert founded himself wondering what it would be like to touch her. He wanted suddenly, urgently, to touch her.[90]

Yet observations of Asian female bodies did not depend upon provocative clothing. The liberal weekly *FEER*'s 'Hongkong Look-See' column, in the context of describing celebrations of China's National Day in 1969, favourably contrasted the bodies of Hong Kong's 'communist girls' with their counterparts in the People's Republic: the former 'actually have something to which Mao badges can be "prominently" pinned. Perhaps a superior diet has something to do with the additional flesh in the right places of the colony's female leftists. Or do they perhaps dream of stopping the parade in Tieanenmin [*sic*] Square in Peking in their new Maidenform bras!'[91]

The easy availability of Chinese women, particularly where a commercial element was present, occasionally led to a moral panic, particularly in the 1970s and later as increasing Chinese affluence led to greater political and social activism. Such views endured not only throughout the colonial period but well beyond, for example in the recurring hand-wringing in the local press or in Bi Guozhi's 2010 Cantonese film *Girl$* about teenage girls engaging in 'paid dating'. On the other hand, not only Asian women but European women as well took advantage of the opportunities to make money in commercial

[92]

sex. Sean O'Callaghan's 1968 account of trafficking and the sex trade in Asia described the emerging market for western and Eurasian prostitutes for whom newly wealthy Chinese men were willing to pay top dollar.[92] A front-page *SCMP* headline in 1975 announced that 'Expat Hookers Invade Wanchai': most were British or Australian; 'Many British girls are secretaries; some are just bored wives of British servicemen.' The same paper reported in 1994 that increasing numbers of young British girls were coming to Hong Kong to make it as hostesses and prostitutes, largely to an 'affluent Chinese clientele', as well as making pornographic films. In the words of one interviewee, 'I wouldn't want my mum to know what I'm doing but I have a good time and I get paid loads of money to do it.'[93]

In contrast to the relative openness with which Hong Kong's status as a heterosexual male playground was discussed, public discourse was significantly more circumspect regarding homosexual opportunity. This is, of course, not surprising, given that homosexuality remained a criminal offence until 1991. Moreover, since the Chinese population was generally disapproving, open British homosexuality threatened to 'let down the side' and undermine the legitimacy of colonial rule. For this reason, the police force's Special Branch monitored homosexual activity, and prosecutions were routine. Open discussion of male homosexuality in English-language publications was most often found in newspaper columns either reporting arrests or blackmail scandals or, occasionally, calling for relaxation of criminalisation; the casual references to easy availability of sex that are common in heterosexual contexts cited above have no homosexual counterpart. For example, although James Kirkup's 1993 memoir, *Me All Over*, describes his Asian homosexual encounters dating back to the 1950s, his 1970 travel book cited above, *Hong Kong and Macau*, includes instructions only for picking up female prostitutes.[94]

Yet the limitations of discourse concerning casual homosexual encounters should not disguise the fact that, if pursued discreetly, similar opportunities existed. Indeed, the occasional arrest or newspaper scandal very likely belied the wider mundane prevalence of clandestine encounters. By their nature, these extraordinary events serve as an uncertain guide to daily life; we have no way of knowing how many illicit episodes occurred for every arrest or blackmail. We do, though, have some grounds for thinking that the police exercised restraint in prosecuting, focusing on those cases that were, for one reason or another, too public to ignore.

The arrest of Gordon Huthart is one case in point. The son of Lane Crawford entrepreneur Robert Huthart, he became an important businessman in his own right: as the founder, at age twenty-eight, of the

New York-style club Disco Disco, he is often regarded as the 'father' of the entertainment district Lan Kwai Fong. Formerly a regular at the nightclub in the Peninsula Hotel, The Scene, where he had frequently been thrown out for dancing with other men, he envisioned Disco Disco as a venue that would serve not only as a safe place for gay revelry, but, according to the *Sunday Morning Post Magazine* at the time of his death in 1996, as a transformative institution. As the paper put it, the younger Huthart 'had a strong conviction that he was in a position to make a real difference to the gay community'. When his club was raided, or when undercover police attempted to infiltrate the club, he became confrontational. Ultimately, in August 1979, eight months after the club's opening, he was arrested and charged with both sexual and drug offences, including '15 counts of buggery involving young Chinese men between the ages of 16 and 20'.[95] Pleading guilty, he served only thirteen weeks in prison, but his arrest, trial, and conviction leave several questions unanswered: how many additional similar encounters did he have, with which he was not charged? Would he have been arrested had he continued to operate discreetly, rather than becoming a major irritant to the police, openly flouting the law? And if the answer to the latter question is negative, then how many other similar offenders, content to remain discreet, were allowed to go about their business?

If Huthart's offences became public because of his operating a prominent club – 'quite literally the only place to go for nearly four years' – police officer John MacLennan's became public because of the mystery surrounding his death. MacLennan, characterised by popular historian Kate Whitehead as an admirer of Winston Churchill and devotee of the royal family, who wore a kilt on formal occasions and often drunkenly listened to bagpipes at loud volumes in his apartment in the wee hours, discreetly slept with young Chinese men arranged by a triad pimp. Following the revelation of a failed attempt to seduce a seventeen-year-old prospective police candidate, MacLennan was dismissed from the police force in late 1978, but Governor MacLehose, through the intervention of Elsie Elliott, ordered the dismissal rescinded. The police, however, embarrassed by this outside interference, used a fortuitous lead to prosecute MacLennan. Warned that the jig was up, MacLennan agreed through a lawyer to turn himself in; when he did not appear as agreed, Special Investigation Unit (SIU) officers went to his apartment, where they found he had been shot dead. The ensuing inquiry ultimately concluded that MacLennan had committed suicide; the fact that he had been shot five times in the chest helped to fuel widespread speculation, reaching all the way to London, that he had been killed in order to prevent his exposure of the SIU's conspiracy against him.[96]

In continuing to prosecute homosexuality nearly a quarter of a century after it had been decriminalised in the UK, the Hong Kong Government was clearly representing Hong Kong's popular opinion, a point of some importance; longstanding colonial governance emphasised respecting local cultural norms unless they were especially offensive to British morality, while the Government's post-1967 efforts to close the 'gap' between itself and the public militated against running too far ahead of public opinion on decriminalisation. This is one of the themes of Chapter 5. What is important in the present context, though, is that the criminal prosecutions and press accounts of male prostitution rings rested upon far more widespread casual homosexual practice. Criminal law forced punters to exercise particular caution, but young Asian male bodies, like their female counterparts, were easily accessible to British men in late colonial Hong Kong. Unlike the enjoyment of Asian women, however, casual access to young Asian men remained mostly outside the public discourse, surfacing only occasionally and then generally in criminal contexts.

Conclusion

It is tempting to see the characterisations of Hong Kong conveyed in this chapter as a counter-narrative to others presented in the book. In contrast to the more ostensibly 'serious' themes of entrepreneurship, modernisation, and good governance, the depictions examined here focus on Hong Kong as a site of male pleasure and leisure. This divergence from the more earnest themes is exemplified by sport and clubs, which constituted attempts to recreate British cultural forms prevalent 'back home' – even if, in practice, club membership would have remained beyond the means of many had they not lived in Hong Kong. The divergence seems even more pronounced in depictions of British male sexuality, in which the easy access to Asian women's (or young men's) bodies created nearly effortless opportunities for sexual pleasure that would have surely been available only to a small percentage of these men back home.

Yet the idea of Hong Kong as a site of pleasure was not only deeply embedded in the British cultural engagement with the colony, but was also thoroughly intertwined with the themes that were more likely to appear in GIS's or British MPs' boasts about the British accomplishments. As already hinted, club and sport constituted venues in which British officials, traders, and servicemen enacted their distinction from their Chinese subjects, and could engage in the informal conversations among officials that facilitated the presentation of a unified front to

Hong Kong people. Sexual encounters with readily available Asian women were less conducive to 'good governance' – and while (as we saw in Chapter 1) the postwar period saw the gradual erosion of the proscription against romantic entanglements between Europeans and Chinese, casual dalliances remained déclassé. If their existence was widely acknowledged in general terms, those partaking were expected to be discreet. On the other hand, it is easier to reconcile the (preferably discreet) enjoyment of Asian women's bodies with the unbridled capitalism described in Chapter 2: what, after all, was the point of making money if not to enjoy life's pleasures?

Perhaps most importantly, these forms of leisure were among the qualities that the British congratulated themselves for having brought to Hong Kong. As we will see in Chapter 7, in those 'narratives of 1997' that conjured up the worst fears of what would happen after the change of sovereignty, fears of Communist puritanism that could endanger the British-influenced Hong Kong way of life rested side by side with perceived threats to freedom of speech, rule of law, good governance, and economic freedom.

Notes

1 Marcus Collins, *Modern Love: An Intimate History of Men and Women in Twentieth-Century Britain* (London: Atlantic Books, 2003).
2 Susanna Hoe, *The Private Life of Old Hong Kong* (Hong Kong: Oxford University Press, 1991).
3 John Tosh, *Manliness and Masculinities in Nineteenth-Century Britain: Essays on Gender, Family and Empire* (London and New York: Routledge, 2004), p. 193.
4 Tosh, *Manliness*, p. 212. Tosh further notes imperialism's association with adventure and toughness.
5 May Holdsworth, *Foreign Devils: Expatriates in Hong Kong* (Oxford: Oxford University Press, 2002), pp. 17, 152.
6 Patrick Abercrombie, *Hong Kong: Preliminary Planning Report* (Hong Kong: Government Printer, 1948), p. 17.
7 ANA, A1838/530/4, Commonwealth of Australia, Trade Commissioner Service, 'Post Report on Hong Kong – January, 1954', p. 9.
8 Susanna Hoe, *Watching the Flag Come Down: An Englishwoman in Hong Kong 1987–1997* (Oxford: Holo Books, 2007), p. 85.
9 Jonathan Dimbleby, *The Last Governor: Chris Patten and the Handover of Hong Kong* (London: Little, Brown, 1997), p. xiii.
10 John Burdett, *The Last Six Million Seconds: A Thriller* (New York: William Morrow, 1997), p. 95.
11 See Mark Hampton, 'Projecting Britishness to Hong Kong: The British Council and Hong Kong House, 1950s–1970s', *Historical Research* 85 (November 2012): 691–709.
12 See also Ackbar Abbas, *Hong Kong: Culture and the Politics of Disappearance* (Minneapolis: University of Minnesota Press, 1997), p. 6; Frank Leeming, *Street Studies in Hong Kong: Localities in a Chinese City* (Oxford: Oxford University Press, 1977), p. 12.
13 Mark Hampton, 'Early Hong Kong Television, 1950s–1970s: Commercialization, Public Service, and Britishness', *Media History* 17 (August 2011): 305–22.

14 WYAS, William Moore collection, 108D77/358, Billy Moore to Vera Moore, 25 September 1945, BFMO Sydney; WYAS, William Moore collection, 108D77/380, Billy Moore to Vera Moore, 12 November 1945, Hong Kong; WYAS, William Moore collection, 108D77/391, Billy Moore to Vera Moore, 7 December 1945, Hong Kong.
15 Patrick F. McDevitt, *May the Best Man Win: Sport, Masculinity, and Nationalism in Great Britain and the Empire, 1880–1935* (Basingstoke: Palgrave, 2004), pp. 2, 4.
16 The place of sport in expatriate life in Hong Kong is discussed in Holdsworth, *Foreign Devils*, pp. 255–72. For a contemporary account from 1961, see Derek Webb, *Hong Kong* (Singapore: Eastern University Press, 1960), pp. 84–8.
17 '1st Battalion News', *The China Dragon* 27 (April 1956), pp. 117, 125–9 (Staffordshire Regiment Museum). Compare to *The Borderers' Chronicle: The Journal of the King's Own Scottish Borderers* 24 (31 December 1949), pp. 107–8. King's Own Scottish Borderers Regimental Museum.
18 'Expedition Crisis', *Queenshill Courier* 2 (October 1961), p. 2; 'Yesterday's News on the Himalayan Expedition', *Queenshill Courier* 2 (October 1961), p. 7. Royal Regiment of Fusiliers Museum (Warwickshire), Warwick, RRF/1998.12. In the event, the expedition was able to go ahead. 'Himalayan Expedition Approaches Everest', *Queenshill Courier* 2 (November 1961), p. 7. Royal Regiment of Fusiliers Museum (Warwickshire), Warwick, RRF/1998.12.
19 *The Antelope* 30 (November 1960), p. 58 (Royal Regiment of Fusiliers Museum (Warwickshire), Warwick).
20 Denys Roberts, *Another Disaster: Hong Kong Sketches* (London and New York: Radcliffe Press, 2006), pp. 160–1.
21 CHAS, C 11, Michael Page to H. J. Collar, 31 January 1966; and Hong Kong General Chamber of Commerce and the Federation of Hong Kong Industries, 'Mr John Baillie Hamilton LECKIE.'
22 *The Clubs of Hong Kong* (Hong Kong: Illustrated Magazine Publishing, 1981), p. 7.
23 Arthur Hacker, 'Rogues to Riches', *Hong Kong Tatler* 21 (June 1997): 124–45 (p. 124).
24 Amy Milne-Smith, *London Clubland: A Cultural History of Gender and Class in Late Victorian Britain* (Basingstoke: Palgrave, 2011), pp. 6, 162–4.
25 John M. Carroll, *Edge of Empires: Chinese Elites and British Colonials in Hong Kong* (Cambridge, MA: Harvard University Press, 2005), pp. 97–101.
26 Hoe, *Watching the Flag Come Down*, p. 50.
27 HKU Special Collections, Hong Kong Club, *Report of the One Hundred and Twenty-Third Ordinary Yearly Meeting of Members Held in the Club House on Wednesday, 7th April 1971, at 5:30 p.m.* (Hong Kong: Hong Kong Club, 1971), pp. 2–3.
28 *The Club: Special Commemorative Issue, 1897–1981* (Hong Kong: Club Publications, 1982), p. 44.
29 *The Club*, pp. 4, 10.
30 Glenn Schloss, 'Hong Kong Club to Let Women Join', *SCMP* (19 May 1997).
31 Roberts, *Another Disaster*, pp. 75–6; Denys Roberts, 'Introduction', in Spencer Robinson (ed.), *A History of the Hong Kong Cricket Club* (London: Centurian Books, 1989), p. 8.
32 Roberts, 'Introduction', p. 7; Roberts, *Another Disaster*, p. 77.
33 Robinson, *A History of the Hong Kong Cricket Club*, pp. 32–8.
34 Roberts, 'Introduction', p. 9; HKU Special Collections, *The Hong Kong Cricket Club, Accounts and Report, 1974/75* (Hong Kong: Green Pagoda Press, [1975]), p. 6.
35 HKU Special Collections, *Memorandum and Articles of Association of the Reform Club of Hong Kong* (Hong Kong: Yau Sang, 1949).
36 HKU Special Collections, *Hong Kong Reform Club, 2nd 10 Years Anniversary Report, 1959–1968* ([Hong Kong]: [Hong Kong Reform Club], [1969?]), p. 24.
37 *Hong Kong Reform Club* (quotation is from p. 23).
38 NLW, Misc. Recs. 358, St David's Society of Hong Kong, pp. 1, 5.
39 NLW, Misc. Recs. 358, President's Speech, St David's Night, 1 March 1961.
40 NLW, Misc. Recs. 358, 'Dance Now – Pay Later'.
41 Ronald Hyam, *Empire and Sexuality* (Manchester: Manchester University Press, 1991), pp. 1, 202.

42 F. D. Ommanney, *Fragrant Harbour: A Private View of Hong Kong* (London: Hutchinson, 1962), p. 24.
43 Ommanney, *Fragrant Harbour*, pp. 101–6.
44 Sean O'Callaghan, *The Yellow Slave Trade: A Survey of the Traffic in Women and Children in the East* (London: Anthony Blond, 1968), p. 27.
45 Private communication from Peter Cunich, 15 September 2014. I am grateful to Cunich for sharing this material from his projected two-volume history of HKU. The first volume has been published: Peter Cunich, *A History of the University of Hong Kong*, Vol. I: *1911–1945* (Hong Kong: Hong Kong University Press, 2013).
46 Jan Morris, *Hong Kong: Epilogue to an Empire* (New York: Random House, 1997), p. 55.
47 O'Callaghan, *The Yellow Slave Trade*, p. 55.
48 WYAS, William Moore collection, 108D77/367, Billy Moore to Vera Moore, 18 October 1945.
49 Ian Fleming, *Thrilling Cities* (London: Jonathan Cape, 1963), p. 24.
50 Jackie Pullinger, *Chasing the Dragon* (London: Hodder and Stoughton, 2010 [1980]), p. 33.
51 According to Nigel Cameron, for the young men among Hong Kong's population, most of whom were transplanted peasants, the temptations could be formidable: 'No village lad ever had such a choice of girls – and such provocative girls taking their manners from Taiwan actresses – to ogle at.' Nigel Cameron, *Hong Kong: The Cultured Pearl* (Hong Kong: Oxford University Press, 1978), pp. 208–9.
52 Harold Ingrams, *Hong Kong* (London: HMSO, 1952), p. 88.
53 George Adams, *The Great Hong Kong Sex Novel: The Rise and Fall of a Hong Kong Chauvinist* (Hong Kong: AIP Publications, 1993), p. 104.
54 Adams, *The Great Hong Kong Sex Novel*, p. 40.
55 Richard Mason, *The World of Suzie Wong* (London: Fontana, 1959 [1957]), p. 74.
56 Hans Lutz and Robert Snow, 'Hard Labour for Life', *FEER* (16 January 1971), p. 18. Sean O'Callaghan describes one Hong Kong girl who worked for low pay in a knitting factory before moving on to a dance hall in order to support her three brothers, for whom she was the sole support after her father developed tuberculosis. See O'Callaghan, *The Yellow Slave Trade*, pp. 35–6.
57 John Gordon Davis, *The Years of the Hungry Tiger* (London: Michael Joseph, 1974), p. 79.
58 Roberts, *Another Disaster*, p. 91.
59 Roberts, *Another Disaster*, pp. 114–15.
60 James Kirkup, *Cities of the World: Hong Kong and Macao* (London: J. M. Dent and Sons, 1970), p. 72.
61 O'Callaghan, *The Yellow Slave Trade*, pp. 30–4, 38–9 (quotations on pp. 33–4).
62 Judy Bonavia, *Essential Hong Kong* (Boston and Toronto: Little, Brown, 1990), pp. 99–100. Patrick Hase notes that when he assumed his junior civil service position in the early 1970s, the buy-out price for a bar girl would have been the equivalent of one month of his salary, and so he very much doubts that many British expatriates could have afforded this option (personal communication, 15 October 2014).
63 Kevin Rafferty, *City on the Rocks: Hong Kong's Uncertain Future* (New York: Viking, 1989), p. 27.
64 Fleming, *Thrilling Cities*, p. 25.
65 Roger Boschman, *Hong Kong by Night* (Hong Kong: CFW Publications, 1981), p. 47.
66 www.perfectloving.org/history4.html (accessed 23 December 2014).
67 Boschman, *Hong Kong by Night*, p. 47.
68 Joe Matyeh, *Bachelor's Guide to Hong Kong* (Hong Kong: Ted Thomas, 1982), p. 3. The publisher, Ted Thomas, was a former Radio Television Hong Kong (RTHK) producer and Government Information Services (GIS) director who founded a public relations firm, Corporate Communication, in 1973. He attained some notoriety in 2009 for allegedly bilking a near-centenarian woman, former war correspondent Clare Hollingworth, of most of her savings. See Emma Hartley, 'Doyenne of War Correspondents Parted from Life's Savings', *Telegraph* (22 October 2009).
69 Matyeh, *Bachelor's Guide*, p. 10.

70 Matyeh, *Bachelor's Guide*, pp. 44–5, 50, 64, 70.
71 FAULDS 3/3/1/6, Russell Johnston to Andrew Faulds, 2 October 1984.
72 Chi-kwan Mark, 'Vietnam War Tourists: US Naval Visits to Hong Kong and British–American–Chinese Relations, 1965–1968', *Cold War History* 10 (February 2010): 1–28. Mark notes that in the year 1966, 185,000 military and naval servicemen, mostly American, contributed some HK$316.9 million to the local economy (p. 4).
73 Mason, *The World of Suzie Wong*, p. 37. For the history of prostitution in late-nineteenth and early-twentieth-century Hong Kong, Australia, Singapore, and India, see Philippa Levine, *Prostitution, Race and Politics: Policing Venereal Disease in the British Empire* (London and New York: Routledge, 2003).
74 Mason, *The World of Suzie Wong*, p. 38.
75 Mason, *The World of Suzie Wong*, pp. 103, 106.
76 O'Callaghan continued: 'My friend thought it would be an excellent idea to photograph the real Suzie Wong, or at least the prostitute of that name, shaking hands with Nancy Kwan. Unfortunately, on the night set for the meeting she got hopelessly drunk on the few Hong Kong dollars he gave her.' O'Callaghan, *The Yellow Slave Trade*, p. 29.
77 Holdsworth, *Foreign Devils*, p. 195.
78 Adams, *The Great Hong Kong Sex Novel*, p. 142. For a post-Handover morality tale about the dangerous side of playing the field in Hong Kong, see Abigail Haworth, 'Dangerous Liaisons', *Marie Claire* (7 January 2009).
79 Adams, *The Great Hong Kong Sex Novel*, pp. 231, 235.
80 Adams, *The Great Hong Kong Sex Novel*, p. 4.
81 Adams, *The Great Hong Kong Sex Novel*, pp. 72–4.
82 Davis, *The Years of the Hungry Tiger*, p. 93.
83 Burdett, *The Last Six Million Seconds*, p. 274.
84 Paul Theroux, *Kowloon Tong* (Boston, MA and New York: Houghton Mifflin, 1997), p. 12.
85 Caroline Knowles and Douglas Harper, *Hong Kong: Migrant Lives, Landscapes, and Journeys* (Chicago: University of Chicago Press, 2009), pp. 180–94 (quotation on p. 194). For the broader context of domestic helpers' lives in Hong Kong, see Nicole Constable, *Maid to Order in Hong Kong: Stories of Migrant Workers*, 2nd edn (Ithaca, NY: Cornell University Press, 2007).
86 Fleming, *Thrilling Cities*, p. 21.
87 Ommanney, *Fragrant Harbour*, p. 48.
88 Mason, *The World of Suzie Wong*, p. 30.
89 Roberts, *Another Disaster*, p. 96.
90 Donald Moore, *The Striking Wind* (London: Hodder and Stoughton, 1959), pp. 25–6.
91 'Hongkong Look-See', *FEER* (9 October 1969), p. 143.
92 O'Callaghan, *The Yellow Slave Trade*, pp. 28, 41.
93 Ian Whalley, 'Expat Hookers Invade Wanchai', *SCMP* (22 June 1975); 'Have Sex … Will Travel', *SCMP* (2 October 1994). See also 'Corrupt Police Shatter Dreams of Prostitutes', *SCMP* (16 May 1991).
94 James Kirkup, *Me All Over: Memoirs of a Misfit* (London: Peter Owen, 1993).
95 Alice Cairns, 'Flash Gordon', *Sunday Morning Post Magazine* (22 September 1996): 12–15. For a contextualisation of the founding of Disco Disco, which also cites the Cairns article, see Sea-ling Cheng, 'Consuming Places in Hong Kong: Experiencing Lan Kwai Fong', in Gordon Mathews and Tai-Lok Lui (eds), *Consuming Hong Kong* (Hong Kong: Hong Kong University Press, 2003), pp. 237–62.
96 Kate Whitehead, *Hong Kong Murders* (Oxford: Oxford University Press, 2001), pp. 19–31; Richard West, 'Overstepping the Oriental Mark', *Spectator* (15 March 1980), p. 11.

CHAPTER FOUR

The discourses of order and modernisation

In a brief 1988 pamphlet written to encourage London parish churches to form a link with the Anglican Church in Hong Kong, following a few sentences of basic explanation of Hong Kong's colonial status, geography, and history, readers learned of Hong Kong's modern trappings: 'First impressions of the Westerner arriving at the modern airport are of a highly urban, industrial city, with skyscrapers and fast moving traffic.' The reader is immediately cautioned, though, that these appearances of modernity could be deceiving: 'But never forget, this is a Chinese city with an overwhelming Chinese population, that still thinks and acts in Chinese.'[1] Chineseness and modernity, the syntax conveys, are disjunctive.

Five years later, an *SCMP* column entitled 'From a Barren Rock to a Modern City' began with a familiar juxtaposition. On the one hand, there was the Hong Kong skyline, 'with its stunning towers of steel and concrete ... perhaps the most dramatic urban landscape in the world ... a complex and highly developed network of roads, underground transport tunnels, drainage and other modern infrastructure systems'. These modern wonders existed, on the other hand, despite the fact that 'little more than 150 years ago Hong Kong was, in the words of the then British Prime Minister Lord Palmerstone [sic], "a barren rock [sic] with hardly a house on it"'. Similar depictions of Hong Kong's wondrous transformation often credited the fortuitous combination of good (minimalist) British government with the entrepreneurial energies and hard work of the Chinese population, themes familiar from Chapter 2. This article, by contrast, more directly credited the Government: 'Underpinning this remarkable transformation, that has completely changed the face of the territory, is the Hong Kong Government's ceaseless commitment to providing good infrastructure and community facilities to support private sector development and to meet the needs and aspirations of the people.' The article went on

[100]

to list seven different areas in which the Government currently contributed to Hong Kong's continual modernisation, while reminding its readers that these achievements occurred notwithstanding 'Hong Kong's very low tax rate'.[2]

Chapter 2 argued that Hong Kong Britishness included a libertarian vision of unconstrained capitalism in which one could sink or swim according to one's own efforts, ability, and luck. The frequent assertion of this vision can only be understood in the context of the emergence of the welfare state in postwar Britain, as a counterpoint to the 'People's Peace'. Yet this was not the only dimension of Hong Kong Britishness; alongside it existed a narrative of the British as modernisers, bringing the blessings of civilisation to a migrant urban population and backward rural villagers.

Modernising the colony meant providing suitable housing for a rapidly growing population, many of whom lived as squatters in ramshackle housing that was subject to periodic landslides and fires, most notably the Shek Kip Mei fire of 1953. Modernisation also entailed the creation of infrastructures, including roads, tunnels, bridges, public transportation, and reservoirs. Such modernising projects, of course, could amount to significant Government interventions in the colony's economy, in apparent defiance of the tropes identified in Chapter 2. These two visions could, in many cases, be reconciled through Government reliance on private contributions to top-down modernisation. At other times they underwrote competing sides in specific controversies, or were allowed to rest in contradiction. It is, no doubt, this sort of contradiction that David Bonavia had in mind in referring to Hong Kong's 'strange combination of prudent, British-style civil service and buccaneering businessmen who are prepared to risk an arm or a leg for a quick, fat profit'.[3]

Whether referring to modernised or still virgin territory, observers frequently noted the natural beauty of Hong Kong, both coastal and inland. Several writers described being overwhelmed by the first sight of the harbour, where nature and civilisation commingled. Alexander Grantham's 1965 memoir, describing his first arrival in Hong Kong in 1922, notes 'We knew that the harbour, enclosed between the island and the mainland, was one of the finest in the world, but were not prepared for the beauty or the bustling activity... It was exhilarating and, strangely enough, seemed to harmonize with the quiet majesty of the hills: nature and man not in conflict but complementing each other.'[4] Jan Morris began her popular history with an elaborate description of arriving by boat from inland. China contained 'many marvels', writes Morris; the 'most astonishing thing of all, though, lies at the southern edge of the Chinese land mass, just below the Tropic of Cancer, where the Zhu Jiang or Pearl River debouches through Guangdong Province into the South China Sea'. For nearly three pages she describes darkness, a 'thick white mist', still water, the occasional fog horn; 'You might be anywhere, or nowhere at all.' As the boat approaches the harbour, 'like the rising of the theatre's curtain the fog begins to lift'; first you see additional boats, then

> buildings of concrete, steel and mirror-glass, with advertisements on them ... taller and taller those buildings turn out to be, each higher than the one before – pressing upon one another, looking over each others' shoulders, immense clean buildings of white, or silver, or even gold, with masses of portholed windows, or great cross-girders, with jagged rooflines and spiky towers – up the city heights until green mountainsides appear behind ... So like a fanfare, as the vapours are burnt away, a last phenomenon of China is revealed to you; a futuristic metropolis, like something from another age or another sensibility, stacked around a harbor jammed fantastically with ships.[5]

But how did this blending of nature and, ultimately, a hyper-civilised city come about? In other contexts, those articulating the British achievement in Hong Kong would point to a benign administration that unleashed individual and voluntary entrepreneurial energies. This chapter will point to a complementary discourse, one that underscored planned modernisation.

Bringing order to the urban jungle

Descriptions of Hong Kong regularly highlighted the confusing, disorderly spectacle of the urban areas, and the role of British administrators or cultural authorities in establishing order in them. Such disorder could vary in danger or intensity, ranging from the merely confusing to criminal or political violence – most significantly in the riots of 1956, 1966, and 1967–68. The more benign disorder was that facing western tourists. In the early 1970s, the *Hong Kong Official Guide* described Kowloon's 'main artery', Nathan Road, as a 'bewildering complex of signs, which at night become an electric rainbow'. Not far from the 'tourist area of Tsimshatsui', in Mongkok, 'the English signs will have totally disappeared and you will be in the bewildering maze of a flourishing Chinese city'.[6] Around the same time, Dorothy Needham, former Associate Director of the Sino-British Cooperation Office and wife of scientist Joseph Needham, describing the less crowded and more Anglicised Victoria (Central) in her diary, confirmed this confusion, noting in particular the heavy traffic and large crowds of pedestrians.[7]

This level of safe disorder required only the services of the Hong Kong Tourist Authority (HKTA), the semi-governmental organisation founded by Government Act in 1957, and its member businesses (only member businesses could advertise in the *Hong Kong Official Guide*). Accordingly, in the section on 'Nightlife', the *Official Guide* introduced the advertisements for escort services with an emphasis not only on 'pleasant company' but also on guidance:

> Visitors to Hong Kong who wish to see the city with somebody who lives here and knows where the good places are, frequently patronise an escort service. These entirely respectable organisations provide partners of all nationalities as guides and companions for unescorted male and female travellers who would like a night out on the town in pleasant company.[8]

The advertisement for 'the Famous Alliance Escorts & Tourist Guide Agency' – 'Members: HKTA' and '(as referred to in Playboy Magazine July 1972)' – posed the rhetorical question: 'Ladies, why have that insecure feeling when one of our male escorts can show you around town at most economical rates?'.[9] For those men who preferred to enjoy nightlife unescorted, the *Official Guide* advised that the 'best ballrooms are Members of the HKTA. The tourist is not recommended to try any of the others where the girls are unlikely to understand English.' Happily, men arriving unaccompanied at the nightclubs in Wanchai or Tsimshatsui 'may even take the girls out if they wish'; in the case of the ballrooms, 'you seldom drink alcohol but you may find pleasant company and again the girls can be taken out – though they will expect you to entertain them quite well'.[10]

Similarly, the HKTA offered guidance for shopping, including its publication of *Stop and Shop*, which listed all shops belonging to the HKTA. Shopping in Hong Kong was not as straightforward as one might hope: 'With the enormous variety of inexpensive and exciting goods before you, shopping in Hong Kong is not for the faint-hearted: indecision can turn this wonderful shopper's paradise into a nightmare.' The *Official Guide* thus offered advice, ranging from 'plan your shopping. Decide what you really want and then look round comparing prices and quality', to distinguishing between department stores where the prices were 'clearly stated' and smaller shops where one could bargain, to avoiding 'touts' who would claim a 15 per cent middle man's fee. The *Official Guide* also warned of 'unscrupulous merchants' who sometimes sold 'imitations for the genuine article'. Happily, this danger could be remedied by perhaps the most important piece of advice: 'Remember that stores who are Associate Members of the HKTA are bound by the rules of the Association to maintain ethical standards at all times in the conduct of their business and to discourage malpractices contrary to the interests of the tourists.'[11]

As noted, this level of disorder or confusion merely required guidance for the bewildered visitor. A deeper level of chaos, by contrast, needed British governance. The confusion was tied both to overcrowding – a frequent topic of commentary – and to the haphazard way in which living, consumption, and production often blended. Leo Goodstadt, at the time Deputy Editor of the *FEER*, in a 1968 academic study blamed crowded housing conditions, particularly in the first generation of public housing estates, for encouraging people to spill out into the streets. The prewar official standard of 35 square feet per inhabitant had dropped to 24 square feet in the initial public housing projects, in order to save costs; but, asked Goodstadt, 'What can a man do in even 35 square feet?'. He continued, arguing that

> The poor conditions make the home very unattractive, and it is a place in which members of the family spend as little time as possible – especially in the summer. This leads, for example, to children wandering unsupervised in the streets where they have plenty of opportunity to observe such undesirable activities as drug-taking.

Urban density, moreover, was exacerbated by a dearth of public parks, gardens, and playgrounds – only about one-third as many as stipulated by the 'town planning standards' to which the Government had ostensibly committed.[12]

The Leeds scholar Frank Leeming, in his 1977 urban geography, similarly related crowding to cost of living, as they reinforced each other in a vicious cycle: 'Life in cubicles is one factor which drives Hong Kong people to live in public, in the streets and in restaurants. The cost of eating in restaurants and sharing the life of the streets is equally a factor which predisposes people not to spend more on housing.' Other than in the 'best suburbs, various impoverished backwaters, and to some extent Central District', congestion was a problem, and 'in most working-class and most business districts, it [was] all-pervading, apparently limitless, and impenetrable'. Central District, the location of the 'head offices of the banks, the big shipping companies, the big Western enterprises, and the property and financial interests', was relatively tame by comparison: 'hawking and other kinds of street congestion [were] reduced to Western levels'.[13]

It was not merely the size of the crowds, but the character of its members, that contributed to the chaos. According to James Pope-Hennessy, 'Generations of British Governors, five-year transients obeying or ignoring the commands of Whitehall, have striven to reconcile the warring interests of commerce and humanity, of education and racial jealousies, and of a bewildering variety of religious creeds. They have tried to impose cohesion and order on a population in its essence inchoate and fluid.'[14] A late 1960s book aimed at recruiting British police officers to Hong Kong noted Kowloon's overcrowding 'with its inevitable squalor and dirt', and pointed out that many who lived in 'suburbs and shanty towns' were 'newcomers to city life', whose transition was 'often complicated by unemployment or the fact that they speak a different Chinese dialect than their neighbours'.[15]

Hong Kong Island, though urban, remained less crowded than Kowloon, offering ample scope for the transferal of rural habits to the modern city. Writing in 1962, F. D. Ommanney described the rural/urban blend of Shun Wan (Sheung Wan), just to the west of the Europeanised Central District:

> There were several rows of houses in Shun Wan. Each had one or two rooms and no sanitary arrangements of any kind. One was a living- and the other a sleeping-room. There was a communal stand-pipe from which water was fetched by the women in buckets hanging from shoulder-poles. In front of the houses there was a rectangular concrete space, bounded by a low wall and divided into sections, one section to each house. These were threshing-floors or drying-floors, and rice was often spread out to dry in the sun upon them.
> The place was full of very evocative and nostalgic smells and homely sounds. There was the universal presence and smell of animal dung. There were pigs, dogs, ducks and chickens everywhere. The pigs were great 'swaybacks' with their dugs dangling in the mud. The dogs were the same variant of the chow that one sees all over the colony and in the junks and sampans on the harbour. There was the smell of hot, rank vegetation and of the sun on old walls, and there were the voices of innumerable totally unwashed children.[16]

The disorderliness resulting from rural migration into the city is likewise a theme in the fond 2004 recollections by poet and novelist Martin Booth of the dangerous chaos of Kowloon during his 1950s childhood:

> Walking along the streets was mildly hazardous. First, one was periodically peppered with bird seed and desiccated droppings as a finch had a scratch-about in the bottom of its cage three floors above. Second, one was dripped on from laundry hanging out to dry over the street on bamboo poles. Third, and less benign, was the fact that one could be hit by a chicken bone or other detritus from a completed meal.

According to a Chinese friend, this puzzle of food dropping from the sky stemmed from Kowloon people's recent emergence from rural China: 'in China, one threw wasted food into the street and the local pigs or dogs ate it. That there were no pigs wandering the streets of Kowloon seemed immaterial to the residents.'[17] Transplanted from their villages, the newly urban Hong Kong residents' rural habits brought a disorder that the older Booth could, through the lens of nostalgia, find charming and that the child Booth could perhaps experience as excitement. For a typical British visitor, they served as chaotic reminders of Hong Kong's foreignness.

Not only did crowding derive from the diversity of people blending together, but it also stemmed from the promiscuous mixture of different types of activities in close quarters. As Leeming put it, hawkers 'often bring total congestion to a climax, because they are attracted to congested streets' – because this was where customers could be found – 'and forthwith greatly increase congestion in them'. Nor was their activity confined purely to selling; rather, '[w]orking a circular saw, storing sheet steel, conducting a circulating library, cleaning fowls, cutting hair, respraying vans, and a hundred other street, pavement and alley activities share with hawking the responsibility for setting up obstacles to public circulation, and creating total congestion'. Much of this congestion, he argued, stemmed either from 'encroachment or multiple use, or both, all in the line of business'. Restaurants, for example, would expand into the alley behind; 'Rather than take bigger and more expensive premises, the restauranter [sic] helps himself to an unauthorized subsidy from the public in the form of getting his scullery work performed in the alley.' Aside from such encroachment, multiple use – e.g. an entrepreneur operating a factory out of his flat, or low-wage workers sleeping at their workplace – further contributed to the congestion.[18]

If Kowloon in general was a disorderly and crowded space in need of British organisation, the extreme case was the Walled City – seemingly doomed to remain chaotic because it was neither under British jurisdiction nor under effective Chinese administration.[19] Originally a Qing fort built in 1846 to confine the British to Hong Kong Island, by the time of the New Territories lease in 1898 it was surrounded on all sides by British authority, yet remained untouched by this authority: a 'world unto its own' in Elizabeth Sinn's words.[20] Described by the journalist David Bonavia as 'a hotbed of drug-pushers, prostitutes, unlicensed doctors and dentists – unsanitary, jerry-built and unsafe', it served in the British imagination, according to Seth Harter, both as the 'dark antithesis of colonial order' and as an 'extreme example of the short-comings of a laissez-faire society'.[21] Jackie Pullinger, who came to live in the Walled City as a young British missionary in 1966, recalled 'the smell and the darkness, a fetid smell of rotten foodstuffs, excrement, offal and general rubbish'.[22] *Financial Times* journalist Kevin Rafferty, describing its last years in the 1980s before the Sino-British Joint Declaration paved the way for the Colonial Government to clear it, emphasised the chaos and disorder of a *'laissez-faire* society, with none of the redeeming features of an established government' and whose 33,000 inhabitants translated into 3 million per square mile. In his words:

> A walk in the Walled City is a real journey through darkness. An imaginative circus or fairground entrepreneur couldn't devise some of the horrors of the place. Only inches above your head there are spiders' webs of wire and cables held together, it often seems, only by real spiders' webs tying up the dirt and grime of decades. It is advisable to wear a waterproof cap to avoid being drenched by the constant drips of water. You also have to watch you don't slip into the puddles of slime and mulched rubbish. Walls are damp and seemingly in the terminal stages of leprosy. Very quickly you lose any sense of direction. It is possible to go in at ground-floor level, wander through the warren-like passages and come out on the sixth floor without apparently having climbed any stairs. These dwellings are built honeycomb-fashion, one backing on to the next without rhyme or reason. They continue a full fifteen storeys high. Police once discovered a heroin factory whose owners had hidden drugs by pushing them through loose bricks in the walls: it took the authorities more than half a day to find the other side of the wall, so chaotically constructed are these dwellings.[23]

Yet if the Walled City constituted an extreme level of disorder, few would have denied that it belonged to a continuum of disorder and density within the urban areas, running the gamut through Mong Kok, other parts of Kowloon, and Central.[24] Naturally, in the context of the 1984 agreement, the British Government sought permission to tear down the wall, so that it would not 'leave behind such an inglorious legacy in 1997'.[25]

The most important means of establishing order was the building of public high-rise housing estates, beginning in the early 1950s and accelerating after the Shek Kip Mei fire of 1953 killed two people and rendered more than 50,000 people, mostly recent immigrants from China, homeless. As Alan Smart has shown, this housing programme was only partly about providing safe housing for shanty town squatters; it was also a means of resettling rural villagers whose land was desired for Government infrastructure projects, for example reservoirs.[26] Indeed, this is one of the areas in which the discrete challenges of the urban and rural areas came together. Nonetheless, in the prevailing discourse concerning the earliest housing estates, the problems of urban disorder, especially the sanitary conditions and fire dangers of squatters' housing, predominated.

Although the squatter problem was often attributed to immigration from China, Goodstadt showed in 1968 that the connection was not

Figure 6 Squatters, Tiu Keng Leng, Kowloon, *c.* 1952. Such ramshackle housing could be devastated by fires, landslides, and other disasters.

as straightforward as people often assumed. Squatters, he wrote, were not necessarily recent immigrants themselves; indeed, immigrants appeared, in the first instance, to choose 'conventional' housing in the overcrowded urban tenements. The proliferation of squatting was, however, related to immigration, because the private housing market had failed to keep up with Hong Kong's burgeoning population. Further, because prewar housing stock was subject to rent controls, landlords did not have an incentive to spend money improving conditions. As a result, a secondary market spread, in which primary tenants sub-let squalid apartments at ever-increasing (and illegal) rents. Squatters were often former private apartment residents who preferred illegal squatting to continued living in expensive yet inadequate apartments. In other cases, tenants who were suddenly evicted lacked the leisure time to search for new accommodation that was, in any case, inadequate. Goodstadt put it starkly: 'When the difference between conditions in conventional [private] housing and those of squatter huts is so small, it is no wonder that people are willing to flee from high rents to wooden shacks.' The rational choice calculation was further skewed by the public housing policies themselves; squatters had a greater chance of being 'resettled' into public housing than tenement dwellers did.[27] No doubt it was for this reason that, by the end of the

[108]

1960s, emphasis increasingly shifted toward making new public housing available for those still living in first-generation public estates.[28]

The discourse also emphasised the tremendous speed with which the housing was built. According to Colonial Secretary C. B. Burgess, speaking in 1962, the Government was at the time of his speech adding a new 'multi-storey block' every nine days, with a total of 200 since 1955.[29] In late 1970, Acting Governor Sir Hugh Norman-Walker commemorated the 500th such block, and the 50th estate school; he cited the Programme, which had been begun in great haste 'with a view to conversion and improvement in future years', as 'characteristic of the hope and energy that have inspired the people of Hong Kong to overcome obstacles, shortages and deprivation and with our sole resource – our people – to create a thriving, vigorous, forward-looking community on barren hillsides and land reclaimed from the sea'. He pointed out that the buildings' standards had risen over time, with new buildings replacing the earlier communal washrooms and water and electricity supplies with private ones, and with the buildings now extending to sixteen storeys to 'free more ground space for public use; schools, restaurants, and welfare premises are provided in separate buildings, and this building which I am opening to-day introduces a further improvement of greater living space for each person'.[30] By 1976, a British Information Services 'fact sheet' on Hong Kong boasted that the Hong Kong Housing Authority directly provided housing for some 1.84 million people in 57 estates, and would be able to house an additional 1.5 million people by 1983. As the fact sheet noted, the Authority 'plans, builds, and manages all public housing estates, with the Housing Department serving as its executive arm'.[31]

Yet if the public housing estates solved the basic problem of shelter for many squatters, they were not without problems. First, as Sir Hugh's speech quoted above acknowledged, the initial standards, though a clear improvement over homelessness and lean-tos, were modest; the flats were small, and offered such basic facilities as water, toilets, and electricity only communally. The increased sturdiness of the shelter compared to squatters' quarters was offset by a decline in hygiene standards. A 1970 Foreign and Commonwealth Office (FCO) brief in preparation for a Hong Kong visit by Parliamentary Undersecretary Anthony Royle referred to many of the estates as 'squalid in the extreme': 'those compelled to occupy these estates seem to have little or no desire to keep the buildings and their surroundings tidy; in the absence of planned facilities (e.g. shops, eating places) hawkers abound'.[32] Leo Goodstadt's 1968 study concurred: hygiene and cleanliness in cooking fell by the wayside in the face of overcrowding, particularly since 'many domestic units are used for industrial and commercial purposes as well as living'.[33]

[109]

Figure 7 The early public housing estates were very basic. Resettlement Estate, Wang Tau Hom, Kowloon, 1960s.

Aside from the flats' modest character, they also could promote anomie. Morris Berkowitz, in a 1968 article in the scholarly *Journal of the Royal Asiatic Society Hong Kong Branch*, wrote that Hakka villagers, relocated to flats near Taipo Market because their ancestral land was needed for the Plover Cove reservoir (see below), failed to integrate into their new urban environments. 'They have not become, in any meaningful sense, urban residents. They are now basically urban villagers living in a ghetto rather far removed from contact with their new physical neighbors in Taipo market.' Not only had they remained mentally and culturally segregated from their neighbours; they also showed 'signs of structural problems in the economic sphere, which may soon spread to other aspects of social life, such as family organisation and social control over children'. Such problems were worst for those unable to speak Cantonese, and for the families in which the male head of household was unemployed (even when an adequate income was available through remissions or collecting rents).[34] Goodstadt, also writing in 1968, made the same point but with opposite language: housing shortages had *prevented* the creation of 'villages' in urban Hong Kong, as people were indiscriminately thrown together without respect to linguistic or family considerations.[35] The resulting potential breakdown of law and order was nearly universal: some squatter areas remained 'largely unpoliced and unregulated by Government'. Goodstadt noted that racketeers proliferated, and there was a 'real danger of open disaffection' and a 'grave political danger that these squatter colonies might become a law unto themselves as one well-known area (Rennies Mill) was until 1961'. By contrast, in the public housing estates, where people could not choose their neighbours, the uprooting from family and other networks had seen the emergence of 'marked "teddy-boy" tendencies' among adolescents.[36]

Similarly, long-time *SCMP* art critic Nigel Cameron, in his 1978 history of Hong Kong, described 'human problems of alarming proportions' in the densely populated high-rises, resulting from the breakdown of previous social bonds:

Especially for people who a few years ago were mostly villagers, the impersonality of life in a forest of high-rise buildings (ill-equipped with shopping, transport, amusement, and other communal facilities) is humanly destructive. For those born and brought up in such an environment the results are unknowable but probably menacing. The problem is not unique to Hong Kong, but in the Colony it is more acute than in many other places because of the high density of people in any given room-space, and because of the basically rural background of the over-twenty-five age group.

[111]

The only defence for the Government, Cameron wrote, was that its leaders simply did not know what else to do in the face of such a large number of squatters and homeless, rendered more pressing in the aftermath of the Shek Kip Mei fire. Nonetheless, the results were dispiriting, and without any 'real excuses' in a city as wealthy as Hong Kong. Cameron highlighted the noise growing out of overcrowded living conditions:

> The radio, the radios of all the neighbours, the TV sets of the better-off, chatter their Chinese, jangle and bang and screech out their Cantonese opera, with remorseless advertising punctuating the programmes every few moments. And the machine-gun clatter of mahjong played at speed and with a verve only the southern Chinese manage to work up, forms a kind of ground base of sound like that in a textile factory. There may indeed be several small factories nearby adding their quota of noise.

More alarming, though, was the breakdown of law and order: 'Gangs of youths terrorize the populace, monopolize play areas to exclusion of younger children, or of rival gangs. The incidence of robberies, murders, and rape rises sharply as old living customs and familiar ways break down under unaccustomed and inconvenient new conditions.'[37]

Naturally, the police were the first line of British contact with criminal urban disorder. According to Georgina Sinclair, Hong Kong's police force blended characteristics of metropolitan-style civil police practice and Irish/colonial-style paramilitary practice, with the former predominating in Victoria and Kowloon and the latter predominating in the rural areas of the New Territories.[38] In the face of extreme events such as riots, though, the distinction could be blurred. A 1988 *New Statesman & Society* article quoted former Hong Kong police commissioner Roy Henry describing the colony's approach to public disorder as 'paramilitary' – and lamented that Hong Kong's methods were, with Henry's help, being transferred to Britain.[39] Fictional depictions of the police emphasised corruption and brutality – sometimes critically, but in other cases as part of the necessary price for maintaining order. One of the themes of John Gordon Davis's 1979 novel *Typhoon* was that even a would-be honest officer in the post-reform 1970s, Bernard Champion, found acceptance of bribery an essential part of his job: accepting bribes allowed staff sergeants to pressure triad syndicates, and the resulting cash reserves allowed the police to offer rewards for information when it was needed quickly. A related theme of *Typhoon* was that, although such instrumental corruption endured, the anti-corruption drive of the early 1970s had weakened the police force's ability to maintain order, allowing the triads to spin out of control.

Beyond policing, the Government could bring zoning laws to bear. Leeming noted that by the early 1970s, the Government had increasingly attempted to separate uses, for example through the use of leases that limited the types of activities permitted. Such actions, in turn, could stem from commercial considerations, such as when those purchasing offices argued that allowing factory work and cooking would reduce the building's value. At the time Leeming wrote, in 1977, 'This kind of separation of uses [was] already common, though not universal, in Central District', and was in the process of spreading into nearby Sheung Wan.[40] The Government's approach to addressing overcrowded streets similarly encompassed attempts to separate uses, notably in its efforts to tackle the 'complex of social utility combined with social disorderliness which is called the hawker problem'. In short, Government promoted hawker licensing, and their relocation from the streets to licensed bazaars.[41]

Some of the problems identified above stemmed from rapid population growth, the failure of the private housing market to keep up with demand, and the initial focus of public housing efforts almost exclusively on the basic problem of shelter. As we will see below, between the late 1950s and early 1970s, the Government shifted its efforts more in the direction of comprehensive town planning. In doing so, it simultaneously sought to relieve urban overcrowding and make use of the 'empty spaces' of the New Territories.

Modernising the New Territories

We have seen that the urban areas, particularly Kowloon, were described as overcrowded and disorderly. By contrast, observers frequently conceptualised the New Territories as virtually empty space; what was not empty was undeveloped. In either case, the New Territories were a canvas on which British administrators could paint in modernising brushstrokes. If Kowloon, in the prevailing discourse, was inherently unknowable because of its chaos, the New Territories were equally unknowable because they belonged to a different time and place. In both cases, British discourse displayed the hard-won accomplishment of knowing the unknowable, even while emphasising the achievement of bringing order and modernity to the chaotic or backward.

According to Denis Bray, the one-time Secretary of Home Affairs, 'In the fifties the New Territories were terra incognita for urban dwellers – and that included everyone of any seniority in the government.' Referring to Tai Po, he writes,

> This was a farming community and village life continued in very much the way that it had done for generations. Few villages had access to roads.

None had electricity, running water, sewage, or refuse collection services. Where communal services were found they had been put in by the people themselves.[42]

Austin Coates, in his autobiography *Myself a Mandarin*, likewise described the New Territories around the time of his arrival in 1949 as a place unsullied by modernity, of either a British or a Chinese variety:

Not exactly China, not exactly Hongkong, this third mental climate was older in its ways of thought, unchanged by the Chinese politics of fifty years, or by the Hongkong sophistications of a century. It was a separate climate, in which emperors were not unknown, since it lived in a corridor of time devolving directly from the distant past.[43]

These postwar descriptions of the contemporary New Territories are not that far removed from Jan Morris's description of their character in the late nineteenth century. Morris treats Boundary Street at the edge of Kowloon as the edge of civilisation: 'Beyond were the mysteries of China, where superstition reigned, where bandits and tigers lurked, where ne'er-do-wells went to gamble with the natives, and unspeakable things went on in opium dens.'[44] Indeed, if 1898 had brought this area under British control, observers continued to focus on its antiquity and bucolic timelessness. Governor Grantham, in his memoirs, emphasised the 'tranquil and ancient' properties of life in the New Territories in the 1950s: 'The hand of the twentieth century had, seemingly, scarcely touched it.'[45] John Gordon Davis, in his 1974 novel *The Years of the Hungry Tiger*, described the New Territories of the late 1950s as 'still the old China of before the battles long ago' – having escaped the alternative modernisations of British Hong Kong and Republican China.[46] Even in the early 1970s, the aforementioned *Hong Kong Official Guide* referred to the 'comparative emptiness of the farming areas to the north of Kowloon, known as the New Territories'. It noted, further, that 'the rural areas correspond much more to the visitor's idea of traditional China than anything else in the Colony'.[47] This image was created not only by the rural landscape, but also by the odd personal appearance of the villagers; for example, in a 1960 book on Hong Kong designed for Malayan English-speaking secondary school students, in a series entitled 'Our Neighbours', Derek Webb lovingly described the 'traditional' clothing of the Hakkas, including the hats and aprons they wove, with 'great pride', on a 'crude hand-loom', despite the 'abundance of cheap, mass-produced clothes, close at hand in the towns'.[48] Even in 1985, in his children's book, Anthony Shang described a modernity that was only beginning to assert itself: 'In villages like Ping Shan toddlers are tended by old women, who chat in alleys while old men sit in tea-houses, talking and playing cards. Senior clansmen and rich farmers form councils to decide village affairs. At night a watchman beats his drum every hour on his rounds.' Shang continued, however, to note that village tradition was quickly being supplanted by modernity with its industrial estates, colour televisions, and Japanese cars.[49]

Not only did the New Territories remain untouched by modernity in the immediate postwar years; they were also remote from urban Hong Kong. A 1956 visit by Australian Wing Commander M. A. Andersen to the RAF Headquarters at Little Sai Wan noted that although the camp was only ten miles from Hong Kong City, a lack of civilian buses made even this distance formidable.[50] A late 1960s book on Hong Kong's police force emphasised that much of the New Territories was 'inaccessible to vehicles', so that 'remote communities are visited by Village Penetration Patrols which go out for two or three days at a time, sleeping and feeding in the villages they visit'.[51] Susanna Hoe, in the context of describing a rare 1997 foray into the New Territories, opined that 'It's always healthy for us colonials to be faced with the fact that Hong Kong did not begin in 1841', implying that modernity had still not quite overcome the pre-1841 way of life. She went on to lament that 'Not having a car, we have not explored the New Territories nearly as well as we should have liked – now time has run out.'[52]

If 'tranquil and ancient' qualities could be attributed to the New Territories, their wildness was also noted. Throughout the 1960s, there were frequent reports of wild animals. For example, Dan Waters recalled an early 1950s rumour of a leopard roaming the New Territories, while a 1965 front-page article in the *SCMP* had to reassure readers that the recent New Territories killer was not a tiger after all, but merely a wild dog.[53] Derek Webb, writing in 1961, insisted that tigers and leopards in the colony were 'visitors' from across the border, but noted that a leopard had been reported in 1957 around Sha Tin: 'It attacked and killed a number of animals before crossing back into China, where it is believed to have been shot, some eight miles from the border.' He also described such animals as the Chinese Spotted Leopard Cat, monkeys, the Scaly Anteater, the Barking Deer, and the wild boar.[54] Not that wild animals always confined themselves to the New Territories; in 1968 the *FEER* reported that a buffalo had made its way to Central's Des Voeux Road.[55]

Beginning in the 1950s, deliberate efforts were made to develop and urbanise the New Territories, building planned towns, roads, reservoirs, and other infrastructure projects. In large part, these actions constituted a response to a refugee crisis that had resulted in overcrowded urban areas and contributed to dangerous and inhumane squatter

areas, as well as water shortages. The latter problem, in turn, necessitated the removal of some long-established villages whose location
interfered with desirable spots for reservoirs. Against these conditions
stood geopolitical realities; because of both China's proximity and the
cold war context, Britain could not afford to neglect the worst effects
of overcrowding.

Yet deliberate, planned modernisation also reflected currents in postwar British culture. If, as Chapter 2 has shown, one strand of British
culture in Hong Kong included the idea of unrestrained capitalism,
another followed the view hegemonic in 1950s Britain that technoc-
racy could bring the benefits of civilisation to colonies, former colonies, and developing countries. Guy Ortolano has written that C. P.
Snow's famous 1959 'Two Cultures' lecture at Cambridge was part of
a wider argument for exactly this line of thinking; not only should sci-
entists and other experts take the lead in planning British society, but
they should encourage industrial development in the Third World as
well. Doing so would not only help people in the former colonies, but
would also extend British influence. F. R. Leavis's blistering response
three years later was part of an argument that the scientific and industrial revolutions had been, in many ways, wrong turns, and battles
that had already been lost in Britain could still be won in undeveloped countries. Ortolano argues that Snow's position was easily the
more influential one in the early 1960s, though within the next decade
the anti-planning and anti-developmentalist positions had both gained
considerable strength within British culture and politics.[56] The modernisation of the New Territories had elements of the British culture
of 'planning'. In addition, both the development of the New Territories
and the use of zoning in Kowloon and Hong Kong Island can also be
seen in the long context of colonial urban planning, in sites as diverse
as India, Nigeria, Zanzibar, and Malaya. Colonial planning could focus
not only on commercial development or separating home and work in
order to relieve urban congestion, but also on sanitation and disease
control, racial segregation, and the use of architecture to project imperial authority.[57]

Modernisation efforts required the Government to retreat significantly from the long-established British imperial practice of allowing
indigenous elites to continue to rule according to 'traditional' laws and
customs, except where their offence against British norms was simply too strong to countenance. This practice was not only accepted
across the Empire as far more cost-effective than a more transfor-
mational governance would have been, but, in the case of the New
Territories, also reflected that the initial British assumption of power
in 1898 had been met with armed resistance.[58] For this reason, as we

will see in Chapter 5, New Territories magistrates worked closely with village leaders, styled themselves as traditional 'mandarins', and sometimes settled disputes according to Chinese statutes. Traditional lineage-based inheritance laws were also left unchanged so that, in contrast to the rest of the territory, the New Territories included villages in which land ownership remained clan-based and restricted to males – indeed, nearly two decades after the change of sovereignty, male villager land ownership remained an anomaly in a SAR in which most property owners leased the land from the Government and legal equality between the sexes was the norm. This non-interference principle had to be compromised when villager land was required for an infrastructure project. The delicate negotiations with village leaders also served as a reminder that the New Territories were not as empty in reality as they could appear in the discourse.

The discursive emphasis on the comparative 'emptiness' of the New Territories shared similarities with the theme of 'virgin lands' within the broader discourse of settler colonialism, a theme that was often applied to such locales as the British Dominions, Israel, or the nineteenth-century United States.[59] However, in contrast to these cases, in Hong Kong's New Territories the evocation of emptiness did not herald the migration of settlers from the colonial metropole itself. Rather, only the development – planned towns, roads, reservoirs, and other infrastructure – was British. The migrants who would populate the virgin lands were Chinese, even if not always indigenous.

The New Territories and town planning

Roger Bristow's academic survey, *Hong Kong's New Towns: A Selective Review* (1989) directly linked the development of town planning to British interwar and postwar models; Kowloon Tong, precluded because of flight paths into and out of nearby Kai Tak airport from building high-rises, remained the province of housing derivative of Raymond Unwin's Letchworth and Hampstead Garden Suburb, though 'for Hong Kong, the introduction of the detached two-storey residence set in its own individual garden, with the adjacent communal open space in the tradition of the English village green, was as revolutionary as it was inappropriate'.[60] By contrast, in the New Towns beginning in the late 1950s, not facing similar constraint on building heights, planners applied models from Britain's own postwar new towns to the density of Hong Kong. Bristow argued that the British model was widely influential internationally, and that Hong Kong, through the 'influence of expatriate British planners, and through the training in Britain of Hong Kong's Chinese professionals', was a key manifestation of

British influence. As Bristow noted, Sir Patrick Abercrombie's *Greater London Plan* (1944) had five key assumptions, four of which were relevant to Hong Kong's new town model: 'that no new industry would be admitted to London and the Home Counties except in special cases; that decentralisation of persons and industry from the congested centre should take place; that the total population of the whole area would not increase; that the port would remain; and that new planning powers would become available'.[61] In a brief report in 1948, Abercrombie applied his vision of town planning directly to an analysis of Hong Kong, noting that in Hong Kong 'two special characteristics of its problems at once emerge, neither of them perhaps unique, but each present to a highly intense degree: firstly the shortage of land for any sort of urban expansion or quarter: secondly an unlimited reservoir of possible immigration'. He explicitly contrasted the land shortage of Hong Kong with Manhattan, 'where space is short, being limited to a peninsula, but where there is plenty of adjacent land available'.[62] In making this statement, he appears not to have envisioned the New Territories as a suitable place for urban expansion; although the colony, with its firm border at the Sham Chun (Shenzhen) River, was certainly much smaller than New York City, other planners would quickly begin to discover that the New Territories had potential for conversion into a series of planned towns.[63]

According to Bristow, both in Britain and in Hong Kong the paramount concern was the congestion of the city centre, and as a result care was taken to place the new towns far enough away from the centre, and including enough employment opportunities, to discourage their simply turning into bedroom communities for the main urban centre – an aim, we might note, that has been by no means entirely realised either in the UK or in Hong Kong. In the case of Hong Kong, of course, land scarcity necessitated a high-rise adaptation of the British new town model – an innovation that, Bristow observed, had been pioneered in Singapore.[64]

The first planned town, Tsuen Wan–Kwai Chung, began development in 1959, in a process that quickly caused tensions between Government officials and villagers who had traditional rights to the land now desired by the Government. As the historian James Hayes, also a former long-time colonial official in the New Territories, points out, relocating the villagers through an exchange of rural land for urban real estate required tedious negotiations. In addition to the villagers, Hayes notes that by the mid-1950s Tsuen Wan's population of 80,000 included a significant contingent who were part of a new 'squatter housing and squatter industry' and who 'had little regard for authority'; they, too, had to be rehoused. Indeed, Hayes suggests that Tsuen

Wan was 'conceivably the most difficult place to start the process'. During the 1960s, similar planned urbanisation took place in Sha Tin and Tuen Mun, necessitating the resettling and compensation of some villagers, while others were able to remain in their villages as the cities grew up around them. In the early 1970s, this often cumbersome early urbanisation of the New Territories was subsumed within a centrally planned New Towns Programme, with these three towns christened as the first New Towns.[65]

As explained in a 1981 memo from the Sha Tin District Office, a Government plan launched in October 1972 to house 1.8 million people by the mid-1980s envisioned placing over half of them in the New Towns already being built at Sha Tin, Tsuen Wan, and Tuen Mun. These New Towns followed a principle of 'balanced development', combining housing, industry, recreational facilities, schools, local shops, playgrounds, and open space. Referring specifically to Sha Tin, the memo noted that the plan was to provide a 50 per cent–10 percent–40 per cent ratio of governmental rental housing, governmental Home Ownership Scheme housing, and private housing; the latter would include luxury accommodation and middle-class housing, with an aim of creating a 'properly balanced community with a complete range of housing options'.[66] Belying its official commitment to laissez-faire, the Government, according to a GIS booklet, proactively addressed the land needs of an expanding industrial sector by building 'new industrial satellites', the first at Kwun Tong, 'where hills were leveled and the soil dumped in the sea to create land for factory sites and housing'. Beyond creating new physical space, the Government went so far as to plan specific population targets, with 530,000 residents planned for Tuen Mun and 550,000 planned for Sha Tin.[67]

Continued population growth combined with Government planning resulted in the thorough transformation of the New Territories before the end of the colonial period, particularly as private developers followed infrastructure developments into previously under-utilised areas. Late-colonial discourse routinely noted the speed of the transformations in language familiar from descriptions of Hong Kong Island and Kowloon. James Kirkup's travel book described the New Territories in 1970 as a rapidly changing area: 'a mountain that was there on my last visit will have been moved away into an inlet of the South China Sea, or a valley of villages will have been inundated to make a reservoir. New apartment blocks for industrial workers, farm workers and refugees are always going up, as are new factories and scientific installations.'[68] Similarly, a 1985 children's book marketed in Britain profiled a recent illegal immigrant living in Tuen Mun as reflecting that the changes were happening at a bewildering pace: 'I grew up in a country where ideas often took years, or even lifetimes, to be developed into working projects. The skyline here in Hong Kong can change overnight.'[69] The aforementioned GIS booklet acknowledged this change, but argued that traditional village life had managed to adapt to this physical modernisation.[70]

Infrastructure

Taking an active governmental role in modernising Hong Kong might seem, in theory, to conflict with the meme of unbridled capitalism explored in Chapter 2. In part, we can attribute this contradiction to officials' simple recognition of the necessity of dealing with disorderliness. In part, it is explained when we recognise that the Colonial Government's role in the economy was always more extensive than advertised, and that promoting an environment conducive to oligopolistic capitalism could, in fact, be compatible with Government intervention. On the other hand, one way in which the preference for 'non-intervention' displayed itself was in the Government's reliance on partnerships between State and private sectors, both commercial and charitable. This was true of small-beer projects. For example, in the mid-1960s when the Urban Council promoted community televisions in public venues, it relied on donations to supply the television sets.[71] Likewise, in the early 1970s, the Department of Textile Industries at Hong Kong Technical College – the forerunner of what would eventually become the Hong Kong Polytechnic University – accepted from the British firm George Hattersley and Sons the permanent loan of a loom.[72] It was, though, also true of large-scale developmental projects, such as the construction of New Towns: as noted in the programme for a 1997 exhibition at the Edinburgh City Art Centre – *Hong Kong: City of Tomorrow* – the eighth New Town, Tin Shui Wai in the Yuen Long District in the northwest New Territories, was a joint project of the Government and Li Ka-shing's company, Cheung Kong (Holdings) Ltd. According to the programme, they had 'jointly provided the substantive investment needed for this new town. In return, the new town is a blend of public sector and private sector accommodation fully supported with community facilities, including schools, provision for the elderly, landscaped areas and amenities for residents.'[73] Such partnerships illustrated the Government's commitment to 'positive non-interventionism' – it acted to create public goods that no business would find profitable to initiate – but also, where possible, to maintaining a limited direct Government role in Hong Kong's economy.[74]

At the same time, these infrastructure projects, along with what Sun Yat-sen called the 'English example of good government',[75] offered the best example of a proactive approach to transforming Hong Kong into a first-tier modern city. This theme can be seen in the discourse surrounding the problem of water supply, specifically during the 1963–64 drought, and the building of the Cross-Harbour Tunnel (opened in 1972), the Mass Transit Railway (MTR) subway system (1979), and the Chek Lap Kok Airport (1998). This chapter will close with a brief examination of the first and last of these.

All four projects grew out of the phenomenon, as Governor Robert Black explained in August 1963 to journalists gathered at the Foreign Correspondents' Club, of Hong Kong's 'spectacle of a great and vital population, confined in a small space which lacks the raw materials necessary for industry, nevertheless making a tremendous success of its community'.[76] This particular speech was delivered against the backdrop of an emergency shortfall in Hong Kong's water supply, resulting from a six-month drought that, according to *The Economist* two months earlier, had led to 'the rare and horrendous nightmare of a modern over-crowded city slipping towards the brink of water famine'. That article noted that those who had their own domestic supply were confined to a 'four-hour ration every fourth day', while those without their own running water 'have indulgence of supply every two days by queueing patiently for hours in the scorched streets with their kerosene tins'.[77] Nearly two decades later, James Clavell's *Noble House* would memorialise this water crisis, depicting Casey, the young American woman in search of quick riches, learning about it the hard way as she struggles with buckets in the lavatory in the eponymous trading company's headquarters. While she feels 'furious that her shoes had got splashed', she unknowingly uses an extravagant amount of water.[78]

The 1963–64 water crisis, aside from being an emergency requiring immediate measures, also underscored longer-term infrastructure needs.[79] As a July 1963 Far Eastern Department confidential memorandum noted, in the immediate crisis the Government had little choice but to turn to neighbouring Guangdong for assistance, both because of actual need and because of the likely reaction of Hong Kong Chinese if mainland offers were rebuffed. In the long term, though, such dependence was unwise because of the threat that China would use it to blackmail the colony for political concessions. As a result, the Government sought to draw on Chinese help in the medium term by building a pipeline from Guangdong, while aiming by 1968 to attain self-sufficiency through building a major new reservoir at Plover Cove. The memorandum held out the prospect that the 'political price to be paid [would be] no more than the favourable publicity in Hong Kong which the CPG [Communist Party Government] can hope to

[121]

extract' – a price that would be much smaller than the 'embarrassment which could result from internal unrest and dissatisfaction' because of unrelieved water shortages.[80]

Governor Black spent most of his Foreign Correspondents' Club speech highlighting the Government's 'Operation Water' – in which the Government was importing large quantities of water from the Pearl River by tanker – along with potential future plans, including the building of additional reservoirs. He also devoted several paragraphs to revisiting the history of the Government's actions since the early 1950s, in which large-scale capital-intensive projects had marched in lock-step with the colony's surging postwar population. It would be easy for a critic to overlook these accomplishments during the present crisis, he noted – he quipped that some may have even blamed the Government for the 'drought itself' – but in fact the accomplishment already had been considerable. In the decade since 1952, the Government had built the Tai Lam Chung reservoir, arranged with the Po On County Government to tap into the Shum Chun (Shenzhen) reservoir, and had begun pumping water from the sea. The filtration capacity had grown from 43 million gallons per day to 97 million, and the service reservoir capacity had grown from 52 million to 150 million.[81]

Despite this ongoing achievement, the recent drought had required the emergency measures of Operation Water, whose implementation had been 'complex to a degree': Black recounted in tedious detail the

> actual chartering of tankers of a tonnage suitable for operation in the Pearl River, the cleaning out of these tankers, the planning, siting and construction of the berths and dolphins to receive them, the laying of pipes to carry the raw water into our supply system, the reconnaissance of the Pearl River to make salinity tests and to determine specific points for drawing the water.

He went into even more technical detail in describing the prospects for rendering sea water drinkable. Ultimately, he invoked the idea of a potentially permanent technical revolution, as he expected that population would continue growing indefinitely. Only briefly, near the end of his speech, did he allude to the 'possibility of obtaining additional supplies of water with the assistance of our neighbor'.[82]

The crisis threatened to present an image of Government inadequacy – always a danger for a government that highlighted its laissez-faire bona fides. This is, no doubt, why Black took such pains to point out what the Government had already been doing for the past decade, along with emergency measures taken and long-range improvements still to come. Likewise, Hong Kong's United Kingdom

[122]

Trade Commissioner emphasised in a June 1963 letter to the Board of Trade in London that the existing infrastructure was more than adequate for a year with normal rainfall; sadly, the 'last "normal" year was 1961'. As happened so often in discussions of living conditions in Hong Kong, the Trade Commissioner made a point of comparing Hong Kong standards to those elsewhere in Asia: even in the unusual times of May 1962–May 1963, the four-hour daily supply did not cause 'undue hardship', and those dependent on communal supplies – 'including 500,000 squatters' – were 'doubtless better off than if they had been imbibing cholera and typhoid in the unrationed supplies provided in most cities of the Far East'. At the same time, industry's water supply had been 'virtually unrestricted'. Indeed, it was only the 'driest ever recorded' winter of 1962–63, coming on the heels of an already low rainfall the previous year, that had rendered the existing arrangements inadequate.[83]

As this example suggests, during the 1963–64 water shortage crisis, the Hong Kong Government carefully managed public opinion. As one Government official noted in a confidential memorandum to the British Chargé d'Affaires in Peking in August 1963, people had generally accepted the water restrictions with 'fortitude'; still, it was 'important to convince them that Government is doing everything possible to alleviate the situation both within the short and long terms'. No doubt the Governor's detailed speech the very next day to the Foreign Correspondents' Club, cited above, was part of this effort; the memorandum noted that the press had been asking questions about the building of the pipeline to China, and 'sooner or later we must expect to come under increasing pressure to comment on the apparent lack of progress'.[84] In explaining developments, the Government's hands were tied somewhat by a fear of wrecking the ongoing negotiations with the Guangdong authorities by revealing too much in public. The Guangdong officials had been encouraging, but needed reassurance that Hong Kong would bear the cost and would not back out if adequate rainfall suddenly appeared. They also rebuffed any suggestion that the project was mutually beneficial, for example by providing irrigation in Guangdong; this meant that the pipeline was being framed as an act of Chinese beneficence, pure and simple.[85] While the negotiations were proceeding, Governor Black felt constrained not to 'make any statement which might be taken to imply criticism of the CPG for the slowness of developments'; as a result, he could not address press speculation.[86]

Still, the GIS frequently released Daily Information Bulletins updating the public on rainfall, the amount of water in the reservoirs, the possibility of relaxing water restrictions, actions the Government was taking, and other water-related topics. For example, a 12 August press release featured an explanation from the Director of Public Works as to why restrictions were tighter in August than they had been in May, even though there was now more water in storage. 'The answer is simple', he explained: in May, the prospect of the rainy season was still ahead, whereas in August it no longer was.[87] In explaining the Government's actions, a balance was constantly struck between dealing with the current crisis and making long-range plans to place Hong Kong on a more secure footing. A 1 October press release announcing immediate plans to launch the 'River Indus Flood Pumping Scheme', designed to extract surplus flood water from the river and be fully operational by late 1965, emphasised the grand scale of the project through mentioning the estimated cost and the eventual annual water yield. It also included both technical and superlative language that highlighted the project's prudent sophistication: a 'low inflatable dam of neoprene-coated nylon'; a 'novel and inexpensive type of dam'. Finally, it linked the project to the Plover Cove reservoir that would be ready by 1968.[88]

The medium-term building of reservoirs, and the short-term measures to address the immediate water crisis, dealt with a basic primary need. By contrast, the last major project undertaken by the Colonial Government, the construction of a new international airport at Chek Lap Kok, aimed more at staking Hong Kong's place as a first-tier city. The Kai Tak airport in the heart of Kowloon was increasingly inadequate to the needs of a major global city, and significant expansion was not feasible. It also was a famously awkward airport in which to land, and numerous writers noted the frightening or disconcerting experience of peering into urban apartment windows while passing by at close distance.[89] As the impending change of sovereignty approached, building a new airport also took on an added symbolic importance as a demonstration of Hong Kong's continued attractiveness for international capital, a vote of confidence in the post-Handover future, and more broadly, Britain's modernising colonial legacy. As a 1981 article in the *FEER* argued, during the period after Governor MacLehose had broached the topic of the expiration of the New Territories lease but before Margaret Thatcher's fabled visit to Beijing, 'In the absence of any clear policy statement on 1997, Tin Shui Wai [the eighth New Town] and the new airport will be the best "money-where-your-mouth-is" gesture that will allow investors to "put their hearts at ease" over Hongkong's future.'[90] Following the 1984 Sino-British Joint Declaration, the airport came to symbolise continuity: by starting a major project that would require debt lasting well beyond the Handover, the Hong Kong Government could provide a tangible demonstration that no radical changes were in store. Finally, in addition to facilitating Hong Kong's postcolonial competitiveness and demonstrating continuity, the airport could cement Britain's legacy as a colonial moderniser. As Jonathan Dimbleby put it in his 1997 history of the Patten years, the 'development of the new airport was a precondition for sustaining the phenomenal growth rates to which [the business community] had become accustomed'.[91] The *SCMP* referred to the project in 1992 as 'the springboard that will launch Hongkong into the next century'.[92] A September 1991 FCO 'Background Brief' underscored the airport's symbolic importance, noting that it would be operational in 1997; it left unsaid the obvious point that this cementing of Britain's claims to have bequeathed its former barren rock with a final, lasting symbol of modernity was timed to coincide with the Handover year. The brief further noted the careful, detailed planning that had already gone into the airport's building. Going back to 1973, the Hong Kong Government had explored alternative sites to the Kai Tak Airport; it had undertaken a 'series of sub-regional studies' leading to a broader 'Territorial Development Strategy'. The brief emphasised the airport's long-term and strategic underpinnings, and framed this discussion by noting that throughout the 1980s, 'considerable thought [had] been given to the question of how best to provide for Hong Kong's further expansion'.[93]

Finally announced by the Governor in October 1989, four short months after the Tiananmen Square killings, the Hong Kong Government's plan to build a new airport immediately became a political football, with the PRC objecting repeatedly to the airport's handling. As numerous commentators have noted, usually in a tone of bemusement at the Chinese Government's unreasonable paranoia, Beijing often accused the British of using the airport as one last grand boondoggle, a way to enrich its companies while leaving the Hong Kong treasury depleted. Frank Welsh, whose previous books had included a 'personal memoir' of the Duke of Westminster, an 'insider's view' of the City of London, two books on public enterprises, and a book of horror-themed short-stories, briefly summarised the airport's politics in the 1997 reissue of his 600-page Hong Kong history: 'Suspicions were aroused – quite wrongly – that the British Government was proposing to empty the colonial coffers for the benefit of British construction companies'.[94] Percy Cradock, who had moved from the Foreign Office to become a political advisor first to Thatcher and then to Major, referred in his memoir to 'ominous mutterings from Peking' by the end of 1989; they 'related to cost, fears that the plan might be over-ambitious and, more precisely, that it could leave the Special Administrative Region in a weaker financial position in 1997'. Noting the relative subtlety of these complaints, he concluded nonetheless that they constituted a 'more refined version of Deng Xiaoping's worries in 1984 that we would deliberately impoverish the territory before leaving; the airport was seen as a means by which British companies would be enriched and Hong Kong's treasury emptied'.[95] Robert Cottrell, writing in the *Spectator*, agreed that Chinese leaders were being paranoid, but pointed out parenthetically that the awarding of early contracts to British companies, combined with British companies exiting Hong Kong since Jardines 'started the trend' in 1984, made it more difficult for Britain to answer such charges.[96]

Ultimately, the Foreign Office's desire to launch the airport project led the British to agree, in a June 1991 'Memorandum of Understanding', to a fixed level of borrowing to which the Colonial Government could commit without Beijing's approval, and to a stipulated level of fiscal reserves that Hong Kong would have at the time of the Handover, two provisions that undermined any claims that the British were fully in charge until 30 June 1997. Even more significantly, in negotiating the memorandum, Cradock persuaded the Prime Minister, John Major, to commit to visiting Beijing, becoming the first important western leader to do so since the Tiananmen Square massacre two years earlier. According to Stephen Vines, Major's distaste for this latter concession was one of the reasons he determined to sack Governor Wilson, whom he closely associated with the Foreign Office's conciliatory approach to China relations.[97] Governor Patten, as we will see, proved much more willing to stand rhetorically for democracy, even at the cost of alienating Beijing. In the summer of 1991, however, the desire to end the colonial era with a high-level infrastructure project took precedence.

Notes

1 LMA, DRO/101/267, *What Is It?*, p. 2.
2 'From a Barren Rock to a Modern City', *SCMP* (11 April 1993).
3 David Bonavia, *Hong Kong 1997: The Final Settlement* (Hong Kong: FEER, 1985), p. 143.
4 Alexander Grantham, *Via Ports: From Hong Kong to Hong Kong* (Hong Kong: Hong Kong University Press, 1965), p. 3.
5 Jan Morris, *Hong Kong: Epilogue to an Empire* (New York: Random House, 1997), pp. 15–17.
6 John Rylands Library, Rupert E. Davies Collection, DDRd4 4/1, 'Explore Kowloon', *Hong Kong Official Guide*, Vol. III, no. 3 (n.d.), p. 36.
7 Girton College, Cambridge, GCPP Needham 5/1/12, Dorothy Needham diary, 6 September 1971.
8 John Rylands Library, Rupert E. Davies Collection, DDRd4 4/1, 'Nightlife', *Hong Kong Official Guide*, Vol. III, no. 3 (n.d.), p. 71.
9 'Nightlife', p. 69.

10 'Nightlife', p. 72.
11 John Rylands Library, Rupert E. Davies Collection, DDRd4 4/1, 'Shopping', *Hong Kong Official Guide*, Vol. III, no. 3 (n.d.), p. 73.
12 L. F. Goodstadt, 'Urban Housing in Hong Kong', in Ian C. Jarvie and Joseph Agassi (eds), *Hong Kong: A Society in Transition* (New York: Frederick A. Praeger, 1968), pp. 257–98 (pp. 284–5).
13 Frank Leeming, *Street Studies in Hong Kong: Localities in a Chinese City* (Oxford: Oxford University Press, 1977), pp. 9, 21, 35.
14 James Pope-Hennessy, *Half-Crown Colony: A Hong Kong Notebook* (London: Cape, 1969), pp. 15–16.
15 TNA, FCO 40/226, *Policing Hong Kong* (n.d., [1968–69?]), p. 13.
16 F. D. Ommanney, *Fragrant Harbour: A Private View of Hong Kong* (London: Hutchinson, 1962), pp. 125–6.
17 Martin Booth, *Golden Boy: Memories of a Hong Kong Childhood* (New York: St Martin's Press, 2004), pp. 57–8.
18 Leeming, *Street Studies*, pp. 39–40.
19 For an articulation of Britain's 'let sleeping dogs lie' policy toward the Walled City, see FAULDS 3/3/1/1, Edward Heath to Joan Vickers, 24 December 1973.
20 Quoted in Seth Harter, 'Hong Kong's Dirty Little Secret', *Journal of Urban History* 27 (November 2000): 92–113 (p. 92).
21 Bonavia, *Hong Kong 1997*, pp. 26–7; Harter, 'Hong Kong's Dirty Little Secret', pp. 94, 110.
22 Jackie Pullinger, *Chasing the Dragon* (London: Hodder and Stoughton, 2010 [1980]), p. 26.
23 Kevin Rafferty, *City on the Rocks: Hong Kong's Uncertain Future* (New York: Viking, 1989), pp. 366, 367, 374.
24 See also Booth, *Golden Boy*, pp. 131–5.
25 Emily Lau, 'United against a Slum', *FEER* (29 January 1987), p. 28.
26 Alan Smart, *The Shek Kip Mei Myth: Squatters, Fires and Colonial Rule in Hong Kong, 1950–1963* (Hong Kong: Hong Kong University Press, 2006).
27 Goodstadt, 'Urban Housing in Hong Kong', p. 280.
28 Hong Kong Government Information Services Bulletin, 'Bigger Flats for Resettled Families: Reasons why Many Prefer Not to Move', 15 May 1970. FCO 40/306, TNA.
29 C. B. Burgess, *A Problem of People: Extracts from a Statement by a Former Colonial Secretary of Hong Kong* (Hong Kong: Government Printer, n.d.), p. 1.
30 TNA, FCO 40/306, Hong Kong Government Information Services Bulletin, 'Acting Governor Opens 500th Resettlement Block and 50th Estate School: Full Text of Sir Hugh's Speech', 19 November 1970, p. 3.
31 *Fact Sheet: Hong Kong* (London: Central Office of Information, 1976), p. 12.
32 TNA, FCO 40/306, 'Visit of Parliamentary Under Secretary Mr Royle, to Hong Kong, October, 1970'.
33 Goodstadt, 'Urban Housing in Hong Kong', p. 281.
34 Morris I. Berkowitz, 'Plover Cove Village to Taipo Market: A Study in Forced Migration', *Journal of the Royal Asiatic Society Hong Kong Branch* 8 (1968), 96–108 (pp. 103, 107).
35 Goodstadt, 'Urban Housing in Hong Kong', pp. 285–6.
36 Goodstadt, 'Urban Housing in Hong Kong', pp. 287–9.
37 Nigel Cameron, *Hong Kong: The Cultured Pearl* (Hong Kong: Oxford University Press, 1978), pp. 178–81, 186. According to former civil servant Patrick Hase, Cameron's description seriously exaggerates violent crime rates on the estates (personal communication, 15 October 2014).
38 Georgina Sinclair, *At the End of the Line: Colonial Policing and the Imperial Endgame 1945–80* (Manchester and New York: Manchester University Press, 2006), pp. 173–4.
39 Gerry Northam, 'Police Get Their Marching Orders', *New Statesman & Society* 1 (23 September 1988), p. 28.
40 Leeming, *Street Studies*, p. 62.

41 Leeming, *Street Studies*, p. 81. On the 'hawker problem', see Josephine Smart, *The Political Economy of Street Hawkers in Hong Kong* (Hong Kong: Centre for Asian Studies, University of Hong Kong, 1989).

42 Denis Bray, 'Recollections of a Cadet Officer Class II', in Elizabeth Sinn (ed.), *Hong Kong: British Crown Colony, Revisited* (Hong Kong: Centre for Asian Studies, University of Hong Kong, 2001), p. 19.

43 Austin Coates, *Myself a Mandarin: Memoirs of a Special Magistrate* (Hong Kong: Oxford University Press, 1987 [1968]), p. 13.

44 Morris, *Hong Kong*, p. 191.

45 Grantham, *Via Ports*, p. 114.

46 John Gordon Davis, *The Years of the Hungry Tiger* (London: Michael Joseph, 1974), p. 23.

47 John Rylands Library, Rupert E. Davies Collection, DDRd4 4/1, 'Explore New Territories', *Hong Kong Official Guide*, Vol. III, no. 3 (n.d.), p. 41.

48 Derek S. Webb, *Hong Kong* (Singapore: Eastern University Press, 1960), p. 26.

49 Anthony Shang, *Living in Hong Kong* (London and Sydney: Macdonald, 1985), p. 17.

50 ANA, A12187 3/5/AIR Part 2, 'Visit to Hong Kong – Wing Commander M. A. Andersen', 30 October 1956. Compare to *The Borderers' Chronicle: The Journal of the King's Own Scottish Borderers* 24 (31 December 1949), p. 110. King's Own Scottish Borderers Regimental Museum.

51 TNA, FCO 40/226, *Policing Hong Kong* (n.d. [1968–69?]), p. 15.

52 Susanna Hoe, *Watching the Flag Come Down: An Englishwoman in Hong Kong 1987–1997* (Oxford: Holo Books, 2007), p. 194.

53 Dan Waters, 'Hong Kong in the 1950s and '60s: Reminiscences', *Journal of the Hong Kong Branch of the Royal Asiatic Society* 42 (2002): 323–43 (p. 328); 'NT Killer not the "Tiger"', *SCMP* (1 November 1965).

54 Webb, *Hong Kong*, p. 90. As of 2015, wild boars, cows, and monkeys were still occasionally seen.

55 'Traveller's Tales', *FEER* (21 March 1968), p. 509.

56 Guy Ortolano, *The Two Cultures Controversy: Science, Literature and Cultural Politics in Postwar Britain* (Cambridge: Cambridge University Press, 2009); Guy Ortolano, 'Planning the Urban Future in 1960s Britain', *The Historical Journal* 54 (2011): 477–50.

57 E.g. William Cunningham Bissell, *Urban Design, Chaos, and Colonial Power in Zanzibar* (Bloomington: Indiana University Press, 2011); Garth Andrew Myers, 'A Stupendous Hammer: Colonial and Post-Colonial Reconstructions of Zanzibar's Other Side', *Urban Studies* 32 (1995): 1345–59; Ambe J. Njoh, 'Urban Planning as a Tool of Power and Social Control in Colonial Africa', *Planning Perspectives* 24 (2009): 301–17; Liora Bigon, 'Sanitation and Street Layout in Early Colonial Lagos: British and Indigenous Conceptions, 1851–1900', *Planning Perspectives* 20 (2005): 247–69.

58 Patrick Hase, *The Six-Day War of 1899: Hong Kong in the Age of Imperialism* (Hong Kong: Hong Kong University Press, 2008).

59 Lorenzo Veracini, ' "Settler Colonialism": Career of a Concept', *Journal of Imperial and Commonwealth History* 41 (2013): 313–33 (p. 324).

60 Roger Bristow, *Hong Kong's New Towns: A Selective Review* (Hong Kong: Oxford University Press, 1989), p. 9.

61 Bristow, *Hong Kong's New Towns*, p. 13. The criterion that was not relevant to new towns was the fourth, concerning the survival of the port.

62 Patrick Abercrombie, *Hong Kong Preliminary Planning Report* (Hong Kong: Government Printer, 1948), p. 4.

63 According to Suzanne Pepper, until the 1971 census surprisingly revealed that over half of Hong Kong's people already lived in the New Territories, developers avoided building beyond Boundary Road because of concerns for the post-1997 lease. See Suzanne Pepper, *Keeping Democracy at Bay: Hong Kong and the Challenge of Chinese Political Reform* (Lanham, MD: Rowman and Littlefield, 2008), pp. 171–2.

64 Bristow, *Hong Kong's New Towns*, pp. 30–3.

65 James Hayes, *The Great Difference: Hong Kong's New Territories and Its People, 1898–2004* (Hong Kong: Hong Kong University Press, 2006), pp. 97–102 (quotations on pp. 97–8).
66 SHORE 13/18, 'The Development of Sha Tin New Town'.
67 *An Introduction to Hong Kong* (Hong Kong: Government Printer, 1983), p. 27.
68 James Kirkup, *Cities of the World: Hong Kong and Macao* (London: J. M. Dent and Sons, 1970), p. 56.
69 Kam Hung Tam, in Chris Fairclough, *We Live in Hong Kong* (Hove: Wayland, 1985), p. 41.
70 *An Introduction to Hong Kong*, p. 32.
71 Mark Hampton, 'Early Hong Kong Television, 1950s–1970s: Commercialization, Public Service, and Britishness', *Media History* 17 (August 2011): 305–22 (p. 313).
72 WYAS, George Hattersley and Sons collection, J. Woolfenden to R. L. Smith, 19 January 1972; Smith to Woolfenden, 27 January 1972; Woolfenden to Smith, 1 February 1972.
73 NLW, *Hong Kong, City of Tomorrow: An Exhibition about the Challenge of High Density Living, City Art Centre, Edinburgh, 26 October 1996–4 January 1997*, p. 26.
74 See Norman Miners, *The Government and Politics of Hong Kong*, 5th edn (Hong Kong: Oxford University Press, 1998), p. 48 for a succinct statement of this point.
75 Dan Waters, quoting Sun Yat-sen, speech to Hong Kong University Students, 1923, in Dan Waters, *Faces of Hong Kong: An Old Hand's Reflections* (New York: Prentice Hall, 1995), p. xiii.
76 TNA, CO 1030/1655, Hong Kong Government Information Services Daily Information Bulletin, 20 August 1963, 'H. E. The Governor's Talk at Luncheon Meeting of Foreign Correspondents Club', 2.
77 'Dry as Dust Politics', *The Economist* (8 June 1963), p. 1005.
78 James Clavell, *Noble House: A Novel of Contemporary Hong Kong* (New York: Delacorte Press, 1981), pp. 103–5.
79 I am grateful to David Clayton for sharing his unpublished paper, 'Water Management in Hong Kong: The Origins, Effects and Legacies of "One Water, Two Systems"'.
80 TNA, CO 1030/1655, Far Eastern Department confidential memorandum, 4 July 1963, 'Water Shortage in Hong Kong: Submission to Minister of State'.
81 TNA, CO 1030/1655, Hong Kong Government Information Services Daily Information Bulletin, 20 August 1963, 'HE The Governor's Talk at Luncheon Meeting of Foreign Correspondents Club', p. 6.
82 TNA, CO 1030/1655, Hong Kong Government Information Services Daily Information Bulletin, Tuesday, 20 August 1963, 'HE The Governor's Talk at Luncheon Meeting of Foreign Correspondents Club', pp. 4–6, 13.
83 TNA, CO 1030/1655, Arthur Wooler to M. S. Trenaman, 24 June 1963.
84 E.g. TNA, CO 1030/1655, E. G. Willan to T. W. Garvey, 19 August 1963 (copied to J. D. Higham, CO).
85 TNA, CO 1030/1655, Secretary of State for the Colonies to Hong Kong (Sir Robert Black), telegram, 5 October 1963.
86 TNA, CO 1030/1655, 'The East River Pipeline' (copy of brief given to Lord Landsdowne by the Governor), n.d. [late August/early September 1963].
87 TNA, CO 1030/1655, Hong Kong Government Information Services Daily Information Bulletin, 12 August 1963, 'Another 1,500 Million Gallons of Water Required by End of Month/for Relaxation of Present Restrictions', 1–2.
88 TNA, CO 1030/1655, Hong Kong Government Information Services Daily Information Bulletin, 1 October 1963, 'River Indus Flood Pumping Scheme: $24 Million Project Will Produce Additional 8,500 Million Gallons of Water Yearly'.
89 E.g. Martin Booth, *The Dragon and the Pearl: A Hong Kong Notebook* (London: Simon and Schuster, 1994), pp. 1–7; Percy Cradock, *Experiences in China*, new edn (London: John Murray, 1999), p. 236; Ommanney, *Fragrant Harbour*, p. 38.
90 Philip Bowring and Mary Lee, 'Mandarin on the Move', *FEER* (25 December 1981), p. 11. The phrase 'put their hearts at ease' referred to Deng Xiaoping's vague assurances in rebuffing MacLehose's request for a clear indication of Hong Kong's post-1997 status.

91 Jonathan Dimbleby, *The Last Governor: Chris Patten and the Handover of Hong Kong* (London: Little, Brown, 1997), p. 68.
92 'Airport Project Puts Spotlight on HK', *SCMP* (31 July 1992).
93 TNA, FO 973/665, 'The New Hong Kong Airport', Foreign and Commonwealth Office Background Brief, September 1991 (quotations from p. 2).
94 Frank Welsh, *A History of Hong Kong* (London: HarperCollins, 1993), p. 535. The sentence continues, however, to acknowledge the reasonableness of China's claims to involvement in such a large-scale project whose importance would last well beyond 1997.
95 Cradock, *Experiences of China*, p. 238.
96 Robert Cottrell, 'Closing Time at the Last Chance Saloon', *Spectator* (3 July 1992), pp. 9–10.
97 Cradock, *Experiences of China*, pp. 242–3; Stephen Vines, *Hong Kong: China's New Colony* (London: Orion Business, 1999), p. 78.

CHAPTER FIVE

Good governance

In the 1997 edition of her history of Hong Kong, in a passage amounting to an elegy, Jan Morris writes:

> On the whole, with many lapses and exceptions, British Government in Hong Kong had been good government. It had risen, as the Empire itself had, from the opportunism of its origins, through the jingo pomp of its climax, to a level of general decency. It had ensured personal freedoms, it had given stability, it had even in its late years made a brave start with social welfare, and tried to live up to the British Empire's truest morality, the morality of fair play. It had demonstrated that in certain circumstances imperialism need not be oppressive, but could be a species of partnership, or a technical service.[1]

The same year, Steve Tsang, in a volume published to mark the change of sovereignty, argued provocatively that taken on specifically Confucian terms, Chinese people were never ruled so well as under British imperialism: 'It is paradoxical that it has taken British imperial rule in Hong Kong to deliver a government which meets the requirements of "as good a government as possible in the Chinese tradition".'[2] A few years later, in a 2001 reflection on his career as a civil servant, Patrick Hase wrote that 'the period of the late 1970s and early 1980s was the period of the all-round best administration Hong Kong has ever had, and I am proud to have served in it'.[3]

This chapter examines the idea of good governance as one of the key British discourses concerning postwar Hong Kong. Similarly to previous chapters, the point here is not to write a comprehensive history of colonial governance; rather, it is to convey how British commentators – both in Hong Kong and in Britain – described what the British themselves were doing. As we will see in Chapter 7, 'good governance' was a key attribute of Britishness that was thought to be in jeopardy with the change of sovereignty.

As we have already seen, the trope of British 'good governance' was intimately linked to the idea of Hong Kong as a neo-Victorian capitalist paradise – John Stuart Mill's other island. The discourse examined in Chapter 2 emphasised those aspects of governance centring on non-intervention and low taxation, and the resulting unleashing of entrepreneurial energies. The discussions of 'good governance' examined in this chapter, by contrast, emphasise the more proactive side of British governance – rule that was credited with producing Hong Kong's economic miracle through unleashing entrepreneurship, but that also was sufficiently adaptable to embrace social welfare and political reforms by the 1970s, even while presiding over continued economic growth. In doing so, numerous British commentators argued, the Government maintained its benevolent authoritarianism even while introducing what Steve Tsang has called 'accountability without democracy'.[4] From this perspective, the efforts of the Patten administration to introduce aggressive democratic reform in the final half-decade of colonial rule represented both a betrayal of what had worked for so long, and a cynical attempt at legacy-building at the expense of the interests of the majority of Hong Kong's Chinese population. This chapter will argue, though, that the discourse of good governance was pragmatic and adaptable throughout the entire postwar period, no less in the Patten era than in previous decades.

Authoritarianism and non-interference

A 1949 pamphlet published by the Hong Kong Government, and addressed to the British soldiers sent to defend the colony, credited British rule (and 'our countrymen') with transforming Hong Kong from a 'barren rock' to the city that 'now commercially dominates the Far East'. In making this claim, the pamphlet emphasised Hong Kong's status as a free port:

> The British have always believed in freedom to travel and trade, and it is through the free interchange of ideas which is possible when men meet to trade that understanding between nations is fostered. We have put no walls or curtains round Hong Kong to shut out truth. Our doors are open.

At the same time, it underscored not the lax regulatory framework, but the more positive manifestation of British governance, without which Hong Kong's favourable geographical position and the 'ingenuity, resilience and hard work of its native peoples' would have amounted to little. The advantage of 'a century of British rule and British traditions' had provided 'stability, security and initiative' that led to an influx of traders and refugees. Asking why such people came, the pamphlet responded with a list of British accomplishments in governance:

> They came because there was impartial justice here, because there was protection from bandits and pirates and pickpockets, because there were laws of health and sanitation which protected them from disease, business laws which protected them from cheats and tricksters; they came because the administration was honest, the banks secure, human rights respected; and they came here finally because in many cases this small Colony provided what their own homes did not.[5]

As other quotations in this book will illustrate, several of these accomplishments would have been, at best, relative. Yet well before the MacLehose reforms of the 1970s, the Hong Kong Government was crediting the very same 'British rule' that had built Hong Kong from a 'barren rock' with providing British justice, law and order, honest government, and individual liberties.

As Tsang points out, the 'good' government with which he credited the colonial administration, which featured non-interference in its subjects' lives as one of its leading virtues, was accomplished by an autocratic, unrepresentative Government. In the period immediately following the Second World War, after British rule was re-established following Japanese occupation, Governor Mark Young had put forward plans to introduce constitutional reform and resulting democratic self-government. The Young Plan was ultimately rejected by London, a decision facilitated by subsequent Governor Alexander Grantham's disapproval. Grantham's logic was that since Hong Kong, unlike other British colonies, was not destined for independence, direct elections did not make sense; second, closely related, that China would interpret the establishment of democracy as a prelude toward independence, and would pre-emptively seize Hong Kong – in other words, continued British rule in Hong Kong precluded democratisation; and third, that if elections were introduced, the conflict between Communists and Nationalists would dominate Hong Kong politics, making Hong Kong ungovernable.[6] The decision not to introduce democratic reform was made easier by the fact that until the late 1960s the majority of people in Hong Kong were refugees who had deliberately chosen to live in undemocratic Hong Kong rather than in Civil War or Communist China, and that many of them considered themselves transients who would either return to China when things had settled down, or would move on to another destination. As *The Economist* noted in 1946, Young's desire to implement reform in order to give 'the citizens of Hong Kong a fuller and more responsible share in the management of their own affairs' exposed the difficulty of 'ascertaining who the citizens of Hongkong really are and how to obtain their "views and wishes"'.[7] The popular lack of interest in constitutional reform was further underwritten, according to the sociologist Lau Siu-kai, by Hong Kong Chinese people's 'utilitarianistic familialism', a tendency that led them to seek redressing of their economic and social needs through extended families rather than through the State.[8]

Not only did Hong Kong's Chinese expect little of their Government; more positively, it could be argued that Hong Kong's non-democratic Government addressed more 'fundamental' needs than democracy itself. Hilton Cheong-Leen, founder and Chairman of the Hong Kong Civic Association and long-time Urban Council member, made this point in speeches in the 1950s and early 1960s. Speaking in 1961 at an Urban Council Annual Conventional Debate, Cheong-Leen asserted that constitutional reform was 'bound to come; that is an absolute certainty!' The main task was to ensure that it happened neither too quickly nor too slowly. In the meantime, Hong Kong was 'in effect one of the most benevolent and progressive dictatorships the world has ever known! For this, let us be thankful!'[9] As he had argued in a speech half a decade earlier, democratic self-government, while a desirable end, was not the most important quality of government. Admittedly, the progress of Hong Kong required that 'we must not merely rely upon a benevolent, fatherly and efficient administration, but we must give our local people more opportunity to gradually assume an increasing amount of responsibility in the management of local affairs'. The people of Hong Kong were not, though, unhappy with the current arrangement, in which the Governor was externally appointed and all of the top posts were held by colonial administrators,

> and the answers are not far to seek: there is personal freedom for the individual, opportunity for him to better himself, and law and order under which he may enjoy the fruits of his labour. Thus we have something which is even more fundamental than a democratic system of government: freedom of the individual, which is the cornerstone of the democratic way of life.[10]

This shifting of focus from democracy itself to the 'democratic way of life' was a familiar rhetorical tactic during the postwar years; it undergirded claims during the 1950s that authoritarian Hong Kong was a 'Chinese "show window for democracy"'.[11]

Hong Kong was ruled in authoritarian fashion by a London-appointed Governor in consultation with appointed Executive and Legislative Councils, which were heavily dominated by trading and industrial interests; the only elected body was the Urban Council, whose purview was mostly limited to municipal services. It combined an official

commitment to laissez-faire government with strategic intervention in cases of perceived market failure, seen most prominently in
a large-scale public housing programme beginning in the early 1950s.
Consultation with the Executive and Legislative Councils was a means
of coopting Chinese elites, allowing what Ambrose King has called the
'administrative absorption of politics', and was generally practiced.[12] It
is worth noting, though, as S. S. Hsueh explained in dead-pan language
in his 1962 primer on the Hong Kong Government, that the Governor
was required to seek counsel from them *except* in cases that he thought
were either too insignificant to merit bothering them, or in cases that
were too urgent to involve them, or if their involvement might be
'materially prejudicial to the service of the Crown'; in other cases the
Governor was expected to consult with these bodies, but was officially
free to ignore their advice.[13] As wide-ranging as these exceptions and
caveats are, King put it in even more universal terms: 'Strictly speaking, the Governor can govern the colony, if he wishes, with his own
will without regard to what the people in the colony think.'[14] Still, as
Peter Harris argued in 1978, custom dictated that the Governor would
normally follow the advice of the Executive Council in particular: 'For
the Governor to exercise these [absolute] powers, except in the most
exceptional circumstances, would be a very grave matter indeed.'[15]
The Governor's consulting with Hong Kong business elites would take
place informally as well as through official channels; we have already
seen the popular quotation that Hong Kong was governed by the Jockey
Club, the Bank, and the Governor, 'in that order', and to that one could
add the broader elite to be found in the Hong Kong Club and regular
dinners at the Governor's home.

The need for an authoritarian Governor to consult with his subjects
in practice was perhaps most pronounced in the New Territories, particularly in the earlier part of the postwar period. As the HKU-based
political scientist Norman Miners noted in the revised 1998 edition
of his classic 1975 textbook, *The Government and Politics of Hong
Kong*, until 1980 the urban areas and the New Territories were governed by 'two completely different systems of local administration',
under two separate authorities, the Home Affairs Department and the
New Territories Administration. During the 1960s and 1970s gradual reforms made them much more similar, until in 1981 both were
incorporated into a 'unified pattern of district administration'.[16] For
the first few postwar decades, the Colonial Government ruled the New
Territories by collaboration with village leaders through the Heung
Yee Kuk, an advisory body initially established in 1926, filled by elections of village representatives from 1948 onward, and turned into a
statutory body by Legislative Council Ordinance in 1959. Although

officially having only an advisory capacity, Miners argued, the Heung Yee Kuk had effective powers that went beyond this role; for example, in the construction of the Tai Lam Chung reservoir, negotiations with this body were crucial to winning the consent of villagers. James Hayes has argued that it is 'doubtful whether the nine New Towns could have been developed without the consultation and compromise' facilitated by the reformed Heung Yee Kuk.[17]

Not only did British governance take place within an authoritarian framework, but it also followed the longstanding principles of colonial trusteeship and non-interference with indigenous customs, except in cases in which British sensibilities were particularly offended. Trusteeship meant that however defined, and even if honoured as often in the breach as in the practice, the Colonial Government would act in the interests of the colony and its people rather than on behalf of London. Colonial officials frequently highlighted their 'relative autonomy' from London, and their championing of Hong Kong's interests.[18] As for non-interference, it was frequently remarked that, following the Nationalist and Communist revolutions on the mainland, traditional Chinese culture existed in the British-governed New Territories more than anywhere else. Traditional clan-based inheritance patterns endured – indeed, they continued even after 1997, in contradiction to the property regime elsewhere in the territory. Concubinage was prohibited only in 1971, and Chinese cultural acceptance of bribery was frequently named as a rationale for Government toleration of a practice that, ostensibly, the British found objectionable. On the other hand, the Colonial Government had abolished the *mui tsai* system of domestic servitude in the late 1920s, largely the result of metropolitan pressure, and the eating of dogs was made illegal in 1950.[19] Moreover, parliamentary activism surfaced periodically between the 1950s and 1970s, reaching a fever pitch in the mid-1970s, raising the prospect that the Colonial Government would lose its relatively free hand, particularly as Hong Kong became Britain's most important remaining colony in a greatly reduced Empire.[20]

Colonial administrators and other commentators went beyond tolerating or even supporting Chinese customs, to the point of identifying with traditional Chinese ruling practices. This has already been seen in Steve Tsang's essay, cited above, in which he favourably evaluated British governance in Confucian terms. It is seen even more vividly in Austin Coates's 1968 memoir, *Myself a Mandarin*. In this book, Coates describes his career as a magistrate in the New Territories between 1949 and 1956, focusing on the practical irrationalities that stemmed from the peculiarities of the Chinese mind. As the terms of the New Territories lease allowed litigants 'to choose whether they would have the magistrate hear their suits according to the common law, or according to Chinese law and custom', he had to be well versed in both.[21] To the difficulty of learning a second legal tradition was added that of understanding the Chinese people, whose reactions to life's events were 'utterly at variance with the reactions of other races ... more akin to the reactions and thoughts of another planet than of another race'.[22] Coates had to become accustomed to the non-linear thought processes of Chinese, a characteristic that led to the 'unusual difficulty Chinese people seemed to have in explaining things, beginning at the beginning'.[23] Chinese litigants not only could not be trusted to tell the truth; they did not even understand the abstract value of telling the truth, but would do so only if doing so would secure an advantage: the idea of 'perjury' as a crime would make no sense to a Chinese. For this reason, Coates objected to colleagues' introducing oaths into a trial because, 'realizing that oaths of this kind would make no difference to the degree of untruth that came into the court, the taking of them at once clothed the proceedings in a veil of hypocrisy'.[24] Finally, unlike Europeans, Chinese would not elucidate their positions precisely and directly, in order 'to avoid all possibility of any kind of confrontation or showdown': rather, according to Coates, the 'perfectly conducted negotiation [was] one in which neither of the principal persons concerned ever has to refer to the matter in hand'.[25]

As condescending as these quotations will sound, Coates presented such Chinese political customs as benign and charming exotica that he was able to accept and master, to the point that he learned to adapt his implementation of law to the Chinese mind as well as culture. One trial, in particular, taught him the valuable lesson

> that Chinese general ideas are less concerned with absolute standards of right and wrong, in the context of specific laws and situations, than with a vague and diffuse principle of general benevolence ... If, instead of pursuing hard and fast legal judgments – good for one party, bad for the other – one aimed for generally unsatisfactory compromises based on this imprecise principle of benevolence, there was a fair likelihood of unexpectedly harmonious results.

He presents himself as having embraced this lesson, though he admits that his compromise solution to that particular trial, 'by Western standards, was not only illegal but immoral'.[26] This statement, which would seem to conflict with the shibboleth of British rule of law, points instead to another frequently cited attribute of governance: its pragmatic nature.

Closing the gap

As Chapter 2 illustrated, for many commentators non-interference and deference to Chinese cultural practice were exemplified above all by Britain's allowing Hong Kong to become a site for unbridled capitalism. Why else, after all, did Hong Kong's immigrant population grow so rapidly after the Second World War and the Chinese Civil War? However, the 1966 and 1967–68 riots undermined this particular construction of good governance. Faced with what the political scientist Ian Scott has called a 'crisis of legitimacy', good governance had to adapt, even if only cosmetically, to the demands of the Hong Kong people. Accordingly, the Colonial Government moved to close the so-called 'gap' that had emerged between itself and its subjects. At the same time, it was clear that large numbers of Hong Kong people, the majority of whom now had been born in Hong Kong and saw it as the only home they had ever known, had begun to expect more from their Government in terms of social welfare. This was particularly the case for university-age students. In this atmosphere, the Government took several measures to indicate its accountability and responsiveness to its subjects – most significantly through expanding public education and public housing, accelerating its move toward localisation of the civil service, introducing Chinese as an official language, and tackling the problem of corruption. Broadly speaking, the Government of the 1970s, under Murray MacLehose, won over the people of Hong Kong. It did so, moreover, without introducing thoroughgoing democratic reform.

Ostensibly, the 1966 Star Ferry riot was a working-class protest over an announced fare increase on first-class (but not standard-class) tickets; the riot was quickly contained. The 1967–68 riots began as a labour strike in an artificial-flower factory; they became, as Ray Yep and Robert Bickers put it, a 'major anti-colonial movement' including 51 deaths, 4,500 arrests, 'and a campaign of bombings which threatened to destabilize the colony'; they were ultimately squashed by a 'full range of emergency and security measures instituted by the colonial administration'. The riots also seriously complicated Sino-British relations, and briefly raised the spectre of an early change of sovereignty.[27] What matters in the present context is how contemporary British discourse assimilated the riots into the theme of good governance. Following the riots, it was apparent to many British observers that they could no longer take Hong Kong Chinese residents' political passivity for granted. As John Cooper noted in 1970, Hong Kong's population had changed. In place of a population disproportionately made up of refugees, many of whom did not necessarily expect to live in Hong

Figure 8 Peaceful protesting by young people during the 1967–68 riots. The crisis would convince the Government that a 'gap' existed between itself and the people.

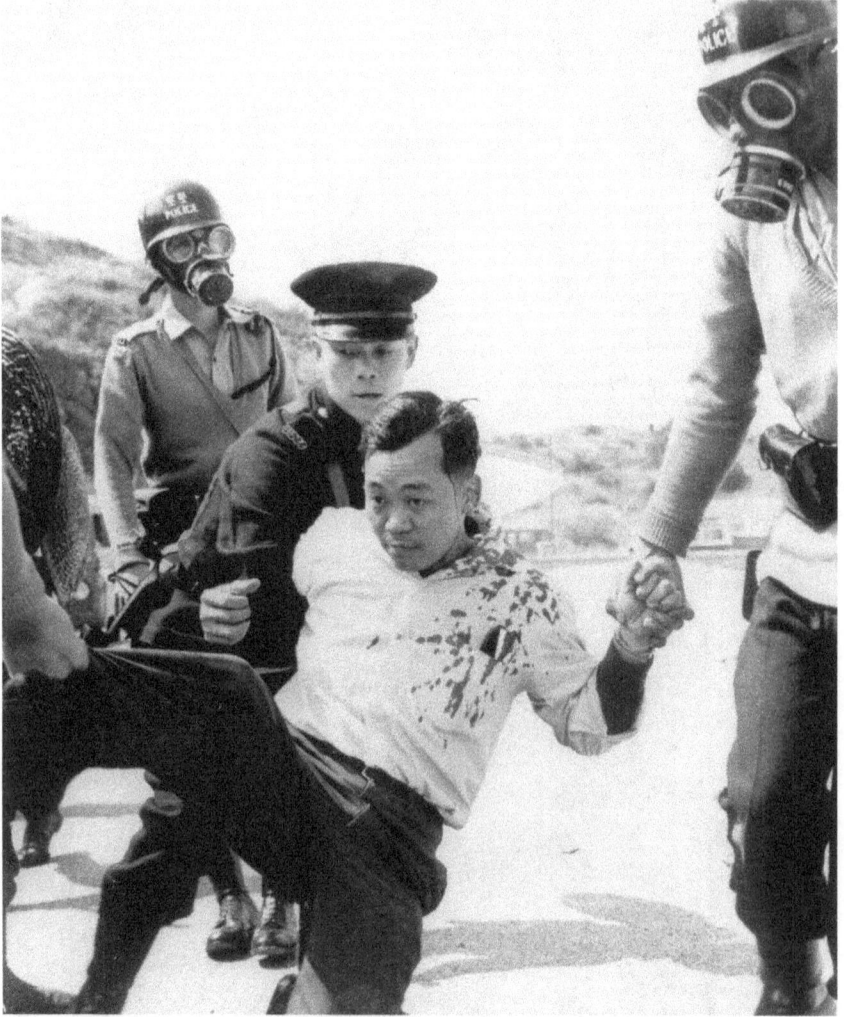

Figure 9 The 1967–68 riots led to 51 deaths, 4,500 arrests, and numerous bombings. The Hong Kong Police Force would have the word 'Royal' added to its title in appreciation for its handling of the crisis.

Kong permanently, there were now 'several hundreds of thousands of young men and women, more often than not born in the Colony, full of the ideas and ambitions which young people invariably have'. Such people would 'not be content to slave away in poor conditions as did their fathers, whose only real concern had been their escape from the mainland'.[28]

Where Cooper emphasised material deprivation, Alec Douglas-Home, former Prime Minister and now FCO Secretary, emphasised the retrograde political system: in a confidential 1973 brief for Prime Minister Edward Heath, he noted 'areas of strain' resulting from Hong Kong's emergence as a 'modern industrial society ... without any hope of constitutional advance'.[29] In fact, as the *FEER* argued in 1968, metropolitan politicians and officials tended to conflate social and constitutional reform in discussing the 'Hong Kong problem' following the riots; so did some commentators in Hong Kong.[30] Colonial officials, by contrast, kept the two issues separate. As the American scholar Suzanne Pepper notes, the 1970s social reform measures were not mere concessions; they followed from a gradual acceptance – 'albeit not without additional prodding throughout five more years of foot-dragging' – that the Hong Kong population had changed and the Government's response had not matched rising expectations. By contrast, colonial authorities did not admit to political obsolescence; rather, they doubled down on maintaining colonial authority. In Pepper's words, the 'police gave up neither their truncheons nor their shoot-to-kill rules of engagement as deemed necessary, and the British never apologized for anything'.[31]

The conflation of the social and the constitutional can be seen in a confidential FCO document from May 1968. In the context of articulating the pros and cons of renewing David Trench's governorship, set to expire the following year, Lord Shepherd, the Minister of State for Commonwealth Affairs, argued, on balance, against his renewal, reasoning that the 'disturbances of last year mark, in some respects, the end of a long chapter of *laissez-faire*. There is a need for change and there is a growing sense of frustration within many influential circles in the Colony that there must be a new drive from above.' There was some doubt that Trench could carry out such a programme.[32] In the event, Trench's governorship was renewed for a year, until April 1970, but the perception that Hong Kong needed to make substantial changes to its established pattern of governing was becoming conventional wisdom in London.

Yet Shepherd did not only call for a change in leadership; he also underscored that Hong Kong needed to create more opening for popular participation in government, particularly for the young. In a June 1969 meeting with Unofficial Members of the Executive and Legislative Councils (UMELCO), he suggested that the 'present composition of the Executive and Legislative Councils' was inadequate for this task. The difficulty was that 'To get on to these Councils one had to be successful – and in Hong Kong that meant being successful in business or industry.' As a result, the youth, the Hong Kong people who were most separated from the establishment by a 'gap', were effectively excluded.[33]

While Shephard called for more direct popular representation, defenders of the Government's record often insisted that the problem was merely one of public relations: a communication gap had grown between the Government and people, and needed to be addressed by a greater provision for consultations, an ombudsman to receive complaints, and similar measures.[34] This view was exemplified by the Government's own publicity arm, the GIS, which in early 1967 highlighted that the *Report of Inquiry Commission* into the causes of the 1966 Star Ferry riots, recently published, had concluded that 'political, economic and social frustrations' had not been the 'direct cause' of the riots. Nor had the popular reaction to the proposed price hikes for first-class seats, during a time of inflation, been a rational one: the committee that had approved the increases 'was considering the problem of what is a fair return, without which the economic machine in Hong Kong will not operate effectively'; by contrast, 'the emotions perhaps more than the thoughts of the public were being enlisted'. The implication was clear: not only had the public responded emotionally rather than to a substantive problem, but the Government itself bore no blame as a result of its substantive decisions. Rather, the Government's problem was one of presentation. Indeed, as the GIS pointed out, the Commission had argued that 'amongst a wide section of the population, little is known of Government's achievements in many fields and that there was much misunderstanding of Government's aims'.[35] Following the more far-reaching 'disturbances' beginning in May of that year, this complacency would seem more difficult to defend. Yet Government spokespeople continued to insist, in the face of criticism, that the problem was mainly one of miscommunication. In late 1969, the *FEER* cited a recent survey of public attitudes revealing that 'people see the administration as at best unsympathetic, at worst corrupt'.[36] When the 1970 anti-bribery law left the task of enforcing anti-corruption in the hands of the police, Elsie Elliott claimed that this provision gave a 'monopoly on corruption to the police'. Responding to such charges, Dennis Bray, the acting Secretary for Home Affairs, replied that

> Hong Kong people deserve and have one of the best governments in Asia. It has a liberal, farsighted and efficient public service which has, in co-operation with the people, turned the war-wrecked tumbledown entrepot of 25 years ago into the thriving industrial city of today. Social progress has been as striking as material progress and the story is well-known [*sic*]. Why else did people come here? Why do they stay?[37]

The meme of a communication 'gap' obscuring otherwise sound British colonial government underwrote the adoption of the City District Officers (CDO) scheme in 1968. Modelled on the New Territories' District Officers, and designed specifically as political officers,[38] in confidential memoranda describing their purpose officials repeatedly emphasised that it was to give a public face to an already smoothly functioning State. Not only did these administrative officers give a specific, local face to Government, but as most were Chinese, they also removed the racial barrier.[39] A January 1969 report from D. R. Holmes, the Secretary for Chinese Affairs, to the Governor, just a few months after the establishment of the CDO, explained their inspiration from the New Territories: when the British had assumed control in 1898, there was 'already in existence a closely knit society which provided a number of administrative and social services for itself', and the British officials assimilated themselves to this existing structure. By contrast, in the urban areas of Hong Kong and Kowloon, administration was conducted by specialised departments; this organisational method met the standards of 'efficiency and economy' but, unfortunately, failed politically, as it contributed to a communication gap. Despite the Government's technical proficiency, therefore, urban officials did not know specific districts well, and the

> people of an urban district [were] confronted with a bewildering array of public services ... there was still no person or office which the residents could recognise as 'the government' in their district. There was no officer responsible for assessing the overall impact of government activities in the urban districts or for gathering opinion and judging popular feeling on local issues.

The report overtly stated that the decision to appoint ten CDOs was political rather than administrative: it was 'to meet the need for a government presence in the various urban districts'. Their task was to 'make themselves as accessible as possible to the people in their districts, and keep in touch with all local organisations'. They were charged with assessing the 'overall impact of government policies' in addition to explaining these policies 'as well as the difficulties and the achievements of the Government to ordinary people'.[40] Governor Trench encouraged the task-defined Government Departments to make use of the CDO network 'in order to ensure that their services and activities are fully understood by the public, and in order to sound out public opinion about existing services or procedures or new ideas as the need arises'.[41] The CDO's physical presence was apparently calculated to integrate within people's daily lives; appropriately for Hong Kong, the offices, by design, looked like 'shops': 'The rather breezy decor has attracted favourable comment and given the impression that a significant step has been taken to bring the government closer to the lives of ordinary people.'[42] A year after the scheme's establishment, one London official indicated that in his view the scheme was working; based on the Officers' reports on what the 'man in the street is saying of Government', he was 'much less apprehensive than before [his] visit about the gap between the "Establishment" and the people in Hong Kong'.[43]

The MacLehose era, lasting from 1970 to 1982, has been frequently cited as the key reform period in modern Hong Kong's history, and MacLehose himself as a major figure in making this happen. Even his frequent critic, Elsie Elliott (by then Elsie Tu), looking back from the vantage point of the late 1980s, acknowledged that under his governorship, 'social justice took root in many fields, and progress was made, to the chagrin of some of the selfish among the wealthy'.[44] Yet when MacLehose was appointed Governor in 1970, the *FEER* feared the opposite, that he would be too dominated by metropolitan rather than local interests. It cautioned that as a career diplomat he had been 'trained to serve British interests', unlike previous Governors who had risen through the colonial service: 'Unless he can learn to put Hongkong first, whatever London's wishes (the hallmark of the best colonial service officer), the colony will come to regret his appointment.'[45] Although in fact MacLehose proved to champion Hong Kong interests, scepticism toward his reformist zeal was well founded. Yep and Lui, drawing on recently available archival material, have shown that far from pushing reform, MacLehose often acted as a break on demands from London, out of a perception that London's vision outpaced the expectations of Hong Kong opinion; they characterise him as a 'reluctant reformer'.[46]

Despite MacLehose's hesitations, the 1970s were marked by extensive social reforms. As John Carroll has pointed out, the MacLehose reforms, coming as they did after the 1967–68 riots, grew out of recognition that improving the living standards of Hong Kong people was a necessary condition of continued British rule.[47] These reforms, drawing on a commissioned report from the consulting firm McKinsey, included increased localisation of civil service, free elementary education, an acceleration of the public housing programme, and the renaming of embarrassingly anachronistic titles: the Colonial Secretary became the Chief Secretary and the Secretary for Chinese Affairs was rechristened the Secretary for Home Affairs, while even the 'colony' itself was now referred to as a 'territory'.[48] At the same time, as we saw in Chapter 4, this is the context in which the underground mass transit railway was first developed. Space does not permit discussing in detail the discourse surrounding all of these reforms. It is, though, worth pausing to consider perhaps the most celebrated reform, the attack on bureaucratic corruption.

The problem of corruption in Hong Kong had been noted for several decades. Often it involved 'satisfied customer' transactions of the sort that led to few complaints, such as hawkers paying 'tea money' to police in exchange for overlooking violations of laws against unlicensed selling; what one person might call 'corruption' was, to another, just a cost of doing business. More notoriously, expectation of payment pervaded those aspects of daily life in which a professional or public ethos should have prevailed: clients assumed that proper hospital care required tipping the nurses or that fire fighters would refuse to turn on the water – and then refuse to turn it off – without payment. Officially, the colonial authorities opposed such practices, but (following the non-interference principle) tolerated them because they were a deeply embedded part of Chinese culture. The reality was that British players were key beneficiaries of the system. In the case of the police, pyramid franchising networks were established, requiring lower-level officers to pay a fee in exchange for the right to collect 'squeeze' in a particular geographical area; 'tea money' went to lower-level Chinese officers, while the more substantial rewards made their way up the hierarchy to British supervisors. When gadflies such as Elsie Elliott and Alan Ellis complained, they were accused of undermining colonial rule.[49]

When it became clear, by the late 1960s, that a significant Chinese constituency for strong anti-corruption measures had emerged, the Colonial Government tried, first, to allow the police to reform itself through its internal anti-corruption branch, which had existed since 1949. Under increasing public pressure, the MacLehose Government, keen to re-establish legitimacy and repair the 'gap' between Government and people, established the ICAC, with extensive powers of subpoena, which began operation in 1974 under the leadership of Jack Cater. The Government's anti-corruption efforts also included the 1968 Prevention of Bribery Ordinance, which provided that officials in possession of wealth that went beyond what their positions had officially paid them were prima facie guilty of a criminal offence, unless they could provide a satisfactory explanation for their wealth. This law marked a clear departure from the metropolitan British understanding of the rights of the accused, because it established presumption of guilt (the charged had to prove innocence) and removed the right not to testify. This deviation from British legal traditions proved troublesome when high-ranking Police Superintendent Peter Godber, hearing in 1973 that he was to be charged under the Prevention of Bribery

[145]

Ordinance, escaped to England; despite clear sympathy for the problems of colonial governance, the British authorities would not extradite Godber to Hong Kong so long as he was accused only of possessing unexplained wealth, since the latter was not a crime in the United Kingdom. MacLehose argued that Chinese opinion – exemplified, for example, in student-led 'Get-Godber-back' rallies – considered such 'legal niceties' as nothing more than rationalisations for old boys taking care of their own. London extradited Godber only when he was charged with actual acceptance of bribery, a charge made on the basis of the suspect testimony of Ernest 'Taffy' Hunt, the first police officer convicted under clause 10 of the Prevention of Bribery Ordinance – testimony offered in exchange for amnesty.

By the end of the colonial period, the dramatic reduction of public corruption and bribery in daily life stood as one of the Government's proudest accomplishments, and the ICAC was one of the most highly esteemed institutions in Hong Kong; the accomplishment rested, though, on a willingness to depart from longstanding British constitutional protections. In the context of wider post-1967 reforms, Government commentary about corruption was routinely presented in principled terms: the authorities were championing longstanding 'British' commitments to anti-corruption as well as responding to public opinion. The attack on corruption was, however, as pragmatic as any other example of 'good governance' considered in this chapter; the official discovery of longstanding British principle occurred only after a crisis of authority had emerged, and one could argue that, despite Godber's widely assumed guilt, the means used to extradite him could have been described by Coates's statement, quoted earlier in a different context: 'by Western standards ... not only illegal but immoral'. Indeed, Elsie Elliott would note in 1981 that it seemed 'certain that the charge on which [Godber] was extradited was a fictitious one', but rationalise that 'it was at least based on the kind of thing he had been doing'.[50] The Colonial Government's pragmatic approach to anti-corruption measures was also seen in MacLehose's extending in 1977 a 'partial amnesty' in response to a large-scale police mutiny, during which they marched on ICAC headquarters.

'Accountability without democracy'

Despite significant post-crisis reforms from above, the crucial point remains that the Colonial Government aimed to remain firmly in control, and largely succeeded. Agnes Ku has argued that the Government's strategy in the 1970s was 'designed to create an image of public consent while containing possible discontents against the administration'.[51] As Ku writes,

> the government took the people to be a mass of subjects under its paternal rule rather than a public of autonomous citizens with equal political rights. As subjects, their opinions were channeled to the government by means of a system of consultation which aimed at minimizing open dissatisfaction with its policies. From the perspective of the government, politics meant the manipulation and display of public consent. Consensus politics was the name of the game.[52]

Ku's argument echoes that made by contemporary scholar Ambrose King, who argued in 1975 that the post-crisis Government tried to build legitimacy by 'claiming to conform to democratic values, if not to a democratic form of government'.[53] From the Government's perspective, maintaining the colony's basic authoritarian structure was essential; for reasons already discussed, democratic self-government could not be entertained.

The Government's attempts to square essential control with more extensive popular engagement were, according to some contemporary academics, aided by popular expectations of politics. Prior to the late 1960s, a lack of popular interest in western conceptions of democracy could be readily attributed to a lack of interest in politics more broadly – Lau Siu-kai's 'utilitarianistic familialism', already mentioned. Following the MacLehose reforms, it could perhaps more convincingly be tied to local understandings of 'democracy'. According to Lau Siu-kai and Kuan Hsin-chi, in a 1986 survey only 23.2 per cent of respondents defined a democratic government as one elected by the people; nearly twice as many, 43.9 per cent, 'would classify a government as democratic if it was willing to consult public opinion, without requiring that public opinion must be followed', while 15.8 per cent defined a democratic government as one that could 'lead the people'. Lau and Kuan concluded, accordingly, that although election was the 'sine qua non of democratic government' in western theory, it did not 'appear to be the crucial element in the mind of the Hong Kong Chinese'.[54]

With democratic constitutional reform off the table, but with a post-1967 perception that Hong Kong's growing population, and especially its youth, risked atomisation, it became increasingly urgent to find ways to coopt Hong Kong people into the existing non-democratic structure of government. As Philip Bowring and Mary Lee noted in a late-1981 article analysing the news of Sir Edward Youde's appointment as Governor, 'Hongkong people are now more conscious of their own interests than ever before.'[55] In 1981 and 1982, accordingly,

[147]

the Government created District Boards and District Management Committees for ten urban districts and eight in the New Territories, with three stated aims:

> First, to create more and better channels of communication between residents of districts and the government.
> Second, to give residents a more direct say in government services and policies affecting their districts, and to ensure that district needs are identified and dealt with effectively.
> Third, to improve co-ordination and response by the administration at district level.[56]

It is instructive that all three of these aims retained the assumption of an appointed, not elected, Government; rather than choosing their Government, Hong Kong people were, in effect, offered a mechanism for petitioning the Government. More broadly, these aims offered a means of attaching people to the Government, and attaching their local and neighbourhood lives to the central administration.

According to a 1981 report from the Sha Tin District Council, community building had to start at the grass roots; 'it must grow up from the residents involved'. Accordingly, the role of the Council was to 'encourage, assist and advise, and to ensure that persons with good community sense are brought together and shown what can be done'. To achieve this aim, the Sha Tin District Council encouraged the residents of each 'multi-storey building' to form 'Mutual Aid Committees or Owners Corporations', as soon as residents occupied the block, in order to promote 'mutual care, a sense of responsibility and a real community spirit among residents'.[57]

In seeking to manage public opinion, the Government was well served by a generally supportive mainstream press. As Governor Trench, in a speech given to the Newspaper Society of Hong Kong in November 1966, put it, journalists played a valuable role in explaining the Government to the people, and he thanked them for their valuable service during the Star Ferry riot the previous April.[58] During the riots of 1967–68, the Government suspended three Communist newspapers, and one publisher and printer 'faced court proceedings for an alleged violation of laws against sedition, inflammatory reports and the spreading of false reports'.[59] Even where the press kept its freedom to publish, dissent could be stifled in other ways; one eighteen-year-old student received a two-year sentence for distributing anti-Government leaflets in school, even though, as Ray Yep notes, many of the leaflets were 'merely cuttings from pro-Peking newspapers that the colonial government allowed to be published in the territory'.[60] More broadly, as Stephen Vines wrote in 1999, for much of the colonial period, until well into the 1970s, the GIS could normally count on the mainstream press to reproduce its press releases virtually unchanged; Vines further quoted a long-time RTHK journalist as saying that in the mid-1960s, 'all broadcast news was government news'. It was only after the mid-1970s, during an era in which the 'colonial government was neither strong enough nor concerned enough to maintain its previous powers of influence', that a more assertive press emerged that would seek to hold the Government accountable, acting in effect in place of an opposition party. Yet even then, the Government continued to use more subtle means to attempt to influence the media.[61]

In addition to the Government's making use of a subservient press for much of the colonial period, until the end of the 1970s the Special Branch of the Police used 'wire taps and street tails' to monitor the activities of various activist groups, including the Hong Kong Observers, the Education Action Group, the Hong Kong Federation of Students, and the Christian Industrial Committee. None of these groups could reasonably be described as radical, but had drawn the attention of Special Branch through such activities as championing the elevation of Cantonese as an official language, writing editorials in the *SCMP*, and trying to spread Christianity by identifying it with the causes of the working class.[62]

Democracy and decolonisation

Not all commentators were content with narrowing the 'gap' between the people and a non-elected Government through coopting and community building. Members of the Urban Council, even before the 1967–68 disturbances, had begun calling for more substantively democratic reforms, reviving ideas that, as Steve Tsang puts it, had been 'shelved' at the beginning of Alexander Grantham's tenure.[63] In 1966, an 'ad hoc committee' of the Urban Council pushed for an expansion of that body's functions, as the one popularly elected Government institution in the colony. Arguing that there was not 'sufficient contact between the Government and the people at the present time', and that increasing education had led the younger generation to take a greater interest in politics, the committee urged steps to 'allow the people of Hong Kong to take a more active part in their own affairs'.[64] The committee called for turning the Urban Council into a territory-wide parliament, a 'Greater Hong Kong Council', that included Hong Kong and Kowloon District Councils, and a 'Rural District Council' comprising the existing Heung Yee Kuk which entailed 27 Rural Committees representing 625 villages. The committee envisioned that the New Towns – Tsuen Wan, Sha Tin, and Tuen Mun, among others – might eventually merit their own district councils. The committee recommended, without actually using the word, something resembling the Dominion idea: this reform would 'give the fullest local representation, whilst at the same time maintain[ing] what we believe to be the wish of the people to remain under the protection and guidance of Britain in external affairs'.[65] The proposed Greater Hong Kong Council would combine direct and indirect elections, and local and territory-wide elections; the Council's chairman should be called 'Mayor'.[66] The committee solicited opinions from various professional and civic organisations in Hong Kong; while some declined to comment and others preferred to continue working through the Legislative Council, the proposal attracted enough interest to suggest that the Government needed to take seriously that discontent could spark concrete proposals for substantive democratisation. Along with the riots themselves, the assertiveness of the Urban Council formed the background to Government attempts to reinvent its image. They also show that the projection of a benignly authoritarian Government that was democratic in its responsiveness without being democratic in form did not go unchallenged.

A 1979 pamphlet signed by seven of the twelve elected Urban Council members, including B. A. Bernacchi and Elsie Elliott, criticised both the Council's narrow remit and the narrow franchise that had elected them, while noting that the other five elected members and the twelve appointed ones stood against them. Echoing late-1960s London claims, the pamphlet argued that election by functional constituencies resulted in an electorate from privileged categories only, perhaps 10 per cent of Hong Kong's population; but because of the 'cumbersome exercise of registration', many qualified people were unable to vote, resulting in elections in which the electoral roll 'seldom rises above 1% of the total population'. This was particularly problematic in that the list of categories clearly excluded 'most of Hong Kong's enormous workforce, its housewives and small businessmen', the unenfranchised categories among which 'injustices are likely to occur'. The pamphlet further complained that while the Urban Council – again, the only elected Government body in Hong Kong – had authority over 'public recreation and amenities, cultural affairs and some aspects of health', its remit excluded 'education, public housing, social welfare, town planning, transport and fire services', all functions reserved for the Government appointed by London.[67] The Urban Council's budget, moreover – most of which was devoted to salaries to personnel of the Urban Services Department – was accountable to the London-appointed Government and, following 1973 reforms, its jurisdiction had been gradually shrunk.[68]

[150]

At the same time that the pamphlet criticised the lack of genuine representation for Hong Kong's masses, it also criticised the Government's attempt to 'bridge the gap' between itself and the public that had been revealed in the riots: not by electoral reform but by such public-relations efforts as establishing a 'so-called "Ombudsman"' to receive public complaints, and subsequently publicising the successful redressing of 'minor matters such as changing names on identity cards, checking on immigration delays, and directing people to relevant Government departments' – the sort of 'routine matters' that could be 'settled without fanfare at any elected Urban Councillor's ward office'.[69]

Between 1979 and 1984, the question of the colony's post-1997 status came to the fore when Governor MacLehose, concerned about the uncertainty of commercial leases, raised the issue during an official visit to Beijing; following tense negotiations between Deng and Thatcher, during which housing and stock-market values fell precipitously, the matter was resolved in late 1984 with the signing of the Sino-British Joint Declaration. As it became clear that Britain would not be able to maintain control of the colony, the question of constitutional reform and the introduction of democratic representation once again surfaced. In a November 1984 White Paper, following up a Green Paper from the previous July, Parliament announced its intention to 'develop progressively a system of representative government at the central level which is more directly accountable to the people of Hong Kong and is firmly rooted in Hong Kong'; the system was to grow out of existing governmental structures and would gradually expand the number of directly elected officials.[70] Similarly, as Michael Chugani expressed it in a November 1985 *SCMP* column, the British Government believed 'that unless Hongkong is allowed to evolve politically at a pace that meets the aspirations of the population', the Territory's recently recovered 'economic viability' as a trading centre, following the crisis of confidence in the early 1980s, would once again 'rapidly diminish'.[71]

Yet long-time Hong Kong civil servant John Walden, in a 1985 lecture given to the Hong Kong Management Association, referred to the democratisation of the territory as a 'grand illusion', and dismissed the 1984 White Paper as mere cover, both to ensure that Parliament agreed to the Sino-British Joint Declaration, and (along with the Chinese and Hong Kong Governments) to 'appease five million free people on whom they have imposed one of the most callous diplomatic accommodations of all time'.[72] He argued against democratisation both on the grounds that the British and Hong Kong Governments were not sincere, and on the grounds that direct elections of the Legislative Council would not be an efficacious way to ensure popular representation. He argued that Hong Kong Government officials had maintained, during his own twenty-nine-year career (1951–80), that 'the introduction of democratic politics into Hong Kong would be the quickest and surest way to ruin Hong Kong's economy and create social and political instability'. Those occasional civil servants, 'usually from former British colonies in Africa', who championed democratic reform were dismissed as 'disloyal or even dangerous'. In his view, nothing had changed since then in the Hong Kong Government's outlook, but far from stifling popular representation, Walden argued that opposition to democracy 'had the whole-hearted consent of the entire business community, all of the professional classes and most of the general public'.[73] In Walden's view, the widespread antipathy to democratic politics reflected a consensus that the growth of prosperity following the Second World War simply would not have been possible without an authoritarian Government. Indeed, Hong Kong people often saw democratic Britain itself as 'an object lesson; a once great country that had ruined its economy and the work ethic of its people by democratic politics'.[74]

Walden did not, however, equate authoritarianism with lack of popular representation. Echoing a theme from his short 1983 book, *Excellency, Your Gap Is Showing!*, Walden asserted that the 'political instincts' of Hong Kong people were 'deeply rooted in the Confucian tradition', and favoured the 'security of authoritarian government and the resolution of conflict by compromise rather than confrontation'. These instincts were well served by the existing Government, in which the civil service made decisions and the Legislative Council approved them (rather than the other way around). A more democratic Legislative Council might have some salutary effects, particularly as the civil service came under increasing pressure from Beijing; electoral democracy in itself would not, though, make the Government more representative. Officials, however empowered, would naturally identify with the longstanding Government goal of maintaining stability. Rather than putting all of their eggs in the basket of elections, then, Hong Kong people would be better served to establish direct mechanisms for maintaining the civil service's accountability to the people. Walden suggested, for example, a statutory right to information from the Government, 'next day publication in Chinese and English of all proceedings of the Legislative Council and important committees', and media coverage of public affairs and improved investigative reporting.[75]

As the 1980s progressed, and particularly after the 1989 Tiananmen Square massacre, the question of democratic reform took on an added urgency, both for Hong Kong's political activists such as Martin Lee, Emily Lau, and Christine Loh, and for British politicians eager to achieve an honourable exit. For example, in a 1990 letter to Robert

Runcie, the Archbishop of Canterbury, Labour leader Neil Kinnock, explaining his opposition to the Thatcher Government's lack of support for democratic reform, blasted the Government's lack of progress toward implementing such reform, asking whether the British were 'simply going to hand over to the Chinese authorities a colonial system in which the ruling power appoints, with no effective accountability, the key figures in the Government and the administration?'.[76] Writing in the *Spectator* half a year earlier, Charles Moore had suggested that this was exactly what Beijing wanted, and that in this regard Beijing and London had a common interest, one contrary to that of the Hong Kong people: 'Peking likes what it sees of British colonial rule. It wants to grab that stability and prosperity, not seeing that those things also depend upon freedom. Britain wants no diminution of her colonial authority before 1997.' Moore's point came in the context, less than six months after Tiananmen, of criticising London for not doing more to protect Hong Kong from 'Chinese tyranny'. His implication was that the PRC would eagerly take over the British dictatorial Colonial State without preserving the British benevolent spirit of freedom that had allowed it to function properly; Britain, for its part, was abandoning its responsibilities.[77]

With the appointment of Chris Patten as the final Governor of British Hong Kong, democratic reform was at last placed firmly on the agenda, specifically with the introduction of direct elections for a significant number of Legislative Council members in the selection of the last Legislative Council before the June 1997 Handover. Officially, this was meant to ensure that the Hong Kong people would be empowered to resist any encroachments by the Chinese Government against Hong Kong's special administrative status. Moreover, since the Joint Declaration had vaguely referred to an 'elected' Government for Hong Kong, and since Britain officially had responsibility for Hong Kong until the Handover, Patten could claim that he was within his rights, was looking to the interests of the Hong Kong people, and was honouring the spirit of the Joint Declaration.

Patten's appointment was fortuitous. Major had already decided to replace David Wilson, who was too closely linked to the Foreign Office 'China hands' that the Prime Minister considered too eager to placate Beijing;[78] Patten was available for the position only through the odd historical contingency of leading the Conservative Party, as Party Chairman, to a surprise electoral victory over Neil Kinnock's Labour Party while losing his own seat in the same election. Had he won re-election to his own seat, he surely would have been appointed to a more desirable post, in the Cabinet; had Labour won the election, Kinnock likely would have appointed someone from his own party (if not a civil servant) as Governor. Popular among the Hong Kong Chinese, who called him Fat Pang, Patten departed from the traditional aloofness of the Governor, rejecting the ceremonial Windsor uniform, and was frequently sighted walking around the colony.[79] In October 1992, in his first policy speech as Governor, Patten announced his goals for democratisation:

(i) to ensure that Hong Kong has a vigorous and effective executive-led government which is accountable to the legislature;
(ii) to broaden the participation of the community in the conduct of Hong Kong's affairs; and
(iii) to devise arrangements for the elections in 1994 and 1995 which command the confidence and support of the community.[80]

It is worth remembering that even though Patten's discourse of democratisation went well beyond that of previous Governors, and even though his 1994 reforms would be reversed after 1 July 1997, they had their limitations from the perspective of most western electoral systems. First, most obviously, Patten did not press the issue of directly electing the top official, the Chief Executive. Second, of the sixty seats in the Legislative Council, only twenty were filled by geographical constituency voting; thirty were filled by functional constituency, ensuring that organised interests rather than individual citizens had the greater representation, and ten were filled by an election committee. The 1995 election, the last under British authority and the only one governed by the 1994 reform, attracted only 35 per cent turn-out overall, with the functional constituency turn-out particularly low because of a 'failure by many voters to identify which of the new functional constituencies was "theirs"'.[81]

In addition to articulating his own views, Patten spoke for a clear constituency of Hong Kong people, and one that had emerged well before his arrival. For example, a statement by a wide range of Hong Kong Chinese Christian leaders, just ahead of a January 1988 parliamentary debate on Hong Kong, argued that Hong Kong people demanded, and the British and Hong Kong Governments had previously promised, direct elections before 1997. Similar arguments were made by a group of medical practitioners, the Hong Kong Professional Teachers' Union, and the Federation of Civil Service Unions, among others. Nor was the issue simply a matter of when to implement direct elections; it also concerned how 'election' would be defined, whether entailing a western-style mass electorate voting for politicians at all levels, or a more limited version favoured by Beijing. In the same context, the Hong Kong Observers, who described themselves as an 'independent, non-partisan group formed ... to comment on the policies and actions of government and other institutions in Hong Kong', made the case that the 'high degree of autonomy' promised in the Joint Declaration depended upon 'no less than true democracy founded on universal suffrage'.[82]

Notwithstanding the Governor's popularity, John Flowerdew notes that Patten was arguably being disingenuous: he knew that his interpretation of 'elections' was not the same as Beijing's, and that Beijing could easily undo the results of the election after June 1997; he would, then, accomplish nothing practical for the people of Hong Kong.[83] What Patten did do, though, was to promote Britain's legacy as having left behind a democracy. One could add, cynically, that so long as Britain ruled Hong Kong, it did not introduce inconvenient democratic reforms, but as soon as the Handover was inevitable, it had no interest in maintaining the authoritarian political system that had served it so well for so long. More charitably, one could argue, as Stephen Vines has, that no previous Governor had faced such an assertive and obvious Hong Kong constituency for participatory democracy, and that even if Patten's specific constitutional reforms could be overturned after 30 June 1997, the 'spirit of greater political independence and self-confidence' that emerged on his watch would be more enduring. As Vines put it, 'By elevating the role of the legislature and local government and encouraging the notion of accountability, Mr Patten created expectations of representative government which are not so easy to suppress.'[84]

One could also argue, though, that despite Patten's elevated tone – invoking such concepts as honour and responsibility to Britain's former subjects – the discourse of good government remained as pragmatic as ever. Austin Coates's self-identification as a Chinese-style mandarin; the replacement of non-interference with limited social welfare following major riots; the governing of the New Territories, before the 1980s, entirely differently from the urban areas; and the introduction of vigorous anti-corruption measures: all of these had been less about any overarching principle than about the pragmatic desire to dampen conflict. In the atmosphere during and after the negotiations leading to the Joint Declaration – and certainly following the events of 4 June 1989 – the introduction of democratic reforms was arguably as much about maintaining Hong Kong's governability while the Colonial Government remained as it was about constructing a fitting colonial legacy; or, more precisely, these two functions were intertwined.

In the early 1990s, the concept of British 'good governance' – an idea that had previously shown itself fully compatible with paternalistic authoritarianism – seemed to require the incorporation of democratic reform. Yet the discourses of both democratic reform and good governance were repositioned to become inextricably bound to what I call the 'narratives of 1997', the contest over shaping the meaning of the Handover – a meaning that went well beyond questions of government. This is the subject of Chapter 7. First, though, we will examine the relationship of Hong Kong's Chinese subjects – and, more briefly, its ethnic-minority subjects – to the idea of Britishness.

Notes

1 Jan Morris, *Hong Kong: Epilogue to an Empire* (New York: Random House, 1997), p. 293.
2 Steve Tsang, 'Government and Politics in Hong Kong: A Colonial Paradox', in Judith M. Brown and Rosemarie Foot (eds), *Hong Kong's Transitions, 1842–1997* (Basingstoke: Macmillan, 1997), p. 79.
3 Patrick Hase, 'The District Office', in Elizabeth Sinn (ed), *Hong Kong, British Crown Colony, Revisited* (Hong Kong: Centre of Asian Studies, University of Hong Kong, 2001), pp. 123–45 (p. 145).
4 Steve Tsang, *Governing Hong Kong: Administrative Officers from the Nineteenth Century to the Handover to China, 1862–1997* (London and New York: I. B. Tauris, 2007), pp. 147–52.
5 ANA, A1838 528/1/5, Part I, *Why Hong Kong?*, pp. 14–15.
6 Steve Tsang, *Democracy Shelved: Great Britain, China, and Attempts at Constitutional Reform in Hong Kong, 1945–1952* (Hong Kong, Oxford, and New York: Oxford University Press, 1988). See also Mss. Brit. Emp. Si 288, Rhodes College, Oxford, Alexander Grantham, interview by D. J. Crozier, 21 August 1968, p. 11; 'Hongkong: The Persistent Colony', *The Economist* (19 January 1957), p. 209; Chan Man-lok, 'Between Red and White: Chinese Communist and Nationalist Movements in Hong Kong, 1945–1958' (M.Phil. thesis, University of Hong Kong, 2011).
7 'Hongkong as a Crown Colony', *The Economist* (19 October 1946), p. 628.
8 Lau Siu-kai, *Society and Politics in Hong Kong* (Hong Kong: Chinese University Press, 1983).
9 HKU Special Collections, Hilton Cheong-Leen, 'Hongkong Urban Council Annual Conventional Debate – 11 April, 1961', in Hilton Cheong-Leen, *Hongkong Tomorrow: A Collection of Speeches* (Hong Kong: self-published, 1962), p. 25.
10 Hilton Cheong-Leen, 'Individual Freedom in a Colonial Society', in *Hongkong Tomorrow*, pp. 12–13.
11 Suzanne Pepper, *Keeping Democracy at Bay: Hong Kong and the Challenge of Chinese Political Reform* (Lanham, MD: Rowman and Littlefield, 2008), p. 127.
12 Ambrose King, 'Administrative Absorption of Politics in Hong Kong: Emphasis on the Grass Roots Level', *Asian Survey* 15 (May 1975): 422–39. See also Ma Ngok, *Political Development in Hong Kong: State, Political Society, and Civil Society* (Hong Kong: Hong Kong University Press, 2007), pp. 17–31.
13 S. S. Hsueh, *Government and Administration of Hong Kong* (Hong Kong: University Book Store, 1962), pp. 22–3; John M. Carroll, *A Concise History of Hong Kong* (Lanham, MD: Rowman and Littlefield, 2007), pp. 117, 163.
14 King, 'Administrative Absorption of Politics', p. 425.
15 Peter Harris, *Hong Kong: A Study in Bureaucratic Politics* (Hong Kong: Heinemann Asia, 1978), p. 74.
16 Norman Miners, *The Government and Politics of Hong Kong*, 5th edn (Hong Kong: Oxford University Press, 1998), p. 169.
17 Miners, *The Government and Politics of Hong Kong*, pp. 177–8; James Hayes, *The Great Difference: Hong Kong's New Territories and Its People, 1898–2004* (Hong Kong: Hong Kong University Press, 2006), p. 83.

18 On autonomy, see Ray Yep (ed.), *Negotiating Autonomy in Greater China: Hong Kong and Its Sovereign before and after 1997* (Copenhagen: NIAS Press, 2013).
19 Susan Pedersen, 'The Maternalist Moment in British Colonial Policy: The Controversy over "Child Slavery" in Hong Kong 1917–1941', *Past & Present* 171 (2001): 161–202; Shuk-wah Poon, 'Dogs and British Colonialism: The Contested Ban on Eating Dogs in Colonial Hong Kong', *Journal of Imperial and Commonwealth History* 42 (2014): 308–28. In addition, 'sweatshop' labour conditions were to a limited extent ameliorated in the early 1960s, in part because of metropolitan activist pressure. David Clayton, 'From "Free" to "Fair" Trade: The Evolution of Labour Laws in Colonial Hong Kong, 1958–62', *Journal of Imperial and Commonwealth History* 35 (2007): 263–82.
20 Ray Yep and Tai-Lok Lui, 'Revisiting the Golden Era of MacLehose and the Dynamics of Social Reforms', in Yep, *Negotiating Autonomy*.
21 Austin Coates, *Myself a Mandarin: Memoirs of a Special Magistrate* (Hong Kong: Oxford University Press, 1987 [1968]), p. 17.
22 Coates, *Myself a Mandarin*, pp. 8–9.
23 Coates, *Myself a Mandarin*, p. 36.
24 Coates, *Myself a Mandarin*, pp. 130–1.
25 Coates, *Myself a Mandarin*, p. 218.
26 Coates, *Myself a Mandarin*, pp. 60–1.
27 Ray Yep and Robert Bickers, 'Studying the 1967 Riots: An Overdue Project', in Robert Bickers and Ray Yep (eds), *May Days in Hong Kong: Emergency and Riot in 1967* (Hong Kong: Hong Kong University Press, 2009), p. 1. For a multi-perspectival analysis of the riots, see Bickers and Yep, *May Days in Hong Kong*; for a narrative of the riots, see Gary Ka-wei Cheung, *Hong Kong's Watershed: The 1967 Riots* (Hong Kong: Hong Kong University Press, 2009).
28 John Cooper, *Colony in Conflict: The Hong Kong Disturbances, May 1967–January 1968* (Hong Kong: Swindon, 1970), p. 312.
29 TNA, PREM 15/1626, Alec Douglas-Home, 'Hong Kong', 20 September 1973.
30 Cited in Pepper, *Keeping Democracy at Bay*, p. 158.
31 Pepper, *Keeping Democracy at Bay*, pp. 149–51.
32 TNA, FCO 40/43, Lord Shepherd to Harold Wilson, 13 May 1968. Emphasis in original.
33 TNA, FCO 40/235, 'Note of a Meeting with Unofficial Members of Executive and Legislative Councils (UMELCO) on Thursday, 5 June, 1969'.
34 The assertion that the main source of popular discontent was a mere communication gap is also noted by Pepper, in *Keeping Democracy at Bay*, Chapter 9.
35 TNA, FCO 40/39, Government Information Services Daily Information Bulletin, Tuesday, 21 February 1967, '1966 Kowloon Riots Not Premeditated: Report of Inquiry Commission Published'. Similar language – in some cases identical language – appears in a GIS press release of three days later, TNA, FCO 40/39, 24 February 1967, 'Commission Reports on Hong Kong Riots: "Invest in Youth"'. For early academic discussions of the Government's predilection for blaming popular dissatisfaction on a 'communication gap' rather than any substantive failures, see King, 'Administrative Absorption of Politics', pp. 430–1; Lau, *Society and Politics*, p. 58.
36 'Sir David Knows Best', *FEER* (4 December 1969), p. 528.
37 Quoted in David Baird, 'On the Cheap', *FEER* (19 December 1970), p. 8.
38 Steve Tsang, *A Modern History of Hong Kong* (London and New York: I. B. Tauris, 2004), p. 190.
39 TNA, FCO 40/235, 'Lord Shepherd's Visit to Hong Kong, June 1969: Reorganisation of Local Administration and related matters', 1.
40 TNA, FCO 40/235, 'The City District Officer Scheme: A Report to the Governor', 24 January 1969, 1–3.
41 TNA, FCO 40/235, 'SCA's Report on the First Year of the City District Office Scheme', 22 February 1969, 1.
42 TNA, FCO 40/235, 'Report by the Secretary for Chinese Affairs on the City District Officer Scheme', 24 January 1969, 9.

43 TNA, FCO 40/235, C. H. Godden, 'Hong Kong', 23 July 1969, 2.

44 Elsie Tu, *An Autobiography* (Hong Kong: Longman Group, 1988), p. 281.

45 'Conservative Choice: By a Correspondent', *FEER* (17 October 1970), p. 8.

46 Yep and Lui, 'Revisiting the Golden Era of MacLehose', pp. 110–11.

47 Carroll, *A Concise History of Hong Kong*, p. 160.

48 For a summary of the MacLehose reforms, see Ian Scott, *Political Change and the Crisis of Legitimacy in Hong Kong* (Hong Kong: Oxford University Press, 1989), pp. 127–70; Tsang, *Governing Hong Kong*, pp. 140–7. According to Duff McDonald, McKinsey got the Hong Kong contract through 'old boy' connections: Alcon Copisarow, the first non-American Senior Partner of McKinsey, 'ran into the British governor of Hong Kong, Murray MacLehose, "in the Club" and walked out with a mandate'. Duff McDonald, *The Firm: The Story of McKinsey and Its Secret Influence on American Business* (New York: Simon and Schuster, 2013), p. 80.

49 This paragraph and the two following ones are extracted from Mark Hampton, 'British Legal Culture and Colonial Governance: The Attack on Corruption in Hong Kong, 1968–1974', *Britain and the World* 5 (September 2012): 223–39; see that article for more detailed footnoting. In addition, see H. J. Lethbridge, *Hard Graft in Hong Kong: Scandal, Corruption, the ICAC* (Hong Kong: Oxford University Press, 1985); Leo Goodstadt, *Uneasy Partners: The Conflict between Public Interest and Private Profit in Hong Kong* (Hong Kong: Hong Kong University Press, 2005), pp. 139–57; Rance P. L. Lee (ed.), *Corruption and Its Control in Hong Kong* (Hong Kong: Chinese University Press, 1981).

50 Elsie Elliott, *Crusade for Justice: An Autobiography* (Hong Kong: Heinemann Asia, 1981), p. 248.

51 Agnes S. M. Ku, *Narratives, Politics, and the Public Sphere: Struggles over Political Reform in the Final Transitional Years in Hong Kong (1992–1994)* (Aldershot: Ashgate, 1999), p. 106.

52 Ku, *Narratives, Politics, and the Public Sphere*, p. 97.

53 King, 'Administrative Absorption of Politics', p. 425.

54 Lau Siu-kai and Kuan Hsin-chi, *The Ethos of the Hong Kong Chinese* (Hong Kong: Chinese University Press, 1988), p. 75. For another reference to this study, see Benjamin K. P. Leung, *Perspectives on Hong Kong Society* (Hong Kong: Oxford University Press, 1996), pp. 61–2. By the early post-1997 period, Stephen Vines described Lau Siu-kai as one of the members of the old order seeking to ingratiate themselves with the 'new masters'. According to Vines, Lau 'has often taken it upon himself to explain Chinese [PRC] policies and has done so with some eloquence. It is hard to imagine that he will be confined to academic life indefinitely.' Stephen Vines, *Hong Kong: China's New Colony* (London: Orion Business, 1999), p. 156.

55 Philip Bowring and Mary Lee, 'Mandarin on the Move', *FEER* (25 December 1981), p. 10.

56 *A Guide to District Administration* (Hong Kong: Government Printer, 1981), p. 8.

57 SHORE 13/18, District Office, Sha Tin, 'The Development of Sha Tin New Town', 15 May 1981.

58 CHAS, C 11, 'HE The Governor Stresses Need for Change in Local Authority System: Annual Dinner of Newspaper Society of Hong Kong', Government Information Services Daily Information Bulletin Supplement, 23 November 1966.

59 Carol P. Lai, *Media in Hong Kong: Press Freedom and Political Change, 1967–2005* (London and New York: Routledge, 2007), p. 39.

60 Ray Yep, ' "Cultural Revolution in Hong Kong": Emergency Powers, Administration of Justice and the Turbulent Year of 1967', *Modern Asian Studies* 46 (July 2012): 1007–32 (p. 1016).

61 Vines, *Hong Kong*, pp. 217–19.

62 Pepper, *Keeping Democracy at Bay*, pp. 177–8.

63 Tsang, *Democracy Shelved*.

64 FS J/74/3, 'Report of the Ad Hoc Committee on the Future Scope and Operation of the Urban Council', p. 4.

65 FS J/74/3, 'Report of the Ad Hoc Committee on the Future Scope and Operation of the Urban Council', pp. 13–14.
66 FS J/74/3, 'Report of the Ad Hoc Committee on the Future Scope and Operation of the Urban Council', pp. 18, 20.
67 SHORE 13/18, *The Hong Kong Urban Council: The Case of the Elected Members* (Hong Kong, 1979), pp. 1–3.
68 *The Hong Kong Urban Council*, p. 4.
69 *The Hong Kong Urban Council*, p. 10. See also SHORE 13/18, Elsie Elliott, Denny Huan, and Tsin Sai Nin to Lord Goronwy-Roberts, 24 June 1978.
70 POLL 3/2/1/77, 'White Paper: The Further Development of Representative Government in Hong Kong', November 1984, 14.
71 POLL 3/2/1/77, Michael Chugani, 'Path to an Early Takeover', *SCMP* (20 November 1985); see also 'Setting the Pace in Hong Kong', *The Times* (4 December 1984).
72 POLL 3/2/1/77, John Walden, 'Towards the Democratisation of Hong Kong: The Grand Illusion' (11 September 1985), pp. 1, 7.
73 Walden, 'Towards the Democratisation of Hong Kong', p. 2.
74 Walden, 'Towards the Democratisation of Hong Kong', p. 4.
75 Walden, 'Towards the Democratisation of Hong Kong', p. 6, Annex.
76 KNKK 1/3/55, Neil Kinnock to Robert Runcie, 19 April 1990.
77 Charles Moore, 'Fiddling while Freedom Fades', *Spectator* (25 November 1989), p. 12. In January 1988, William McGurn had made a similar point: the colonial system entailed an 'oligarchy of British civil servants in collusion with the local wealthy', but it 'worked well chiefly because British administrators were disinclined to exercise the vast powers they had reserved for themselves. But the same system in other hands would most likely not have transformed what Lord Palmerston in 1841 contemptuously dismissed as a "barren island with hardly a house upon it" into a world financial centre. Whatever else the PRC might be, its leaders have never stood accused of a reluctance to invoke their power.' William McGurn, 'Divorcing Hong Kong', *Spectator* (30 January 1988), p. 13.
78 Vines, *Hong Kong*, p. 79.
79 Jonathan Dimbleby, *The Last Governor: Chris Patten and the Handover of Hong Kong* (London: Little, Brown, 1997).
80 FAULDS 3/3/1/15, 'The Governor's Address to the Legislative Council, 7th October, 1992: The Constitutional Package', p. 1.
81 Dimbleby, *The Last Governor*, pp. 293, 301.
82 FAULDS 3/3/1/10, 'Lobbying Letter to MPs', 13 January 1988; Hong Kong Observers to Andrew Faulds, 12 January 1988; Anthony Ng, C. Y. Huang, and C. H. Leong to Andrew Faulds, 15 January 1988; Wong Wai-hung to Andrew Faulds, 12 January 1988; Szeto Wah to Andrew Faulds, 13 January 1988.
83 John Flowerdew, *The Final Years of British Hong Kong: The Discourse of Colonial Withdrawal* (New York: St Martin's Press, 1997). For a less academic and more acerbic indictment of Patten's introduction of direct elections, see FAULDS 3/3/1/16, Elsie Elliott to Tony Blair, 9 January 1997 (copy). See also Percy Cradock, *Experiences of China*, new edn (London: John Murray, 1999), 228; Vines, *Hong Kong*, pp. 87–90.
84 Vines, *Hong Kong*, pp. 90–1.

CHAPTER SIX

Chinese Britishness

In the June 1997 issue of *Hong Kong Tatler*, the magazine, which by this point articulated a largely postcolonial, elite 'Hong Konger' voice, took stock of the 'good', the 'bad', and the 'ugly' legacies of British colonial rule. The 'good' included British etiquette, the British legal system ('despite the silly wigs'), gin and tonics, Marks and Spencer underwear, and taxi queues. Among the 'bad' legacies cited were a lingering 'colonial us-and-them mentality' in which a 'remarkable lack of racial intermingling' had taken place, British snobbery, and British pop culture, in which phenomena such as the Spice Girls and *Loaded* magazine had 'managed to infiltrate and subvert 5,000 years of glorious Chinese culture'.[1] These lists are striking for the relative lack of penetration most of these British manifestations had made into wider Hong Kong culture compared, say, to Cantopop, Chinese opera, or the films of John Woo. Moreover, arguably, many of them would have been practised or consumed in open understanding that they were cultural imports attracting the thinnest of allegiance, not evidence of any kind of wholesale transformation of Hong Kong's population into culturally 'British' people. Above all, they do not move beyond caricature.

Previous chapters have focused on the interaction between Hong Kong and British culture, including the relationship of Hong Kong to Britishness. As we have seen, Hong Kong was a canvas on which particular British values were projected: unbridled capitalism, modernisation, and good governance, among others. It was also a site for distinct leisure practices, including those relating to sport, clubs, and sexuality. But in what ways did Britain's Chinese subjects participate in British culture? To what extent did they identify with British values? And how did British discourse treat the prospect of Chinese inclusion within the community of Britons?

Affective Britishness?

According to available evidence,[2] very few of Hong Kong's Chinese residents self-identified as 'British' in any cultural sense. This should not be confused with a lack of admiration for some elements of British culture, or even for 'British culture' as a comprehensive phenomenon. What I mean, rather, is that little evidence suggests that many Hong Kong Chinese embraced Britishness as a key component of their subjective identities. This is not surprising. To start, most of Hong Kong's early postwar residents spoke little English, a point frequently remarked upon by western commentators. A 1957 BBC Audience Research Report compared the level of English in Hong Kong unfavourably with that in India and Pakistan, though it noted that interest in English was relatively high.[3] According to Judith Agassi, writing in 1968, while 86.2 per cent of Hong Kong's people 'usually' spoke Cantonese, only 8.78 per cent of Hong Kong's population could speak both Cantonese and English.[4] Nor was the lack of English limited to the working classes. The Cambridge historian Herbert Butterfield, when serving in 1970 as a consultant at the Chinese University – one of only two universities in the colony at the time – noted that 'many of the students are unable to cope with English lectures and are almost incredibly slow in handling books in English'.[5] If the English language had limited penetration, then so, too, did other aspects of British culture, as numerous observers noted. One British writer in the early 1960s claimed that whereas the 'well-to-do classes' had an 'occidental veneer' belying their oriental core, 'The poorer classes do not even have the Western veneer and in the back streets of Hong Kong – the tenements, the restaurants and the tea-houses – you are in a foreign country, surrounded by an alien culture.'[6] A 1964 *Economist* article, in the context of trying to explain Hong Kong's economic miracle, denied that the territory was 'a British colony at all'; rather, it was 'just a part of China with British colonial managers, typewriters, judges' wigs, lighthouses, policemen, animal protection societies and press button A telephone boxes'.[7] The philosophers Joseph Agassi and I. C. Jarvie in 1968 distinguished between Hong Kong's 'surface' westernisation and the still thoroughly Chinese social and cultural practices, including education, the concept of face, and the conduct of business.[8] Frank Leeming noted in 1978 that Hong Kong remained 'overwhelmingly a Chinese [society] in language, social habit both public and private, and the social consciousness of the people'.[9] The Canadian-born Roger Boschman's guidebook *Hong Kong by Night*, in the context of revealing a 'Nightlife for Chinese Only', warned tourists visiting

Kowloon that 'You need only walk up Nathan Road's "Golden Mile" a little farther than usual and you soon find there are more signs in Chinese than in English. And after another few hundred yards you see almost no English at all. It's time to turn around and head back.'[10]

Even as the period of colonial rule wound down, British commentators continued to note the lack of British cultural penetration. As a leaflet from a Church of England Bishops' Council put it in 1988 – in the context of encouraging a link between its diocese and that of Hong Kong – despite trappings of modernity, 'this is a Chinese city with an overwhelming Chinese population, that still thinks and acts in Chinese'.[11] The actor-turned-Labour MP Andrew Faulds, writing in the mid-1980s, distinguished between, on the one hand, a small minority who held western travel documents and championed the quick introduction of direct elections, and on the other, 'the great bulk of the populace who still feel the ancient attachment to China and Chinese values' and would be better served by a more gradual approach to reform.[12] Kevin Rafferty put it succinctly: 'Hong Kong really is a slice of China in western disguise.'[13] Moreover, if British cultural penetration had been limited, then not surprisingly the prospect for post-1997 nostalgia was limited. *Sunday Times* correspondent Michael Sheridan, writing in the *New Statesman* ten days before the 1997 Handover, argued that unlike the end of British India in 1947, the loss of Hong Kong would not be the 'end of an affair', as the British and Cantonese had 'never developed the mutual affection that marked the Raj'.[14]

In his 1952 book *Black Skin, White Masks*, Frantz Fanon argued that an inferiority complex was inherent in all colonial subjects, producing a loss of their 'local cultural originality' and leading them to adopt the cultural values of the colonial power.[15] Similar claims have been made for overseas Chinese, for example in some Chinese-Americans' use of the derogatory term 'banana' to criticise those who had embraced mainstream white culture. This analytical frame would seem, though, to have limited applicability to the Hong Kong Chinese engagement with British culture. Far from developing feelings of inferiority, Chinese in Hong Kong remained famously chauvinistic, a point frequently remarked by western commentators. As Austin Coates put it in 1968,

> The ambassador of the most powerful nation, with nuclear warheads and other mighty armament, is basically, from the instant of setting foot on the soil of China, and despite anything that may suggest to the contrary, just another foreigner, i.e. inferior to the humblest farmer or shop assistant. A foreigner in China *is* inferior. He is inferior because more than 700,000,000 people all around him think so.[16]

The same year, Agassi and Jarvie noted the Chinese 'comforting reassurance that simply having been born Chinese amounts to being

[162]

inestimably superior to all other forms of life on earth'.[17] Similarly, Jan Morris (1997) argued that Hong Kong's lack of assimilation to British imperial culture in the late nineteenth century derived from Chinese racial self-confidence:

> The Chinese were very different from flexible Bengalis, naive Africans, charming Malays or frankly hostile Pathans. They infiltrated everything with a peculiar air of self-sufficient calculation, and seemed hardly like subjects at all. Several hundred million of their compatriots lived just across the water, and they had been brought up one and all in the conviction that every Chinese ever born was superior to every foreigner.[18]

Nor were European observers the only ones to note the Chineseness of Hong Kong. Moreover, beyond a practical lack of British cultural penetration, it was not uncommon for even better educated, English-speaking Chinese actively to repudiate any claim to Britishness. For example, Stanley Kwan, the banker who helped to create the Hang Seng Index, claims in his memoirs to have had a life-long ambivalence about his relationship to Britain. Born in 1925 to a Hong Kong filled with British symbols, he nonetheless recalls growing up with a reflexive loyalty not to Britain but to 'five thousand years of Chinese tradition and history'. The British monarchy, by contrast, was 'far removed from our daily lives'. Attending a colonial school in the late 1930s and early 1940s, he resented being forced to learn European history with a smattering of Chinese history only 'through the filter of British lenses', but he had difficulty reconciling these feelings with his being a beneficiary of a British education at a British school. He describes watching British Information Service films with his classmates during the early part of the Second World War, and, to the horror of his headmaster, they booed at the sight of George VI and applauded Adolf Hitler. He also describes sneaking out of cinemas before the end, so as to avoid having to stand for 'God Save the King'.[19] Even nearly half a century later, when his public service to the colony was rewarded with an MBE, he remained ambivalent. During the ceremony, as 'God Save the Queen' was played, he noticed that the

> metal cross of the medal was capped by the Royal Crown and hung from a red ribbon with gold trimming; inscribed around the centre of the cross were the words: 'For God and the Empire'. I was suddenly overcome by a surge of mixed emotions. I had enjoyed a productive and fulfilling life in the colony and was gratified by this public recognition of my services, but I also recalled how deeply I resented the British Empire's exploits in China and how its 'gunboat policy' had forced open China's ports for British merchants.[20]

[163]

One of Hong Kong's most famous Anglophiles, Sir David Tang, provides another example of an avowed lack of subjective Britishness. Sir David, founder of Shanghai Tang, has long been active in promoting Anglo-Chinese relations and British–Hong Kong relations, and advocating improved English-language proficiency in Hong Kong; the journalist Stephen Vines has described him as possessing the 'distinctive English accent of the British public school which tried to drum his Chinese-ness out of him'. Awarded an OBE on the eve of the Handover, in 2008 he was elevated to a KBE. In a 2012 interview with *Asia Tatler* he sounded very much like one of the stock British characters in le Carré's *The Honourable Schoolboy*: despite Britain's great civilisation, he said, Britain itself had lost its greatness because of its laziness and political correctness. Asked to describe Queen Elizabeth in five words, he replied 'she is absolutely bloody marvelous'.[21] Yet even Sir David, before the Handover, stated that 'I don't feel British in the slightest' and pointed to a basic gulf between the Chinese and British people.[22]

If even the English-speaking, elite-educated Chinese subjects in Hong Kong did not self-identify with Britishness, then it should be noted that this was consistent with British and Hong Kong Government priorities. Law Wing Sang has argued that the Hong Kong project of 'collaborative colonial power' did not centre on a sharing of British cultural values. Rather, the Hong Kong Government was interested in a governmentality that was unconcerned with spreading British values to the Chinese community, and indeed often gave positive support to Confucian values in opposition to modern Chinese nationalism or communism emanating from mainland China.[23] British wartime prisoners in occupied Hong Kong contemplated postwar constitutional reform and representative government in part as a means of helping Hong Kong's Chinese population to identify with the British Empire, and these ideas were briefly pursued by Governor Sir Mark Young; the abandonment of this reform by subsequent Governor Alexander Grantham rested in part on Grantham's belief that Hong Kong people would never identify with the British.[24] Moreover, as I have argued elsewhere, the Hong Kong Government's efforts to promote British culture among its subjects were limited at best, with neither early television policy nor the activities of the British Council in Hong Kong (at least after the 1960s) significantly aiming to promote British values within the colony.[25] A similar lack of interest in Hong Kong Britishness was on display in Britain's higher education policy; a 1979 decision to increase university fees for overseas students exempted those from European Economic Community (EEC) member states and those with refugee status, who were classified as 'home students'; Hong Kong students, by contrast, did not receive this status. According to the Hong

Kong Government, in 1980 this increase led to a 42 per cent drop in the number of British visas issued to first-time Hong Kong students.[26]

Not only did Hong Kong's Chinese have little subjective identification with 'Britishness', even as British and colonial authorities made little effort to inculcate such an identity, but even those Hong Kong people who emigrated to Britain in the first few postwar decades apparently felt little connection to their host country.[27] Between 1951 and 1971, emigrants from Hong Kong made up between a quarter and a third of Britain's Chinese population, growing from 3,459 in 1951 to 29,520 in 1971, figures not dissimilar to those of emigrants from Malaysia and Singapore; by 1981, Hong Kong had decisively surpassed Malaysia and Singapore as the leading source of the Chinese population in Britain, with a total of 58,917.[28] According to research by the anthropologist James Watson, Hong Kong's diaspora to the United Kingdom was shaped by the contingency of changes in the agricultural economy of Hong Kong's New Territories in the 1950s and the effects of the 1962 Commonwealth Immigrants Act. The new availability of imported rice, particularly from Thailand, undermined the New Territories' rice economy. While inhabitants of some villages responded by shifting to factory jobs in Kowloon, or becoming day labourers, hawkers, or domestic servants for British army camps, the Mans, the dominant lineage of San Tin, largely chose emigration to Britain (and, to a lesser extent, the Netherlands, West Germany, and Belgium). With the passage of the Commonwealth Immigrants Act – a measure aimed less at the Chinese than at West Indian and South Asian populations – a voucher system was established, in which the highest priority went to those immigrants who were hired to a specific job before arriving in Britain. This system privileged those who had connections to the UK, and specifically in the restaurant industry in which Chinese immigrants had already established themselves. Because of the Mans' early presence in this industry, and the strength of the lineage, they were able to predominate among Hong Kong immigrants to Britain during the 1960s.[29]

More pertinent to the present discussion, according to Watson the Mans used emigration not to establish new lives in Britain, but as a way of preserving village life in San Tin. Because of their higher incomes, restaurant workers (not to mention owners) were able to provide significant remittances to San Tin on a scale that not only made it one of the richer villages in the New Territories, but made themselves – despite their absence – leading figures within the village. In addition to remittances, immigrants to Britain remained tied to the village through regular visits (facilitated by a Man-operated travel agency and charter flights) and, often, through leaving wives and children behind. Beyond the positive attractions of continuing identification with their village in rural Hong Kong, where they hoped to retire, Man immigrants' identification with Britishness was hindered by the fact that they generally spoke little English.[30] Indeed, both because of their lack of English skills, and because they overwhelmingly worked in an isolated and largely 'invisible' industry, Gregor Benton and Edmund Terence Gomez conclude more broadly that the Chinese postwar migrant generation remained among the least assimilated of Britain's immigrant communities. In addition, as the incidence of family immigration grew after primary immigration became more restricted in the late 1960s, this generation's children, in many cases, underperformed in school and appeared in danger of relegation to the same catering industry in which their parents worked. Only in the 1990s and afterward did this change.[31] For this reason, a 1990 *New Statesman & Society* article, reporting that 90 per cent of 'people of Hong Kong extraction' worked in the catering trade while only about 3 per cent were professionals, quoted one recent immigrant from Hong Kong who argued that he was more 'British' than those immigrants from Hong Kong who had been in the UK for thirty years.[32]

This cultural distance of New Territories villager immigrants from their British hosts received dramatisation in Timothy Mo's 1982 novel, *Sour Sweet*. Mo, born in Hong Kong of mixed Anglo-Welsh and Chinese ancestry and educated at Oxford, depicted a young immigrant couple, Chen and Lily, who attempt to make their way in the London catering industry. Chen is at home neither in Britain nor in Hong Kong; in Britain he feels himself an 'interloper', and he has no claim to clan land in his ancestral village: 'He was remembered there in the shape of the money order he remitted to his father every month, and would truly have been remembered only if that order had failed to arrive.'[33] Despite operating a modestly successful take-away, he cannot stay on top of his gambling debts, and eventually is killed by triads who, in addition to smuggling heroin, prey upon unassimilated Chinese immigrants. Lily, herself not a native of the New Territories, but an immigrant from Kwangsi province who became a Tsuen Wan factory worker before marrying Chen and moving to London, desperately tries to preserve her family's Chinese character. She requires her young son, Man Kee, to attend Chinese school weekly. When he is bullied at school, Lily teaches him the rudiments of Chinese boxing, preferring not to draw the attention of school authorities by complaining; when Man Kee is scolded for fighting unfairly, Lily scorns the English concern for fair play.

Lily's lack of assimilation reflects, among other factors, a distrust of British government and a failure to understand British concepts of law and government. She does her best to evade the electoral-registration worker who visits her family. She tries to avoid the tax authorities, but when an Inland Revenue official patiently explains income and deductions, she finds the latter an incredible instance of a tax official teaching her how to evade taxes. She assumes that it will be possible to bribe British officials, whether police officers or immigration officers, despite her older sister Mui's admonishing her that government does not work that way in Britain.

Indeed, of the novel's main characters, Mui is the most assimilated. She befriends the English lorry drivers who frequent the take-away; this connection helpfully leads to stolen foodstuffs that enhance the take-away's profits, but also leads to Mui's unwed pregnancy. Structurally, Mo has linked impropriety to Englishness or the loss of Chineseness. Well before Mui's pregnancy, Lily had observed the young English girls in her shop with disgust: unlike her own case at their age, when she had worked in the Tsuen Wan factory, these English girls had 'extra money for take-away meals ... [and] nail varnish'. They seemed to lack all 'sense of decency and family honour':

> All running round together until a scandalous hour. It was after ten o'clock when they came in. No wonder they were always getting themselves pregnant. And she thought complacently of her own little family. Really, there was no question how superior Chinese people were to the foreign devils.[34]

To Lily, then, Mui's pregnancy is not mere misfortune but represents the very deracination that Lily is attempting to avoid.

Instrumental Britishness

Although Hong Kong's adoption of cultural Britishness, let alone a subjective identification with Britishness, remained severely limited, in particular contexts Britishness held an instrumental attraction to Hong Kong's Chinese activists. Hilton Cheong-Leen, born in British Guyana, founding Chairman of the Hong Kong Civic Association (1954) and a long-time Urban Council member beginning in 1957, frequently evoked Britishness in his calls for constitutional and economic reform in Hong Kong. Speaking in 1960 to the Hong Kong Y's Men's Club, Cheong-Leen heralded the colony's recent industrialisation and called for a strengthening of trade among Commonwealth countries. While urging more investment in Hong Kong on the part of the United Kingdom, Canada, and Australia – a step that 'would incidentally serve to keep pace with growing American and other foreign investments in Hongkong industries' – he also emphasised that

Hong Kong's emergence as an industrial power could 'in the coming years contribute a more substantial share in the economic development of the newly emerging Commonwealth countries in Africa and elsewhere'. Cheong-Leen presented Hong Kong as a site in which the 'best in Chinese and British cultures' could blend, contributing to a 'deeper and more lasting understanding' between Asians and westerners. In making this case, he highlighted the role of Britishness both in his motivation – that Hong Kong should attain its 'rightful place in the Commonwealth sun' – and in the factors enabling Hong Kong's success – the 'framework of British justice, law and order, and respect for freedom of expression and thought'.[35] Similarly, in a 1966 debate on constitutional reform in Hong Kong, recognising that independence was off the table, he called for an elected Legislative Council that would contribute to a 'local identity for Hongkong people in which they would be proud to be called "Hongkong Citizens" and at the same time retain a common citizenship with people of Britain'.[36]

With the signing of the Joint Declaration in December 1984, and the firm commitment to the transfer of sovereignty in 1997, the question of Chinese Britishness took on a very practical quality; this gained an added urgency with the Tiananmen Square crackdown in June 1989.[37] The basic charge is familiar: unlike the typical colonial exit, which resulted in independence, in this case Britain – 'perfidious Albion' in the title of one book – was retreating from Hong Kong shamefully, abandoning its loyal subjects to a tyrannical, arbitrary, and murderous Communist regime.[38] The question of Chinese Britishness in the second half of the 1980s and in the 1990s was foregrounded by the fact that, as a result of the 1962 Commonwealth Immigrants Act and 1981 British Nationality Act, Hong Kong's British nationals – in the late 1980s numbering around 3.5 million out of the colony's 6 million people – had no automatic right of abode in the UK.[39] As Dick Wilson, former editor of the *FEER*, noted in 1990, Hong Kong residents' status as British subjects

> used in the first half of this century to confer the right of abode in the UK, under the extraordinary imperial self-delusion by which a piece of Palmerstonian unreality, acceptable before the aeroplane, was cruelly maintained for several decades after international aviation began to affect population movements. After 1961 this right of abode was progressively restricted.[40]

Hong Kong people's post-1961 lack of a right of abode had almost immediate consequences, as the 1967 Kowloon 'disturbances' briefly raised the prospect of PRC takeover. However, as Labour politician and Home Office Undersecretary David Ennals argued at the end of that year, 'the fact is that during the troubled period of the past seven months, the Chinese Government have at no time demanded the return of Hong Kong to China and we have no reason to suppose that they have any intention of invading the Colony.' He went on to assert, on the one hand, that 'people in Hong Kong who are anxious about their future may rely on the British Government in power at the time to do everything possible to assist those in Hong Kong who may be placed in difficult circumstances', but, on the other hand, that unrestricted admittance to the UK would not be forthcoming.[41]

At the time the 1981 Nationality Bill was passed, according to a report by the Hong Kong Commissioner, Hong Kong people interpreted it as being primarily aimed at themselves: two-thirds of the holders of the 'UK and Colonies Citizenship' set to be redefined as British Dependent Territories Citizens (BDTCs) lived in Hong Kong. As the Commissioner noted, 'There is a widespread belief in Hong Kong that the Bill is a move by the Government to make clear that Britain does not accept responsibility for Hong Kong citizens and in particular that if the status of Hong Kong were to change Britain would be under no obligation to safeguard the position of Hong Kong Citizens *in any way*.'[42] The Commissioner noted further that most people in Hong Kong accepted that it was unreasonable to expect that a few million Hong Kong people would have the right of abode in the UK, nor would they want to move there: 'most of them who might wish to leave Hong Kong in the future would prefer to settle in America'. Rather, they objected to the way in which the bill symbolically 'distanced' the British Government from responsibility for Hong Kong.[43] It was to forestall exactly this sort of distancing that UMELCO, in May 1984 during the debates over what would become the Joint Declaration, issued a statement on 'The Future of Hong Kong'. Citing the value of Hong Kong's 143-year 'constitutional link' with the British Crown in providing an 'effective external insulator against interference from the ruling government on the Mainland', the UMELCO statement noted the 'essential incompatibility' between the contemporary Chinese Government to which Hong Kong was to be delivered and the 'liberal traditions of a capitalist society'. Accordingly, UMELCO articulated six 'worries' and posed two 'questions', which among them sought to ascertain whether Britain would insist on some kind of presence in Hong Kong after 1997 in order to ensure that Hong Kong's freedoms were honoured, whether Britain had a mechanism in place for preventing Chinese encroachment on British rule during the final thirteen years, and whether Britain would provide right of abode to its Hong Kong nationals: 'Hong Kong belongers who cannot accept the idea of living under Communist authority'.[44]

As Ian Scott has pointed out, most Hong Kong residents accepted that China was the 'legitimate sovereign power in the territory', and held 'strong feelings of patriotism toward the country ... enhanced by cultural and family ties'. Yet, he argues, 'most Hong Kong people seemed to feel that allegiance to their country need not extend to approval of its government'.[45] Similarly, Frank Leeming wrote in 1977 that 'The people do not shake off, or even wish to shake off, the commitment of loyalty to China – loyalty not primarily or mainly to the Chinese government, but to the mainland community.'[46] In the words of Lee Cheuk Yan, a trade union spokesman, quoted in the *New Statesman* in 1984, 'Local people dislike the British but at the same time they are afraid of the communists, although they recognise Chinese sovereignty over Hong Kong.'[47]

Scott's argument is further borne out by political discourse from the late 1980s, in which prominent Hong Kong Chinese activists sought to assert rights as loyal British subjects, using the language of British national character, while nonetheless affirming their affective commitment to Hong Kong and China. In addition, sympathetic British activists based in the UK articulated similar views on behalf of Hong Kong's residents. In essence, the position argued was that Britain's treaty commitment in the Joint Declaration called for it to safeguard Hong Kong's prosperity and stability; yet, particularly in the aftermath of the Tiananmen Square incident, Hong Kong was facing a brain drain as 1,000 people per week were emigrating, thereby undermining that prosperity and stability. This was more than a question of British 'honour' and duty to its subjects. For one thing, Britain's achievement in Hong Kong – the latter's often-remarked transformation from a 'barren rock' to one of the world's most prosperous cities – had depended upon creating a space in which the energies of the Chinese people could flourish.[48] Allowing, instead, an environment from which Hong Kong's Chinese residents wished to flee would, therefore, undermine this British achievement. At the same time, as Chapter 7 will explore, the safeguarding of Hong Kong's 'one country, two systems' settlement was thought to depend upon its remaining a golden goose from which China prospered; a decline in Hong Kong's prosperity would make Beijing far less likely to honour the agreement.

The solution to this problem, according to activist groups both in Hong Kong and in the United Kingdom, including Honour Hong Kong, Hong Kong Link, and British Citizens for Hong Kong, was to restore the 'right of abode' to the 3.5 million British nationals in Hong Kong who had in 1981 been redefined as BDTCs. Such activists argued that this escape valve would, paradoxically, increase the likelihood of those nationals' remaining in Hong Kong.[49] Moreover, according to Kenneth Leech, an opinion poll by Hong Kong Radio less than three weeks after the Tiananmen Square killings suggested that only 6 per cent of

British passport holders would want to move to Britain, while more than three times as many would go to other countries, and well over half would want to stay in Hong Kong. These poll results may have reflected a sense that the Hong Kong people were unwelcome; according to Leech, in 1988, of the nearly 50,000 people who had left Hong Kong, around half had gone to Canada, while only 776 had come to Britain.[50] Yet British opponents of Hong Kong people's 'right of abode' successfully raised the spectre of 3.5 million Chinese descending upon the United Kingdom, and in the event, the British Government granted full British passports to only some 50,000 Chinese households (comprising potentially 225,000 individuals) containing members in particularly sensitive positions who, it was feared, might be likely targets for retaliation by the PRC after 1997. Labour Party leader Neil Kinnock, in a 1990 letter to the Archibishop of Canterbury, called the plan 'utterly cynical'.[51] In the context of debate on the bill, Hong Kong Link denounced the package as a violation of the 'constitutional right' to 'full British nationality' that all British nationals possessed: 'We believe the Government's scheme is discriminatory in principle, offensive to human dignity, unworkable in practice, and bitterly divisive in effect.'[52] Percy Cradock, former Ambassador to China, wrote in 1994 that the figure of 50,000 households was a necessary compromise: a 'balance between moral obligation and political practicality'. Failure to have awarded even that limited number of passports, he insisted, would have threatened continuing exodus of professionals and entrepreneurs who were vital to Hong Kong's economic performance; giving significantly more was simply not realistic in the context of British electoral and parliamentary politics.[53] Lydia Dunn, writing for the Office of the Members of the Executive and Legislative Councils (OMELCO) (the organisation previously named the Unofficial Members of the Hong Kong Executive and Legislative Council (UMELCO)) during the bill's debate, argued that failure to pass it would make Hong Kong virtually ungovernable and would also send the 'wrong message' to other sympathetic countries.[54] Andrew Faulds, the only Labour MP to vote for the bill, nonetheless called it 'disgraceful' even after the fact, and indicated that he had voted for it only because failure to pass any bill could have had devastating consequences for Hong Kong's economy.[55]

What is interesting about these arguments for the present purpose is their implication for Chinese Britishness. On the one hand, British opponents of the right of abode argued that Hong Kong Chinese had no real loyalty to Britain, nor did they self-identify as British; they would very likely emigrate en masse to Britain if given the opportunity, but only for narrowly self-interested reasons: for example, to escape Communist tyranny, or to take advantage of the British Welfare State.

In Stuart Ward's terms, Hong Kong's Chinese were among the 'rejected Britons'; or, as Werner Menski put it, 'If "there ain't no black in the Union Jack", there is no space for yellow, either.'[56] That this rejection was racial can hardly be doubted; as some British defenders of Hong Kong Chinese right of abode pointed out, some 300 million Europeans already had the right of abode in Britain thanks to the EEC, not to mention the much smaller number of people from Gibraltar or the Falkland Islands.[57] In contrast to Hong Kong, the whiteness of these populations, along with the greater stability of their countries, meant that few Britons expressed worry about them swamping the British Isles. Yet somewhat ironically, because Macau's ethnic Chinese had full right of abode in Portugal, Portugal's prospective membership in the EEC would mean that Macau's Chinese would enjoy the right of abode in Britain that was denied to Hong Kong's Chinese.[58]

Popular fears of Britons' being swamped by immigrants from Hong Kong, often directly linked to Hong Kong people's alien race or culture, can be seen in the correspondence of Conservative MP Enoch Powell. As Bill Schwarz has argued, Powell, famously the author of the so-called 'Rivers of Blood' speech (1968) embodied, for many Britons, the defence of whiteness against mainstream politicians too willing to betray the race; accordingly, it is not surprising that Britons alarmed about the prospect of a mass Hong Kong immigration would have chosen him as their champion.[59] A July 1984 correspondent from Manchester forwarded to Powell a letter he had originally sent to his MP Fred Silvester, along with Silvester's reply. The correspondent worried that in the event of a Chinese Idi Amin figure arising, those Hong Kong people holding a British passport would be allowed to immigrate. In this case, the 'already disillusioned' (white) British people would 'lose their will to exist as a separate people'.[60] A September 1984 correspondent praised Powell's prescient warning of future immigration from Hong Kong, particularly among police and officials who could be targeted for punishment by the PRC. He opposed such immigration, arguing that Asians, whether from India or Hong Kong, 'will not and *cannot* be English. Their cultures remain Asian.'[61] A June 1989 correspondent, addressing the 'still young and handsome looking right honourable Enoch Powell MP and Genius' argued incoherently against allowing Hong Kong Chinese to settle in Britain on the grounds that Chinese people displayed their immorality by shooting 'their own dissidents'. This correspondent argued that Australia or the Falkland Islands would make a better home for Hong Kong Chinese, and suggested for good measure that Britain's West Indian population could be swapped with South Africa's white population.[62] At least one of Powell's correspondents, a Hong Kong Chinese writing from Hong

Kong, insisted that the Joint Declaration would satisfy Hong Kong people, few of whom would want to leave their familiar life and work for crime- and strike-ridden England.[63] Still, most of Powell's correspondents exemplified what one 1985 pamphlet, issued by the Joint Council for the Welfare of Immigrants (JCWI), called 'Britain's insensitive and pathological fear of non-white immigration'.[64]

Auberon Waugh, writing in the *Spectator* in June 1989, a few short weeks after the Tiananmen Square massacre – and, amazingly, without directly mentioning it – pitched his objection to right of abode at a higher level of bonhomie than did Powell's typical correspondent. In a column published under the heading 'Another Voice' – it disputed the magazine's unsigned leading article of the previous week – he admitted that to see 'the miracle of Hong Kong handed over to these incompetents and barbarians is undoubtedly a bleeding shame', but denied there was really anything the British could do about it. He acknowledged that 'all the best people' in Britain felt good about themselves for calling upon the British Government to extend right of abode to 3.2 million Hong Kong Chinese, but concluded that it was 'absurd' to 'pretend that the Hong Kong Chinese have some mystical right of abode beyond the dictates of charity, pity and possible advantage'. He gave short shrift to their Britishness: not least because

> although they may technically be British subjects, they do not actually pay British taxes nor take any part in British elections. A surprising number of them do not talk any English, and few have any particular regard for Britain. We are not even their biggest trading partners, trailing behind the USA, China and West Germany.

He admitted that the 'obligations of charity and pity' were 'less easy to laugh off', but noted the 'unfortunate accident' that at the exact moment that the British were debating their moral obligations, the Hong Kong Government was agitating to be freed from its own 'charitable obligation to accept further refugees from Vietnam'. With the same rhetorical prowess that prompted him to leave the post-Tiananmen context out of his framing, he also neglected to mention that Hong Kong hardly had played the same effective role in having created the post-Vietnam War refugee crisis that Britain had played in creating a British colony on the edge of Communist China; to his claim that Hong Kong's Chinese were not Britain's problem, he added by implication that they were not particularly deserving.[65] One of Andrew Faulds's correspondents in early July 1989, citing the 'Rushdie affair', worried about the prospect of non-Christian Hong Kong immigration; she suggested that Britain's 'responsibility' for Hong Kong, which Faulds had referenced in his reply to her previous letter, was 'slightly' altered by 'the fact that we only leased Hong Kong'. At the very least, that might make Britain's responsibility only 'temporary'.[66]

It is not surprising that opponents of immigration noted Hong Kong people's otherness. Yet supporters of the right of abode – both those in Britain and those in Hong Kong – while insisting on Hong Kong people's 'British' rights, very similarly articulated their subjective non-identification as British, an identity that made large-scale migration to the UK unlikely. For example, a 1985 JCWI pamphlet took exception to the assumption that 'non-white people, once given the right to enter Britain, will automatically and almost immediately seek to exercise it'.[67] Indeed, Hilton Cheong-Leen, by now a Legislative Council member as well as remaining Chairman of the Hongkong Civic Association, wrote to the Minister of State for Foreign and Commonwealth Affairs in early 1986 urging him to use his 'good offices to reduce the "invasion bogey" of the British Isles by 3¼ million Hong Kong ethnic BDTCs to its minimal and insignificant proportions'.[68] Similarly, a 1989 position paper by OMELCO was provocatively entitled 'Hong Kong Is Our Home'. It pointed out that before 1962, British subjects in Hong Kong 'shared a common citizenship with British subjects in the UK and had the unfettered right to enter, work and remain in the UK'; this right 'was taken away'. Adding further insult, in 1997 even the BDTCs status would be taken away, to be replaced – only for those who applied for it on time – with a new status of British National (Overseas) (BNO). Not only would this status afford 'very little protection', but it would not give them the right of abode anywhere – not even in Hong Kong. This poor treatment occurred, the pamphlet argued, despite the fact that 'Like British subjects everywhere they owe loyalty and allegiance to their sovereign.'[69] Arguably, the criticism that the BNO passport did not provide the right of abode even in Hong Kong was more theatre than substance: the 1984 Joint Declaration spelled out who possessed the post-Handover right of abode in Hong Kong, and this status did not in any way depend on the possession of post-Handover British nationality (for obvious reasons, given that Hong Kong would no longer be a British territory).[70] On the other hand, as the JCWI argued in 1985, the fact that the BNO passport was not attached to the right of abode (in Hong Kong any more than in the UK) rendered the passport fairly ineffective as a travel document, since third countries would not allow entry without proof of the right to return to *somewhere*. The suggestion that the passport include a 'reference to the holder's identity card' entailed, in effect, that the identity card itself would serve as the travel document.[71] Yet in the present context, the relevant point to make about the 1989 OMELCO pamphlet is its strident (if instrumental) appeal to British rights.

[174]

At the same time, loyalty to the British sovereign did not imply the desire actually to live in the United Kingdom; as the pamphlet argued, '[v]ery few people here wish to leave the flourishing, exciting city that they look on as their home'. Rather, insecurity led them to seek a second passport – a quest that, absent the right of abode, required emigration; Stanley Kwan, for example, ultimately emigrated to Canada. Nor did OMELCO accept the suggestion that all that was necessary was for Britain to secure 'guarantees from countries throughout the world to take large numbers of people from Hong Kong' in an 'Armageddon Scenario'; the confidence necessary to prevent 'Brain Drain' required 'immediate, concrete guarantees – in the form of passports'.[72] A November 1989 pamphlet published by the JCWI argued that the lack of an overseas passport prompted the mass exodus that was occurring: 'a record 55,000 people left this year, and the numbers are limited only by the quotas set by other countries'. The result was that estimated staff turnover in business was around 25–30 per cent, a proportion that was even worse in middle management and specialised technical areas.[73] Several months later, the Archbishop of York, shortly after returning from a visit to Hong Kong as leader of a British Council of Churches delegation, pointed to Hong Kong churches that had lost 30 per cent of their membership to emigration in just a few months, as well as a growing shortage of doctors.[74] The quality of the émigrés was as alarming as their quantity; not all of the reported one-third of Hong Kong's overall population who, in May 1989, were considering emigrating ahead of the Handover would have been able to do so in practice.[75]

Not only would the right of abode likely prevent the continuing exodus from Hong Kong, allowing Hong Kong's Chinese to remain in the city they called home, but some critics of the UK Government's policy argued that a mass migration to the UK, even if it did occur, would actually redound to the latter's benefit. At the time the Draft Agreement of the Joint Declaration was presented, in September 1984, Liberal MP Russell Johnston suggested that immigration from Hong Kong would 'do the UK economy a power of good', since such immigrants could provide what the UK economy lacked: 'innovation, energy and commitment to work hard'.[76] A May 1989 *Spectator* article similarly argued that 'the loss of confidence in Britain of the many talented and industrious individuals in Hong Kong who are seeking another base in another country' would cost Britain dearly. Not only did most of them merely want a guarantee so that they could stay in Hong Kong, but even if they were to immigrate to Britain, it would not be cause for alarm: 'we did quite well from letting in Jewish refugees from Central Europe in the 1930s and 1940s (though we were scarcely generous about it), Hungarians in the 1950s and Ugandan Asians in the 1970s'.[77] Not quite two months later, writing in the *New Statesman & Society* just a few days after Tiananmen, H. A. Turner predicted that by 1997 'well over a million people' would have established a claim to 'refuge outside Britain', for example in North America and Australasia; these would be,

> in effect, the most able, educated and enterprising members of Hong Kong society, the products of an advanced education, a civilised and orderly life-style, and a culture orientated to industrious self-improvement, to mutual family support and to community interest and works. They have also been the agents, under a regime mostly benevolent and non-interventionist towards business, of a remarkable economic dynamism which has made Hong Kong the cited paradigm of Mrs Thatcher's ideological mentor, Milton Friedman.

How ironic, Turner noted, if 'they should be excluded by the government which most lauds the ideals they embody'.[78] To which we might add, how ironic given that, as Chapter 2 argued, Hong Kong had, by Thatcherite logic, been more British in character than Britain itself during the heyday of postwar Welfare State consensus.

Although this chapter's primary focus is on Chinese Britishness, Hong Kong's Chinese residents were not the only group affected by the British Government's desire to ensure that future events in Hong Kong did not result in unwanted immigrants. Whatever the injustice of their being denied British rights and being involuntarily transferred from one governmental jurisdiction to another, they were, in theory, being upgraded from colonial subjects to citizens in a republic run by their countrymen. Many of Hong Kong's non-Chinese (and non-European) subjects, by contrast, faced the prospect of statelessness.[79] Like Chinese activists, the Council of Hong Kong Indian Associations asserted both their rights as loyal British subjects and the ultimate desire of most Hong Kong Indians to remain in Hong Kong. Yet as the organisation's Acting President, K. Sital, argued in a 1985 petition to the House of Lords, even if Hong Kong's potentially stateless Indians did wish to move to the UK, their small number – approximately 6,000 – meant that they did not pose the same risk of swamping Britain as the Hong Kong Chinese did. The statement cited MP Andrew Faulds's assertion in the House of Commons that although the Indian community constituted only about 1 per cent of Hong Kong's population, it accounted for between 12 and 14 per cent of the territory's trade and that, moreover, it was the wealthier Indians who disproportionately stood to become stateless, as the poorer Indians were more likely to carry Indian passports.

Although the emphasis on the Indian community's small numbers, economic contribution to Hong Kong, and desire to continue living in Hong Kong was chiefly pragmatic, the Council's petition closed by appealing, as many Chinese activists did, to the 'rights and freedom of British Subjects'.[80] The British Government disputed the Council's summary of the Indians' plight. As Foreign Office Minister Richard Luce argued, the Sino-British Joint Declaration provided for non-Chinese current British Dependent Territory Citizens to have the right of abode in Hong Kong; their new BNO status would entitle them to passports on which they could travel outside Hong Kong; and they were entitled to British consular protection within Hong Kong. Aside from that, a path was available under Chinese law for them to become Chinese nationals.[81] The British Government's position, then, was that it was fulfilling its obligation to its non-Chinese subjects in Hong Kong.[82]

Significantly, Hong Kong's UMELCO supported the right of abode in Britain of non-Chinese residents. In January 1986, in the context of Parliament's debating the Hong Kong (British Nationality) Order 1986, UMELCO stated that its members were 'profoundly disappointed' with the British Government's approach to the 'compelling case' of ethnic minorities and former servicemen, and accused the Government of failing to discharge their moral responsibility to British nationals who have made valuable contributions to Britain and the Commonwealth'. UMELCO asserted the right of all BNO passport holders (both Chinese and ethnic minorities) to travel freely in the UK and called for a passport that made this right explicit; in this pre-Tiananmen period it did not yet assert the right of abode for Hong Kong's Chinese, and insisted that such a passport would not circumvent the normal immigration rules. In the case of ethnic minorities, however, UMELCO called for full British citizenship. Moreover, echoing a linkage familiar in western culture at least since the French Revolution, it called for those who had defended Hong Kong – 'British territory' – militarily during the Second World War to be awarded full citizenship.[83]

Chinese Britishness was an identity to be asserted for instrumental reasons, not, in most cases, a subjective self-identification. Hong Kong is hardly unique in this regard: Lynn Hollen Lees has made a similar point about articulations of Britishness in Malaya between 1890 and 1940, distinguishing between a 'subjective definition of identity' and 'one that is performative and related to particular situations'.[84]

But is that all there is to it? I would suggest that a subjective self-identification that *had* become prominent by the mid-1980s – that of Hong Konger – contained a great deal of Britishness within it, even if not generally articulated as such. To be sure, much of the resentment

'Hong Kongers' exhibited toward two successive waves of 'new immigrants' from the PRC in the 1978–81 period and in the early 1990s reflected economic competition as well as a not untypical urban disdain for less sophisticated rural transplants – both of which sat uneasily with the fairly brief roots most of them had in Hong Kong themselves.[85] Yet the binary between Hong Kong and mainland had a distinct, and frequently articulated, cultural element in it as well. In a summary of a Legislative Council debate in March 1984, in the context of the negotiations that would ultimately lead to the Joint Declaration, S. Y. Chung and R. H. Lobo, respectively Senior Unoffical Member of the Executive Council and Senior Unofficial Member of the Legislative Council, noted that the 'systems of Hong Kong and China are fundamentally different', leading Hong Kong people, who valued 'personal freedom' above all other rights, to fear the prospects of a handover to China. They argued that the 'great majority of Hong Kong people wish[ed] to maintain their existing life-style, social, legal and economic systems'.[86] Although they did not make this explicit, the last two systems named were direct legacies of British rule, while the first two named arguably depended upon it. Two months later, a UMELCO statement, already cited, foregrounded its implicit calls for right of abode in Britain for Hong Kong people and a post-1997 role for the British Government in Hong Kong by pointing to the 'historical reality that Hong Kong has developed over many years as a recognisable community in its own right with its own distinctive lifestyle'.[87] The scholar Sea-ling Cheng, describing the reinvention of Lan Kwai Fong in the 1990s as a space in which affluent Chinese and westerners freely intermingled, noted that its Chinese denizens often adopted westernised fashion sensibilities; one informant, pointing to her friend's revealing clothing, told Cheng that 'we obviously can't go to Chinese restaurants without getting stared at. We dress in such a way that the locals may think we look like prostitutes. But for the *gwailou*, they're used to it – it's no big deal.' These young women, argues Cheng, had effectively become 'half-Chinese half-*gwailou*', and regarded Lan Kwai Fong as a 'haven for their no-longer-fully-Chinese selves'.[88]

To be sure, this westernised lifestyle was not merely British; it owed a great deal to American influences, for example. Yet the British contribution to the making of the Hong Konger went well beyond merely creating the structure in which such interactions could occur. It also included specific shaping of the cultural fabric of their society, and one that Hong Kong's Chinese have often asserted. For example, Hilton Cheon-Leen, in a 1966 speech to students at the Chinese University – the same university whose students' English proficiency so disappointed Herbert Butterfield four years later – claimed that the colony's

Figure 10 Hong Kong youth greet the Beatles, July 1965.

young population was 'absorbing a full torrent of British, American and other types of Western culture'. Despite his inclusive label for these cultural imports, three of his five examples were British, including English classical literature, 'Beatle-singing', and 'James Bond 007 thrillers', while his more inclusive examples – western science and 'bowling dates', reflected arenas in which even Britain itself was arguably less distinctive.[89] A Hong Kong Government publication from the early 1990s asserted that many of Hong Kong's young executives were British-educated, while British retailers had recently expanded to the colony, and Hong Kong's workers had 'grown accustomed to British banking systems, British laws and British corporate structure'. At a more mundane level, perhaps, 'Britain's famous double decker buses' were a 'familiar sight' on Hong Kong streets.[90] Equally mundane, in 1994, just a few short years before the Handover, surveys about the Hong Kong legal system indicated 'strong public support for retaining wigs and gowns'.[91] The trappings of Britishness, both superficial and substantive, remained central to the conception of the Hong Kong person, even when not articulated as such. Christine Loh, writing in 1994 in the short-lived *Eastern Express*, argued that the territory had grown up in a very different direction to the mainland, resulting in a very different culture: 'Hong Kong has found its interests best served by a combination of liberal values, non-interventionist government, free trade and the rule of law.' Hong Kong people were pragmatic. Happily, the British colonisers had 'let Hong Kong go much its own way' in developing such values; she doubted that the PRC would follow suit.[92] Even Stanley Kwan, despite his self-conscious 'ambivalence' about Britain's role in China and Hong Kong, named among his reasons for choosing Canada as his new home: the 'common heritage in British based systems and institutions and the use of English as an official language', and a 'wide range of constitutional rights and personal freedoms'.[93]

More broadly, when Chinese Hong Kong people, nearly two decades after the Handover, publicly articulated a civic identity, often in opposition to mainland Chinese, they frequently emphasised one or more categories that were, in fact, fundamental to Hong Kong Britishness: rule of law, anti-corruption, fair play, modernisation (including, for example, not eating dogs, lining up in queues correctly), efficient but minimal government, even democratisation. In many cases, such attributes were cited without mention of their British provenance.[94] In the case of cultural theorist Law Wing Sang, by contrast, the very definition of contemporary Hong Kong Chineseness is bound up with the colonial experience, a colonial identity that continues to 'linger in the absence of a discernible colonizer'; for Law, it is less the content of British culture than the internalisation of a collaborative mentality that is crucial.[95] Whether articulating 'British' values apart from British people, or articulating a lingering colonialism without colonisers, it remains difficult to articulate a Hong Kong identity without smuggling in a substantial dose of Britishness.

Notes

1 'British Legacy in Hong Kong', *Hong Kong Tatler* 21 (June 1997), p. 158.
2 As noted in the introduction, this chapter, like the rest of the book, is based on English-language evidence. Among all of the chapters, this is the one in which the lack of Chinese sources is most notable. I have made some effort to locate Chinese sources with the help of research assistants, to no avail. I have also consulted with Cantonese-speaking experts on recent Hong Kong history who expressed doubt that Chinese sources would add substantively to this analysis.
3 BBC WAC, E3/1, 391/1, Far East Hong Kong, 1 January 1955 to 31 December 1996, 'Overseas Audience Research Report/Survey of Listening in Hong Kong, December 1957', p. 1.
4 Judith Agassi, 'Social Structure and Social Stratification in Hong Kong', in Ian C. Jarvie and Joseph Agassi (eds), *Hong Kong: A Society in Transition* (New York: Frederick A. Praeger, 1968), pp. 65–75 (p. 75).

CHINESE BRITISHNESS

5 BUTT/21/5, Herbert Butterfield, 'The Chinese University of Hong Kong'.
6 F. D. Ommanney, *Fragrant Harbour: A Private View of Hong Kong* (London: Hutchinson, 1962), p. 41. Nigel Cameron's 1978 history similarly argued that from 'almost every vantage point overlooking the harbour of Hong Kong the visitor has to remind himself that this is the East and that he is gazing on an oriental city. Almost everything in sight is occidental.' Nigel Cameron, *Hong Kong: The Cultured Pearl* (Hong Kong: Oxford University Press, 1978), p. 200.
7 'How Hongkong Does It', *The Economist* (14 November 1964), p. 725.
8 Joseph Agassi and Ian C. Jarvie, 'A Study in Westernization', in Jarvie and Agassi, *Hong Kong: A Society in Transition*, pp. 129–63.
9 Frank Leeming, *Street Studies in Hong Kong: Localities in a Chinese City* (Oxford: Oxford University Press, 1977), quoted in Joe England, *Industrial Relations and Law in Hong Kong*, 2nd edn (Hong Kong: Oxford University Press, 1989), p. 39.
10 Roger Boschman, *Hong Kong by Night* (Hong Kong: CFW Publications, 1981), p. 21.
11 LMA, DRO/101/267, *What Is It?*, p. 2. See also Jan Morris, *Hong Kong: Epilogue to an Empire* (New York: Random House, 1997), p. 130.
12 FAULDS 4/9/8, File 2/2, unpublished handwritten manuscript, untitled, n.d., p. 7. See also FAULDS 4/9/4, unpublished handwritten manuscript (speech), untitled, n.d. [1996–97], p. 4.
13 Kevin Rafferty, *City on the Rocks: Hong Kong's Uncertain Future* (New York: Viking, 1989), p. 7. See also, from the same year, Ian Buruma, 'This Colony is Full of Voices', *Spectator* (8 July 1989), pp. 8–9.
14 Michael Sheridan, 'Close of Business', *New Statesman* (20 June 1997), p. 45.
15 Frantz Fanon, *Black Skin, White Masks*, trans. Richard Philcox (New York: Grove Press, 2008), p. 2.
16 Austin Coates, *Myself a Mandarin: Memoirs of a Special Magistrate* (Hong Kong: Oxford University Press, 1987 [1968]), pp. 225–6.
17 Agassi and Jarvie, 'A Study in Westernization', p. 158.
18 Morris, *Hong Kong*, p. 78.
19 Stanley S. K. Kwan with Nicole Kwan, *The Dragon and the Crown: Hong Kong Memoirs* (Hong Kong: Hong Kong University Press, 2008), pp. 1, 24, 26, 27.
20 Kwan, *The Dragon and the Crown*, p. 166.
21 Stephen Vines, *Hong Kong: China's New Colony* (London: Orion Business, 1999), p. 71; 'Interview: David Tang on All Things British', *Hong Kong Tatler* (11 June 2012), available at http://hk.asiatatler.com/culture-lifestyle/arts/interview-david-tang-on-all-things-british (accessed 30 August 2014); Beryl Cook, 'Business Hit by Low Level of English', *SCMP* (2 April 1993); Beryl Cook, 'British Connection: English Campaign a Big Hit', *SCMP* (26 March 1993); Oliver Poole, 'Sir Donald Tsang Tops Honours', *SCMP* (14 June 1997).
22 Vines, *Hong Kong*, p. 71.
23 Law Wing Sang, *Collaborative Colonial Power: The Making of the Hong Kong Chinese* (Hong Kong: Hong Kong University Press, 2009). See Grace Ai-Ling Chou, *Confucianism, Colonialism, and the Cold War: Chinese Cultural Education at Hong Kong's New Asia College, 1949–1963* (Leiden: Brill, 2011) for the role of such policies in the creation of the Chinese University of Hong Kong (CUHK).
24 Felicia Yap, 'A "New Angle of Vision": British Imperial Reappraisal of Hong Kong during the Second World War', *The Journal of Imperial and Commonwealth History* 42 (2014): 86–113; Steve Tsang, *Democracy Shelved: Great Britain, China, and Attempts at Constitutional Reform in Hong Kong, 1945–1952* (Hong Kong, Oxford, and New York: Oxford University Press, 1988).
25 Mark Hampton, 'Early Hong Kong Television, 1950s–1970s: Commercialization, Public Service, and Britishness', *Media History* 17 (August 2011): 305–22; Mark Hampton, 'Projecting Britishness to Hong Kong: The British Council and Hong Kong House, 1950s–1970s', *Historical Research* 85 (November 2012): 691–709.
26 SHORE 13/18, 'Note for Rt Hon. Peter Shore MP: Fees for Hong Kong Students in Britain'.

27 For the wider context of emigration from Hong Kong during this period, see Ronald Skeldon, 'Emigration from Hong Kong, 1945–1994: The Demographic Lead-up to 1997', in Ronald Skeldon (ed.), *Emigration from Hong Kong: Tendencies and Impacts* (Hong Kong: Chinese University Press, 1995).

28 Monica J. Taylor, *Chinese Pupils in Britain: A Review of Research into the Education of Pupils of Chinese Origin* (Windsor: NFER Nelson, 1987), cited in Gregor Benton and Edmund Terence Gomez, *The Chinese in Britain, 1800 – Present: Economy, Transnationalism, Identity* (Basingstoke: Palgrave Macmillan, 2008), p. 51.

29 James L. Watson, *Emigration and the Chinese Lineage: The Mans in Hong Kong and London* (Berkeley, Los Angeles, and London: University of California Press, 1975). For the wider context of postwar immigration policy, see Kathleen Paul, *Whitewashing Britain: Race and Citizenship in the Postwar Era* (Ithaca, NY: Cornell University Press, 1997).

30 Watson, *Emigration and the Chinese Lineage*.

31 Benton and Gomez, *The Chinese in Britain*, pp. 321–60.

32 Jolyon Jenkins, 'The Dream of Sami-Si', *New Statesman & Society* (19 January 1990), p. 11.

33 Timothy Mo, *Sour Sweet* (London: Paddleless Press, 1999 [1982]) p. 5.

34 Mo, *Sour Sweet*, p. 143.

35 HKU Special Collections, Hilton Cheong-Leen, 'Hongkong in the Changing Commonwealth', in *Hongkong Tomorrow: A Collection of Speeches* (Hong Kong: self-published, 1962), pp. 10–11.

36 FS J/74/1, Hilton Cheong-Leen, 'Debate on Report of the Ad Hoc Committee on the Future Scope and Operation of the Urban Council', 4 October 1966.

37 The landscape concerning this issue changed immediately after the Tiananmen Square incident. See, for example, Woodrow Wyatt, 'Passports against Slaughter', *The Times* (6 June 1989); 'The Hong Kong Crisis: Duty and Honour', *The Times* (8 June 1989).

38 William McGurn, *Perfidious Albion: The Abandonment of Hong Kong 1997* (Washington: Ethics and Public Policy Center, 1992).

39 Hong Kong's Chinese population consisted both of British nationals, generally born in the colony, and non-nationals, generally more recent immigrants from China. The number who, as British nationals, would have had right of abode in Britain before the legal change in 1961 is frequently cited by period sources; the number fluctuates from source to source. For example, a 1992 memorandum from the Hong Kong Freedom Association stated that 'Hong Kong is currently a free and prosperous society of over 6 million people of whom some 3.5 million are British Nationals and entitled to the protection of the Crown.' Bishopsgate Institute, BG/P/18/2/148, Hong Kong Freedom Association to Bernie Grant, 25 February 1992.

40 Dick Wilson, *Hong Kong's Future: Realistic Grounds for Optimism?* (London: Royal Institute of International Affairs, 1990), p. 25.

41 TNA, FCO 40/130, David Ennals to Sir George Sinclair, n.d. [late 1967]. This letter came in response to an exchange initially launched by a letter from M. H. Jackson-Lipkin to Home Secretary Roy Jenkins in September, complaining that Hong Kong medical doctors carrying 'so-called British passports' were told they needed a visa to enter the UK. TNA, FCO 40/30, Jackson-Lipkin to Jenkins, 19 September 1967.

42 SHORE 13/18, 'The Nationality Bill – A Note by the Hong Kong Commissioner', p. 2. Emphasis in original. See also 'Hong Kong's Human Factor', *The Times* (11 May 1986).

43 SHORE 13/18, 'The Nationality Bill – A Note by the Hong Kong Commissioner', pp. 3–4.

44 FAULDS 3/3/1/6, UMELCO, 'The Future of Hong Kong', 8 May 1984.

45 Ian Scott, *Political Change and the Crisis of Legitimacy in Hong Kong* (Hong Kong: Oxford University Press, 1989), p. 11.

46 Leeming, *Street Studies*, p. 14.

47 Quoted in Kevin Toolis, 'Colonial Cold Feet', *New Statesman* (4 May 1984), p. 21.

48 See, e.g., Bishopsgate Institute, BG/P/18/2/148, OMELCO, 'Hong Kong Now and beyond 1997', October 1989.
49 Bishopsgate Institute, BG/P/18/2/148, British Citizens for Hong Kong, 'Hong Kong's Future Is in Your Hands', 21 December 1989. See also BG/P/18/2/148, OMELCO, 'Hong Kong', 15 December 1989.
50 Bishopsgate Institute, BG/P/18/2/148, Kenneth Leech, Runnymede Briefing Paper, New Series no. 1, 'Immigration, Nationality and Hong Kong: Some Underlying Issues', 1.
51 KNKK 1/3/55, Neil Kinnock to Robert Runcie, 19 April 1990.
52 FAULDS 3/3/1/10, Hong Kong Link, Press Release, 'The British Government's Nationality Package', 20 December 1989.
53 Percy Cradock, *Experiences of China*, new edn (London: John Murray, 1999), p. 236. A leading article in the *Spectator* in June 1989, very shortly after Tiananmen, argued that, at least, the British Government could have *tried* to influence public opinion toward accepting Britain's moral responsibility to its Hong Kong Chinese subjects. 'What Are Leaders For?', *Spectator* (17 June 1989), p. 5.
54 FAULDS 3/3/1/10, Lydia Dunn to Andrew Faulds, 17 April 1990.
55 FAULDS 3/3/1/10, Andrew Faulds to J. T. Thacker, 1 May 1990.
56 Stuart Ward, 'The End of Empire and the Fate of Britishness', in Helen Brocklehurst and Robert Phillips (eds), *History, Nationhood and the Question of Britain* (Basingstoke: Palgrave, 2004), pp. 242–58 (p. 246); Werner Menski, 'Conclusions: Coping with the Cost of Mistakes', in Werner Menski (ed.), *Coping with 1997: The Reaction of the Hong Kong People to the Transfer of Power* (Stoke on Trent: Trentham Books, 1995), pp. 185–201 (p. 197).
57 E.g. KNKK 1/3/42, Humphry Berkeley, 'Draft Proposal for a Settlement of the Future of Hong Kong Submitted to the Shadow Cabinet', 24 April 1990; FAULDS 4/9/4, Andrew Faulds, speech, n.d. [c. 1996–97]; JCWI, *A Question of Belonging: British Nationality Law and the Future of Hong Kong* (London: JCWI, 1985), p. 14; Bishopsgate Institute, BG/P/18/2/148, Kenneth Leech, Runnymede Briefing Paper, New Series no. 1, 'Immigration, Nationality and Hong Kong: Some Underlying Issues', p. 2.
58 Jolyon Jenkins, 'Hong Kong Deal "Leaves Grave Nationality Problems"', *New Statesman* (29 November 1985), p. 5. See also JCWI, *A Matter of Honour: The Nationality Question in Hong Kong* (London: JCWI, 1989), pp. 4–5; Mary Dejevsky, 'Hong Kong Chinese Accuse Mother Country of Betrayal', *The Times* (20 March 1989), 15.
59 Bill Schwarz, *The White Man's World* (Oxford: Oxford University Press, 2011), pp. 34–52. See also Camilla Schofield, *Enoch Powell and the Making of Postcolonial Britain* (Cambridge: Cambridge University Press, 2013).
60 POLL 3/2/1/76, Harold Berriman to Fred Silvester, 27 July 1984 (copy).
61 POLL 3/2/1/76, Robert Row to Enoch Powell, 29 September 1984.
62 POLL 3/2/1/76, [anon.] to Enoch Powell, 20 June 1989.
63 POLL 3/2/1/76, Polly Lo to Enoch Powell, 11 October 1984.
64 JCWI, *A Question of Belonging*, p. 9.
65 Auberon Waugh, 'Trying Not to Laugh off the Obligations of Charity and Pity', *Spectator* (24 June 1989), p. 8. This column came one week after the *Spectator's* unsigned leading article calling upon politicians to lead the public in accepting Britain's moral duty to 'defend the freedom of those for whom it responsible'. Such moral arguments could be supplemented, the leader urged, by pointing out 'that it is very unlikely that anything like the full number will want to come, and that most of those who come will be the sort of people who could do Britain a lot of good'. See 'What Are Leaders For?'. For a fictitious account of the politics of the refugee crisis, see Anthony G. Cooper, *The Sanctuary* (Hong Kong: Communication Management, 1989). On the experience of post-Vietnam War refugees in Hong Kong, see Sophia Law, *The Invisible Citizens of Hong Kong: Art and Stories of Vietnamese Boatpeople* (Hong Kong: Chinese University Press, 2014).
66 FAULDS 3/3/1/10, Pam Hillier to Andrew Faulds, 6 July 1989. See also Pam Hillier to Andrew Faulds, 11 June 1989; Andrew Faulds to Pam Hillier, 3 July 1989.
67 JCWI, *A Matter of Honour*, p. 20.

68 LSE, Finsberg 2/2/3, Hilton Cheong-Leen to Timothy Renton, 24 January 1986.
69 Bishopsgate Institute, BG/P/18/2/148, 'Hong Kong Is Our Home'.
70 See *A Draft Agreement between the Government of the United Kingdom of Great Britain and Northern Ireland and the Government of the People's Republic of China on the Future of Hong Kong. Presented to Parliament by the Secretary of State for Foreign and Commonwealth Affairs by Command of Her Majesty, September 1984* (London: HMSO, 1984), p. 37.
71 JCWI, *Passports to Somewhere* (London: JCWI, 1984), p. 5.
72 Bishopsgate Institute, BG/P/18/2/148, 'Hong Kong Is Our Home'.
73 JCWI, *A Matter of Honour*, pp. 11–12. See also FAULDS 3/3/1/10, Simon Murray to Andrew Faulds, 8 December 1989. Murray was the Chairman of Honour Hong Kong.
74 KNKK 1/3/55, John Habgood to Neil Kinnock, 11 April 1990.
75 'More Say They Will Leave the Territory before 1997', *SCMP* (15 May 1989).
76 Jill Hartley, 'Our Workers Would Do UK a "Power of Good"', *SCMP* (7 October 1984), p. 11. This argument was echoed five years later by the Hong Kong Freedom Association; see Bishopsgate Institute, BG/P/18/2/148, 'Hong Kong and British Nationality', n.d. [1989]. See also Michael Trend, 'The Sun that Needn't Set', *Spectator* (10 December 1988), p. 15.
77 'Breaking Eastern Promise', *Spectator* (13 May 1989), p. 5.
78 H. A. Turner, 'Eastern Promises', *New Statesman & Society* 2 (7 July 1989), p. 11. See also JCWI, *A Matter of Honour*, pp. 20–1, for a summary of the Corry Report, which argued for the likelihood that mass immigration of Hong Kong people to the UK would be highly beneficial to the British economy.
79 For a useful survey of the history of ethnic minorities in Hong Kong, see John Nguyet Erni and Lisa Yuk-ming Leung, *Understanding South Asian Minorities in Hong Kong* (Hong Kong: Hong Kong University Press, 2014), pp. 17–50.
80 FAULDS 3/3/1/9/i, Council of Hong Kong Indian Associations, 'Hong Kong Bill', 12 February 1985. According to journalist David Bonavia, the total number of Indians in Hong Kong was between 14,000 and 15,000, but over half already held Indian passports. FAULDS 3/3/1/9/I, David Bonavia, 'Hong Kong Indians Plead for UK Right of Abode', *The Times* (20 February 1985), p. 9. See also FAULDS 3/3/1/10, H. N. Harilela to Andrew Faulds, 11 November 1989; and a speech by Faulds about five years later addressing the non-Chinese British nationals in Hong Kong, FAULDS 4/9/4, n.d. See also FAULDS 3/3/1/16, Christine Loh to Members of Parliament, 24 April 1995.
81 'Britain "Tangled" over BNO Issue', *SCMP* (8 February 1985); FAULDS 3/3/1/9/i, Richard Luce to Andrew Faulds, 1 March 1985.
82 The Council of Hong Kong Indian Associations' critique of this position appears in FAULDS 3/3/1/9/i, President H. N. Harilela's letter to Andrew Faulds, 27 April 1985. This letter also repeats the assertion that Hong Kong's Indian community did not, in any case, wish to live in the UK. See also FAULDS 3/3/1/9/i, Richard Luce to Andrew Faulds, 20 May 1985; K. Sital to Andrew Faulds, 10 July 1985.
83 FAULDS 3/3/1/9/i, 'Legco Vote as One over Nationality', *SCMP* (9 January 1986); 'UK's Nationality Stance Leaves Hong Kong Disappointed', *Dateline Hong Kong* (24 January 1986); Lydia Dunn to Andrew Faulds, 3 January 1986; 'Statement by Unofficial Members of the Executive and Legislative Councils on 17 January 1986' (quotation is from this document). On the links between military service and citizenship see, e.g., Jean Bethke Elshtain, *Women and War* (Chicago: University of Chicago Press, 1995).
84 Lynn Hollen Lees, 'Being British in Malaya, 1890–1940', *Journal of British Studies* 48 (2009): 76–101.
85 Helen F. Siu, 'Positioning "Hong Kongers" and "New Immigrants"', in Helen F. Siu and Agnes S. Ku (eds), *Hong Kong Mobile: Making a Global Population* (Hong Kong: Hong Kong University Press, 2008), pp. 117–47.
86 SHORE 14/28, 'Debate on Hong Kong's Future in the Hong Kong Legislative Council on 14th March 1984', included with S. Y. Chung and R. H. Lobo to Peter Shore, 26 March 1984.

87 FAULDS 3/3/1/6, UMELCO, 'The Future of Hong Kong', 8 May 1984.
88 Sea-ling Cheng, 'Consuming Places in Hong Kong: Experiencing Lan Kwai Fong', in Gordon Mathews and Tai-Lok Lui (eds), *Consuming Hong Kong* (Hong Kong: Hong Kong University Press, 2003), pp. 237–62 (pp. 248–9).
89 FS J/74/1, Hilton Cheong-Leen, 'Hongkong's Role in Asia', address to the Chung Chi College Assembly of the Chinese University of Hong Kong, 13 May 1966. In this speech he defended an 'internationalist' outlook that appropriated the best of western culture while continuing to 'preserve and adapt the best aspects of Chinese culture to living in the twentieth century'.
90 *Hong Kong: Its Value to Britain* (Hong Kong: Government Printer, 1992), pp. 5, 10.
91 Jason Gagliardi, 'Gowned, Bewigged and Sitting in Judgement from an Ivory Tower', *Eastern Express* 1 (4 February 1994), p. 1.
92 Christine Loh, 'The First Line of Defence', *Eastern Express* (3 February 1994), p. 18.
93 Kwan, *The Dragon and the Crown*, p. 173.
94 For example, see Ho Lok Sang, 'New Govt's Cultural Policy Must Uphold Hong Kong's Core Values', *Chinadaily*, 22 May 2012, www.chinadaily.com.cn/hke-dition/2012-05/22/content_15351143.htm?goback=%2Egde_4279340_member_119472971#%21 (accessed 20 October 2013). The distinctiveness of Hong Kong identity in opposition to a mainland reference point is a key theme in Lau Siu-kai and Kuan Hsin-chi, *The Ethos of the Hong Kong Chinese* (Hong Kong: Chinese University Press, 1988).
95 Law Wing Sang, *Collaborative Colonial Power*, p. 3.

CHAPTER SEVEN

Narratives of 1997

A June 1997 Independent Television News segment opened with scenes from Hong Kong's *Tatler* Ball – 'the only invitation that counts'. With an elegiac quality typical of that month's news coverage, the narrator pointed out that in this 'scene dominated for years by British expatriates, now all that glitters here belongs to local Chinese'. The viewer was next introduced to barrister Gilbert Rodway, who had 'never missed the occasion', but learned that 'this is his last appearance: he's leaving Hong Kong, believing that for the British, the good days are over'. Rodway's view is not surprising, of course. The disappearance of Britons' official status seemed likely to mean loss of position and prestige, while the new business environment seemed unlikely to favour British expatriates and companies; for this very reason, Jardines and the Hong Kong Shanghai Bank had moved their incorporation to Bermuda. But as the scene shifted from the *Tatler* Ball to an interview with Rodway on his boat, gin and tonic in hand, the viewer learned that Rodway was pessimistic about more than the fate of British expatriates. Not only did he fear that the 'well-oiled machine' of the British legal system would deteriorate, but he doubted that Hong Kong would be ruled well without British tutelage: 'I doubt [the Chinese] will have the capacity; the whole of their history shows that they're incapable of administration on a broad scale.'[1]

Postwar British discussions of Hong Kong highlighted Britain's achievements – modernisation, good governance, and the creation of a colonial space in which unbridled capitalism could flourish – while at the same time projecting a site for the British at play. Much of this discourse noted the transience of this 'borrowed' place and time, whether because the Chinese could seize it back at any moment or because 1997 seemed, even in the immediate postwar years, a likely terminal date. Remarkably, even in the 1960s and 1970s such acknowledgements of Hong Kong's finality had a complacent air, as if in expectation that something would, after all, turn up – or, perhaps, in agreement with Richard Hughes's statement that 'borrowed time is as good as any'. Yet with the Thatcher Government's failure to negotiate an extension of the British presence after 1997, resulting in the 1984 Joint Declaration and an unequivocal countdown to the Handover, British discourse began to consider the meaning of the Handover itself. Much of the discussion turned shrill, particularly after the Tiananmen Square massacre in June 1989, with novelists, journalists, and memoirists evoking apocalyptic scenarios. On the other hand, British officials, both in London and in the Hong Kong Government, insisted that they had secured a good deal for the colony and that there were strong grounds for optimism about Hong Kong after the Handover. This chapter will examine the competing narratives of 1997 that emerged in the final decade and a half of British Hong Kong.

The debates over the meaning of 1997 began in earnest as it became clear in 1982 that Hong Kong's return to Chinese sovereignty would inevitably follow upon the expiration of the New Territories lease. The Thatcher Government had initially hoped to renew the lease, or failing that, to trade sovereignty for continued administration; Deng Xiaoping quickly put that idea to rest, leaving the British Government nothing more to do than to try to negotiate the best terms of transfer. The resulting late-1984 Sino-British Joint Declaration committed China to allowing a 'high degree of autonomy' for Hong Kong for fifty years following China's resumption of sovereignty; China would not impose the socialist economic system, and Hong Kong people would continue to enjoy the personal and civic freedoms to which they had become accustomed.[2] As the *New Statesman* argued in October 1982, 'If China wants to re-establish its legal overlordship, there is nothing that any British government can do about it.' Nor, the journal argued, should it. Nearly two years later, following a period of intense negotiations, the journal in August 1984 credited Thatcher, after initially insisting upon the sanctity of the treaties permanently ceding Hong Kong Island and Kowloon, with having 'the good sense to recognise an irresistible force when it hits her in the face'. The colony was anachronistic, Britain had no national interest in maintaining it (even if expatriate Britons had a personal interest), and in any case there was no realistic way of defending it.[3]

For British officials, both in London and Hong Kong, there was an obvious incentive to emphasise British achievements and the 'honourable' way in which they delivered Hong Kong's six million residents to the PRC. Not only were they bidding for Britain's historical legacy as they prepared to exit the last significant British colony, but they were doing so in the context of their consistent unwillingness to consider mass immigration of Hong Kong Chinese to the UK. The linguist John Flowerdew has eloquently described two different discursive approaches to the Handover. The approach exemplified by the Sinologists and 'friends of China', Governor Sir David Wilson (1987–92) and Foreign Office negotiator Percy Cradock, emphasised British relations with China, a large and potentially important trading partner, and promoted 'convergence' between British and Chinese policies, before and after the Handover. Following Wilson's replacement by Chris Patten, the British approach changed dramatically – a change that Cradock, uncharacteristically for a retired diplomat, criticised publicly. Patten's approach was more confrontational, and in contrast to the Sinologists who exchanged Chinese proverbs with PRC officials in private, his method often relied on 'megaphone diplomacy' through the Hong Kong and international media. Not only did Patten employ a different style, but he also attached less significance to Sino-British relations than to publicising Britain's historical legacy. Flowerdew emphasises the rhetorical aspects of Patten's projection of Britain's honourable withdrawal, a rhetoric focusing on four British bequests: free trade, the rule of law, individual freedom, and democracy. He rightly points out, moreover, that all four of these themes were problematic in light of Britain's actual record in Hong Kong.[4]

Despite their significant differences, what both approaches had in common was that they emphasised the strong position of Britain's legacy as the Handover approached, and optimism about the future. To be sure, this optimism could be a cautiously guarded one, based on assessments of China's economic self-interest or on the warning the Chinese that 'the world will be watching' to ensure that they did not violate the Joint Declaration or Basic Law. Still, it amounted to a claim that Hong Kong would continue to prosper after 1997 – a claim that was asserted repeatedly in the final decade and a half of British rule.[5]

This narrative began during the negotiations leading to the signing of the Joint Declaration in December 1984. A few months prior to the signature, in September, Labour Party spokesperson George Robertson, despite a couple of digs aimed at Margaret Thatcher, complimented the 'skill and local knowledge of the professional negotiators' who had produced a Draft Agreement that incorporated 'great efforts to guarantee the independence of the judiciary and the process of law'.[6] In her press conference in Hong Kong following the signing, Thatcher 'treated her questioners with harsh and sardonic self-righteousness'. Asked by *FEER* correspondent Emily Lau about the morality of handing over five million people to a Communist dictatorship, Thatcher 'said the overwhelming majority of people in Hong Kong were glad Britain had acted when it did to get an agreement on 1997, and added: "You may be a solitary

Figure 11 Visit of Margaret Thatcher to Hong Kong, September 1982. At the time, the Prime Minister still hoped to negotiate a continued British administration of Hong Kong.

exception." [7] Thatcher's barb glossed over the distinction between popular support for a Joint Declaration, given the fact of Britain's departure, on the one hand, and support for or optimism about the change of sovereignty itself, on the other. [8] Yet as Russell Johnston, Liberal MP and party spokesman on Foreign and Commonwealth affairs, had argued

[189]

in September, given China's refusal to extend the lease of the New Territories, Britain's only real choice was returning it to China 'with agreement or without agreement'.[9] Likewise, a few days after Thatcher's December press conference, Foreign Secretary Sir Geoffrey Howe told the House of Commons 'that the agreement provided sufficient detail in the many areas it covers to give confidence, both internationally as well as in Hong Kong itself, that the future was a secure one'.[10]

The final Governor, Chris Patten, was equally sanguine in his public assessments of Hong Kong's prospects. In a series of twenty-eight ten-minute talks broadcast on RTHK in 1995 and 1996 he presented a narrative of Hong Kong history and expressed optimism that its prosperity and freedom would endure beyond the Handover. For example, in April 1995 he congratulated Hong Kong on having little corruption: '... not much, and we crack down on corruption very hard wherever we find it'. In the same talk, he emphasised that Hong Kong did not 'suffer from over-government', a quality that not only tied directly to the British cultural legacy described in Chapter 2, but directly linked to the character of Hong Kong's people: 'We don't allow envy to masquerade as economic policy. I'm sure you know what I mean. We're not jealous of others who get on, make a fortune, buy a big car. Class-war isn't the root of our politics, thank heavens.'[11] But what about after the change of sovereignty? Patten asserted his belief that Hong Kong would remain 'a free, prosperous, decent society, living with the rule of law – under a Chinese flag'. The only way this would fail to happen, indeed, would be if the people of Hong Kong allowed it to happen: 'I don't think Hong Kong will change fundamentally if the men and women who live here don't want it to change. Fatalism, thinking there's nothing you can do, expecting the worst, is self-fulfilling.'[12]

Two months later, Patten elaborated on the prospect that British legal traditions would survive after Britain's exit. For starters, he insisted that the Colonial Government would continue to govern in reality as well as in name until the change of sovereignty:

> We don't intend to put off the tough challenges, the unpopular choices, just because 1997 is coming up fast. That would be fatal for the authority of government. Not particularly the authority of this government, but of government itself. It would corrode the morale of our excellent civil service. It would leave our successors with a bucketful of problems. And which problems ever got easier by putting off doing anything about them?[13]

Taken in context, Patten was referring not only to day-to-day governing, but also to controversial larger initiatives, such as the building of the new airport at Chek Lap Kok and the expansion of the franchise.

But he also responded to those who predicted that China would simply undo any changes that it did not like, or would undo the British legacy. Referring specifically to the implied conflict between British Hong Kong's legal inheritance and the prospective post-1997 administration, he argued:

> Any tension between the Basic Law and the common law in Hong Kong has to be dealt with in the courts after 1997. I can't for the life of me see the good in running up the white flag now – as some people seem to be doing – by claiming that the Basic Law will simply punch holes in the common law after 1997. What's the gain for Hong Kong in telling the world that the rule of law is finished here, that this is what the 1990 Basic Law means, when that very rule of law can and will survive provided we continue to have courts which can test it and a community that supports it?[14]

Patten's optimism was wilful and difficult to credit.[15] With arbitrary Chinese government, most notably the Tiananmen Square killings of 1989, in the background, it would surely be difficult for very many listeners to believe that Hong Kong people's continuing to 'want' to live in a free society, or their refusal to be 'fatalistic', would be a sufficient guarantee against tyranny. Similarly, his argument that there was no 'gain for Hong Kong' in predicting the worst was hardly an argument that the worst would not *actually* happen. Yet Patten was not alone in articulating optimism. Andrew Faulds, in responding to a confidential 1996 'Perception Survey' commissioned by the Hong Kong Government and administered by the University of Sheffield, indicated an overall optimism buttressed by a belief that China would honour the Joint Declaration and was concerned to protect its Hong Kong investments, that law and order would not deteriorate after the Handover, that media freedom would not be 'curtailed', and that Hong Kong would remain a 'relatively corruption free society'.[16] In one of his public speeches around the same time, Faulds referred to the Sino-British Agreement as a 'historic achievement' that he believed was 'working out well', and blamed 'a few colonial types' in the media for provoking trouble between Britain and China.[17] Faulds's optimism about Hong Kong's future came despite his disgust with the 'arrogant and ill informed' Patten's constitutional reform, which had effectively 'derailed' the 'through train' that would have ensured continuity of the Legislative Council's composition beyond June 1997.[18] Yet if the politicians were to change with the change of sovereignty, Jonathan Fenby, writing on the eve of the Handover, saw 'perhaps the most telling argument for at least measured optimism' in the continuity of the senior civil servants.[19]

[191]

Yet not every observer, either before or after June 1989, was so optimistic. The *SCMP* art critic Nigel Cameron, writing in 1978, compared Hong Kong's future to post-1949 Shanghai. Anticipating the 1997 Handover, he called Hong Kong 'an eccentric paragraph of extreme interest, brief as the detonation of a Chinese cracker, in the span of Oriental history'. The obvious continuation of investment activity was, he argued, a sign that Hong Kong, 'doomed perhaps to paralysis by a commercial coronary thrombosis in 1997, has entered, in the last decade or so, on a terminal phase of frenetic, bizarre activity'. The only hope he held out was that China would be reluctant to take over Hong Kong given that its culturally foreign residents were potentially troublesome dissidents.[20] Similarly, Walter Easey, the Hong Kong police inspector turned implacable enemy of the colonial regime, predicted in 1980 that the PRC would take over Hong Kong suddenly within the next few years – though it is difficult to call this pessimism given Easey's pro-Beijing politics. His logic in expecting a sudden takeover stemmed from the crisis of business confidence as the New Territories lease approached its expiration, meaning that leases and contracts of medium duration could not be entered; Easey expected the British and Chinese to remain at an impasse given their irreconcilable views of the nineteenth-century treaties, and argued that this impasse could be solved only by a sudden Chinese takeover as the British washed their hands of Hong Kong. For the British expatriates accustomed to the good life, the prospect would be ruinous – a fate about which Easey seemed gleeful – but he acknowledged that among 'civil (sic) servants', seniority would have its benefits:

> Departmental heads and officers nearing pension will get fabulous tax-free golden handshakes – some of them for the third, fourth or fifth time. The younger ones (mostly the police) will fare rather poorly on handshakes and little chance of re-employment in similar jobs – the world-wide requirement for englishmen [*sic*] with small brains, thick skins, long arms, big pockets, a smattering of para-military training and even less cantonese [*sic*] being at an all time low in the 1980s.

Despite his opposition to the British presence in Hong Kong, he also did not think the takeover bode well for the Hong Kong Chinese. He expected an absorption of Hong Kong similar to that of Shanghai in 1949–50, complete with 'population transfer'. He further expected an end to tourism's 'prostitution-oriented component' and severe limitations on the 'shopping-spree type of trip'.[21]

Easey was ultimately wrong about both the nature of the transfer of power, and its timing.[22] Moreover, he differs from many of the other commentators in this chapter in that he welcomed the demise of British

Hong Kong. Still, it is notable that he was in broad agreement with many of the more pessimistic commentators about what was likely to happen as a result of Britain's loss of sovereignty. Regardless of their political views, there was a broad agreement that the Handover would mean the end of the Hong Kong that has been described in earlier chapters, the Hong Kong of unrestrained capitalism, orderly law, freedom, and modernisation. Leyland Otter, writing in 1984, saw the decision of Jardines to relocate to Bermuda as a 'particularly serious blow to business confidence, promoting speculation of a general corporate exodus'. Felix Patrikeeff, writing in late 1988, described a generalised nervousness about the future. People speculated that the reason the new Hongkong Bank had a helicopter platform was so that the bank's gold reserves could be transferred out of Hong Kong at a moment's notice. More generally, he described anxieties leading those who could do so to try to arrange an escape 'bolt hole'. Not only did the wealthy divest part of their business holdings, and the upper middle class raise cash to be able to make an escape, but, Patrikeeff noted, one 'very senior' Chinese police superintendent, fearing reprisals by the PRC for his role in colonial administration, claimed that 'If he did not get a full [British] passport, or was able to purchase similar rights somewhere by 1995 … he would come down to Kai Tak (the airport) with a group of armed police officers and take a plane at gunpoint to Taiwan, considered by most as a sanctuary of last resort.'[23]

Peter Dally, Chairman of the obscure British Anti-Communist Council, would probably have found Patrikeeff's description, if anything, an understatement.[24] In a substantive 1984 pamphlet, written while the Joint Declaration was still in negotiations, Dally invoked the prospect of mass purges that would 'undoubtedly' follow the Handover; not only would many people die in these purges, but still others would die trying to escape by sea. The PRC could not possibly maintain Hong Kong's existing capitalist system, both because of ideological incompatibility and because of economic incompetence. In view of this certain future of doom, Britain's betrayal of its Hong Kong subjects was unforgiveable; moreover, it was gratuitous. Almost uniquely, Dally argued the preferability of war with China over agreeing to a handover. He dismissed China's military threat to Hong Kong, arguing that if Britain showed determination to resist, China was unlikely to invade because of the unreliability of its army. Even if China did attempt to invade, the British need not fear war; after all, the Chinese had been unable to take Quemoy from Taiwan. In fact, if the PRC did invade, then Britain could probably count on help from Taipei – particularly if it offered to recognise the Republic of China as the Government of China. For that matter, the people of Hong Kong would resist, and

[193]

other countries, such as Vietnam and India, might well take the opportunity to make war on China.

Throughout his pamphlet, Dally made two recurring comparisons: to the lessons of Munich concerning appeasement and to the British resolve during the Falklands crisis. As in Munich, the desire to appease a dictator would prove to be a mistake. The PRC, like Hitler, was incapable of acting in good faith, and respected only strength. As in the 1930s, appeasing the dictator would only lead to a humanitarian crisis. By contrast, the Falklands war had arisen only because the Argentinians had assumed – falsely, it turned out – that Britain lacked the political will to project military power 8,000 miles away from home. Yet by showing that Britain could stand up for principle, two results followed: first, signalling to China that Britain would defend its position in Hong Kong would now likely be credible; and second, failure to do so could only be an act of racism, a 'double standard' because Britain's Hong Kong subjects were non-white. Nor was Dally alone. In a proposal submitted to the Labour Shadow Cabinet in 1990, Humphry Berkeley, a Labour (and former Conservative and SDP) Member of Parliament, similarly contrasted the 'craven' willingness to turn over several million Hong Kong citizens to 'the most repressive Communist country in the world' with the spilling of British blood just a few years earlier in defence of 1,800 Falklanders' self-determination. He argued, moreover, that if the Chinese Government were unwilling to ensure the rights of Hong Kong's citizens in a negotiated treaty, the British should dramatically increase its military strength and prepare, if necessary, to defend its Hong Kong citizens' rights.[25]

Where Dally argued that the PRC could never tolerate a capitalist Hong Kong, George Hicks, an Australian political scientist living in Hong Kong, did not envision Beijing's deliberately imposing its Communist system on Hong Kong: too much was at stake both economically and in terms of Chinese prestige to risk the city's collapse. Nonetheless, in a short book in 1989 collecting a series of academic articles and editorials originally published in 1987 and 1988 – significantly, before the Tiananmen Square massacre – he argued that Beijing lacked the capacity to govern Hong Kong effectively, and the discipline to allow the city truly to govern itself. The vast difference in income levels between Hong Kong and the rest of China, moreover, would tempt emigrants to flood to the city, the party leadership to redistribute the city's wealth to other parts of China, and well-positioned party members to turn their political influence into wealth at the city's expense. Part of the problem was a simple difference in culture: Hong Kong's economy worked well because it was embedded within a larger culture that was alien to China:

Although Hong Kong is 98 percent Chinese, its tradition, culture, belief, attitudes, and ethics are often different from those of Communist-ruled China. This difference is not surprising after 143 years of British rule. The deep-rooted Chinese Communist way of doing things, through personal influence and 'backdoorism', is generally hated in Hong Kong, which is much more of a meritocracy where regulations are followed and there is respect for the rule of law. Hong Kong culture is based on a combination of extremely hard work and the freedom to act in unproductive ways. Horse racing, Macao casinos, gambling in general, lotteries, nightclubs, and so on give people a zest for life and are the essential other side of the work–ethics coin. Hong Kong's culture is 'all of a piece' and has a unity that Beijing can hardly be expected to understand.[26]

Elsewhere, he argued that China possessed a '2,000-year-old belief in the virtues of benevolent interventionism and a capacity to engineer it, unshaken by a parallel record of failure'. For this reason, he worried that even if Chinese leaders accepted in principle the desirability of allowing Hong Kong to remain autonomous, their very culture would make it unlikely in practice that they would maintain the British separation between politics and economics.[27] This sharp difference between Hong Kong and mainland cultures was similarly argued, the same year, by Ian Buruma in the *Spectator*:

> For Hong Kong represents everything the current rulers of China hate most. It is Milton Freedman's idea of capitalist heaven; it is largely Cantonese (disliked by most non-Cantonese); it is deeply contaminated by spiritual pollution, meaning anything from horse racing and discotheques to free discussion of ideas that are anathema to communist dictators.

Like Hicks, Buruma argued that such a cultural clash would, despite China's material interest in maintaining Hong Kong's autonomy, make it difficult to do so in practice.[28]

In the decade leading up to the Handover, Hicks argued, Hong Kong's ruling triumvirate – Beijing, London, and the Hong Kong business elite – were desperately trying to maintain stability in order to keep profits flowing. In the absence of adequate opportunity for small businessmen and professionals to prosper, emigration was 'Hong Kong's great safety valve'; should that fail, he noted, there were plans afoot to double the size of the police force. Not only did emigration provide a safety valve, but it also gave ordinary Hong Kong residents some leverage over Beijing's policies, for Hong Kong's continuing prosperity obviously required its skilled workers and entrepreneurs to remain. Hicks argued, though, that relying on Beijing's good intentions and capacity for government was too risky, and so he wrote in his introduction: 'The message of this book to these people is simple: Get out while the going is good.'[29]

Much of the language of Hicks's essays is far from catastrophist: the demise of British culture and values in Hong Kong will lead to a gradual deterioration of civil liberties as an authoritarian capitalism is ensconced; Hong Kong will lose its position as a regional financial capital but will remain a manufacturing hub. Yet in places (including the book's introduction), he compared the likely effect of the Chinese take-over to Nazi policies toward European Jews:

> There is no close historical analogy to the Hong Kong case, but the experience of the European Jews who fled from Hitler in the 1930s might be pondered. Consider the case of those who could have left but didn't and the reasons for staying they gave at the time. As in the 1930s, the danger is that when the Hong Kong exodus really gets underway, the world's doors will slam shut.[30]

Indeed, he warned that the window might not remain open until 1997; although the British would remain in Hong Kong officially until 1997, and the Chinese 'would insist on a white governor handing over the keys', it was quite plausible that a 'massive running down of the British presence, leaving China in early and total control', would occur.[31] Similarly, the 1997 edition of Jan Morris's history of Hong Kong notes that even before Patten's 1992 arrival, it was 'fashionable' to say that the Chinese were already in control of Hong Kong, so that 'nothing much would happen when the Chinese arrived – it had happened already'.[32] Nor was Hicks the only one to compare the fate of the Hong Kong Chinese to the fate of Europe's Jews. Legislative Council member and democratic activist Martin Lee told the BBC's Jonathan Dimbleby, on 13 June 1989, barely a week after the massacre in Beijing, that 'Handing over 5½ million people to China who are deemed to be counter-revolutionary is like handing over 5½ million Jews to Nazi Germany during the Second World War, when they were born in a British territory.'[33] The *New Statesman & Society* in 1993 was comparatively moderate in arguing only that Margaret Thatcher had betrayed Hong Kong people when she 'bullied and harassed civil servants into negotiating a treaty ... that gave the Chinese totalitarians everything they wanted'.[34]

The Tiananmen Square crackdown, combined with the imminent approach of the Handover, only lent an urgency to fears that were as much about the events of the early 1950s as they were about more recent history. Speaking to an American filmmaker in 1997, Christine Loh and Emily Lau both expressed concern about their future safety, though Loh acknowledged that she could not say definitively whether the fears were justified or merely 'shadows of the past'. Nonetheless, she noted that under British rule, one never worried that political activism would cause harm to befall oneself or one's family, implying that she was not willing to make the same prediction for Hong Kong politics after the resumption of Chinese sovereignty. She also indicated that she worried that the annual 4 June vigil in Victoria Park commemorating the Tiananmen Square massacre would be prohibited with the Handover.[35]

For Martin Booth, who, as we have seen, spent much of his youth in Hong Kong in the 1950s and early 1960s, the post-1997 prospects were daunting, as much a result of the erasure of border control as due to distinctly Chinese policies. Writing in 1998, he predicted that within about a decade Hong Kong would become absorbed into a 'Pearl River delta megalopolis' stretching as far as Guangzhou, characterised by high crime rates, 'endemic' corruption, and 'dangerous' levels of pollution. Beyond its human cost, Booth argued, this development might influence the future of the Chinese novel, possibly leading to the emergence of the Hong Kong science-fiction novel.[36] In addition to its wider effects on the city, Booth believed that Hong Kong's demise could be seen in the fate of the Gurkha soldiers. Not only were they to be given a shameful pension based on pre-1947 Indian army rates, but as Booth told the BBC in 1998, those who sought employment in Hong Kong to supplement their meagre pensions, or their younger relatives, faced the prospect of menial and poorly paid jobs as 'chauffeurs, messengers, nightwatchmen and gold shop guards'.[37]

The vision of the loss of British expatriates' status in post-Handover Hong Kong is, of course, a fundamentally different matter than whether the Chinese resumption of sovereignty would mean the end of Hong Kong as a lawful, capitalist, modern city – though one suspects that, as suggested in the Gilbert Rodway interview cited above, these two concerns often blended together in the minds of expatriates. Certainly it is worth recognising that, regardless of predictions for the future of Hong Kong itself, there was a sense by the early 1990s that *la belle époque* was over for British expatriates. Indeed, even in 1985, one British sailor, Stephen Brook, noted that when his family arrived in Hong Kong two years earlier, they were 'bitterly disappointed', having 'expected life here to be much more "colonial"', like Singapore used to be'.[38] At the higher end, a raft of articles in the *SCMP* warned that high times were over for colonial FILTH. The expatriate package was becoming more rare, and competition more keen. As a result, one 1989 article noted that while the number of expatriates was expanding, 'most notably the Filipino and the Japanese', the British civilian expatriate population had dropped by a third during the 1980s. The same article quoted a restaurateur as saying 'It is a very different situation from the old days when many of the expats came here because

[197]

they couldn't hold a decent job down anywhere else.'[39] A 1994 headline simply stated 'Expats' Golden Era at an End'. The article pointed out that not only was localisation eroding the need for expatriates but, as one interviewee noted, 'It will become increasingly difficult to justify having someone who can't post a letter or buy a bar of soap from a shop.' But increasingly, competition meant that the British were not even the most privileged expatriates. A report revealed that the average British expatriate enjoyed a package worth HK$2.1 million, compared to about $2.5 million for their American counterparts, largely because the American companies' housing allowances were more generous.[40] Not that Americans found it particularly easy to secure such packages in this increasingly competitive period. One Princeton history gradu-ate in the late 1980s cold-called Jardine Fleming, with unhappy results:

> I can remember getting through to someone with a very thick English accent. And I said, 'Hi, my name is Ted Pulling. I'm from Princeton University, and I'm out here looking for a job. I was wondering if I could come over and talk to you?' The response was, 'Do you really think you can simply telephone Jardine Fleming and obtain an interview?' I was very put off by that; my heart sank. At that point Hong Kong struck me as a very English enclave.[41]

The articles cited above mainly referred to middle- and upper-middle-class Britons, but the localisation policies and increasing prosperity opened up new possibilities for unemployed Britons to take jobs seen as undesirable by Hong Kong Chinese; Britons, then, in an unwelcome role reversal, were the new desperate immigrants.[42] A 1996 *Independent* article noted that, in contrast with the easy-going, gentle-manly 'FILTH' positions of the past, 'Hong Kong sees young British men and women fresh from the dole queue and ready to do work which many Chinese think distinctly inferior.' Such positions as door-keeper, leaflet distributor, food deliverer, and courier offered pay that was 'not spectacular', but was 'far higher than most of them could expect to earn at home'. Many of these British 'coolies' were 'well-qualified but inexperienced', including those who worked for a sandwich shop whose owner 'boast[ed] that he only employ[ed] British graduates with a good degree to deliver his sandwiches to the surrounding offices'.[43] Liam Parker, writing in June 1997, traced the decline of Britons' pos-ition in Hong Kong through 'the evolution of this popular joke':

1965
    Q: What do you say to a *gweilo* who speaks perfect Cantonese?
    A: Here's your cut from the prostitution and drugs racket, officer …
1988

Q: What do you say to a *gweilo* who has been forced to learn one sentence of Cantonese?

A: Very good. No, you can't marry my daughter.

1997

Q: What do you say to a *gweilo* who speaks no Cantonese?

A: Soup of the day and the duck confit, please.[44]

Novelising 1997

Narratives of 1997 not only featured in political and journalistic discourse, but also showed up in fiction, both before and after the Handover. Examples include Stephen Leather's *The Vets* (1993), John Burdett's *The Last Six Million Seconds* (1997), Paul Theroux's *Kowloon Tong* (1997), John Gordon Davis's *The Year of Dangerous Loving* (1997), Robert Elegant's *Last Year in Hong Kong: A Love Story* (1997), and American writer Muhammad Cohen's *Hong Kong on Air* (2007).[45] This chapter will conclude with an examination of some of these fictitious portrayals of colonial Hong Kong's final days, emphasising the continuities and discontinuities each projected.

Stephen Leather's *The Vets* (1993) describes a complicated scheme, instigated by the PRC leadership, to take over one of the British banks and gain the public-relations value of restoring order when the British were unable to do so. They seek to accomplish this goal by using American Vietnam War veterans as a decoy: the veterans stage a robbery of the last Hong Kong Jockey Club race of the season using a helicopter and insider connections; but they're distracting attention from the robbery of much of the gold belonging to the Kowloon and Canton Bank, a thinly disguised stand-in for the Hongkong and Shanghai Bank. The scheme involves a partnership between Beijing and Hong Kong triads, and the key figure, Anthony Chung, who proposes it, does so in exchange for the release from prison of his father, a former leading party official who was on the wrong side during the Tiananmen Square massacre. Chung accomplishes his task in part by blackmail: he seduces Anne Fielding, the wife of the bank director, and tapes their lovemaking. Fielding goes along with the takeover because of blackmail, but also because he is enticed by the prospect of staying on as a director following the Handover. The clear message is that those British who cooperate with Beijing are rewarded, while those who do not are punished. In addition, it presents the Chinese leaders as unprincipled seekers of wealth and power: they have no compunction against working with organised criminals, and in order to further their goals are willing to release a dissident who is, according to their own views, a traitor.

[199]

Even beyond the plot, the novel's general tone repeatedly suggests an awareness that Hong Kong is finished. For example, we see Chung visiting a couple of night-clubs, the first called Nineteen 97:

> It seemed to Anthony Chung that only someone with a particularly British sense of humor could have given the name Nineteen 97 to a bar frequented by Hong Kong's beautiful people. The average Hong Konger had nothing to celebrate about the date when the British colony was to be handed back to its true owners, but the bar cum disco was nevertheless packed with young, exuberant expatriates and affluent Chinese, dancing themselves senseless to the driving beat of the latest Canto-pop hits.[46]

After leaving this bar, he walks into another:

> The volume of the music was lower than in Nineteen 97, but the clientele was similar, young men and women dressed in expensive designer clothes, partying as if there were no tomorrow, trying to squeeze as much enjoyment out of the place as they could in the little time they had left. Chung knew that most of them reckoned that under Chinese rule the good times would soon be over. The frantic excitement of the Lan Kwai Fong revelers reminded Chung of nothing so much as the band playing as the *Titanic* went down.[47]

Similarly, one dinner party is described as follows: 'The food was superb and the conversation was typical of any Hong Kong gathering: the future of the colony after 1997; falling property values; the disintegration of law and order; and who was leaving.'[48]

The most evocative description of the breakdown of law and order as the British era ends occurs when three characters discuss the police commissioner's house being robbed in broad daylight:

> 'Yeah, and he assigned four uniformed constables to stand guard, round the clock', said Cormack. 'That's more than they have patrolling most of the housing estates in Hong Kong. The man has no shame.'
> 'Who has, these days?' said Donaldson. 'It's every man for himself. And the last one out's a sissy. I tell you, there's going to be blood on the streets before long. Full-scale riots, the works. You know, Hong Kong used to be one of the safest places in the world, for expats anyway. There was trouble among the triads, sure, but they kept the violence among themselves. Europeans never got mugged, tourists could walk through the streets at midnight and be one hundred percent safe, guaranteed, and it was almost unheard of for an expat's house to be broken into. Now look at it. That woman on Disco Bay, the New Zealander, gang-raped and cut up with a machete. Her house smashed to bits. That was just mindless. The Cathay Pacific pilot who was robbed at gunpoint. They roughed him up and trashed his house as well as robbing him. Tourists are being mugged every day, cars owned by Brits are being vandalized in

front of their homes, their kids are getting roughed up at school. There's an anti-British feeling the like of which we've never seen before, and it's going to explode. And who's going to contain it when it does? The Army's pulling out, the police are leaving in droves. I tell you, it'll be the little yellow men in green uniforms, they'll be the ones restoring law and order, and they'll do it like they did in Tiananmen Square.'

One listener, Coleman, protests this characterisation of Chinese behaviour, and Donaldson continues:

'They own this place, remember? That's what Thatcher confirmed when she said they could have it in 1997. They're the landlords and we're the tenants, and if we can't keep the place in order, they'll do it themselves. Trust me on this. You know that new highway that cuts right through Shenzhen? Tailor-made for tanks.'[49]

For Donaldson, Chinese tyranny and the breakdown of order go hand in hand, along with the loss of Britons' privileges.

John Burdett's *The Last Six Million Seconds*, published in February 1997, can only be described as apocalyptic. The book's title refers to the final seventy days before the Handover, and clearly refers to the end not only of the colonial administration, but, for all practical purposes, of Hong Kong. The novel centres on the investigation by an honest and incorruptible Eurasian police inspector, Chan Siu-kai, of a gruesome triple murder. Through the course of Chan's investigation, he learns that the murders are part of a struggle over who will control post-Handover Hong Kong: the Beijing Government; south-Chinese warlords led by a General Xian, reminiscent in many ways of those of the 1920s; or effete British diplomats who can do nothing more than try to cast an honourable gloss on their delivery of six million British subjects to a tyrannical Government. General Xian's PLA troops control much of the Southeast Asian heroin trade and the general has connections to organised crime in the United States.[50] At the same time, General Xian has aspirations to greater power, exemplified above all by his attempt to acquire a nuclear weapon.

Burdett, who spent over a decade working as a lawyer in Hong Kong before becoming a full-time novelist, makes frequent commentary on the meaning of the Handover, often through the voices of his characters.[51] For example, Aston, an English police officer (and a clear example of FILTH) who faces redundancy within a couple of months, thinks that in Hong Kong 'you could feel the pressure of uncontainable envy, loathing and longing pressing in from over the border', emotions that would be given an outlet after the Handover. For Aston, it is not British rule of law and modernisation that are the worst of the casualties. He considers himself fortunate to have had three years in Hong Kong; he had 'been drunk with excitement since arrival'. An exchange with a colleague captures what he will miss about Hong Kong:

> 'I tell you, honest, I'd give ten years of my life to stay on here' ... 'You know why? Life! The place is buzzing with it, night and day. It's crawling with it, bursting. People flying all over the place earning a crust, nobody has time to sit around moaning. England's on Valium, America's on Prozac, here people still act human. There's youth, ambition, drive. Eighty percent of the population is under thirty.'

Pressed by his colleague, Aston admits that he will also miss the Asian women.[52]

Inspector Chan, called 'Charlie' by his British colleagues, is the product of a Chinese mother and an Irish father who used to go 'whoring in Wanchai' on weeknights before disappearing one day. If Aston is philosophical, Chan views the Handover with more alarm. For example, on observing mostly Chinese students at the UHK, he 'wondered how they felt, growing up under one of the most aggressive capitalist systems in the world, knowing that within two months they would have to learn a new system under new masters. Probably they felt the way he felt: cheated and scared.'[53]

As Chan begins his investigation, his superiors – primarily the London-appointed political advisor (Milton Cuthbert) whose chief concern is to provide Britain a politically palatable way of exiting Hong Kong – try to remove him from the case. The PLA, Cuthbert knows, is the 'largest criminal organization in the history of the world' or, as some call it, the 'biggest triad of all'. Although the fact that the PLA is essentially a ruthless mafia is an open secret in diplomatic circles, it is important for British public relations that this truth not be acknowledged:

> If that news emerged from an official source – a medium-ranking Hong Kong policeman would do – even at this eleventh hour Britain might be expected to do something to protect the six million people who lived in Hong Kong from the predators over the border. But London wanted most not to have to do anything at all until the colony had been safely handed over to Beijing at midnight on June 30. After that the UK could deplore the growth of corruption and the likely loss of human rights in its ex-colony from a position of zero responsibility.[54]

If the British diplomats are knowingly surrendering Hong Kong to tyranny and willingly acquiescing in the destruction of rule of law, at least there is nothing 'communist' about the new arrangement. Perhaps most tellingly, at the novel's denouement, as General Xian's warlords have succeeded in effectively taking over Hong Kong, in advance of the

Handover, the General informs his audience (in which Inspector Chan is present), that the West has won the ideological cold war: capitalism is triumphant. But now, he warns, China is going to beat the West on its own terms, and succeed in it the same way the West did: 'Slaves and narcotics. After the slaves and narcotics phase of capitalism, who knows, we might even have democracy in China. But we're a long way behind, and we have to start in the way approved by history. Aren't you pleased we've taken the path to freedom?'[55] The Handover, then, does not merely mean the end of a free Hong Kong; it is emblematic of the demise of western dominance. Beyond that, it may even portend the demise of western civilisation itself: whereas Britain weakened China in the nineteenth century through the importing of opium, now the Chinese are returning the favour by smuggling heroin into western countries.

Paul Theroux's *Kowloon Tong*, also published in early 1997 – a 'novelist's equivalent of a hack's cuttings job, rushed out in 213 large-print pages to exploit the moment', suggested Michael Sheridan in the *New Statesman* – is similarly apocalyptic, but it presents a more micro-themed depiction of the Chinese takeover of Hong Kong: a PLA officer, Mr Hung, schemes by a combination of generosity and threats to take over the factory owned by an Englishman, Bunt, and his mother – characters depicted, according to Sheridan, as 'pasty-faced, lazy, furtive, prejudiced and cowardly'.[56] Bunt is the familiar name of a bachelor in his forties named Neville Mullard, who is utterly dominated by his mother and whose childhood fantasies of having a sexually voracious Chinese mistress are, by the end of the novel, being fulfilled by one of his factory workers, Mei-ping. He is the worst sort of expatriate: 'His hatred for Chinese food extended to the plants, the fruit, the trees that were native to the country, and the country itself, the whole of it. He had no interest.'[57] He takes full advantage of the easy accessibility of Asian women to the expatriate man that was discussed in Chapter 3, but unlike John Burdett's Aston, Bunt also takes pride in Britain's contribution to the rule of law. Bunt's thoughts on visiting the police station in Kowloon Tong:

> He was proud of the place. Here, Hong Kong was not a frenzy of marketers and plonkers yattering on cellular phones; it was the rule of law, it was decorum and order. It was the solid building with its serious entrances and its scowling windows, all bars and screens, the dark uniforms, the black boots, the swept floor, the row of chairs, another flag inside, and the portrait of the Queen that was hung on the wall beside the sergeant at the desk.[58]

If, given Bunt's character, it is difficult to sympathise with the loss of his privileged status or even of his family business, Theroux's clear message is not only that the good times are over, but that British rectitude is being transformed into corruption and tyranny.

Robert Elegant's *Last Year in Hong Kong: A Love Story* lacks either the dramatic violence or the demonstrated malign results of Chinese takeover that Leather's, Burdett's, and Theroux's novels portray. Elegant, an American-born former Fellow of the American Enterprise Institute, who spent much of his career in East Asia before settling in London, presents the worst fears for Hong Kong's future through predictions in characters' speech or thoughts, not as accomplished events. The story, reminiscent of Han Suyin's *A Many Splendoured Thing*, centres on the love affair of recently divorced American woman, Lucretia, and a man of mixed Tibetan and English parentage, Dorje. Their love is problematic because Lucretia has been a vocal critic of Beijing, supporting Martin Lee's Democratic Party, and Dorje, as an architect, is dependent for business upon remaining in favour – but also because of his loyalty to Tibet and the expectation that he would marry a Tibetan woman.

On the eve of the Handover, serious crime in Hong Kong is rising, Lucretia reflects, because of British subservience to Beijing, symbolised by dropping the title 'Royal' from the police force and 'rather comically' replacing the red postboxes that displayed the royal crown. 'Such crawling had engendered scorn for the outgoing British administration, despite the courageous stand of the last British Governor. Since the public were now contemptuous of British law and the British-trained police, serious crime was increasing throughout the territory.'[59] Already there are signs of increased corruption in political and business life. But the terrors that are to come are presented as unknowns, rather than an inevitable trajectory. As Lucretia, contemplating her own future in Hong Kong, muses:

> Yet, who could say exactly how Hong Kong's new rulers would behave? There was apparently no precedent. Nothing remotely similar had ever occurred. Never had a democratic country like Britain voluntarily delivered seven million subjects to a tyrannical dictatorship! Never had the rich, the entrepreneurs, the managers, the professional classes, and the natural leaders of the community thus betrayed and abandoned the common people.

She takes no comfort in the often-repeated arguments for why Beijing would behave with restraint:

> Only fools now argued that Beijing must honor its pledge to give the former Colony fifty years of semi-autonomy with unchanged economic and social systems – because of the pressure of world opinion and also because Beijing would not kill the goose that laid the golden eggs. Just so had Old Hong Kong hands assured each other decades earlier that

[204]

the Communists would never demand direct control of the Colony, but would preserve it as a separate entity under British rule because it was so useful to them.[60]

Elsewhere she considers that she may want to stay in Hong Kong after the Handover, if only to 'see what would become of the people of Hong Kong under a Communist regime'.[61]

Yet if Lucretia only fears the worst, her worldly-wise friend, Selma Lotz, warns her exactly what to expect: 'It's no great mystery.' Lotz, a Russian Jew who escaped Russia to Shanghai with her parents as a young girl in the late 1920s, had married another Russian Jewish refugee in 1937. Her husband's costume-jewellery exporting business had prospered, and even the Japanese occupation had barely slowed it. Yet the Communist triumph in 1949 had turned the Lotzes into penniless refugees in Hong Kong – where they had once again prospered. In Selma Lotz's view, the Communists' behaviour in Shanghai in the early 1950s provided a precise blueprint for what would happen to Hong Kong within a few years after 1997: the banning of the Democratic Party, a controlled press, purged textbooks, a subdued Legislature and Courts. True, Beijing promised otherwise: 'So many promises, just like Shanghai. But they're already doing almost exactly the same as they did in Shanghai.'[62]

John Gordon Davis's *The Year of Dangerous Loving*, like the other novels cited above, opportunistically capitalised on the Handover. Unlike the others, though, this was not the author's first Hong Kong-related novel; it came nearly a quarter-century after *The Years of the Tiger*, discussed in previous chapters. Nor was it, properly speaking, a Handover-themed novel. Where Leather, Burdett, Elegant, and Theroux focus their plots on the deleterious effects of the Chinese take-over of Hong Kong, in Davis's novel the Handover is closer to the background. To be sure, the novel includes the inevitable monologues about how justice and the rule of law will be destroyed once Beijing is in control, and about Britain's betrayal of its Chinese subjects as it turns them over to a post-Tiananmen Square murderous regime. The destruction of British Hong Kong is symbolised by protagonist Ian Hargreave, a Canadian expatriate whose adventure begins as he is shot by his wife during an argument precipitated by her finding lipstick on his collar. This is particularly unfair; as Hargreave explains to Jake McAdam: 'Oh Christ. That was just some Wanchai whore trying to be persuasive. Nothing happened, didn't even buy her a drink.'[63] During the course of the novel, Hargreave degenerates from an honourable prosecutor into someone willing to betray the rule of law he has henceforth championed.

But what ultimately leads to Hargreave's compromise of principle is not the encroachment of Chinese Communism, but the collapse of

Soviet Communism and the resulting emergence of an internationally active Russian mafia. The plot centres on the interaction between
two initially discrete story-lines: Hargreave's love affair with Olga, a
Macau-based Russian prostitute half his age, and his attempt to free
her from her mafia captors; and police inspector Bernard Champion's
attempt, in cooperation with one of Russia's few honest police officers, to thwart a Russian gangster's attempt to import uranium into
Hong Kong. Although the Russian's putative buyers are, unsurpris-
ingly, Hong Kong triads, neither the CCP, nor the PLA, nor the fact
of the Handover itself, plays a decisive role in the story. Rather, the
Russian uranium supplier attempts to use Hargreave's love for Olga –
and the threat of cutting off her breast – to blackmail Hargreave into
throwing the case. Happily, this result is forestalled thanks to a heroic
Moscow rescue by Hargreave and Champion. Unlike the novels previously cited, the message in this one is less that the Chinese takeover
has destroyed British Hong Kong, than that Hong Kong is now being
subsumed into an internationally grounded corruption of justice. For
Davis, who began his Hong Kong career as Crown Counsel in the
pre-ICAC 1960s, Hong Kong has perhaps come full circle.

If Hong Kong has ceased to be a British space, perhaps it is not that it
has been absorbed by China but that it has become a truly global city.[64]
Accordingly, it is fitting that the Handover has found an American
novelist, Muhammad Cohen, whose 2007 novel *Hong Kong on Air*
depicts the Handover and a few months on either side from the perspective of an American couple and a television news network for
which one of them works. Whereas the Leather, Burdett, and Theroux
novels appear to give the authors' endorsement of the worst fears concerning the change of sovereignty, Cohen, writing several years later
when the worst fears clearly had not been borne out, merely allows
one of his characters, Laura, to imagine them, while the actual changes
that are portrayed are far more subtle. Laura, an American television
producer who has come to Hong Kong in order to participate in the
Handover, is dumb-struck by the seeming 'unconsciousness' of Hong
Kong's Chinese people toward their takeover by 'Red China, for god's
sake'; for her part, although she thinks expatriates such as herself
will be fine, she is 'certain things will change dramatically for people
who really live here. How can they not?'. Later, she expresses to her
British colleague, Edie, her concern about Hong Kong's takeover by
'Communist dictators'; Edie shrugs the latter off as mere politicians,
similar to those anywhere else.[65] Indeed, Laura's occasional remarks
about Communist tyranny are overwhelmed by the novel's plot,
which suggests that the changes in store for her relate more to inter-
personal culture than to high politics. For example, one of the reasons

that Laura's career stalls is that she tells a mainland executive what she thinks is a helpful truth. The executive responds to Laura's honesty with politeness and apparent gratitude. Later, Edie chides her for misunderstanding the Chinese concept of face. 'A key element of giving face is to allow [the executive] to continue to ignore the bad news undisturbed, to tell the emperor that his new clothes are beautiful not that he's standing there in nature's own.'[66]

A more serious blunder on her part concerns her lack of journalistic skill, which is shown up by her husband, Jeff. Overhearing her telephone conversation with a source suggesting that the Thai Government may be on the verge of running out of cash reserves, Jeff sees an opportunity to make money. Although he knows little about finance, he knows enough to mention this tip to his mistress, Yogi, a Japanese investment banker, who tells him how to profit from the Thai Baht's possible devaluation: short the Indonesian currency, which is likely to follow it down. Jeff makes some four million US dollars from the Asian financial crisis; Laura's employer is disappointed, not that Jeff profited from her source, but that she entirely missed the story. Ultimately, the news organisation relocates to China, and Laura is, mercifully, allowed to remain within the company, taking a position in the States.

In contrast to the other novels cited here, Hong Kong's takeover by China does not, in Cohen's novel, threaten the crushing of Hong Kong freedoms. Rather, what is striking is how much remains the same, even with new masters to court. This is perhaps best seen in the dissolution of Laura's marriage. The details are not important to the present argument, but the final, and rather sudden, break comes not because of Jeff's infidelity (which he successfully keeps a secret), nor from his abusing her journalistic source, but from his unwillingness to follow her back to New York when her Hong Kong career implodes. Ultimately, he refuses to share the money, and even refuses her suggestion that she could stay with him in Hong Kong as a housewife. As he walks away from his apartment and his marriage, his thoughts wander:

> Outside, before his workout, Jeff can call one of those Filipinas he met yesterday. He can call Yogi, tell her Laura is out of the picture, and he can come to Japan, or go to Bali, and buy a sailboat and tie a surfboard to the stern. Or he can go to Bali without Yogi and get his own sailboat ... With his wife throwing him out and $4 million to burn, Jeff realizes he's done what he set out to do when he left Long Island a year ago. He's restarted his life, and he likes the way it's turning out.[67]

The days of FILTH may be over, but the imagined Hong Kong remains, as always, a site in which a person can make a lot of money quickly and a western man can find easy access to Asian female bodies.

Notes

1 Mark Austin (reporter), 'Hong Kong: Expats', 24 June 1997, ITV News. NewsFilm Online archive, www.nfo.ac.uk (accessed 1 July 2009). Rodway was involved in the founding of the Hong Kong Family Law Association in 1986; see 'A Decade of Action', *Hong Kong Lawyer* (February 1997), p. 14, available at http://sunzi.lib.hku.hk/hkjo/view/15/1501044.pdf (accessed 5 August 2011).

2 On the negotiations, see Percy Cradock, *Experiences of China*, new edn (London: John Murray, 1999), pp. 161–215; Ian Scott, *Political Change and the Crisis of Legitimacy in Hong Kong* (Hong Kong: Oxford University press, 1989), pp. 171–219; Steve Tsang, *A Modern History of Hong Kong* (London and New York: I. B. Tauris, 2004), pp. 211–27.

3 'Britain's Other Islands', *New Statesman* 104 (8 October 1982), p. 2; 'A Tale of Two Colonies', *New Statesman* 108 (3 August 1984), p. 3.

4 John Flowerdew, *The Final Years of British Hong Kong: The Discourse of Colonial Withdrawal* (New York: St Martin's Press, 1997). See also Agnes S. M. Ku, *Narratives, Politics, and the Public Sphere: Struggles over Political Reform in the Final Transitional Years in Hong Kong (1992–1994)* (Aldershot: Ashgate, 1999), pp. 117–18; Christopher Patten, *Our Next Five Years: The Agenda for Hong Kong. Address by the Governor the Right Honourable Christopher Patten at the Opening of the 1992/93 Session of the Legislative Council, 7 October 1992* (Hong Kong: Hong Kong Government Office, 1992), p. 1.

5 See, e.g., Kevin Toolis, 'Colonial Cold Feet', *New Statesman* (4 May 1984), p. 21.

6 FAULDS 3/3/1/6, 'Statement on Hong Kong', 26 September 1984.

7 David Bonavia, *Hong Kong 1997: The Final Settlement* (Hong Kong: FEER, 1985), p. 162.

8 Indeed, Lau made exactly this point in her rebuttal in the pages of the *FEER*. See Emily Lau, 'Assessment Assessed', *FEER* (13 December 1984), pp. 26–7.

9 FAULDS 3/3/1/6, 'Statement by Russell Johnston, MP, Liberal Spokesman on Foreign & Commonwealth Affairs on the Government White Paper Describing the Draft Agreement between HMG and the Government of the People's Republic of China on the Future of Hong Kong', 26 September 1984.

10 University of Oxford, Conservative Party Archive, 'International Review', *Politics Today* 1 (21 January 1985), p. 17.

11 Christopher Patten, *Letters to Hong Kong* (Hong Kong: Information Services Department, 1997), p. 6.

12 Patten, *Letters to Hong Kong*, pp. 8, 10.

13 Patten, *Letters to Hong Kong*, p. 25.

14 Patten, *Letters to Hong Kong*, p. 28.

15 See also 'Hong Kong's Tory Betrayal', *New Statesman & Society* 6 (30 July 1993), p. 11; Werner Menski, 'Conclusions: Coping with the Cost of Mistakes', in Werner Menski (ed.), *Coping with 1997: The Reaction of the Hong Kong People to the Transfer of Power* (Stoke on Trent: Trentham Books, 1995).

16 FAULDS 03/42, 'Perception Survey'.

17 FAULDS 4/9/4, Andrew Faulds, speech, n.d. This speech exhibits an optimism he had held for more than a decade; he told a press conference in Hong Kong in 1984 that the not-yet-signed Joint Declaration would work because China had historically honoured all of its international agreements. See Jill Hartley, 'Nationality Not a Big Issue', *SCMP* (10 October 1984), p. 14.

18 FAULDS 4/9/7, Andrew Faulds, unpublished speech notes, n.d.

19 Jonathan Fenby, 'Enter the Dragon', *New Statesman* 10 (27 June 1997), p. 9.

20 Nigel Cameron, *Hong Kong: The Cultured Pearl* (Hong Kong: Oxford University Press, 1978), pp. 258–62, 265.

21 Walter Easey, *Ducking Responsibility: Britain and Hong Kong in the '80s* (Manchester: Christian Statesman, 1980), pp. 22–33, 45, 46.

22 Of his prediction that Hong Kong would revert to China suddenly during the early 1980s, he said he hoped he would be proven wrong: 'If I am wrong, there is no harm

done. Walter Easey will simply be seen as an alarmist, a poor analyst and ultimately, a fool. No matter, this is a risk that anyone who takes on the task of political prediction accepts. This possibility does not alarm me, I can live with it.' Easey, *Ducking Responsibility*, pp. 22–3.

23 Leyland Otter, *Special Study, August 1984: The Future of Hong Kong* (London: Bank of Credit and Commerce International, 1984), p. 5; Felix Patrikeeff, *Mouldering Pearl: Hong Kong at the Crossroads* (London: George Philip, 1989), pp. 169–70, 184.

24 Indeed, in Dally's framing, the PRC's Communist character was its defining quality, and Dally portrayed the CCP essentially as an arm of the international Communist conspiracy; this was highly unusual among the sources cited in this chapter. This paragraph and the subsequent one summarise his pamphlet; see Peter Dally, *Hong Kong Time Bomb* (Cheltenham: British Anti-Communist Council, 1984).

25 KNKK 1/3/42, Humphry Berkeley, 'Draft Proposal for a Settlement of the Future of Hong Kong Submitted to the Shadow Cabinet', 24 April 1990.

26 George L. Hicks, 'Hong Kong on the Eve of Communist Rule', in George L. Hicks, *Hong Kong Countdown* (Hong Kong: Writers' and Publishers' Cooperative, 1989), pp. 7–8.

27 'Red Capitalism', in Hicks, *Hong Kong Countdown*, pp. 118–19.

28 Ian Buruma, 'Hong Kong Finds Its Pride', *Spectator* (17 June 1989), p. 14.

29 Hicks, *Hong Kong Countdown*, pp. ii, x.

30 Hicks, *Hong Kong Countdown*, p. ii. See also 'The Selling of Hong Kong', in Hicks, *Hong Kong Countdown*, p. 88.

31 Hicks, *Hong Kong Countdown*, p. xi.

32 Jan Morris, *Hong Kong: Epilogue to an Empire* (New York: Random House, 1997), p. 300. For examples of Morris's point, see Kevin Rafferty, *City on the Rocks: Hong Kong's Uncertain Future* (New York: Viking, 1989), pp. 319–20; Menski, 'Conclusions'. See also the interview with Father John Ahearn in the American documentary *No Longer Colonies* (Maryknoll, NY: Maryknoll Fathers and Brothers, 1993); viewed at the CUHK library. Jeremy Irons's character in Wayne Wang's *Chinese Box* (Trimark Pictures, 1997), near the film's beginning, similarly predicts post-Handover continuity on the grounds that the Chinese have already effectively taken over the colony.

33 'Hong Kong: A Matter of Honour?', *Panorama* (13 June 1989), re-broadcast later the same day on RTHK. Viewed at the HKBU Library. See also Lee, ' "One Country, Two Systems" – But No Sense of Humour', Foreword to Larry Feign, *Banned in Hong Kong* (Hong Kong: Hambalan Press, 1995), pp. 3–4.

34 'Hong Kong's Tory Betrayal', *New Statesman & Society* 6 (30 July 1993), p. 10.

35 J. Tobin Rothlein, *Eyes of the Storm* (New York: Filmakers Library, 1997); viewed at the CUHK library.

36 University of Birmingham, Martin Booth Papers, 1998/67, Box 6, Martin Booth, typed MS of commissioned article for *FEER*, undated manuscript.

37 University of Birmingham, Martin Booth Papers, 1998/67, Box 6, Martin Booth, 'BBC – From Our Own Correspondent', undated manuscript.

38 Chris Fairclough, *We Live in Hong Kong* (Hove: Wayland, 1985), p. 49.

39 'Expats Mean Business as Their Role Expands', *SCMP* (29 December 1989).

40 'Expats' Golden Era at an End', *SCMP* (25 September 1994). See also 'Expats Get 16 PC Rise in Package', *SCMP* (25 September 1994).

41 Quoted in May Holdsworth, *Foreign Devils: Expatriates in Hong Kong* (Oxford: Oxford University Press, 2002), p. 94.

42 For the story of a young Briton in Hong Kong who had a particularly bad time of it in the mid-1990s, see Chris Thrall, *Eating Smoke: One Man's Descent into Drug Psychosis in Hong Kong's Triad Heartland* (Hong Kong: Blacksmith Books, 2011).

43 Stephen Vines, 'In Hong Kong Today, It's the Brits who Are the "Coolies" ', *Independent* (2 June 1996).

44 Liam Parker, 'Multiple Exit Visas', *Hong Kong Tatler* 21 (June 1997), p. 106.

45 Another notable novel is Christopher New's *A Change of Flag* (Hong Kong: Asia2000, 2000), set against the backdrop of the Deng–Thatcher negotiations.

46 Stephen Leather, *The Vets* (New York: Simon and Schuster, 1993), p. 47.

47 Leather, *The Vets*, p. 49.
48 Leather, *The Vets*, p. 272.
49 Leather, *The Vets*, pp. 263–4.
50 On the role of Hong Kong-based triads in the international heroin trade of the 1960s and 1970s, see Fenton Bresler, *The Trail of the Triads: An Investigation into International Crime* (London: Weidenfeld and Nicolson, 1980).
51 *The Last Six Million Seconds* was his first novel. His later, better-known novels centring on Bangkok also feature a Eurasian, Royal Thai Police detective, Sonchai Jitpleecheep.
52 John Burdett, *The Last Six Million Seconds: A Thriller* (New York: William Morrow, 1997), pp. 14–15, 48–9.
53 Burdett, *The Last Six Million Seconds*, p. 194.
54 Burdett, *The Last Six Million Seconds*, pp. 32, 44–5.
55 Burdett, *The Last Six Million Seconds*, pp. 383–4.
56 Michael Sheridan, 'Close of Business', *New Statesman* (20 June 1997), p. 44.
57 Paul Theroux, *Kowloon Tong* (Boston, MA and New York: Houghton Mifflin, 1997), p. 39.
58 Theroux, *Kowloon Tong*, p. 176.
59 Robert Elegant, *Last Year in Hong Kong: A Love Story* (New York: William Morrow, 1997), pp. 60–1.
60 Elegant, *Last Year in Hong Kong*, p. 172.
61 Elegant, *Last Year in Hong Kong*, p. 11.
62 Elegant, *Last Year in Hong Kong*, pp. 174–80 (quotations on pp. 174 and 180).
63 John Gordon Davis, *The Year of Dangerous Loving* (London: HarperCollins, 1997), p. 8.
64 David R. Meyer, *Hong Kong as a Global Metropolis* (Cambridge: Cambridge University Press, 2000); Stephen Chiu and Tai-Lok Lui, *Hong Kong: Becoming a Chinese Global City* (London and New York: Routledge, 2009); Gary McDonogh and Cindy Wong, *Global Hong Kong* (London and New York: Routledge, 2005); Gordon Mathews, *Ghetto at the Center of the World: Chungking Mansions, Hong Kong* (Chicago: University of Chicago Press, 2011).
65 Muhammad Cohen, *Hong Kong on Air* (Hong Kong: Blacksmith Books, 2007), pp. 93, 246.
66 Cohen, *Hong Kong on Air*, p. 378.
67 Cohen, *Hong Kong on Air*, p. 454.

Epilogue: postcolonial hangovers

In August 2013, while entering the home stretch of writing this book, I took on a twenty-four-year-old post-graduate student named Peter Law. A native of Hong Kong, he was too young to have strong memories of life under British authority; English was not spoken regularly in his home, and he had never travelled to the United Kingdom. His research topic concerned British rule in early-twentieth-century Shanghai; during his undergraduate studies, he had written a senior thesis on the Raj. Nothing about this profile surprised me; I had begun my own post-graduate studies torn between researching British and French history, even though I had travelled to neither country and had no personal connections to either place. What did surprise me was the intensity of Peter's identification with British culture and history – an identification that threatened to make Sir David Tang's famed Anglophilia seem almost detached by comparison. I began to receive emails signed 'God save the Queen', and to notice British photographs and memorabilia decorating his office desk: images of men in kilts, regimental symbolism, and of course the Queen. At an orientation for new undergraduates, he introduced himself as a 'loyal servant of the Queen' – to the bewilderment of the English exchange student sitting next to him.

There is no doubt that Peter is an outlier – and a rather far one, at that. Yet at the time of writing, seventeen years after the resumption of Chinese sovereignty, it was easy to see the lingering British cultural presence, in ways both superficial and substantive. There remained, of course, a sizeable number of British expatriates and long-term residents in Hong Kong, but the 19,000 Britons in Hong Kong in 2009 paled beside the estimated 50,000 Americans, to say nothing of the much larger number of non-Chinese Asians including Filipinos, Indonesians, Thais, and Indians.[1] Certainly in the context of a city of more than seven million people, the vast majority Chinese, the number of Britons was not the main source of continuing British influence. Rather, the combination of inertia, the association of colonialism with Hong Kong's 1980s 'golden age', and the relatively cautious approach of the SAR to major changes allowed the British cultural presence to endure, more as a legacy than as a manifestation of ongoing transnational engagement.

It is easy to see the lingering British presence if one looks for it. Despite fears of encroaching mainland political influence – which often seemed to elide with complaints about mainland tourists' crude behaviour and the reshaping of entire neighbourhoods to accommodate their shopping needs – Hong Kong's Government in 2014 remained very much the bureaucratic, rules-oriented body that the British established.[2] The press remained free and lively, though critics pointed to creeping self-censorship as well as financial pressure from Beijing to refrain from criticising PRC policies; there was also speculation that occasional physical attacks on Hong Kong journalists could be traced to Beijing's orders.[3] The transition toward universal suffrage had not, by September 2014, kept pace with popular expectations, as evidenced by student strikes and the beginning of the 'Occupy Central' movement in defiance of PRC restrictions on the electoral system. The independent judiciary remained well established, even if many people assumed its continuation was precarious. Yet paradoxically the single most prominent challenge to the independent judiciary during the SAR's first fifteen years, concerning the case of whether Filipina and Indonesian domestic helpers should be entitled to the right of abode, saw Hong Kong public opinion and the Government's position allied in opposing the verdict of the lower court; before the Court of Final Appeal sided with the Government, it was widely suggested that the Government could appeal over the court's heads to Beijing for a reinterpretation of the Basic Law.[4] Beijing's June 2014 publication of a 'White Paper' articulating that Hong Kong enjoyed its relative autonomy only as a gift from the Chinese Government seemed to many to herald the long-anticipated clampdown on Hong Kong's rights, but clearly nothing quite like the apocalyptic scenarios conjured by Leather, Burdett, and Theroux's Handover novels had transpired one-third of the way through the SAR's fifty-year term. Even the annual vigil in remembrance of the Tiananmen Square massacre, which Christine Loh and others had expected to be suppressed after 1997, endured – held, one might add, at a site still called Victoria Park and under the watchful eyes of Queen Victoria's statue.

This is not to say that fears were misplaced. As an increasingly assertive China threw its weight around the region, contributing to clashes with Japan, Vietnam, and the Philippines, even as steady mainland immigration offset Hong Kong's own exceptionally low birthrate, Hong Kong people were understandably nervous about Beijing's intentions to their own territory.[5] Far from exhibiting paranoia about PRC encroachment, one could argue that Hong Kong people's vigilance in asserting their territory's difference had been the very reason for the preservation of Hong Kong's political and economic system after 1997; the back-down by Chief Executive Tung Chee-wah (and implicitly by Beijing) over the proposed 'anti-sedition law' based on Article 23 of the Basic Law, following massive demonstrations on 1 July 2003, was the most important example, but not the only one. While this demonstration centred on political freedoms, the 2012 demonstrations against the adoption of a 'patriotic' school curriculum seemed to be at least as much about Hong Kong people's articulation of cultural difference from mainlanders as it was about the existence of propaganda itself. At the same time, as Leo Goodstadt has argued, such defence of political rights came at the expense of vigorous assertion of social rights; in the absence of a dynamic 'welfare lobby', and with a narrowly elected, executive-led Government beholden to the territory's 'tycoons', no obvious channel existed to address popular discontent concerning spiralling housing costs, the erosion of services, and extreme levels of income inequality. As Goodstadt notes, following budget cuts Chief Executive Donald Tsang complacently denied that Hospital Authority services were inadequate; rather, the elderly exaggerated their medical problems, and long queues at government clinics merely reflected older people's sociability.[6]

Surprisingly, from about 2011 pro-democracy and anti-PRC protests were often accompanied by Hong Kong's colonial-era flag, alongside the contemporary Hong Kong flag that included a bauhinia in the centre of a red field.[7] Yet although this appropriation suggests, if not identification with the former colonial power, at least a nostalgia for a golden age before overcrowding and post-industrial income stagnation, it bears remembering that the Hong Kong people's restricted proposed role in selecting their 2017 Chief Executive would be, by any reasonable standard, far greater than their role in selecting their last Colonial Governor. If Hong Kong people felt betrayed by PRC stall tactics, they could not reasonably say that a British-era democracy had been overturned. If what Stephen Vines called the 'spirit of greater political independence and self-confidence' which the Patten Government facilitated was a British legacy, then so too was the Government's ultimate appointment by a committee outside Hong Kong; nor was Special Branch's spying on dissident political groups at the height of Hong Kong's 'golden age' a compelling reason for democrats to wave the colonial flag.[8] There was more than a little irony, moreover, in using the colonial flag in support of democracy and 'Hongkongian' identity, especially to the extent that economic grievances blended with political ones; Britain's own democracy had produced, after 2010, an austerity budget featuring social security cutbacks, high university fees, zero-hour contracts, and 'workfare', and had met with major demonstrations in March 2011 with as many 500,000 protestors taking to London's streets.[9] At the same time, while Hong Kong enjoyed some of the world's most modern infrastructure, and its MTR Corporation had even been contracted to run a London overground rail line, British economics journalists would claim, in 2012, that the UK was a mere two years away from having a 'third world economy'.[10]

Other British legacies may be more superficial, but remained part of the local cultural identity. The Hong Kong Sevens rugby tournament was approaching its fortieth anniversary, maintaining the city's links to British sport, as well as an occasion for laddish revelry; the police helpfully warned in 2014 that punters were vulnerable to 'powerfully built women who prey on drinkers'.[11] Eventually, perhaps, colonial-era currency notes would disappear from circulation; as of 2014 it was not uncommon to see notes still bearing the Queen's image. Some of the most important streets in Hong Kong and Kowloon continued to recall the colonial era – Queen's Road, Nathan Road, Hennessy Road, Salisbury Road – though as one western journalist pointed out when Occupy Central began in late September 2014, the centrally located 'Hong Kong barracks of the People's Liberation Army', formerly called the Prince of Wales Building, was 'one colonial-era name that the new rulers did erase after the handover'.[12] The 2007 demolition of the Queen's Ferry Pier, 'a traditional landing point for British Governors and royalty when they arrived on Hong Kong Island during Colonial times', and its replacement by Pier Number Nine, occurred only after protests, hunger strikes, and court challenges.[13] When signing a lease for a flat in 2007, I was surprised that my realtor used a colonial-era boilerplate form with the Queen's name at the top of the page. When buying my first Hong Kong flat in 2009, I had to sign both English and Chinese versions; both said – though I had to trust my wife's reading of one of them – that in the event of any discrepancies between the two versions, the English one would prevail.

Earlier chapters have already suggested that western cultural imports into Hong Kong in the postwar era went well beyond strictly British influences. The founding of CUHK owed at least as much to American influences as British ones, and American television and film imports often crowded out their British counterparts, even during the colonial era. In the second decade of the SAR's existence, even the university system increasingly drew on American or 'international' standards rather than strictly British ones, most symbolically in the 2012 implementation of a four-year curriculum including a significant core curriculum, replacing the three-year discipline-dominated course of study; at the same time, the British cult of outcomes-based approaches that had overtaken Hong Kong was increasingly prevalent in the United States, at least outside elite private universities.[14] British iconography in Hong Kong was equally swallowed up within wider global forms. Sir David Tang has referred to the Union Flag as Britain's most important symbol; in post-Handover Hong Kong, though, it has become one brand among many. The young girl that I saw on the MTR, with Union Flag toenail polish juxtaposed with shades and a tee-shirt reading 'Black is my colour and my attitude', sat next to a boy whose own tee-shirt advertised the US Army. Nor did western culture have a monopoly on Hong Kong's global engagement. For example, as cultural theorist Meaghan Morris noted in 2006, Hong Kong students were at least as engaged with Korean and Japanese cultures as western ones.[15]

In Britain, Hong Kong remained, as it had for much of the twentieth century, more often on the margins than at the centre of the public mind. The occasional novel, such as John Lanchester's *Fragrant Harbour* (2002) or Jane Gardam's *Old Filth* (2006), reminded at least some readers of Britain's history with Hong Kong. As we have seen, though, much of the British cultural engagement with Hong Kong had long since ceased to be distinctly 'British', well before the Handover. Even if newspapers routinely included the obligatory phrase 'the former British colony' in most stories about Hong Kong, it was not uncommon for commentators to treat the territory less as a British legacy than as a *sui generis* global city. For example, even in 1997, James Dale Davidson and Lord William Rees-Mogg suggested Hong Kong as a 'mental model of the kind of jurisdiction that we expect to see flourish in the Information Age' – a low-tax, non-democratic home in which the post-national 'sovereign individual' could flourish.[16] Davidson and Rees-Mogg referred to the first tier of global elites, but a similar point could be made about the professional and managerial class. One could still see greying (or grey) Britons, colonial hold-overs, frequenting Wanchai's Old China Hand and other pubs, or waxing nostalgic in the Hong Kong Club, but one got the strong sense that the typical short-term British expatriate's connection to Hong Kong was not particularly greater than that of other English-speaking expatriates. As Caroline Knowles and Douglas Harper have written of one type of post-Handover British expatriate, 'Those who see Hong Kong as a high-status job locale do equally well elsewhere. They do not necessarily have a special connection with Hong Kong. Specific places don't matter so much in migrant calculations and connections. The mobile can always, well, move.'[17]

Yet one can argue that Hong Kong's position as a global city is itself an enduring British legacy. Gary Magee and Andrew Thompson have demonstrated that the British Empire in the nineteenth and early twentieth centuries facilitated and grew out of British business, social, and professional networks, migrations, and material cultures that collectively helped to fashion a global culture.[18] Gregory Barton argues that metropolitan cultural forms constituted an informal empire that coopted elites both within Britain's formal Empire and outside it, an 'empire' in which British influence was ultimately superseded by American. The result, Barton argues, is that 'there is one world culture and this one world culture is Western'. He points to the global hegemony of technocratic elites, the widespread ideal of parliamentary government, mixed economies, the colonisation by western images of the 'mental landscape of nearly the entire global village'.[19] Whatever the more specific variations – local dialects and food cultures, for example – it is not a stretch to locate Hong Kong within Barton's model of the 'one world culture'.

John Carroll entitled his book about the relationships between Hong Kong's colonial and Chinese elites in the nineteenth and early twentieth centuries *The Edge of Empires*; Hong Kong existed at the intersection between a global British Empire and a dying Qing agrarian empire. Carroll's title could perhaps extend to contemporary Hong Kong. Barton, in his elucidation of the characteristics of the 'one world culture', makes a telling qualification, in asking 'Why, except for a Western and Marxist bureaucracy in China, is parliamentary government the dominant ideal almost everywhere?'.[20] The pressing question is whether Barton's caveat highlights merely a minor variation in China's broader absorption into a global culture, in which a Chinese adoption of markets, the penchant for studying at western universities, and even western forms of romantic relationships are increasingly prominent. In this scenario, China and the United States could struggle over their countries' relative positions within the 'one world culture', much as Britain and the United States did in the mid-twentieth century. An alternative scenario posits the Chinese form of government not as a mere caveat, but as the centrepiece of an alternative empire: one in which China's emergence as the world's most important creditor nation, global projection of 'soft power' as well as hard, infrastructure projects in Africa, and securing of food and mineral supplies around the world raise the prospects of an entirely different model of statist capitalism that can at best peacefully coexist with Barton's 'one world culture'.[21] In this alternative vision, Hong Kong's place at the 'edge of empires' would suggest that Occupy Central will not be the final border skirmish.

Notes

1 Caroline Knowles and Douglas Harper, *Hong Kong: Migrant Lives, Landscapes, and Journeys* (Chicago: University of Chicago Press, 2009), pp. 12–13.
2 On Hong Kong's relationship with the mainland following 1997, see Gordon Mathews, Eric Kit-wai Ma, and Tai-Lok Lui, *Hong Kong, China: Learning to Belong to a Nation* (London and New York: Routledge, 2008).
3 See Carol P. Lai, *Media in Hong Kong: Press Freedom and Political Change, 1967–2005* (London and New York: Routledge, 2007); Martin Lee, 'Hong Kong's Shaky Democratic Future', *New York Times* (13 March 2014), www.nytimes.com/2014/03/14/opinion/hong-kongs-shaky-democratic-future.html (accessed 1 October 2014). Lai's study skilfully draws on framing developed in western contexts, particularly the radical and liberal traditions of media studies. A Hong Kong newspaper's self-censoring to avoid offending China, Inc. in order to protect advertising revenues and mainland deals for the paper's parent company is not unlike American media's studiously avoiding offending corporate sponsors, or NBC News discreetly failing to report unfavourable news concerning parent company General Electric; the difference, though, was that China, Inc. was locally far more dominant than any single Fortune 500 company was in the United States. Lai's book also shows considerable continuity between the mainstream press in colonial Hong Kong, which was relatively uncritical of the Colonial Government, and the mainstream press in post-1997 Hong Kong, which was relatively accommodating to Beijing. For a comparison with media in a democratic western country, see, e.g., Robert W. McChesney, *Rich Media, Poor Democracy: Communication Politics in Dubious Times* (New York: New Press, 2000).
4 Lau Nai-Keung, 'Govt Should Stop Passing Buck on Basic Law Interpretation', *China Daily Asia* (4 October 2011), www.chinadailyasia.com/opinion/2011-10/04/content_69666.html (accessed 1 October 2014).
5 Robert Kaplan, *Asia's Cauldron: The South China Sea and the End of a Stable Pacific* (New York: Random House, 2014).
6 Leo Goodstadt, *Poverty in the Midst of Affluence: How Hong Kong Mismanaged Its Prosperity* (Hong Kong: Hong Kong University Press, 2013). (Tsang's statement on health care appears on pp. 140–1.)
7 *SCMP Debate, SCMP* (19 November 2002): 8.
8 Stephen Vines, *Hong Kong: China's New Colony* (London: Orion Business, 1999), pp. 90–1.
9 Mary O'Hara, *Austerity Bites: A Journey to the Sharp End of Cuts in the UK* (Chicago: University of Chicago Press, 2014).
10 Larry Elliott and Dan Atkinson, *Going South: Why Britain Will Have a Third World Economy by 2014* (Basingstoke: Palgrave Macmillan, 2012).
11 Clifford Lo, 'Rugby Sevens Revellers Warned of Powerfully Built Women who Prey on Drinkers', *SCMP* (28 March 2014).
12 Bruce Einhorn, 'Hong Kong's Angry Protests: What Now?', *Bloomsberg Businessweek* (29 September 2014), www.businessweek.com/articles/2014-09-29/protests-rock-hong-kong and-china-dot-what-comes-next (accessed 30 September 2014).
13 Chloe Lai, 'Declaration Challenges Queen's Pier Demolition', *SCMP* (19 April 2007); 'HK "Can Demolish" Colonial Pier', BBC News (10 August 2007), http://news.bbc.co.uk/2/hi/asia-pacific/6940160.stm (accessed 1 October 2014); Richard Spencer, 'Hong Kong to Lose Historic Pier', *Telegraph* (1 August 2007; quotation from Lai).
14 See Mark Hampton and Carol C. L. Tsang, 'Colonial Legacies and Internationalization: British History in Contemporary Hong Kong', *Twentieth Century British History* 23.4 (2012): 563–74.
15 John Sutherland, 'The Ideas Interview: Meaghan Morris', *Guardian* (16 May 2006), www.theguardian.com/education/2006/may/16/internationaleducationnews.highereducation (accessed 30 September 2014).

16 James Dale Davidson and Lord William Rees-Mogg, *The Sovereign Individual: How to Survive and Thrive during the Collapse of the Welfare State* (New York: Simon and Schuster, 1997), p. 311.
17 Knowles and Harper, *Hong Kong*, p. 235. See also James Pomfret, 'British Influence in HK Wanes, but Far from Dead', *SCMP* (27 June 2007).
18 Gary B. Magee and Andrew S. Thompson, *Empire and Globalisation: Networks of People, Goods and Capital in the British World, c. 1850–1914* (Cambridge: Cambridge University Press, 2010).
19 Gregory A. Barton, *Informal Empire and the Rise of One World Culture* (Basingstoke: Palgrave, 2014), p. 1.
20 Barton, *Informal Empire*, p. 1.
21 Howard French, *China's Second Continent: How a Million Migrants Are Building a New Empire in Africa* (New York: Knopf, 2014); Joshua Kurlantzick, *Charm Offensive: How China's Soft Power Is Transforming the World* (New Haven: Yale University Press, 2008); Ian Bremmer, *The End of the Free Market: Who Wins the War between States and Corporations?* (New York: Penguin, 2010); Martin Jacques, *When China Rules the World: The End of the Western World and the Birth of a New Global Order*, 2nd edn (New York: Penguin, 2009).

SELECT BIBLIOGRAPHY

This select bibliography includes a list of the archives and periodicals consulted, and a sampling of the most important published sources for understanding this book's topic.

Archives consulted

Australian National Archive
Birmingham University Information Services
   Church Missionary Society Archives
   Martin Booth Papers
Bishopsgate Institute
   Bernie Grant Collection
Boston University, Howard Gotlieb Archival Research Center
   Han Suyin Collection
   James Clavell Collection
British Broadcasting Corporation Written Archives Centre
Cardiff University
   Hugh Cudlipp Collection
Hong Kong Baptist University Special Collections
   Elsie (Elliott) Tu Archive
Hong Kong Government Records Office
Hong Kong Museum of History
Hong Kong University Special Collections
King's Own Scottish Borderers Regimental Museum
Labour History Museum
Leicestershire, Leicester, and Rutland Record Office
London Metropolitan Archives
London School of Economics
   Alfred Morris collection
   Andrew Faulds collection
   Fabian Society collection
   Geoffrey Finsberg collection
   Pamphlet collection
   Peter Shore collection
Modern Records Centre, University of Warwick
The National Archives, Kew, London
National Library of Wales
Oldham Local Studies and Archives

Royal Regiment of Fusiliers Museum (Royal Warwickshire)
Queen's Lancashire Regiment Museum
School of Oriental and African Studies
    China Association collection
Seven Stories Archive, Newcastle
    Kaye Webb collection
Surrey History Centre
University of Bournemouth
    Independent Television Authority Archive
University of Cambridge
    Herbert Butterfield Papers
University of Cambridge, Churchill College
    Duncan Sandys papers
    Enoch Powell collection
    Neil Kinnock collection
University of Cambridge, Girton College
    Dorothy Needham collection
University of Manchester, John R. Rylands Library
    Association of Operative Cotton Spinners and Twiners
    Rupert E. Davies Collection
University of Oxford, Bodleian Library
    Conservative Party papers
University of Oxford, Rhodes College
    Interview transcripts for Governors Alexander Grantham, Robert Black,
        and David Trench
West Yorkshire Records Office, Bradford
    George Hattersley and Sons collection
    William Moore collection

Official publications

A Draft Agreement between the Government of the United Kingdom of Great
    Britain and Northern Ireland and the Government of the People's Republic
    of China on the Future of Hong Kong. Presented to Parliament by the
    Secretary of State for Foreign and Commonwealth Affairs by Command of
    Her Majesty, September 1984. London: HMSO, 1984.
Hong Kong. Hong Kong: Public Relations Office, annual.
Hong Kong. London: HMSO, 1976.

Periodicals

China Daily
Daily Herald
Daily Mail
Daily Mirror
Eastern Express
Economist

Far Eastern Economic Review
Guardian
Hong Kong Tatler
Independent
New Statesman/New Statesman and Society
South China Morning Post
Spectator
Sun
Telegraph
The Times

Other key published works

Abercrombie, Patrick. *Hong Kong: Preliminary Planning Report*. Hong Kong: Government Printer, 1948.

Adams, George. *The Great Hong Kong Sex Novel: The Rise and Fall of a Hong Kong Chauvinist*. Hong Kong: AIP Publications, 1993.

Akers-Jones, David. *Feeling the Stones*. Hong Kong: Hong Kong University Press, 2004.

Benton, Gregor. *The Hongkong Crisis*. London: Pluto Press, 1983.

Benton, Gregor and Edmund Terence Gomez. *The Chinese in Britain, 1800–Present: Economy, Transnationalism, Identity*. Basingstoke, Palgrave Macmillan, 2008.

Bickers, Robert. *Britain in China: Community, Culture and Colonialism, 1900–1949*. Manchester and New York: Manchester University Press, 1999.

Bickers, Robert and Ray Yep (eds). *May Days in Hong Kong: Emergency and Riot in 1967*. Hong Kong: Hong Kong University Press, 2009.

Bonavia, David. *Hong Kong 1997: The Final Settlement*. Hong Kong: FEER, 1985.

Booth, Martin. *The Dragon and the Pearl: A Hong Kong Notebook*. London: Simon and Schuster, 1994.

— *Golden Boy: Memories of a Hong Kong Childhood*. New York: St Martin's Press, 2004.

Boschman, Roger. *Hong Kong by Night*. Hong Kong: CFW Publications, 1981.

Bray, Denis. *Hong Kong Metamorphosis*. Hong Kong: Hong Kong University Press, 2001.

Bristow, Roger. *Hong Kong's New Towns: A Selective Review*. Hong Kong: Oxford University Press, 1989.

Britain and Hong Kong. London: HMSO, 1992.

Brown, Judith M. and Rosemary Foot (eds). *Hong Kong's Transitions, 1842–1997*. Basingstoke: Macmillan, 1997.

Brown, Judith M. and Wm. Roger Louis (eds). *The Oxford History of the British Empire: The Twentieth Century*. Oxford: Oxford University Press, 2001.

Buchanan, Tom. *East Wind: China and the British Left, 1925–1976*. Oxford: Oxford University Press, 2012.

Buckley, Roger. *Hong Kong: The Road to 1997*. Cambridge: Cambridge University Press, 1997.

SELECT BIBLIOGRAPHY

Burdett, John. *The Last Six Million Seconds: A Thriller*. New York: William Morrow, 1997.

Cameron, Nigel. *Hong Kong: The Cultured Pearl*. Hong Kong: Oxford University Press, 1978.

Carroll, John M. *A Concise History of Hong Kong*. Lanham, MD: Rowman and Littlefield, 2007.

— *Edge of Empires: Chinese Elites and British Colonials in Hong Kong*. Cambridge, MA: Harvard University Press, 2005.

— 'The Peak: Residential Segregation in Colonial Hong Kong'. In David S. G. Goodman and Bryna Goodman (eds), *Twentieth-Century Colonialism and China: Localities, the Everyday, and the World*. Oxford: Routledge, 2012, pp. 81–91.

— 'Ten Years Later: 1997–2007 as History.' In Kam Louie (ed.), *Hong Kong Culture: Word and Image*. Hong Kong: Hong Kong University Press, 2010, pp. 9–23, 247, 263–4.

Cartland, Barbara. *Heaven in Hong Kong*. Wallington: Severn House Publishers, 1990.

Cayrol, Pierre. *Hong Kong in the Mouth of the Dragon*. Rutland, VT and Tokyo: Charles E. Tuttle, 1998.

Chan Cheuk-wah. *The Myth of Hong Kong's 'Laissez-faire' Economic Governance, 1960s and 1970s*. Hong Kong: Hong Kong Institute of Asia-Pacific Studies, 1998.

Cheek-Milby, Kathleen. *A Legislature Comes of Age: Hong Kong's Search for Influence and Identity*. Hong Kong: Oxford University Press, 1995.

Cheng, Irene. *Intercultural Reminiscences*. Hong Kong: David C. Lam Institute for East–West Studies, 1997.

Cheng, Sea-ling. 'Consuming Places in Hong Kong: Experiencing Lan Kwai Fong'. In Gordon Mathews and Tai-lok Lui (eds), *Consuming Hong Kong*. Hong Kong: Hong Kong University Press, 2003, pp. 237–62.

Cheung, Gary Ka-wei. *Hong Kong's Watershed: The 1967 Riots*. Hong Kong: Hong Kong University Press, 2009.

Chou, Grace Ai-Ling. *Confucianism, Colonialism, and the Cold War: Chinese Cultural Education at Hong Kong's New Asia College, 1949–1963*. Leiden: Brill, 2011.

Chu, Cindy Yik-yi. *Chinese Communists and Hong Kong Capitalists: 1937–1997*. Basingstoke: Palgrave Macmillan, 2010.

Clavell, James. *Noble House: A Novel of Contemporary Hong Kong*. New York: Delacorte Press, 1981.

— *Tai-Pan: A Novel of Hong Kong*. London: Michael Joseph, 1966.

Clayton, David. 'From "Free" to "Fair" Trade: The Evolution of Labour Laws in Colonial Hong Kong, 1958–62'. *Journal of Imperial and Commonwealth History* 35 (June 2007): 263–82.

— *Imperialism Revisited: Political and Economic Relations between Britain and China, 1950–54*. Basingstoke: Macmillan, 1997.

— 'Trade-Offs and Rip-Offs: Imitation-Led Industrialisation and the Evolution of Trademark Law in Hong Kong'. *Australian Economic History Review* 51 (July 2011): 178–98.

[222]

Coates, Austin. *Myself a Mandarin: Memoirs of a Special Magistrate*. Hong Kong: Oxford University Press, 1987 [1968].

— *The Road*. London: Hutchinson, 1959.

Cooper, Anthony G. *The Sanctuary*. Hong Kong: Communication Management, 1984.

Cooper, John. *Colony in Conflict: The Hong Kong Disturbances, May 1967–January 1968*. Hong Kong: Swindon, 1970.

Cottrell, Robert. *The End of Hong Kong: The Secret Diplomacy of Imperial Retreat*. London: John Murray, 1993.

Cradock, Percy. *Experiences of China*. New edn. London: John Murray, 1999.

Darwin, John. *The Empire Project: The Rise and Fall of the British World-System, 1830–1970*. Cambridge: Cambridge University Press, 2009.

Davis, John Gordon. *Typhoon*. New York: Dutton, 1979.

— *The Year of Dangerous Loving*. London: HarperCollins, 1997.

— *The Years of the Hungry Tiger*. London: Michael Joseph, 1974.

Davis, S. G. *Hong Kong in Its Geographical Setting*. London: Collins, 1949.

Dimbleby, Jonathan. *The Last Governor: Chris Patten and the Handover of Hong Kong*. London: Little, Brown, 1997.

Duara, Prasenjit. 'Hong Kong and the New Imperialism in East Asia, 1941–66'. In David S. G. Goodman and Bryna Goodman (eds), *Twentieth-Century Colonialism and China: Localities, the Everyday, and the World*. Oxford: Routledge, 2012, pp. 197–211.

Easey, Walter. *Ducking Responsibility: Britain and Hong Kong in the '80s*. Manchester: *Christian Statesman*, 1980.

Elliott, Elsie. *An Autobiography*. Hong Kong: Longman Group, 1988.

— *The Avarice, Bureaucracy and Corruption of Hong Kong*. Hong Kong: Friends Commercial Printing Factory, 1971.

— *Crusade for Justice: An Autobiography*. Hong Kong: Heinemann Asia, 1981.

England, Joe. *Hong Kong: Britain's Responsibility*. Fabian Research Series 324. London: Fabian Society, 1976.

— *Industrial Relations and Law in Hong Kong*. 2nd edn. Hong Kong: Oxford University Press, 1989.

England, Joe and John Rear. *Chinese Labour under British Rule: A Critical Study of Labour Relations and Law in Hong Kong*. Hong Kong: Oxford University Press, 1975.

— *Industrial Relations and Law in Hong Kong: An Extensively Rewritten Version of Chinese Labour under British Rule*. Hong Kong: Oxford University Press, 1981.

Fairclough, Chris. *We Live in Hong Kong*. Hove: Wayland, 1985.

Faure, David. *Colonialism and the Hong Kong Mentality*. Hong Kong: Hong Kong University Press, 2003.

Fedorowich, Kent. 'Decolonization Deferred? The Re-Establishment of Colonial Rule in Hong Kong, 1942–45'. In Kent Fedorowich and Martin Thomas (eds), *International Diplomacy and Colonial Retreat*. London: Frank Cass, 2001.

— 'Doomed from the Outset? Internment and Civilian Exchange in the Far East: The British Failure over Hong Kong, 1941–45'. *The Journal of Imperial and Commonwealth History* 25 (1997): 113–40.

Fellows, James. 'Colonial Autonomy and Cold War Diplomacy: Hong Kong and the case of Anthony Grey, 1967–69'. *Historical Research* (forthcoming).

Fenby, Jonathan. *Dealing with the Dragon: A Year in the New Hong Kong*. London: Little, Brown, 2000.

Fleming, Ian. *Thrilling Cities*. London: Jonathan Cape, 1963.

Flowerdew, John. *The Final Years of British Hong Kong: The Discourse of Colonial Withdrawal*. New York: St Martin's Press, 1997.

Goodstadt, Leo. *Poverty in the Midst of Affluence: How Hong Kong Mismanaged Its Prosperity*. Hong Kong: Hong Kong University Press, 2013.

— *Profits, Politics and Panics: Hong Kong's Banks and the Making of a Miracle Economy, 1935–1985*. Hong Kong: Hong Kong University Press, 2007.

— *Uneasy Partners: The Conflict between Public Interest and Private Profit in Hong Kong*. Hong Kong: Hong Kong University Press, 2005.

Grantham, Alexander. *Via Ports: From Hong Kong to Hong Kong*. Hong Kong: Hong Kong University Press, 1965.

[Halliday, Jon]. *Hong Kong: A Case to Answer*. Hong Kong: Hong Kong Research Project, 1974.

Hampton, Mark. 'British Legal Culture and Colonial Governance: The Attack on Corruption in Hong Kong, 1968–1974'. *Britain and the World* 5 (September 2012): 223–39.

— 'Early Hong Kong Television, 1950s–1970s: Commercialization, Public Service, and Britishness'. *Media History* 17 (August 2011): 305–22.

— 'Projecting Britishness to Hong Kong: The British Council and Hong Kong House, 1950s–1970s'. *Historical Research* 85 (November 2012): 691–709.

Hampton, Mark and Carol C. L. Tsang. 'Colonial Legacies and Internationalization: British History in Contemporary Hong Kong'. *Twentieth Century British History* 23.4 (2012): 563–74.

Han Suyin. *A Many-Splendored Thing*. Boston, MA: Little, Brown, 1952.

Harris, Peter. *Hong Kong: A Study in Bureaucratic Politics*. Hong Kong: Heinemann Asia, 1978.

Harter, Seth. 'Hong Kong's Dirty Little Secret'. *Journal of Urban History* 27 (November 2000): 92–113.

Hayes, James. *Friends and Teachers: Hong Kong and Its People, 1953–87*. Hong Kong: Hong Kong University Press, 1996.

— *The Great Difference: Hong Kong's New Territories and Its People, 1898–2004*. Hong Kong: Hong Kong University Press, 2006.

Hicks, George L. *Hong Kong Countdown*. Hong Kong: Writers' and Publishers' Cooperative, 1989.

Hoe, Susanna. *Watching the Flag Come Down: An Englishwoman in Hong Kong 1987–1997*. Oxford: Holo Books, 2007.

Hong Kong: Its Value to Britain. Hong Kong: Government Printer, 1992.

Hong Kong Reform Club, 2nd 10 Years Anniversary Report, 1959–1968. Hong Kong: Reform Club, 1969.

Hopkins, Keith, ed. *Hong Kong: The Industrial Colony*. Hong Kong: Oxford University Press, 1971.

Hughes, Richard. *Borrowed Place, Borrowed Time: Hong Kong and Its Many Faces*. 2nd edn. London: André Deutsch, 1976.

Ingham, Mike. *Hong Kong: A Cultural History*. Oxford: Oxford University Press, 2007.

Ingrams, Harold. *Hong Kong*. London: HMSO, 1952.

Jarvie, Ian C. and Joseph Agassi (eds). *Hong Kong: A Society in Transition*. New York: Frederick A. Praeger, 1968.

Jones, Catherine. *Promoting Prosperity: The Hong Kong Way of Social Policy*. Hong Kong: Chinese University Press, 1990.

King, Ambrose. 'Administrative Absorption of Politics in Hong Kong: Emphasis on the Grass Roots Level'. *Asian Survey* 15 (May 1975): 422–39.

Kirkup, James. *Cities of the World: Hong Kong and Macao*. London: J. M. Dent and Sons, 1970.

Knowles, Caroline and Douglas Harper. *Hong Kong: Migrant Lives, Landscapes, and Journeys*. Chicago: University of Chicago Press, 2009.

Kowloon Disturbances 1966: Report of Commission of Inquiry. Hong Kong: J. R. Lee, Acting Government Printer at the Government Press, 1967.

Kwan, Stanley S. K. with Nicole Kwan. *The Dragon and the Crown: Hong Kong Memoirs*. Hong Kong: Hong Kong University Press, 2008.

Ku, Agnes S. M. *Narratives, Politics, and the Public Sphere: Struggles over Political Reform in the Final Transitional Years in Hong Kong (1992–1994)*. Aldershot: Ashgate, 1999.

Lanchester, John. *Fragrant Harbor*. New York: Penguin, 2002.

Lau, C. K. *Hong Kong's Colonial Legacy: A Hong Kong Chinese's View of the British Heritage*. Hong Kong: Chinese University Press, 1997.

Lau Siu-kai. *Society and Politics in Hong Kong*. Hong Kong: Chinese University Press, 1983.

Lau Siu-kai and Kuan Hsin-chi. *The Ethos of the Hong Kong Chinese*. Hong Kong: Chinese University Press, 1988.

Law Wing Sang. *Collaborative Colonial Power: The Making of the Hong Kong Chinese*. Hong Kong: Hong Kong University Press, 2009.

Leather, Stephen. *The Vets*. New York: Simon and Schuster, 1993.

Lee, Rance P. L. (ed.). *Corruption and Its Control in Hong Kong*. Hong Kong: Chinese University Press, 1981.

Leeming, Frank. *Street Studies in Hong Kong: Localities in a Chinese City*. Oxford: Oxford University Press, 1977.

Lethbridge, H. J. *Hard Graft in Hong Kong: Scandal, Corruption, the ICAC*. Hong Kong: Oxford University Press, 1985.

Leung, Benjamin K. P. *Perspectives on Hong Kong Society*. Hong Kong: Oxford University Press, 1996.

Littlewood, Michael. *Taxation without Representation: The History of Hong Kong's Troublingly Successful Tax System*. Hong Kong: Hong Kong University Press, 2010.

Loh, Christine. *Being Here: Shaping a Preferred Future*. Hong Kong: SCMP Books, 2006.

Ma, Eric Kit-wai. *Desiring Hong Kong, Consuming South China: Transborder Cultural Politics, 1970–2010*. Hong Kong: Hong Kong University Press, 2011.

Ma Ngok. *Political Development in Hong Kong: State, Political Society, and Civil Society*. Hong Kong: Hong Kong University Press, 2007.

McGurn, William. *Perfidious Albion: The Abandonment of Hong Kong 1997*. Washington: Ethics and Public Policy Center, 1992.

— 'The Widows' [*sic*] Mite'. *Spectator* (7 July 1990): 17–18.

McLaren, Robin. *Britain's Record in Hong Kong*. London: Royal Institute of International Affairs, 1997.

Mark, Chi-kwan. *Hong Kong and the Cold War: Anglo-American Relations, 1949–1957*. Oxford: Clarendon Press, 2004.

— 'Lack of Means or Loss of Will? The United Kingdom and the Decolonization of Hong Kong, 1957–1967'. *The International History Review* 31 (March 2009): 45–71.

— ' "The Problem of People": British Colonials, Cold War Powers, and the Chinese Refugees in Hong Kong, 1949–62'. *Modern Asian Studies* 41.6 (2007): 1145–81.

—'Vietnam War Tourists: US Naval Visits to Hong Kong and British–American–Chinese Relations, 1965–1968'. *Cold War History* 10 (February 2010): 1–28.

Marshall, William. *Yellowthread Street*. New York: Felony and Mayhem Press, 2006 [1975].

Martin, Stella. *Adventure in Hong Kong*. London and Basingstoke: Macmillan, 1991.

Mason, Richard. *The World of Suzie Wong*. London: Fontana, 1959 [1957].

Menski, Werner (ed.). *Coping with 1997: The Reaction of the Hong Kong People to the Transfer of Power*. Stoke on Trent: Trentham Books, 1995.

Miners, Norman. *The Government and Politics of Hong Kong*. 5th edn. Hong Kong: Oxford University Press, 1998.

— *Hong Kong under Imperial Rule, 1912–1941*. Hong Kong: Oxford University Press, 1987.

Mo, Timothy. *An Insular Possession*. London: Paddleless Press, 2012 [1986].

— *Sour Sweet*. London: Paddleless Press, 1999 [1982].

Moore, Donald. *The Striking Wind*. London: Hodder and Stoughton, 1959.

Morris, Jan. *Hong Kong: Epilogue to an Empire*. New York: Random House, 1997 [1988].

New, Christopher. *A Change of Flag*. Hong Kong: Asia2000, 2000.

— *The Chinese Box*. Hong Kong: Orchid Pavilion, 2001.

Ng., Maria N. *Pilgramages: Memories of Colonial Macau and Hong Kong*. Hong Kong: Hong Kong University Press, 2009.

Ngo, Tak-Wing. *Hong Kong's History: State and Society under Colonial Rule*. London and New York: Routledge, 1999.

— 'Industrial History and the Artifice of *Laissez-Faire* Colonialism'. In David Faure (ed.), *Hong Kong: A Reader in Social History*. Hong Kong: Oxford University Press, 2003, pp. 543–71.

Ommanney, F. D. *Fragrant Harbour: A Private View of Hong Kong*. London: Hutchinson, 1962.

Otter, Leyland. *Special Study, August 1984: The Future of Hong Kong*. London: Bank of Credit and Commerce International, 1984.

Patten, Christopher. *Letters to Hong Kong*. Hong Kong: Information Services Department, 1997.

— *Our Next Five Years: The Agenda for Hong Kong. Address by the Governor the Right Honourable Christopher Patten at the Opening of the 1992/93 Session of the Legislative Council, 7 October 1992*. Hong Kong: Hong Kong Government Office, 1992.

Patrikeeff, Felix. *Mouldering Pearl: Hong Kong at the Crossroads*. London: George Philip, 1989.

Pepper, Suzanne. *Keeping Democracy at Bay: Hong Kong and the Challenge of Chinese Political Reform*. Lanham, MD: Rowman and Littlefield, 2008.

Peterson, Glen. 'To Be or Not to Be a Refugee: The International Politics of the Hong Kong Refugee Crisis, 1949–55'. *The Journal of Imperial and Commonwealth History* 36 (June 2008): 171–95.

Poon, Shuk-wah. 'Dogs and British Colonialism: The Contested Ban on Eating Dogs in Colonial Hong Kong', *Journal of Imperial and Commonwealth History* 42 (2014): 308–28.

Pope-Hennessy, James. *Half-Crown Colony: A Hong Kong Notebook*. London: Cape, 1969.

Pressure Points: A Social Critique by the Hong Kong Observers. 2nd edn. Hong Kong: Summerson Educational Research Centre, 1983.

Pullinger, Jackie. *Chasing the Dragon*. London: Hodder and Stoughton, 2010 [1980].

Rabushka, Alvin. *Freedom's Fall in Hong Kong*. Essays in Public Policy 79. Stanford, CA: Hoover Institution on War, Revolution, and Peace, 1997.

— *Hong Kong: A Study in Economic Freedom*. Chicago: University of Chicago Press, 1979.

Rafferty, Kevin. *City on the Rocks: Hong Kong's Uncertain Future*. New York: Viking, 1989.

Rainbird, S. W. *The Problem of Narcotic Drugs in Hong Kong*. Hong Kong: Wing Tai Cheung Printing, 1971.

Representative Government in Hong Kong. Hong Kong: Government Printer, 1994.

Roberti, Mark. *The Fall of Hong Kong: Britain's Betrayal and China's Triumph*. New York: John Wiley and Sons, 1996.

Roberts, Denys. *Another Disaster: Hong Kong Sketches*. London and New York: Radcliffe Press, 2006.

Schenk, Catherine R. 'The Empire Strikes Back: Hong Kong and the Decline of Sterling in the 1960s'. *Economic History Review* 57 (August 2004): 551–80.

— *Hong Kong as an International Financial Centre: Emergence and Development, 1945–1965*. London and New York: Routledge, 2002.

Schwarz, Bill. *The White Man's World*. Oxford: Oxford University Press, 2011.

Scott, Ian. *Political Change and the Crisis of Legitimacy in Hong Kong*. Hong Kong: Oxford University Press, 1989.

— *The Public Sector in Hong Kong: Government, Policy, People*. Hong Kong: Hong Kong University Press, 2010.

SELECT BIBLIOGRAPHY

Sinn, Elizabeth (ed). *Between East and West: Aspects of Social and Political Development in Hong Kong*. Hong Kong: Centre for Asian Studies, University of Hong Kong, 1990.

—(ed). *Hong Kong, British Crown Colony, Revisited*. Hong Kong: Centre of Asian Studies, University of Hong Kong, 2001.

Siu, Helen F. and Agnes S. Ku (eds). *Hong Kong Mobile: Making a Global Population*. Hong Kong: Hong Kong University Press, 2008.

Skeldon, Ronald. 'Emigration from Hong Kong, 1945–1994: The Demographic Lead-up to 1997'. In Ronald Skeldon (ed.), *Emigration from Hong Kong: Tendencies and Impacts*. Hong Kong: Chinese University Press, 1995, pp. 51–77.

Smart, Alan. 'Hong Kong's Twenty-First Century Seen from 1997'. *City and Society 9* (1997): 97–115.

— *The Skek Kip Mei Myth: Squatters, Fires and Colonial Rule in Hong Kong, 1950–1963*. Hong Kong: Hong Kong University Press, 2006.

Smith, Henry. *John Stuart Mill's Other Island: A Study of the Development of Hong Kong*. London: Institute of Economic Affairs, 1966.

Snow, Philip. *The Fall of Hong Kong: Britain, China and the Japanese Occupation*. New Haven and London: Yale University Press, 2003.

Szczepanik, Edward F. *The Cost of Living in Hong Kong*. Hong Kong: Hong Kong University Press, 1956.

— *The Economic Growth of Hong Kong*. Westport, CT: Greenwood Press, 1986.

Theroux, Paul. *Kowloon Tong*. Boston, MA and New York: Houghton Mifflin, 1997.

Topley, Marjorie. *Cantonese Society in Hong Kong and Singapore: Gender, Religion, Medicine and Money*. Ed. and intro. Jean DeBernardi. Hong Kong: Hong Kong University Press, 2011.

Tsang, Steve. *Democracy Shelved: Great Britain, China, and Attempts at Constitutional Reform in Hong Kong, 1945–1952*. Hong Kong, Oxford, and New York: Oxford University Press, 1988.

— *Governing Hong Kong: Administrative Officers from the Nineteenth Century to the Handover to China, 1862–1997*. London and New York: I. B. Tauris, 2007.

— *Hong Kong: An Appointment with China*. London and New York: I. B. Tauris, 1997.

— *A Modern History of Hong Kong*. London and New York: I. B. Tauris, 2004.

Turner, H. A. *The Last Colony: But Whose? A Study of the Labour Movement, Labour Market and Labour Relations in Hong Kong*. Cambridge: Cambridge University Press, 1980.

Ure, Gavin. *Governors, Politics and the Colonial Office: Public Policy in Hong Kong, 1918–1958*. Hong Kong: Hong Kong University Press, 2012.

Vines, Stephen. *Hong Kong: China's New Colony*. London: Orion Business, 1999.

Walden, John. *Excellency, Your Gap Is Showing! Six Critiques on British Colonial Government in Hong Kong*. Hong Kong: Corporate Communications, 1983.

Walker, J. *Under the Whitewash*. Rev. and enlarged edn. Hong Kong: *70s Biweekly*, 1972.

Ward, Stuart (ed.). *British Culture and the End of Empire*. Manchester and New York: Manchester University Press, 2001.

Waters, Dan. *Faces of Hong Kong: An Old Hand's Reflections*. New York: Prentice Hall, 1995.

— 'Hong Kong in the 1950s and '60s: Reminiscences'. *Journal of the Hong Kong Branch of the Royal Asiatic Society* 42 (2002): 323–43.

— *One Couple, Two Cultures: 81 Western–Chinese Couples Talk about Love and Marriage*. Hong Kong: MCCM Creations, 2005.

Whitfield, Andrew. *Hong Kong, Empire and the Anglo-American Alliance at War, 1941–1945*. Basingstoke: Palgrave Macmillan, 2001.

Whittle, Andrew. *The Hong Kong Club*. London: Hay Three, 1990.

Wilson, Dick. *Hong Kong's Future: Realistic Grounds for Optimism?* London: Royal Institute of International Affairs, 1990.

Woronoff, Jon. *Hong Kong: Capitalist Paradise*. Hong Kong: Heinemann Asia, 1980.

Yap, Felicia. 'A "New Angle of Vision": British Imperial Reappraisal of Hong Kong during the Second World War'. *The Journal of Imperial and Commonwealth History* 42 (2014): 86–113.

Yep, Ray. '"Cultural Revolution in Hong Kong": Emergency Powers, Administration of Justice and the Turbulent Year of 1967'. *Modern Asian Studies* 46 (July 2012): 1007–32.

Yep, Ray (ed.). *Negotiating Autonomy in Greater China: Hong Kong and Its Sovereign before and after 1997*. Copenhagen: NIAS Press, 2013.

Young, Jingan MacPherson. *FILTH: Failed in London, Try Hong Kong*. Hong Kong: Hong Kong Arts Festival, 2014.

INDEX

airports 100, 117, 121, 124, 125, 126, 190, 193
  Chek Lap Kok airport 121, 124, 125, 126, 190
  Kai Tak airport 117, 124, 125, 193
authoritarianism 47, 54, 132–7, 147, 150, 152, 155, 196

banking 16, 27, 29, 60, 61, 65, 69n, 104, 133, 135, 163, 179, 186, 193, 199
  Hong Kong and Shanghai Bank 60, 61, 65, 135, 186, 193, 199
Black, Robert (Governor of Hong Kong, 1958–64) 79, 121, 122, 123
British Broadcasting Corporation (BBC) 7, 8, 15, 18, 30, 58, 161, 196, 197
British Council 10, 20, 42, 46–7, 53, 74, 164
British Nationality Act (1981) 168, 169, 170
Britishness 3, 4, 6, 8, 11, 31, 44, 46, 47, 48, 50, 101, 131, 160, 161–80, 196, 211, 212
  "British genius" x, 43, 44, 56
British world system 1–2
business 27, 34, 36, 45, 52, 53, 55, 61, 63, 67n19, 86, 101, 103, 104, 106, 120, 125, 133, 135, 141, 145, 150, 152, 161, 175, 176, 186, 192, 193, 195, 204, 205, 216

Cameron, Nigel 5, 48, 59, 98n51, 111, 112, 181n6, 192
capitalism 10, 36, 42–66, 72, 73, 96, 101, 116, 120, 138, 160, 186, 193, 196, 203, 216
Chiang Kai-shek 16, 17
Chinese Britishness 11, 160–80
Chinese Civil War 21, 133, 138
Chinese Communist Party 2, 66n, 121, 194, 199, 206, 209n
Chinese character ("Chinese industrious-ness") 42, 43, 56, 57, 58, 59, 60, 61, 66n, 100, 132, 175, 176, 195
Clavell, James 9, 32, 43, 50–6, 68n42, 121

clubs 2, 11, 15, 25, 27, 29, 30, 33, 35, 46, 48, 60, 61, 72, 73, 74–80, 85, 86, 91, 94, 95, 103, 121, 122, 123, 135, 158n, 160, 167, 195, 199, 215
  Chinese Club 77
  Chinese Recreation Club 77
  Cricket Club 76, 77
  Foreign Correspondents' Club 121, 122, 123
  Hong Kong Club 15, 46, 60, 76, 77, 78, 135, 158n, 215
  Hong Kong Highlanders 79
  Hong Kong Jockey Club 48, 61, 135, 199
  Hong Kong Rotary Club 27
  Hong Kong St Andrew's Society 79
  Hong Kong St David's Society 79
  Hong Kong Y's Men's Club 167
  Ladies' Recreation Club 77
  nightclubs 2, 35, 83, 84, 85, 86, 87, 94, 103, 195, 200
  Reform Club 78, 79
Cold War 10, 11, 17, 19, 22, 23, 35, 44, 87, 116, 203
Colonial Office 3, 16, 21, 44, 76, 82
Commonwealth 6, 16, 26, 27, 109, 141, 165, 167, 168, 174, 177, 189
Commonwealth Immigrants Act (1962) 165, 168
Communism 1, 2, 3, 9, 17, 18, 19, 20, 21, 22, 23, 26, 28, 33, 42, 52, 57, 58, 62, 66n, 82, 84–5, 92, 96, 121, 123, 125, 133, 136, 148, 153, 164, 168, 169, 170, 171, 172, 173, 178, 180, 187, 188, 192, 193, 194, 195, 199, 202, 204–5, 206, 209n24, 212, 213
Confucianism 45, 131, 136, 152, 164
Conservative Party 44, 53, 62, 63, 153, 172, 187, 194
corruption 2, 5, 6, 9, 44, 48, 49, 53, 54, 55, 112, 136, 138, 142, 145, 146, 155, 158n48, 167, 180, 190, 191, 197, 198, 202, 204, 206
  anti-corruption 2, 6, 9, 49, 54, 112, 142, 145, 146, 155, 158n48, 180, 190, 191

Independent Commission against Corruption (ICAC) 49, 145, 146, 206
Prevention of Bribery Ordinance (1968) 145–6
Council of Hong Kong Indian Associations 176, 177, 184n82
Cradock, Percy 21, 125, 126, 171, 188
crime 29, 48, 78, 102, 106, 111, 112, 114, 127n37, 137, 145, 146, 173, 197, 199, 200, 201, 202, 204, 214
organised crime 5, 48, 65, 78, 89, 94, 112, 166, 199, 200, 201, 202, 206
Cultural Revolution 21, 24

decolonisation 3, 4, 11, 12n17, 13n33, 22, 23, 35, 73
democracy 3, 10, 49, 126, 132, 133, 134, 138, 142, 146–56, 164, 180, 188, 190, 196, 203, 204, 212, 213, 214, 215
Deng Xiaoping 20, 21, 126, 129, 151, 187, 209
drugs 5, 50, 64, 65, 68n45, 94, 104, 106, 107, 166, 198, 201, 203
drug trade 5, 50, 68n45, 166, 201, 203
heroin 64, 65, 107, 166, 201, 203
opium 10, 50, 51, 56, 63, 68n45, 72, 114, 203

Easey, Walter 29, 48, 64, 192, 208–9n22
economic development 2, 6, 20, 23, 25, 42, 43, 44, 45, 47, 54, 58, 62, 65, 100, 109, 115, 116, 117, 118, 119, 120, 125, 128n63, 132, 136, 144, 152, 168
'economic miracle' 11, 30, 35, 42, 43, 55, 56, 132, 161, 173
education 25, 34, 54, 56, 67n19, 72, 73, 78, 104, 109, 119, 120, 138, 144, 149, 150, 161, 163, 164, 165, 176, 178, 179, 213, 214, 215, 216
Elliot, Charles 10
Elliott, Elsie 16, 54, 56, 62, 72, 94, 142, 144, 145, 146, 150
Ellis, Alan 145
entrepreneurship 46, 55, 66, 72, 95, 100, 102, 106, 107, 132, 171, 195, 204
expatriates 6, 7, 9, 15, 25, 28, 29, 30, 31, 34, 35, 36, 46, 56, 60, 73, 78, 82, 91, 93, 117, 186, 187, 192, 197, 198, 200, 203, 205, 206, 211, 215

Far Eastern Economic Review (FEER) 5, 27, 32, 34, 45, 53, 92, 104, 115, 124, 141, 142, 144, 168, 188
Faulds, Andrew (Labour MP) 86, 162, 171, 173, 176, 191, 208n17
Foreign Office 16, 125, 126, 153, 177, 188
Foreign and Commonwealth Office 109, 174
freedom 2, 44, 46, 50, 51, 52, 53, 54, 64, 66, 96, 131, 132, 134, 151, 153, 168, 169, 177, 178, 180, 188, 190, 191, 193, 203, 207, 212, 213
economic freedom 44, 46, 49, 96
free market 2, 23, 47, 73
free trade 50, 52, 132, 180, 188

Goodstadt, Leo 45, 60, 68n28, 104, 107–8, 109, 111, 213
government
Executive Council 23, 134, 135, 141, 169, 171, 174, 175, 177, 178
'good government' 10, 44, 45, 79, 95, 96, 100, 120, 131–55, 160, 180, 186
Heung Yee Kuk (New Territories) 135–6, 149
Legislative Council, 23, 78, 134, 135, 141, 150, 151, 152, 153, 154, 168, 169, 171, 174, 175, 177, 178, 191, 196
non-interference 23, 45, 46, 47, 48, 49, 52, 56–61, 62, 106, 107, 117, 119, 120, 122, 132–7, 138, 141, 145, 155, 176, 180, 190
Office of the Members of the Executive and Legislative Councils (OMELCO) 171, 174, 175
Unofficial Members of the Hong Kong Executive and Legislative Council (UMELCO) 141, 169, 171, 177, 178
Urban Council 23, 59, 65, 78, 120, 134, 149, 150, 151, 167
Government Information Services 43, 64, 95, 98n, 119, 120, 123, 142, 148–9, 157n
Grantham, Alexander (Governor of Hong Kong, 1947–57) 3, 16, 33, 57, 101, 114, 133, 149, 164

Handover 1, 2, 3, 6, 7, 11, 12n17, 20, 21, 22, 35, 37n, 42, 43, 49, 76, 90, 91, 124, 125, 126, 129n90, 153, 155, 156, 162, 164,

168, 169, 173, 174, 175, 176, 178, 179, 180, 186–207, 208–9n22, 212, 214, 215
Han, Suyin 33, 40n93, 43
Harcourt, Cecil (Vice-Admiral, Commander-in-Chief of the post-war Hong Kong military Government) 43
homosexuality 33, 35, 93, 94, 95
housing 25, 45, 61, 65, 67n19, 78, 101, 104, 105, 107, 108, 109, 110, 111, 112, 113, 115–16, 117, 118, 119, 120, 135, 138, 144, 150, 151, 198, 213
    public housing 65, 67n19, 104, 108, 109, 110, 111, 113, 118, 119, 120, 135, 138, 144, 150
    squatter housing 59, 65, 78, 87, 101, 107, 108, 109, 111, 112, 115–16, 118, 123
    Shek Kip Mei fire (1953) 13n26, 101, 107, 112

industry 5, 20, 21, 23, 25, 42, 43, 44, 46, 53, 57, 59, 62, 63, 64, 84, 100, 109, 115, 116, 118, 119, 120, 121, 123, 134, 141, 142, 165, 166, 167, 168, 213
interracial marriage 32, 33, 34, 35, 80, 91, 199

Jardine Matheson 50, 68n45, 73, 126, 186, 193, 198
Jiang Zemin 2
Johnston, Russell (Liberal MP) 86, 175, 189

Keynesian economics 23, 44, 62
Kinnock, Neil 153, 154, 171
Korean War 23, 25, 64
    United States embargo of China 23, 25, 64
Kowloon Walled City 56, 82, 106, 107

labour 5, 22, 23, 25, 26, 29, 42, 43, 44, 46, 57, 59, 61, 62, 63, 64, 98n56, 138, 157n, 165
    child labour 59, 62, 63
Labour Party, 22, 49, 52, 53, 86, 153, 154, 162, 168–9, 171, 173, 188, 194
laissez-faire 23, 45, 46, 47, 48, 49, 52, 56–61, 62, 106, 107, 119, 122, 132, 134–5, 141
Lan Kwai Fong 35, 94, 178, 200
law 6, 24, 27, 32, 33, 44, 49, 50, 51, 54, 56, 62, 78, 87, 94, 95, 96, 111, 112, 113, 116, 117, 133, 134, 137, 142, 145, 148,

166–7, 168, 177, 179, 180, 188, 190, 191, 193, 195, 197, 200, 201, 202, 203, 204, 205, 212, 213
Basic Law 188, 191, 212, 213
legitimacy 10, 21, 25, 65, 93, 138, 145, 147
Liberal Party 86, 175, 189

MacLehose, Murray (Governor of Hong Kong, 1971–82) 20, 45, 53, 61, 94, 124, 129n, 133, 138, 144, 145, 146, 147, 151, 158n48
Major, John 125, 126, 153
Mao Zedong 17, 18, 21, 58, 60, 92
media 7, 8, 9, 15, 18, 30, 58, 74, 98n, 149, 152, 161, 188, 190, 191, 196, 197, 217n
migration 21, 22, 23, 24, 25, 42, 53, 107–8, 118, 132–3, 138, 142, 151, 165, 166, 170, 171, 172, 173, 174, 175, 176, 177, 178, 182n39, 183n65, 187–8, 194, 195, 198, 212–13
    emigration from Hong Kong 43, 73, 165, 170, 171, 175, 195, 196
    immigration to Britain 22, 165, 166, 168, 169, 170, 171, 172, 173, 174, 175, 176, 177, 178, 182n39, 183n65, 184n82, 187–8
    immigration to Hong Kong 21, 23, 24, 25, 42, 107–8, 118, 132–3, 138, 142, 178, 182, 194, 198, 212–13
missionaries 7, 10, 16, 21, 34, 54, 56, 65, 82, 106
modernisation 10, 43, 44, 62, 79, 95, 100–26, 141, 160, 162, 180, 186, 193, 197, 201, 214
mui tsai 72, 136

nationalism 9, 17, 23, 164
New Territories lease 17, 18, 20, 21, 37n, 53, 78, 106, 124, 128n63, 136, 173–4, 187, 189–90, 192
new towns 45, 117, 118, 119, 120, 124, 136, 149

Opium War 10

Palmerston, (Henry John Temple) (Third Viscount Palmerston) 10, 11
Patten, Chris 1, 9, 43, 73, 125, 126, 132, 153, 154, 155, 188, 190, 191, 196, 213
People's Liberation Army (PLA) 2, 201, 202, 203, 206, 214

police 5, 6, 7, 26, 27, 29, 48, 49, 54, 64, 75, 84, 87–8, 93, 94, 105, 107, 112, 115, 140, 141, 142, 145, 146, 149, 161, 172, 192, 193, 195, 200, 201, 204, 213
Special Branch 93, 149, 213
population 6, 15, 16, 18, 23, 24, 25, 28, 31, 35, 73, 101, 105, 113, 118, 119, 122, 138, 141, 147, 150, 175, 176, 192, 197, 202
poverty 44, 58, 59, 64, 65, 82, 89, 105, 106, 107, 108, 109
Powell, Enoch 172, 173
press 1, 2, 3, 5, 54, 61, 85, 92, 95, 123, 124, 148, 149, 152, 188, 205, 212, 215, 217n3
  censorship 149, 205, 212, 217n3
  freedom of the press 54, 148, 149, 191, 205, 212
prostitution 29, 56, 64, 72, 80, 81, 82, 83, 84, 85, 86, 87, 88, 89, 90, 92, 93, 95, 106, 192, 198, 202, 206
Public Relations Office 44
Pullinger, Jackie 56, 72, 82, 106

race 31, 32, 33, 34, 35, 42, 43, 56, 57, 58, 59, 60, 61, 66n10, 77, 100, 132, 137, 143, 160, 162, 163, 172, 173, 174, 175, 176, 177, 178, 194, 195
reform 3, 34, 53, 61, 62, 65, 72, 78, 79, 132–4, 138, 141, 144, 145, 146, 147, 149, 150, 151, 152, 153, 154, 155, 162, 164, 167, 168, 191
  MacLehose reforms 133, 144, 147, 158n
refugees 16, 19, 24, 28, 42, 57, 58, 59, 63, 64, 65, 82, 87, 115, 119, 133, 138, 164, 173, 175, 205
right of abode 168–78, 182n39, 212
riots 5, 7, 18, 21, 25, 26, 27, 34, 52, 57, 64, 65, 78, 102, 112, 138–40, 141, 142, 144, 148, 150, 151, 155, 168, 169, 200
  Hong Kong 1967–68 Riots 5, 7, 18, 21, 25, 26, 27, 34, 57, 65, 78, 102, 138–40, 142, 144, 148, 168, 169
  Kowloon riot (1956) 64, 102
  Star Ferry riot (1966) 65, 78, 102, 138, 138, 142, 142, 148, 148
rule of law 6, 50, 62, 96, 137, 180, 188, 190, 191, 193, 195, 197, 201, 202, 203, 205

segregation 32, 33, 34, 35, 91, 111, 116, 160
sex 80, 81, 82, 83, 84, 85, 86, 87, 88, 89, 90, 91, 92–3, 94, 95, 96, 203

sexuality 11, 32, 80, 81, 82, 83, 84, 85, 86, 87, 88, 89, 90, 91, 92, 93, 94, 95, 96, 98n51, 203
Shepherd, Malcolm (Second Baron Shepherd) (Minister of State and Commonwealth Affairs, 1968–70) 141, 142
Sino-British Joint Declaration (1984) 2, 6, 12n, 21, 42, 106–7, 124, 151, 153, 154, 155, 168, 169, 170, 172–3, 174, 175, 177, 178, 187, 188, 189, 190, 191, 193, 208n17
Six Day War (1899) 116
social welfare 3, 4, 22, 44, 45, 46, 48, 53, 57, 59, 63, 65, 66, 72, 101, 109, 131, 132, 138, 142, 150, 155, 171, 176, 213, 214
sport 11, 25, 29, 61, 72, 73, 74–80, 95, 160, 214
  cricket 74, 75, 76, 78
  horse racing 61, 195
  rugby 75, 214
  swimming 29, 33, 75
South China Morning Post (SCMP) 48, 93, 100, 111, 115, 125, 149, 151, 192, 197
Sun Yat-sen 17, 120

television 7, 74, 115, 120, 164, 186, 206, 214
textiles 5, 64, 112, 120
Thatcherism 44, 176
Thatcher Government 44, 53, 62, 63, 153, 187
Thatcher, Margaret 2, 20, 53, 62, 63, 68n45, 124, 125, 151, 153, 176, 187, 188, 189, 190, 196, 201
Tiananmen Square Massacre 2, 21, 22, 35, 125, 126, 152, 153, 168, 170, 171, 173, 176, 177, 182n37, 183n53, 187, 191, 192, 194, 196, 197, 199, 201, 205, 212
  vigil in Victoria Park 197, 212
tourism 30, 84, 85, 87, 102, 103, 104, 161–2, 192, 200, 212
trade 5, 16, 17, 21, 23, 25, 44, 50, 51, 52, 64, 68n, 73, 123, 132–3, 167, 176, 180, 188
transport 57, 63, 100, 101, 111, 121, 150, 214
  Mass Transit Railway (MTR) 121, 214
Trench, David (Governor of Hong Kong, 1964–71) 18, 45, 53, 141, 143, 148
triads 5, 48, 65, 89, 94, 112, 166, 199, 200, 202, 206

INDEX

'unbridled capitalism' 10, 36, 42–66, 72, 73, 96, 101, 116, 120, 138, 160, 186, 193
United States Information Service 10

Vietnam War 10, 23, 87, 99n72, 173

water 19, 65, 105, 109, 114, 116, 121, 122, 123, 124
  drought 116, 121, 122, 123, 124
  reservoirs 101, 107, 111, 115, 116, 117, 119, 121, 122, 123, 124, 136

Welfare State 3, 4, 22, 44, 45, 46, 48, 57, 59, 63, 66, 67n19, 72, 171, 176
Wilson, David (Governor of Hong Kong, 1987–92) 125, 126, 153, 188
working hours 50, 57, 59, 60

Youde, Edward (Governor of Hong Kong, 1982–86) 147
Young, Mark (Governor of Hong Kong, 1946–47) 133, 164

EU authorised representative for GPSR:
Easy Access System Europe, Mustamäe tee 50,
10621 Tallinn, Estonia
gpsr.requests@easproject.com

www.ingramcontent.com/pod-product-compliance
Lightning Source LLC
Chambersburg PA
CBHW031128270326
41929CB00011B/1538